SURVEILLANCE
AND SECURITY

SURVEILLANCE
AND SECURITY

TECHNOLOGICAL POLITICS AND

POWER IN EVERYDAY LIFE

EDITED BY TORIN MONAHAN

Routledge
Taylor & Francis Group
New York   London

Routledge is an imprint of the
Taylor & Francis Group, an informa business

Routledge
Taylor & Francis Group
270 Madison Avenue
New York, NY 10016

Routledge
Taylor & Francis Group
2 Park Square
Milton Park, Abingdon
Oxon OX14 4RN

© 2006 by Taylor & Francis Group, LLC
Routledge is an imprint of Taylor & Francis Group, an Informa business

Printed in the United States of America on acid-free paper
10 9 8 7 6 5 4 3 2 1

International Standard Book Number-10: 0-415-95393-6 (Softcover) 0-415-95392-8 (Hardcover)
International Standard Book Number-13: 978-0-415-95393-1 (Softcover) 978-0-415-95392-4 (Hardcover)

Library of Congress Cataloging-in-Publication Data

Surveillance and security : technological politics and power in everyday life / Torin
    Monahan, editor.
        p. cm.
    Includes bibliographical references and index.
    ISBN 0-415-95392-8 (hardback : alk. paper) -- ISBN 0-415-95393-6 (pbk. : alk.
    paper)
        1. Electronic surveillance--Social aspects. 2. Technology--Social aspects. 3. Social
    control. 4. Privacy, Right of. 5. Neoliberalism. I. Monahan, Torin.

    HM846.S87 2006
    303.48'3--dc22   2006004475

**Visit the Taylor & Francis Web site at
http://www.taylorandfrancis.com**

**and the Routledge Web site at
http://www.routledge-ny.com**

Contents

Preface

The desire for security permeates modern life. In a world perceived as increasingly unstable and insecure, surveillance has become a key mechanism for contending with threats of terrorism and crime. But just what is being secured by modern surveillance technologies? Beyond the literal and figurative borderlands are multiple territories of social life, which are being transfigured by new technologies of identification, monitoring, tracking, and control. Recognizing the inherent politics of technologies, or their capacity to generate power relations and possibilities, renders these other worlds of surveillance and security both visible and analytically important. The chapters in this book probe the everyday practices of surveillance in this way. They find that what is being secured are social relations, institutional structures, and cultural dispositions that—more often than not—aggravate existing social inequalities and establish rationales for increased, invasive surveillance of marginalized groups.

Some of the newly secured (and largely hidden) territories include cultures of fear, gender inequalities, differential mobilities, vast industry profits, and states of legal exception. Also secured are practices of micropolicing the poor, dismantling the welfare state, spying on citizens, and interrogating enemies. It is important to note that many of these operations occur under the rubric of national and international security, recasting any opposition to these emergent systems as suspect and possibly terrorist. Against this backdrop, this book shifts the focus and the debate on surveillance and security. It seeks to draw attention to the need for global "human security," or freedom from fear and want, which is a mode of security becoming more unstable with every passing day.

The chapters that follow engage in this broader conversation. They present a range of surveillance technologies used in everyday life and critically investigate the politics of their use. From biometric technologies at airports and borders, to video surveillance in schools, to radio frequency identification tags in hospitals, to magnetic strips on welfare food cards, surveillance technologies integrate into all aspects of modern life, but with varied effects for different populations. For our purposes, surveillance technologies are those that facilitate the identification, monitoring, tracking, and control of people. It must also be recognized, of course, that the surveillance of abstract data, objects, or flows can easily translate into embodied power relations for individuals or social groups. Thus, these practices must be included within the purview of research on surveillance. Finally, because all information and communication technologies possess a surveillance modality, it may not be analytically useful to employ "intentionality" as the primary criterion for whether surveillance is occurring. One can experience the effects of surveillance systems without being an explicit target of them, their designers, or their operators.

The book is divided into two broad sections: (1) Neoliberal States and (2) Mobilities and Insecurities. Neoliberalism is understood here to indicate the simultaneous advancement of social control mechanisms and retreat from social programs in societies. It manifests in *policies*, such as those for the privatization or elimination of public goods, services, or spaces; in *technological systems*, such as surveillance architectures or inadequate public transportation; and in *cultural dispositions*, such as widespread beliefs about the inefficiencies of public programs and the necessity of individualized responsibility. As a cultural shift, neoliberalism advances new social and moral orders that normalize its assumptions as fundamental truths. The first section of the book focuses on the social control dimension of neoliberal surveillance and queries some of the ways that neoliberal logics are embedded into durable technological forms and institutional practices. Some of the cases analyzed in this section include surveillance of childcare providers, welfare recipients, students, hospital workers and patients, identity-theft victims, and police.

The second section of the book builds on and overlaps with this general critique of neoliberal surveillance to analyze the governance of mobilities, identities, and securities. In this emergent terrain, the passive tracking of individuals is becoming a mere by-product of (seemingly) ubiquitous information technologies such as mobile phones, global positioning systems, smart cards, and the Internet. The filtering of identities into categories of inclusion and exclusion based on informational data, however, promises to enforce and naturalize social inequalities. Unless technological systems and security policies are designed and regulated to minimize social sorting functions, they will likely continue to engender greater human insecurity into the future. Some of the cases analyzed in this section include the surveillance and sorting of bodies along borders and in airports, the generation of locational data by everyday technologies and infrastructures (e.g., mobile phones and public buses), and the mobilization of "preparedness" and "terrorism" as discourses shaping public policy in disturbingly nondemocratic ways.

The contributors to this volume represent some of the very best researchers studying surveillance and security today—from pioneers in the field of technology studies to younger scholars taking the field in new directions. To provide a multidimensional perspective on the complex issues at stake, the contributors represent as well a range of disciplinary perspectives and backgrounds: sociology, criminology, anthropology, science and technology studies, women's studies, geography, philosophy, political science, and new media studies. It is our hope that others will join us in questioning, critiquing, and intervening in surveillance and security regimes in everyday life.

T.M.

CHAPTER 1

Questioning Surveillance and Security

TORIN MONAHAN

Unfortunately, security and liberty form a zero-sum equation. The inevitable trade-off: To increase security is to decrease liberty and vice versa.

Walter Cronkite, journalist

Now we all know that in times of war and certainly in this post-9/11 world, one of the most difficult questions we face is how to balance security and liberty.

Charles E. Schumer, U.S. senator

Since the 9/11 terrorist attacks, the government is charged with protecting the rights of the individual as well as ensuring our collective safety. The antiterrorist policies the government institutes will, by necessity, be more invasive.

Lynn M. Kuzma, political scientist

Why are questions about surveillance and security always framed in terms of trade-offs? Regardless of the forum, from popular media broadcasts to political speeches to academic publications, trade-offs are taken as the starting point for any discussion. Some of the most common expressions of trade-offs are security versus liberty, security versus privacy, security versus freedom, and security versus cost. But, seemingly, once the issues are presented in these terms, the only thing left to decide is whether the public is willing to make the necessary sacrifices to bring about greater national security. Absent are discussions about the politics behind surveillance and security systems, what one means by "security," what (or who) gets left out of the conversation, and the veracity of such assumptions about trade-offs to begin with. Occasionally, more astute critics will ask about the efficacy of surveillance systems in bringing about greater national security. The question is usually along the lines of "Do they work?"—meaning, are surveillance systems efficacious at preventing crime or terrorism? Although important, this type of question is really just an extension of the logic of trade-offs proffered in the opening quotes, because the implication is that if systems are not sufficiently effective, then they are not worth the sacrifice or investment.

This book argues that these are the wrong questions because they obscure the real changes underway and issues at play with the incorporation of surveillance technologies into public life. The questions, in other words, function as a rhetorical smoke screen, hiding deeper motivations and logics behind surveillance and security. Some of the obvious issues not discussed when talking about trade-offs are how surveillance contributes to spatial segregation and social inequality, how private high-tech industries are benefiting from the public revenue generated for these systems, and what the ramifications are of quantifying "security" (e.g., by the number of video cameras) for political purposes.

This chapter—along with the book as a whole—aims to dispel some of the smoke concealing deeper issues about surveillance and security. It starts, for the sake of fairness, by taking the wrong questions seriously, with a specific focus on the question of how efficacious surveillance systems are at bringing about greater security. Next, it proposes and discusses some of the questions that I see as being the right ones: why do we believe in trade-offs, what social relations are produced by surveillance systems, and how can surveillance be used to increase security without sacrificing civil liberties, if at all? In raising alternative questions of this sort, my goal is not to provide definitive answers but instead to open up the field of inquiry and to move beyond the fog surrounding current debates over these critically important topics.

Taking the Wrong Questions Seriously

On February 12, 1993, two ten-year-old schoolboys kidnapped and murdered two-year-old Jamie Bulger in Merseyside, United Kingdom.

Closed-circuit television (CCTV) footage showed Bulger being led by the hand out of a shopping center unbeknownst to his distracted mother. The boys proceeded to take him on a two-and-a-half mile walk, periodically beating him and taunting him along the way. When confronted by several concerned bystanders, the boys claimed that Jamie was their younger brother and that they were looking out for him, and no one intervened. When they reached a secluded railway line, the boys threw paint in Jamie's face and then beat him with stones, bricks, and an iron bar. Finally, he was laid across the railroad tracks with stones stacked on his head and was later run over by a train (Wikipedia 2004). The assailants could not be identified in the grainy video footage from the shopping center, but friends later turned them in. Nevertheless, the media played the tape countless times to a shocked public, and this had the effect of galvanizing tremendous support for public video surveillance in the United Kingdom (Rosen 2001).

Now, more than ten years after the Jamie Bulger killing, Great Britain boasts the most extensive system of public surveillance in the world, with more than four million cameras throughout the United Kingdom (Rice-Oxley 2004) and more than half a million in London alone (Norris 2004).[1] With the equivalent of one camera for every fourteen people, it is estimated that the average person in a large city like London is filmed three hundred times a day (Coaffee 2004). Yet in spite of this proliferation of video surveillance, surprisingly little evaluative research has been conducted on the effectiveness of surveillance in preventing crime, and the independent research that has been done is largely inconclusive.

Two of the most cited studies about surveillance efficacy were carried out in Airdrie and Glasgow, Scotland, in the mid-1990s. The Airdrie research compared total recorded crimes from two years before and two years after 1992—the year when twelve open street CCTV cameras were installed. The research found a 21 percent drop in recorded crimes in the area, so surveillance was determined to be a "success" (Short and Ditton 1995). Nonetheless, the report raises some doubts because it did not explicitly make mention of social factors such as population changes and unemployment rates in the area, which criminologists consider to be crucially important variables in explaining crime rates (Reiman 2000; LaFree 1998; Collins and Weatherburn 1995). The issue of geographical displacement of crime from one area to another is also problematic in this study, even though the authors claim otherwise:

> [Adjacent] areas recorded slight increases in total crimes and offenses in the 2 years following the installation of CCTV. This increase is almost entirely accounted for by the growth in crimes relating to the possession or supply of drugs and to offences committed whilst on

bail. Displacement would be suggested if these crimes declined in the CCTV area. However this was not the case. (Short and Ditton 1995: 3)

The interpretation here is that even though crimes did increase in surrounding areas, these were "natural" occurrences and therefore should not be attributed to displacement. In other words, drug offenses or offenses perpetrated while on bail do not count as crimes unless they are occurring (or declining) in CCTV areas. Because these crimes do not seem to fit the researchers' model of displacement, they are discounted.[2] Still, this can be considered a qualified success for surveillance.

The Glasgow research compared recorded crime offenses from two years before and one year after the installation of thirty-two open street CCTV cameras in 1994. In addition to looking at crime occurrences, this study also measured public perceptions of the system and observed camera monitoring by security personnel in a control room. The findings with regard to efficacy were a wash. As the report states, "The researchers suggest that the cameras were relatively successful, with some reductions in certain crime categories. Overall, however, the reductions in crime are no more significant than those in the control areas outwith [beyond] the camera locations" (Ditton et al. 1999: 1). Thus, the report continues, "CCTV cameras could not be said to have had a significant impact overall in reducing recorded crimes and offences" (Ditton et al. 1999: 2). The explanation provided for this lack of success is that people were generally unaware of the cameras, and without awareness there is no deterrence.

More recent research does nothing to clear up this muddy water about video surveillance efficacy. The *Christian Science Monitor* reports that after ten years of CCTV projects in the United Kingdom at a publicly funded cost of £250 million ($460 million)[3] that

research has yet to support the case for CCTV. A government review 18 months ago [in 2002] found that security cameras were effective in tackling vehicle crime but had limited effect on other crimes. Improved streetlighting recorded better results. (Rice-Oxley 2004: 1–2)

In a government review, which was mandated by the Home Office (the U.K. department in charge of public security) to see what general conclusions could be drawn from existing research, only twenty-four studies were found to be methodologically sound, and the overall outcome was that "CCTV appears to have no effect on violent crimes, a significant effect on vehicle crimes and it is most effective when used in car parks" (Armitage 2002: 5).

On the whole, what these studies from the United Kingdom indicate is that as gruesome as the Jamie Bulger murder was, it would not have been prevented with a more comprehensive system of video surveillance. Indeed, most crimes—violent or otherwise—are not prevented by surveillance. One bright spot within the evaluation literature on video surveillance is that it does appear to enable apprehending and convicting criminals after the fact (Gill 2004). But if the criterion for a worthwhile trade-off (of civil liberties, of privacy, of cost, etc.) is *prevention* of crime, then one must respond negatively to the question "Is it worth it?"

Oddly enough, given the astronomical crime rates in the United States, relatively speaking, one is hard pressed to find *any* independent evaluations of video surveillance in that country. There are several reasons for this. First, unlike many CCTV schemes in the United Kingdom, video surveillance in the United States is largely implemented in an ad hoc way by private companies rather than through public funds or with public oversight. This makes it difficult to even locate where the operational cameras are, let alone evaluate their effectiveness in some controlled way.[4] Second, the most obvious governmental agency for evaluating surveillance—the federal Office of Technology Assessment—was dissolved in 1995 because, as some say, they too often produced reports that suggested politically unattractive regulation of private industries (Coates 1995).[5]

Third, in the United States, publicly funded video surveillance is most often used for generating revenue from traffic violations, such as running red lights, or it is trained on the urban poor on streets, on public transit, or in schools (Nieto, Johnston-Dodds, and Simmons 2002; Monahan, Chapter 7, this volume). Because of the stigma attached to poor minorities in the United States and the public's perception of surveillance systems as crime deterrents, it is highly unlikely that the general public would demand evaluation and oversight of surveillance, especially when those "public" systems are seldom focused on the more affluent.[6] Finally, for reasons that are explored in the next section, evaluations of technological systems, generally speaking, are simply not funded. Thus, of the more than 200 U.S. police agencies that employ CCTV systems, 96 percent conduct *no evaluation* of their effectiveness (Nieto, Johnston-Dodds, and Simmons 2002: 13).

One of the most well-known studies of video surveillance efficacy in the United States was conducted in low-income public housing in the late 1970s (Musheno, Levine, and Palumbo 1978). The researchers found that the use of video surveillance in New York City's public housing did not reduce crime or fear of it, even though CCTV's implementation came at great public cost of an estimated $10,000 per apartment (in three public buildings). The reasons for this "failure," the authors explain, stemmed from a conceptual deficiency as much as from technical limitations. The design strategy in public housing was predicated on the concept of "defensible space" (O. Newman 1972), implying that the agents of crime existed outside of the immediate community and that close collaboration between community members and police officers would keep deviants out. In fact, crime emerged from within the community, poor relations between residents and police prevented community members from contacting the police, vandals routinely disabled the surveillance equipment, and residents chose not to watch the video feeds, which were routed through their television sets.

There is more recent evidence to suggest that criminals are appropriating video surveillance systems that were originally intended to thwart them.[7] In the Frederick Douglas Towers, a public housing complex for seniors in Buffalo, New York, drug dealers established a crack cocaine operation using existing CCTV systems to monitor customers and keep a lookout for police. According to one law enforcement official, "The dealers were using all the security features of the senior apartments at Douglas to their advantage ... to screen who was coming up to the apartment and buzzing people inside the building" (Herbeck 2004). In another case in Virginia, four teenagers were "arrested on charges of operating a large-scale, well-organized crime ring that used surveillance, two-way radios, lookouts and disguises to stage at least 17 commercial burglaries over a 14-month period" (Branigin 2003). As an added twist to this story, the teenagers established their base of operations within a private, fortified, gated community with its own police force (Aquia Harbour 2004). When surveillance technologies originally intended to prevent crime are employed to facilitate crime or protect criminals, it lends a whole different meaning to the question of "Do they work?"

On the subject of traffic violations, cities with red-light surveillance programs do report a significant reduction in red-light runners at those intersections. A Washington, D.C., program reported a 63 percent decrease in red-light runners; Oxnard, California, reported a 42 percent decrease; and Fairfax, Virginia, reported a 40 percent decrease (Nieto, Johnston-Dodds, and Simmons 2002: 20). So, at least for this type of traffic crime, there has been demonstrated effectiveness. This conclusion is somewhat complicated, however, by the potential for increased rear-end collisions when people brake abruptly to avoid fines (Nieto, Johnston-Dodds, and Simmons 2002: 21).[8]

The history of eschewing publicly funded surveillance and security systems in the United States is shifting rapidly in the wake of the 9/11 attacks. Instead of being conceived of as deterrents to ordinary crimes, these systems are now being embraced by policy makers as counterterrorism and intelligence-gathering tools (Lyon 2003b). Perhaps the hottest area of development, along these lines, is in biometrics, meaning the range of technologies designed to measure and classify unique human attributes. Biometrics can include fingerprinting systems, face-recognition technologies, hand-geometry scanning, iris and/or retinal scans, odor identification, thermal face print scans, voice recognition, and so on (Woodward, Orlans, and Higgins 2002). These technologies are varied and complex and present many sociotechnical obstacles for "successful" use (contingent on the social context, the goals of the system designers and users, the interoperability of systems, etc.). The professional biometrics community, for instance, actively debates the appropriateness of some systems versus others (e.g., whether identifiers should be stored in a general database or within portable documents), and they frequently criticize each other for trying to push proprietary biometric "solutions" from which individual companies stand to benefit enormously should their technologies become industry standards.[9] In this respect, knowledge of these technologies is carefully regulated by a professional group, much like with the construction of "facts" in other scientific fields (Latour 1987; D. Hess 1997; M. Fortun and Bernstein 1998). The primary policy goal in the United States is to integrate unique biometric markers into identification documents, such as passports or national ID cards, and then harmonize these identity tokens with massive databases designed to screen for potential terrorists or to monitor the movements and activities of people more broadly. It is worthwhile noting that U.S. security agencies and industries were already moving toward the widespread application of biometric and other surveillance systems prior to 9/11. The attacks, however, provided the impetus for rapidly deploying the systems with as little public scrutiny or debate as possible (Lyon 2003e; Winner 2004).

But do biometrics work for the purpose of locating and stopping terrorists? According to the U.S. General Accounting Office,[10] although "the desired benefit is the prevention of the entry of travelers who are inadmissible to the United States" (Kingsbury 2003: 6), or "keeping the bad guys out" in President George W. Bush's parlance, the challenges to the success of biometric systems are manifold. Obstacles include labor increases, travel delays, tourism reduction, inadequate training, grandfathering arrangements, reciprocal requirements from other countries, exemptions, false IDs, "significant" costs, and circumvention of border systems by more than 350,000 illegal entries a year (U.S. Citizenship and Immigration Services 2002). In addition, more technical obstacles include managing a massive database of up to 240 million records and maintaining accurate "watch lists" for suspected terrorists.

A recent report by Privacy International is forceful in its denunciation of biometrics and national identity cards. The report argues that because no evidence exists that these systems can or do prevent terrorism, any link between these systems and antiterrorism is merely rhetorical:

> Of the 25 countries that have been most adversely affected by terrorism since 1986, eighty per cent have national identity cards, one third of which incorporate biometrics. This research was unable to uncover any instance where the presence of an identity card system in those countries was seen as a significant deterrent to terrorist activity. Almost two thirds of known terrorists operate under their true identity ... It is possible that the existence of a high integrity identity card would provide a measure of improved legitimacy for these people. (Privacy International 2004a: 2)

Thus, not only might biometric systems fail to perform their intended functions, they might have the opposite effect of deflecting inquiry away from terrorists who possess *valid* high-tech biometric IDs. This point should give policy makers pause, because all of the 9/11 attackers entered the United States legally with the requisite visas (Seghetti 2002). Finally, even with completely operational biometric and national ID systems in place, there are numerous ways to circumvent them, for instance, by pretending to be an "outlier" (or a person unable to provide accurate biometric data), acquiring a false identity, escaping watch lists (by providing false information or by virtue of being a "new recruit"), or spoofing identity (for instance, by using custom-made contact lenses to fool iris scanners) (Privacy International 2004a: 7–8). Regardless of the cost or complexity of implementing and harmonizing biometric systems across countries, it is clear that they can never be foolproof, and it is questionable whether they would even diminish threats (see Van der Ploeg [Chapter 11, this volume] for a detailed inquiry into the social effects of some of these systems along borders).

This section has sought to take seriously some of the questions about surveillance and security, as they are typically mobilized. Although the technologies discussed are clearly varied, complex, and contextually dependent, the purpose has been to probe the common underlying assumption of effectiveness that undergirds their deployment. *Efficacy operates, in a sense, as a prerequisite for any determination of whether trade-offs are worth it.* Concerning crime, evaluative studies of video surveillance indicate some success with car burglaries or traffic-related crimes but little or no success with the prevention of other crimes. The general inadequacy of surveillance for stopping violent crime has been acknowledged for some time and is usually attributed to the spontaneous nature of these crimes, which are often called "crimes of passion." One unanticipated consequence of CCTV, then, is that it may provide people with a false sense of security whereby they expose themselves to increased risks. With regard to terrorism, new biometric systems appear even more ill conceived: the technical and social difficulties are seemingly insurmountable, borders are porous (if incredibly dangerous for illegal immigrants), and costs are significant. Most important, when terrorists can and have entered countries like the United States and United Kingdom legally (or when they are already legal citizens or residents), then complex systems of documentation may do little to prevent legal entry in the future.

If we are to take the question "Do they work?" on its own terms, we are led to other questions: Why are there so few evaluative studies? And why are more independent evaluative studies not funded? One possible answer is that most people do not really want to know if surveillance and security systems work; people are afraid to hear that they might not work or that they are as (or more) vulnerable with them as without them. Although this may be true, it is perhaps too individualistic a response, which neglects the political and institutional forces at work. Another answer, engaged within the following chapters, is that *surveillance and security are important components of emerging neoliberal sensibilities and structures.* Contracts for surveillance systems are enormously lucrative for private industries, the likes of which influence local and national security policies. There are also overtly political reasons for the lack of evaluation studies. For example, in January 2004, the U.S. Department of Homeland Security disbanded an independent task force charged with evaluating security systems at U.S. points of entry. This move baffled some lawmakers, because the task force had "a lengthy research agenda, dedicated staff and budget to carry its work through 2004" (Strohm 2004). It seems that the fatal move of this group was to recommend an independent evaluation of the "U.S. Visitor and Immigrant Status Indicator Technology [US-VISIT] program, a biometric entry–exit system for the nation's borders" (Strohm 2004). By dissolving the task force, the Department of Homeland Security was able to postpone any conversation of US-VISIT's inadequacies and thereby avoid the need to justify the agency's (and the administration's) commitment to a flawed system.

Another related explanation for (inter)national commitment to systems with no demonstrable efficacy at preventing crime or terrorism could be strong cultural desires for retaliatory criminal justice, for catching and punishing criminals after the fact. Even if violent crimes like the murder of Jamie Bulger cannot be prevented, surveillance technologies nourish retributive impulses in societies by supporting judicial mechanisms of payback. Thus, punitive tendencies gain strength when the public, the media, politicians, and academics continue to ask questions that presume the effectiveness of technologies for meeting intended purposes but ignore unintended social changes. Surveillance and security systems may, of course, serve a largely symbolic function. If publics perceive enhanced safety, then this may ensure social order and renew faith in policy makers. Unfortunately, such widespread awareness of and subjection to invasive surveillance may actually increase public fears and aggravate existing social and economic vulnerabilities, as the chapters in this book show.

The belief in trade-offs is contingent on efficacy, so questions about efficacy can potentially undermine the dominant political discourse about what we are willing to give up to achieve security. This, in turn, would require a more nuanced political debate about security. Efficacy questions can also challenge widespread faith in technological progress by implying that real answers to threats of crime or terrorism will involve complex social arrangements that defy quick technological fixes. However, as the next section takes up, even if the answer was "Yes, they do work for their intended purposes," questions about efficacy and trade-offs are dangerously reductive to begin with.[11]

Asking the Right Questions

The main problems with questions about trade-offs or efficacy are that root causes for crime or terrorism are not engaged and that deeper social changes brought about by surveillance and security systems are left uninterrogated. One need not embrace technological determinism—or the simplistic belief that technology drives social change of its own accord without any human agency or intervention—to recognize the profound effects that security regimes have on social life. Surveillance and security systems are simultaneously social and technical, and in some ways this is not a new phenomenon: even before the automation of surveillance, modern bureaucracies and architectures functioned as pervasive technical systems of social control (Weber 2000; Foucault 1977). Technologies are neither separate from society nor are they neutral tools that can be applied discretely to social problems (e.g., crime or terrorism). Instead, technologies are thoroughly social inventions to begin with and are part of the social problems they are intended to correct (Winner 1977). As sociotechnical systems, then, surveillance and security are intimately intertwined with institutions, ideologies, and a long history of social inequality (Lyon 2001; Gandy 1993). From this standpoint, one can begin to ask the kinds of questions worth asking and answering—questions about power.

Why Do We Believe in Trade-offs?

A simple answer to the question of why we believe in trade-offs is that, generally speaking, most people—academics included—think badly about technology. Popular opinion perceives technologies as somehow separate from society; they are neutral, efficient, accurate, and discrete tools used to achieve rational and intentional ends. When technologies fail, people blame "human error" or insufficiently evolved social institutions. And when technologies create more problems, sometimes disastrous ones, they are labeled as "side effects" or "unintended consequences" rather than addressed as problems inherent in the design of technologies themselves (Winner 1986).

Take the following argument as an example of how narrow conceptions of surveillance technologies promulgate the logic of trade-offs. In *The Costs of Privacy,* Steven Nock (1993) claims that surveillance arises out of necessity in modern societies, as a way to simulate traditional monitoring by people and to regulate social norms in a society now based on anonymity. Nock writes,

> As traditional methods of family supervision decline, institutional methods of surveillance arise that serve the same social control functions … New methods of information-gathering and dissemination by employers, creditors, and governments that strike many as worrisome, are not necessarily violations of privacy … Almost all [of these developments] depend on *voluntary self-disclosure* (the completion of credit, insurance or drivers license, or employment forms, for example) … It is certainly legitimate to be concerned about the elaboration of computerized methods of monitoring and tracking people. The use of those techniques, however, is governed by widespread standards of propriety and personal autonomy. (Nock 1993: 4, 13–14; italics added)

In Nock's formulation, surveillance technologies simply automate social control functions that existed previously, without any other meaningful changes in social relations. Moreover, as rational actors, each of us has evaluated the options and voluntarily chosen to participate in new surveillance regimes, seemingly without any coercion or without any sanctions if we had (somehow) chosen to opt out instead.

This view of surveillance technologies lends itself to a discussion of trade-offs because it implies that individuals have total control and intentionality with technology use. It perceives all people as equal rational actors, without any power asymmetries, and intimates that social relations or spaces cannot be altered unintentionally. Technological fixes, from this perspective, are natural social progressions, but—at the same time—technologies somehow operate outside of society, as tools that can be applied to social problems (Weinberg 2003). All that is left to do is for societies to collectively weigh the options and choose intelligently.

What is left out of this view of surveillance? Mainly, all the ways that technological systems produce social relations or have the capacity for such production.[12] The pure view of technology articulated by Nock ignores—is bound to ignore—ways that technologies operate not only as tools but as creators of social worlds.[13] For instance, much like architecture, surveillance "programs" spaces for particular, acceptable activities so that non-sanctioned uses of space are discouraged by the environment. So, schools are for learning, malls are for shopping, streets are for driving, and so on. Provided that one adhere to the official program of a space, he or she will encounter little resistance, but should one try to appropriate a space for other uses, such as socializing, sleeping, or protesting, surveillance systems will be employed to discipline those activities. Thus, surveillance on college campuses is intended to protect property and provide public safety, but security personnel freely admit that they also monitor and record public protests and rallies, just to keep people in line (Brat 2004).

Surveillance technologies clearly alter social behavior and are intended to do so, usually as planned deterrents to deviant behavior *but not always with the outcomes intended.* They act as forms of social engineering that legislate norms for acceptable and unacceptable behaviors and actions, and they accomplish this task by individualizing people. As Jason Patton (2000) explains, when people cannot adjust their behavior to the reactions they perceive in others (i.e., physically removed observers), the social context becomes an ambiguous one where everyone is presumed to be individually deviant until proved otherwise. The result is a "panoptic" effect on social behavior (Foucault 1977), meaning that people tend to police themselves and refrain from any actions that might verify their presumed status as deviants in the eyes of unseen others. Rather than surveillance indicating a rationalized and distributed imposition on individual privacy,[14] however, surveillance is often applied selectively and with varying intensities according to one's social address (Phillips and Curry 2003); as such, surveillance can—and does—structure unequal power relations in societies (Cameron 2004; Van der Ploeg 2005; Kupchik and Monahan forthcoming).

Hille Koskela (2000), writing about video surveillance in Finland, adds to these observations a strong feminist critique. She finds that public surveillance does not deter violent crime against women, but the use of cameras does tend to objectify women, sterilize actions, and thereby masculinize space. The emphasis on visual surveillance is completely gendered, with women more often than not subjected to the disembodied gaze of men who operate the cameras that are concentrated in public spheres frequented by women (e.g., shopping malls, public transportation). Furthermore, even while under the presumably paternalistic eye of security cameras, any nonvisual harassment of women remains undocumented and uncorrected—from the official viewpoint, then, verbal abuse or threats never happen. The masculinization of space, which makes women the objects of surveillance, may be completely unintentional but is nevertheless a real production of social relations brought about by surveillance.

We can believe in trade-offs so long as we pretend that the only affective powers technologies have on social spaces, relations, or meanings are rationally chosen and intended. Thus, surveillance advocates can say, "A camera is just like having another officer on the beat" (Conde 2004: 1) or "There is no theoretical difference between surveillance through a camera lens and a naked eye" (Conde 2004: 2). And these conclusions are believable to the extent that any unintended social effects of the kinds described previously are discounted as side effects and to the extent that data are analyzed from afar without delving into the messy materialities of how surveillance systems work. Whereas side effects are seen as *unintended* consequences of surveillance systems, trade-offs are presented as *anticipated* undesirable outcomes, such as the loss of privacy or civil liberties. Contrary to this position, ethnographic studies of the coordination of CCTV security forces and the police in the United Kingdom reveal labor intensification rather than reduction for police personnel who must now respond to additional disturbances witnessed by camera operators (Goold 2004). Another compelling study finds antagonism caused by competing forms of expertise, such that CCTV operators tell the police to mind their own business, try to take credit for arrests, and sometimes come to blows—quite literally—fighting over jurisdiction (McCahill and Norris 2003). These observations reveal one dimension of how surveillance systems are thoroughly social and could never be just like having more police on the street.

Thinking badly about technology is only one answer for why people believe in trade-offs between what are seen as two goods, such as security and liberty. A perhaps more deep-rooted reason has to do with Western systems of logic predicated on dualities: good–bad, black–white, friend–enemy, and so on. This ingrained way of looking at the world explains the rhetorical power of statements such as President Bush's "Either you're for us, or you're against us" (G.W. Bush 2001), and it also explains the social value attributed to clarity and rationality. It is unfortunate that dualistic thinking also instills a profound intolerance for ambiguity and for the necessary messiness that characterizes social worlds (Derrida 1988). Social perceptions of technology are certainly not immune to dualistic logics, which are usually articulated as being "for" technological progress or being "anti-technology," with no middle ground in between. But there are many ways to measure progress (e.g., social, economic, environmental, emotional) and many possibilities for the design and incorporation of surveillance technologies into social spaces and public institutions.

What Social Relations Do Surveillance and Security Systems Produce?

The question of what social relations are produced through the incorporation of surveillance into daily life directs inquiry toward a rich set of data, far less constrained than questions about trade-offs or efficacy. A different way of phrasing the question might be, "What effects do surveillance and security systems have on power, inequality, or democracy?" This question is intended to be not an argument for causality or determinism but, instead, following Foucault's lead, a recognition of the capacity of power to manifest in quotidian institutional operations that simultaneously generate and sustain social relations apart from any property of control that might be possessed by individuals (Foucault 1977, 1980). Clearly, surveillance is part of larger trends toward sociospatial segregation in modern societies (Caldeira 2000; Low 2003), but the social relations produced by these technologies may be difficult to spot when looking at high-tech systems (such as biometrics or video surveillance) alone. Instead, *by attending to the embedding of surveillance technologies into existing institutional systems and social practices, power relations are much easier to detect.*

Consider the following superb example of asking some of the right questions about everyday surveillance. Virginia Eubanks (2004; Chapter 6, this volume) writes about a small urban city in upstate New York where welfare and food stamp recipients have had their lives dramatically altered by the introduction of "electronic benefit transfer" (EBT) systems. Mandated of all states by the Welfare Reform Act of 1996, these systems signify an effort to crack down on food stamp fraud and, ostensibly, to reduce the stigma attached to using food stamps in public places. The EBT tracking, as a form of electronic surveillance, is intended to increase efficiency and reduce fraud, but at what social and financial cost?

Whereas current holders of EBT cards, who are more often than not women, were previously able to walk to local grocery stores to purchase food as they and their families needed it, they now must endure the added expense and inconvenience of hiring a cab or taking a bus some three miles to the nearest large-chain supermarket that accepts the magnetic-strip EBT cards. The local markets cannot afford, or choose not to implement, the systems necessary to accept the welfare cards as a method of payment. Even if the cardholders did elect to walk the additional distance, the main street that one must use to get to the large supermarket doubles as a state highway, at times without sidewalks, making the trip virtually impossible by foot, especially in winter months. This situation is certainly an impediment to "normal" living or economic assimilation, and the burdens of this card system are unduly shouldered by the poor.

EBT systems can be seen as important precursors to biometric national IDs, where the technologies are tested on the most vulnerable members of society first (Gilliom 2001). These systems can integrate biometric identifiers, as has been proposed by the General Accounting Office (1995), and they have the potential to track the movements and spending habits of individuals. Meanwhile, as public agencies and private companies slowly work out flaws in the system, they are draining much needed resources from the poor. For instance, the cards also double as mechanisms for receiving welfare benefits other than food stamps, and people are charged fees for requesting "cash back" at stores or withdrawing cash from ATMs. A *New York Times* article reports that a mother allotted $448 a month for her family to live on pays up to $2.35 for each transaction and that in 1999 the total number of fees charged to the poor per month was around $275,000 (Barstow 1999). A 2001 audit of the New York EBT system placed the surcharges at up to $700,151 per month (Feig 2001: 13). Moreover, few ATM machines accept the cards, cards often do not work across state lines, and—unlike ATM cards—no protections are offered if the cards are stolen and used by others.[15]

The EBT system serves as a case study of the complex deployment of surveillance technologies in everyday life. The question remains, What social relations are produced by it? Reinforced sociospatial segregation of and increased burden on the poor are two clear outcomes. This is seen with the ghettoizing of the poor in upstate New York: they must now endure added inconvenience and cost to purchase food from grocery stores in more affluent areas and then return to their economically segregated downtown apartments. This example also reveals one more dimension to the radically asymmetrical monitoring and tracking of the poor in the United States, whether in public schools, public transportation, public housing, or places of commerce. Finally, *this example draws attention to the vast profits that private companies stand to accrue at public expense.* As an example, with the privatization of the food stamp program, Citicorp Services, Inc., has been awarded lucrative contracts with 34 states, as well as with Guam and the Virgin Islands (Stegman, Lobenhofer, and Quinterno 2003: 14). And although the outsourcing of public services by states makes it difficult to determine total public costs, Citicorp's contract with California alone is for $250 million over seven years (Bartholow and Garcia 2002), with the potential for up to $450 million (*San Francisco Bay Guardian* 2001).

Pursuing the question of "What social relations are produced?" into the arena of privatized surveillance and security systems reveals a pattern of increased dependency and disempowerment of the poor, coupled with the state's relinquishment of its responsibility to meet the basic needs of citizens. A New York audit of Citicorp and Continental Card Services concluded that

> neither contractor produced all of the contract deliverables or regularly met performance standards. As a result, the EBT system is not meeting client expectations, is not providing the level of service to its users that was anticipated, and may be resulting in clients needlessly incurring surcharge fees to access their benefits. (Feig 2001: 4)

Although purportedly saving money for the public, privatization leaves little recourse to the poor when the system imposes serious difficulties or fails. Furthermore, once states have awarded contracts, costly and protracted legal action is their only alternative if they wish to correct problems. This example illustrates the destructiveness of neoliberal ideologies as they are hardwired into institutions and technological systems. The dual outcome of such arrangements is increased profitability for private companies and increased surveillance and marginalization of the poor (Duggan 2003; Comaroff and Comaroff 2000; Giroux 2004).

This is but one example, taken in detail to show how different surveillance and security regimes could be analyzed from a perspective of social change rather than from one of trade-offs or efficacy. Inquiry into border control and biometrics would likely yield similar findings. For example, the U.S. Department of Homeland Security has awarded a 10-year contract of up to $10 billion to the private company Accenture for biometric systems at U.S. ports of entry (Lichtblau and Markoff 2004). Meanwhile, the increased militarization of the border in California and Texas has produced a funnel effect with immigrants crossing in the most dangerous parts of the desert in Arizona and dying at record rates (Cornelius 2001). The social relations produced are those of empowerment for private industries, disempowerment, dependency, and danger for poor or marginalized groups, and inflexibility for the nation-state to provide both police security and human security for the people within—and outside—its borders. Indeed, security in terms of providing for the well-being of people (i.e., "human security" or "population security") has recently been fused with and largely eclipsed by national security apparatuses and logics (Collier, Lakoff, and Rabinow 2004). Thus, "natural" disasters like those caused by Hurricane Katrina serve both as symbols of this lack of institutional "preparedness" and, strangely enough, as rationales for further neoliberal undermining of social and environmental support mechanisms (Lakoff, Chapter 16, this volume).

How Can Surveillance Be Used to Increase Security without Sacrificing Civil Liberties?

If the important questions about surveillance and security revolve around the production of social relations, as I have claimed, and if trade-offs are attractive, in part, because technologies are seen as somehow divorced from society, then the challenge lies in how to govern surveillance technologies well—with an awareness of their social embeddedness and an eye toward their social ramifications. It may be that most public surveillance systems are misguided and inappropriate to begin with. Clearly, mechanisms for evaluating and contesting such systems need to be developed. Nonetheless, civil libertarians, academics, and progressively minded citizens have been able to make precious few inroads in this direction given the current political climate of "the war on terror." Democratizing surveillance practices—in addition to strategic opposition—may be a second, complementary strategy for intelligent technology design and use.

The question of how to govern surveillance technologies well does not imply seeking a *balance* between security and liberty, because this scale metaphor connotes the same either–or logic of trade-offs: an increase on one side necessarily diminishes the other. Rather, it means asking questions about how surveillance can be used to increase security without sacrificing liberties, if at all, and perhaps even to augment liberties. Jeffrey Rosen (2004) writes, as a telling example of a technical solution to this problem, about two different kinds of body screening technologies for passengers at airports. The first displays naked bodies in anatomically correct detail, including any hidden objects that people may be carrying; the second "extracts the images of concealed objects and projects them onto a sexless mannequin" (Rosen 2004: 4). Both systems, which Rosen refers to as "the naked machine" and "the blob machine," respectively, provide the same degree of security, but the blob machine is less invasive by design. This example demonstrates that there are social and technical choices to be made when it comes to surveillance and security, should we take the time to inquire.

The comparison between the "naked" and the "blob" machines is intended to illustrate both the contingency of technological systems and the need for alternatives. It may be the case that neither machine is desirable or sufficiently democratic, for even the blob machine objectifies, scrutinizes, and individualizes people while shifting power to those doing the monitoring. If democratic or liberty-safeguarding designs are not readily available, then perhaps societies should insist on them before proceeding further. Most of the time, there will not be easy answers to the question of how to ensure national security without sacrificing liberties, but until this is seen as a question worth asking, it is likely that surveillance and security systems will continue to disproportionately impose upon and discriminate against women and poor, ethnic minorities.

A starting point would be to make surveillance systems more transparent and democratic. For most people, especially in the United States, surveillance is inherently ambiguous. It is unclear where the cameras (or other information-gathering devices) are, who owns the equipment, who is watching, what the policies are for collecting and disposing of data, to what use data will be put, and what rights people have. In the United Kingdom, under the Data Protection Act of 2000, there are strict rules governing data collection and retention,[16] including the disclosure of surveillance monitoring through signage (e.g., signs telling people when they are under surveillance), but even so, it is estimated that 73 percent of CCTV cameras in London alone are in noncompliance with these rules (McCahill and Norris 2002: 21).[17] The United States is far behind in even establishing basic disclosure policies and does not appear to be interested in catching up. Transparency would mean dissolving some of the many layers of ambiguity around surveillance and recognizing that just because data can be collected and saved indefinitely does not mean that they should be or that collecting and saving data is productive for maintaining and protecting civil society. Indeed, social forgetfulness is a core value in American society, tied to its frontier history (seen in idioms such as "a clean slate," "a fresh start," "forgive and forget"), so data collection, retention, and disposal policies should be critical elements in the governance of surveillance systems (Blanchette and Johnson 2002).

It stands to reason that the best way to increase transparency is to increase public participation in the governance of surveillance. From a policy perspective, this could be done by conducting surveys or interviews about the social effects of surveillance systems (not just about public approval) and using that data to inform public policy. It could be done by requiring a public vote on all surveillance systems and policies, just like for other infrastructure-related projects, but with choices that extend beyond "yes" or "no" to provide a range of options concerning the policies for such systems. Informational pamphlets on ballot initiatives could be distributed wherein one could find evaluations of existing systems elsewhere, discussions of the pros and cons, and so forth. Or, in a much stronger vein, incentives could be provided to enroll citizens of all walks of life into the policy-making process, including participation on subcommittees, citizen review panels, and oversight committees (Sclove 1995).

Some might argue that democratic transparency and participation may work well for local contexts and for relatively mundane purposes but not for national security, where secrecy is somehow mandated. I disagree with this objection. Greater transparency is needed on the level of national security so that individuals know their rights, security agents are held accountable, and contracts with private security industries are kept in check. Given recent revelations that President Bush authorized the U.S. National Security Agency to spy on citizens illegally, the pressing need for transparency and accountability to preserve civil liberties could not be more apparent. Moreover, the call for secrecy with national security neglects (rather than cultivates) public expertise—effectively forcing the public into passive identity roles instead of those of active, democratic agents. Although the U.S. Department of Homeland Security's efforts to enroll citizens into surveillance operations are obviously misguided and problematic, especially for their authoritarian approach to "participation" (see Marx, Chapter 3, this volume), members of the public are often acutely aware of security vulnerabilities but simply do not communicate them for fear of becoming targets of increased suspicion or legal retaliation (see Winner, Chapter 17, this volume). Public involvement may, in fact, help to limit violations of civil liberties, detect fraud, correct security vulnerabilities, and decrease the need for extensive surveillance systems.

Public involvement in data monitoring presents another venue for increasing transparency through participation. In combination with neighborhood-watch initiatives, the public could assist with monitoring cameras, as has been tried with reported success in public housing communities in Boston (Nieto 1997), or could get involved with "copwatch" organizations, which, if sensitive to community needs, could help protect vulnerable members of society (see Huey, Walby, and Doyle, Chapter 9, this volume). Unlike the case described earlier, where community members did not watch surveillance feeds on their television sets (Musheno, Levine, and Palumbo 1978), far better results could likely be produced by designating responsibility to specific community members (or to volunteers) in on-site control rooms or on the streets. The difference revolves around the "valence" (C.G. Bush 1997) of sociotechnical systems: watching television is a passive and removed social experience, but being directly responsible for community safety is a uniquely active experience. At the very least, security personnel doing the monitoring can remain proximate to communities, visible to and approachable by people within communities rather than located in remote "surveillance farms" far away both physically and socially from the people they observe. Naturally, an informed public debate about the merits of public surveillance should precede any community-watching scenario. Part of this should include asking questions of how to provide adequate oversight of surveillance practices, identifying—in advance—specific criteria for "successful" surveillance interventions, and specifying when and under what conditions the systems will be disabled. Absent such discussions, this recommendation could easily fold into a "snitch" or "tattling" culture, where community members spy on each other and contribute to a society of widespread suspicion, discrimination, and social control (see Marx, Chapter 3, this volume).

Unfortunately, efforts at achieving transparency and democracy are not only absent from the current surveillance landscape but being pushed further beyond the horizon, making them harder to imagine, let alone attain, with every passing moment. As the example of the EBT system for welfare recipients demonstrates, the privatization of surveillance, security, and public services delegates technical decisions to companies with profit imperatives rather than social equality agendas. The same could be said of private security forces in malls, gated communities, business improvement districts, war zones, and disaster areas. And the same could be said of vast urban surveillance systems outsourced to private companies by cities or implemented by the private sector without any public oversight or jurisdiction. Finally, the policy aftershocks of 9/11—namely, the USA PATRIOT and Homeland Security Acts—have made public surveillance at once more secretive and pervasive, so the public sector does not exactly provide a model worth emulating in this regard.

Increasing transparency and democratic participation in the governance of surveillance systems are not guaranteed mechanisms for achieving national security or human security or for preserving civil liberties, of course, but they are surely steps in the right direction. The approach advocated here, then, takes the social embeddedness and anticipated ramifications of technologies as a departure point and is therefore predisposed to notice social inequalities earlier in the process and better equipped to mitigate them (Woodhouse and Nieusma 2001; Guston and Sarewitz 2002). The key is seeing surveillance systems as political entities with the capacity to produce social relations—whether intended or not—and then asking how they can be employed to achieve democratic outcomes. From this perspective, "good" surveillance systems would be those that corrected power asymmetries and increased human security in societies. One example might be the website Scorecard.org, which collects and disseminates information about toxic releases in local neighborhoods, assigns blame for environmental contamination (when possible), and provides action items for people to get involved in monitoring industries and cleaning up their communities (K. Fortun 2004). Surveillance systems are more likely to meet the goal of power correction if they are designed for "structural

flexibility" (Monahan 2005a), meaning that they are democratic, participatory, localized, and open to alteration.

Conclusion

This chapter has set out to destabilize the framing of surveillance and
security in terms of trade-offs. Although conversations about trade-offs—
between security and liberty, for example—may serve a strategic purpose
of drawing attention to matters of importance and values worth preserving, these debates artificially constrain inquiry by offering little room
to talk about deeper social changes underway with the incorporation of
surveillance technologies into everyday life. These changes include the
ongoing privatization of public spaces and services; increased social and
spatial segregation along class, race, and gender lines; and disproportionate burdens and risks placed on marginalized groups in society. Moreover,
questions about trade-offs or balances or efficacy are all predicated on an
uninterrogated assumption that taking national security seriously must
perforce threaten liberty or other social goods. It is worth probing the
veracity of such assumptions and the reasons why they are so attractive.

I began by taking questions about trade-offs on their own terms, specifically evaluating the efficacy of surveillance systems in preventing crime
or terrorism. It turns out that there are very few independent evaluative
studies and that they are inconclusive at best. There is evidence to suggest
that surveillance systems may deter vehicular and traffic crimes but that
they do not deter violent crimes at all. In the domain of national security,
there is no evidence to suggest efficacy, in spite of the great financial costs,
institutional labor, and public inconvenience. In fact, surveillance and biometric systems may provide a false sense of security, thereby increasing
vulnerability across the board. The absence of studies and debates about
efficacy could mean that most people—or at least most policy makers and
industry contractors—do not really want to know if surveillance and security systems work.

Even if surveillance and security systems were highly effective, I assert
that questions about trade-offs are still misguided. Better questions worth
asking include the following: Why do we believe in trade-offs? What social
relations are produced by surveillance systems? How can surveillance
be used to increase security without sacrificing civil liberties? Tentative
answers might be that relations of inequality are produced, that technologies are not seen as the social and political agents that they are, and that
transparent policies and democratic governance of surveillance would help
amend the situation. My purpose has been not to present these alternative
questions as the only ones worth asking or to answer them definitively but

instead to open up the conversation, moving beyond trade-offs to a fuller consideration of the role of surveillance in society. The chapters that follow extend the conversation in this way by analyzing the politics of surveillance and security in everyday life.

Acknowledgments

Special thanks to Gary T. Marx and Michael Musheno for their generous comments on this chapter and on the volume as a whole.

Notes

1. This is not meant to imply direct causality between the Bulger killing and the rise of CCTV systems in the United Kingdom, because certainly other factors such as fear of terrorists contribute to this trend. That said, immediately following the Bulger murder, "John Major's Conservative government decided to devote more than three-quarters of its crime-prevention budget to encourage local authorities to install CCTV" (Rosen 2001).
2. Other scholars have criticized the Airdrie study for similar reasons: that crime did rise in peripheral areas and even increased in the district by 20 percent (S. Graham 1998; Dawson 1994; Davies 1995).
3. Other reports calculating public and private expenditures on CCTV put the figure at anywhere from £225 million to £450 million being spent *per year* in the United Kingdom (Nieto, Johnston-Dodds, and Simmons 2002: 9).
4. In fact, a few activist countersurveillance groups have emerged to respond to this lack of knowledge and oversight with cameras monitoring public spaces (Monahan forthcoming; Institute for Applied Autonomy 2004; New York Surveillance Camera Players 2002).
5. It is more likely that the Office of Technology Assessment (OTA) produced balanced reports about the complexity of technologies and that policy makers were frustrated that these reports could not translate into simple or clear-cut policy recommendations (Bimber 1996; Sarewitz 1996).
6. Of course the affluent are filmed regularly in places of commerce, like shopping malls or banks, but these are almost exclusively privately owned surveillance systems deployed on private property, not public systems monitoring public space. A similar observation could be made of the monitoring of the affluent in private gated communities.
7. I would categorize these appropriations of surveillance systems as instances of *countersurveillance:* intentional, tactical uses or disruptions of surveillance technologies to correct institutional power asymmetries (Monahan forthcoming). Like other appropriations of technology (Eglash et al. 2004), countersurveillance reveals the underdetermination of technology and destabilizes deterministic views of technological progress. Gary T. Marx (2003b) calls such acts of resistance to dominant uses of surveillance "a tack in the shoe," exploiting ironic vulnerabilities in larger projects of total public surveillance.
8. Potential conflicts of interest also exist when cities and private companies profit handsomely from the operation of these red-light systems. As a California report relates, "In San Diego, a judge dismissed nearly 300 tickets in a class-action lawsuit, ruling that the evidence was unreliable because the system is privately run and the company is paid through a percentage of the fines" (Nieto, Johnston-Dodds, and Simmons 2002: 21).
9. For an example of one such professional community, see http://biometrics.propagation.net/forums/.
10. In 2004, the U.S. General Accounting Office was officially renamed the "Government Accountability Office." The legislation that enacted this change was the "GAO Human Capital Reform Act," which was signed into law by President Bush on July 7, 2004. Among other things, this legislation "will allow the agency [the Government Accountability Office] to break its link to the federal employee pay system and adopt compensation prac-

tices that are more closely tied to job performance and other factors" (Barr 2004). This means increased instability for government workers and signals the gradual elimination of unionized labor in the federal government. Of course, the symbolism of the name change is crucial: it signals the embracing of neoliberal ideologies, new managerial practices, and disciplinary organizational structures. Elsewhere, I have called these trends *fragmented centralization*, indicating the simultaneous centralization of decision-making authority and decentralization of accountability for (and instability brought about by) those decisions (Monahan 2005a, 2005b).

11. Some technology critics may instead seek to question the purposes served by surveillance—or the stated intended goals of these technologies in specific contexts. This line of inquiry would be a fine starting point if surveillance policies were transparent and rationales were clear. For almost all deployments of surveillance on the public (whether by state agents or by industry agents), this is not the case. There is no enlightened, objective perspective one could achieve to parse policy goals, technologies, and social contexts. Questions of power are more complicated than that, and policy motives are often obscure, influenced by multiple ideological and professional interests.

12. A recognition of the contingent design of all technologies is also often absent from these formulations. This perspective is known as the "social construction of technology" (e.g., Bijker, Hughes, and Pinch 1987; Bijker and Law 1992) and is one way to track the complex design processes that lead to the systems that we often take for granted. Rather than being outside of society and impinging on it in some deterministic way, technologies and social practices exist in dynamic and mutually shaping relationships.

13. Staples (2000) offers a compelling case for the many ways that new forms of electronic, "postmodern" surveillance are radically different from previous, "modern" ones. Mainly, contemporary surveillance is systematic and impersonal, targets bodies more than people, is locally integrated into everyday practices, and scrutinizes and profiles everyone as potentially "deviant," in advance of any evidence or informed suspicion to that effect. Haggerty and Ericson (2000) similarly theorize the distributed, decentralized power and politics of contemporary surveillance regimes. The potential of electronic surveillance for monitoring everyone equally, however, should not imply the removal of asymmetrical power relations, discrimination, or profiling; if anything, these particularistic inequalities are perpetuated, extended, and simultaneously masked by the rhetoric of universalistic (read "objective") surveillance and security (Curry 2004).

14. Privacy is, of course, an ambiguous and hyperindividualized concept that does not account very well for encroachments on social spaces and practices absent targeted individual scrutiny, usually in "private" domains. One way to overcome the limitations of privacy as a conceptual category is to expand it beyond legal definitions to include multiple forms of information generation, access, and expression in modern societies (DeCew 1997; Phillips forthcoming). Another approach is to focus on trust relations, which hold communities and cultures together—manifested either in contestations of social power or in voluntary disclosures for the sake of intimacy or social cohesion (Bourdieu 1977; de Certeau 1984; de Certeau, Giard, and Mayol 1998).

15. In another example, in August 2001, a computer glitch incorrectly registered close to six thousand EBT transactions, double-charging many people (Shesgreen and Hollinshed 2001).

16. The data protection guidelines issued by the Organization for Economic Cooperation and Development provide a related template for regulating surveillance technologies; however, such guidelines were crafted with the primary aim of facilitating trade, not protecting privacy, so their use may be limited for thinking about the power relations engendered by new technologies (Clarke 1989).

17. Goold (2004) also cautions that police officers may require additional oversight to ensure that they do not interfere with control room operators or tamper with surveillance data—two practices that were identified in a study he carried out in the United Kingdom.

Neoliberal States

CHAPTER **2**

The State Goes Home

Local Hypervigilance of Children and the
Global Retreat from Social Reproduction

CINDI KATZ

In an early scene in *The Terminator,* the cyborgian played by Arnold Schwarzenegger walks into an L.A. gun shop and asks to see the wares. The shopkeeper lays out Uzis, submachine guns, rocket launchers, and other sophisticated means of overkill, nervously understating, "Any one of these will suit you for home defense purposes." The situation is likewise in the growing child protection industry. In keeping with the shopkeeper's sly comment, these businesses feast on an all-pervasive culture of fear, while creating a mockery, alibi, and distraction out of what they are really about—to remake the home as a citadel through the peddling of private protective technologies that reinforce it against various forms of intrusion. These industries offer utterly inappropriate technocratic solutions for broad social problems. More important, the growth of the child protection industry is yet another response to the venomous and slippery fear-of-crime discourse that has become one of the key stocks in trade of the neoliberal state. Retrenching on its commitments to the social wage, the contemporary state has not reneged at all, of course, on its commitments to social order.

The commitment to order is legitimated through a tedium of pronouncements concerning crime that creates an aura of fearfulness and distrust while naturalizing increasingly virulent policing, stepped-up prison construction, stricter sentencing policies, and the like, as responses. As the circular discourse of crime, fear, law, and order—propounded at all scales of the U.S. state and largely unquestioned in conventional media—has burgeoned, there has been little willingness to address whether these measures actually have any impact on crime or the creation of genuine public safety. But one thing is certain: the discourse of fear has provoked an increasingly serious domestic response to the perceived dangers in our midst. It is no small irony, then, that as the state pumps up fear to legitimate itself and its skewed expenditures, the loathing it simultaneously produces and the distrust it stokes have encouraged the proliferation of privatized strategies of coping. From the explosion in the production of household armaments to the alarming of all personal property, many Americans seem intent on taking the law into their own hands. This tendency, coupled with the sort of precious concern for children's well-being that has become prevalent in the United States since the late 1970s (cf. C. Katz 1995; Ivy 1993; Cahill 1990), has created the ideal conditions for the emergence and growth of the child protection industry.

The child protection industry is part of the $1.1 billion home surveillance industry brought about by the migration of spy technologies and logics across the domestic frontier. Its products enable parents to monitor from afar their children, childcare workers, and others interacting with their kids. Selling technologies such as "nanny cams" and child-watch monitors, among an arsenal of home security accessories—tasers, pepper spray, maces (including "child-size mace with a mini alarm"), stun guns, crossbows, animal repellents, electronic barking dogs, door braces, telephone voice changers, all manner of safes, infrared alarms, wrist rockets—these businesses render something like a burglar alarm almost quaint, to say nothing of the notion that technologies appropriate for the home should encompass things like vacuum cleaners.

The child protection industry markets its products by tapping into a great and growing anxiety that children can and should be protected from everything. But the anxiety is papered over with disingenuous claims about family life. For instance, "at Securityke we are intent upon reducing the amount of child abuse in America by empowering parents with the appropriate equipment needed to survey your child's surroundings."[1] This claim neatly glides over the fact that nearly all child abuse is perpetrated by members of the child's family. Other companies trade on purveying a family ideal that attempts to overcome, if not ignore entirely, all the ways in which family life has changed over the past few decades. "What we're doing is re-creating the nuclear family from a distance," insists Jack Martin of Simplex Knowledge. With his wife, Patti, Martin invented "I See You," a camera that posts intermittent photographs of childcare settings on a website accessible only to parents and others with a password so that they can check in on their child from work, home, or elsewhere to ensure that the day is going smoothly (Lombardi 1997). Although these cameras in day-cares do enable parents to reassure themselves that, indeed, their children stopped crying after they left or to have a moment of pleasure by observing their children in the middle of the workday, the substantial investment on the part of childcare centers is not to "re-create the nuclear family from a distance" but to demonstrate that their services are safe, reliable, and—one hopes—stimulating. Others hawking the technologies disavow that they are pandering to parental anxiety about their children's safety and use familiarization as a selling point. They suggest that if parents know what their children are doing in daycare, they will find it easier to strike up an evening conversation with them. Other businesses invoke consumer sovereignty as a selling point for getting cameras in daycares, exclaiming that because parents pay so much for childcare and their children's educa-tions, they deserve to know whether they are getting good value for the money. No matter what they claim in their materials, however, virtually all of these businesses are willing to prey on parental fears and use sen-sationalized accounts of children putatively abused by nonfamilial care providers to sell their wares. The murderous nanny Louise Woodward is never far from the scene.

None of these technologies—no matter how strange or impractical—offer anything more than microscale and private solutions to what are social and political-economic problems. Of course, in the contemporary neoliberal climate, that is precisely their allure. Rather than agitating for safer public environments or socially provided childcare, individual house-holds can purchase or rent an array of technologies designed to reassure them that their private strategies for minding their children are at the very least doing them no harm. Such privatized strategies sidestep the social issues of social reproduction in the contemporary United States, including the lack of public or corporate support for childcare or other social benefits and the largely unaltered gender division of household labor that contin-ues to hold women responsible for childcare whether they provide it them-selves or organize and schedule others to do so. They also take for granted the enormous gaps between wealthy and poor households, both nationally and internationally, that enable households of one class to employ mem-bers of another. Yet it is in part these inequalities that foster the distrust and animosity that lead to investments in surveillance technologies.

Among the technologies for sale or rent are "nanny cams," which are miniature wireless or wired devices that can be mounted in the home or come concealed in teddy bears, air purifiers, lamps, clocks, and the like. The cameras enable parents to produce a covert tape or live video of their child and his or her minder. Some systems are motion activated, and some record sound as well as image, but most provide a simple visual record of the scene. Most of those who deploy these technologies do not like what they see. Of course, these parents are a suspicious lot to begin with, but according to one purveyor of nanny cams in the United States, 70 percent of users fire their nanny. They rarely find evidence of abuse but rather degrees of benign neglect—nannies who let children watch television rather than playing with them, who talk on the telephone rather than with their charges, who let children cry rather than attend to them, or who nap while kids are left to their own devices. Although these issues can be serious, they often are not, and taking such extreme action as firing the caregiver rather than clarifying expectations begs the question of how most parents would fare under the disciplining gaze of such scrutiny. Perhaps after breaching the trust one might expect in such an intimate employer–employee relationship, there is no going back to a discussion of work expectations.

Other surveillance technologies include sophisticated ambulatory child monitors that take to new heights the sound monitors many parents now routinely place in children's rooms so they can hear the slightest whimper from elsewhere in the home. The new monitors can be belted onto children so that parents can hear them from distances of up to 50 meters away. Using the ambulatory monitor, parents can hear all of their child's interactions as he or she roams autonomously. The monitor will beep the child minder if the child wanders more than 50 meters away or, most reassuringly, if the child falls into water. In theory, the child has independent mobility while the parent can relax or do other things, reassured in the knowledge that he or she will hear if the child talks with anyone, falls, or gets too far afield. As anyone who has ever minded a young child outdoors will attest, this prospect is unrealistic at best, and it is difficult to imagine an older child agreeing to wear the monitor. As children become more autonomous, however, many contemporary U.S. families invest in beepers or cell phones so that parents and children can always be in contact. Apart from these individualized devices, daycare-based camera systems like "I See You" provide rapidly changing still photographs or, with the more sophisticated systems, videos of the childcare setting that parents can watch on a password-accessible site on the Internet. A growing number of childcare centers have installed these systems; they report that 30 percent of households sign up for it. Checking on one's child throughout the day seems to provide many parents with just the right balm to soothe their anxieties about their child's well-being and ease their guilt about keeping children in care for long periods of time. Of course, a quick glance at their child also gives parents a little boost and a pleasurable distraction at work.

The latest child monitoring technologies are electronic tracking systems. These systems, which involve the use of a chip that can be located with global positioning systems, were initially developed for tracing merchandise in warehouses or on delivery routes. They have begun to be used in some large private parks for keeping a watch on children "freely" wandering on the grounds, and they recently came on the market for individual use. In parks, parents rent a wrist or ankle band with an embedded chip that can be removed from their child only with a special device. Child minders can then visit kiosks outfitted with video monitors that reveal their child's location anywhere on the property. The next iteration of this technology, already dubbed "Digital Angel," involves placing the chip subcutaneously in the child for constant vigilance. Marketing has been stalled by the legal privacy issues raised by embedding a chip in another person, even one's own child.

Any one of these technologies is suitable for "home defense purposes." What is being defended against? For one, guilt and anxiety are frequently the prime emotions of two-career couples, but evidence suggests that these emotions affect women more deeply than they do their male partners (cf. Lombardi 1997; Wrigley 1999). The technologies also "defend" against the absence of state- or business-subsidized high-quality daycare in either neighborhood or work settings, because they offer a way to ensure that whatever childcare services are purchased by those who can afford them are high quality. Such individualized strategies sidestep the question of why these issues are so vexed in the United States. Not coincidentally, the struggle for widely available and affordable childcare is no longer much on the agenda of middle-class and professional people, who have come to take care of their childcare needs through private means and then invest in surveillance technologies to ensure their quality. These technologies are also a defense against the scattering of the extended family and the increased hours of parental work outside the home that characterized the late twentieth century.

These forays into hypervigilance are a portal into a host of larger issues and questions that have precipitated the very problems against which home surveillance technologies and other micropractices of childcare are purportedly defending. In part, I wish to show that microdefenses will never be adequate to the task. I also attempt to understand why these sorts of hypervigilant strategies have arisen in the realm of social reproduction and to link this phenomenon to the rise in "terror talk" concerning children's safety and vulnerability more generally (C. Katz 1995). It must be noted how privileged it is to fetishize certain children's well-being, while at the same time—thanks to broad retreats in social reproduction—other children are vulnerable to risks of an entirely different order. These risks, such as homelessness, poor schools, lack of health care, and unsafe and understimulating public environments, not only go largely unremarked but also are largely made invisible by the resolutely narrow focus of hypervigilance, as if individual issues of children's safety are the only ones that matter. Moreover, part of the anxiety that drives hypervigilance is the result of hiring childcare workers across the income gap created by uneven capitalist development and nourished by globalized capitalist production. Children are vulnerable, north, south, east, and west, because of the crumbling of the social wage and the retreat from social reproduction enabled by the globalization of capitalist production. This is much more dangerous than an understimulating nanny, even a murderous one.

A hallmark of the globalization of capitalist production has been a retreat by capital from its prior commitments to place. Reproducing a labor force and the conditions of production in any particular locale is less germane to enduring economic growth than it was in the past. Workers—unionized or not—have suffered the consequences of the reneging by capitalists on the promises of Fordism and retreats from earlier gains in the social wage. The heightened mobility of capital investment has also led various public authorities to reduce or abate corporate taxes, which, among other things, has reduced public monies available for social welfare. Responsibility for social reproduction has shifted increasingly to private domains, where it is accomplished through household labor—still largely women's—or is purchased. As a result, the nature, scope, and material social practices of social reproduction have become increasingly uneven, such that wealth is transferred to capital from private households and poorer areas near and far.

For instance, as feminist geographers have made clear in studies of the questions of social reproduction associated with childcare, the transnational migration of childcare workers of various types represents a subsidy to wealthier "first world" women (and, by extension, their employers). The subsidy comes from young "first world" women or, more commonly, from women from the global South whose own children are often left behind with relatives, enabling the women to work longer hours but also to receive less compensation in the process (e.g., D. Rose 1993; Pulsipher 1993). The state plays a role in this process. In the United States and Canada, immigration policies admit lone women workers from certain poorer nations (most often in the global South) and simultaneously prevent their families from joining them. Various visa programs in both countries ensure a continuous supply of cheap domestic labor, including nannies and other child minders. The state is also involved in other politico-economic aspects of social reproduction. From state-subsidized electrification, water supplies, and sewage treatment to schools and health care services, as well as a variety of goods and services associated with the "welfare state," the state has long been implicated in social reproduction. The varying role of the state across history and geography also affects the balance between the various constituencies. Recent trends toward privatization, for example, have created sharp distinctions between rich and poor households in how the work of social reproduction is carried out.

Another aspect of hypervigilance is that globalized production promulgates an illusion of placelessness for capitalism. That has enabled it to renege on many of its commitments to particular locales, leading to state and selective corporate disinvestment in social reproduction and to the privatization of many elements of social reproduction, through either household labor or purchase. At the same time, the unevenness of capitalist production gone global has produced an uneven landscape of work, ready workers, compensation, and the like that is partially recalibrated through international labor migration, itself a response to and a promulgator of this unevenness. Due to a gendered pattern of migration, childcare workers and domestic laborers tend to be women whose ability to leave their own children behind in networks of family care reduces the cost of their labor and enables them to work relatively unencumbered for longer hours caring for other people's children.

Home-based childcare, then, works across globalized income and service inequalities, producing and drawing on differentiated cultures of care. In these ways, it brings to the fore in the most intimate setting questions of cultural difference, identity, and the exchange of "love" for money and money for "love." Although most childcare workers do their jobs well, it appears that many parents expect the women they employ to "love" and attend to the children in their care as they would. Many of these women, of course, do love the children they care for, and they often report trying to discipline them as the parents want, even when this runs counter to the ways they would discipline their own children (Wrigley 1999; Hochschild 2000). Yet such intimate wranglings have largely unrecognized and often deep psychic costs. As a result, some nannies may indeed be neglectful, resentful, or even abusive, but most are the opposite, even when they suffer the absence of their own families (Hochschild 2000). However disquieting and tragic the rare instance of caregiver violence, it is noteworthy that the anxiety many employers feel about the safety of their children in these intimate strangers' hands perhaps stems from their having internalized the ghastly truth of the inequalities that make this labor exchange possible.

Finally, as I noted previously, the availability of relatively cheap domestic workers enables families in the global North to enlist a private solution to their childcare problems. These middle-class parents do not advocate for social or public provision of childcare services, which in earlier periods of feminist and progressive activism in the United States were on the agenda. Neither does the situation alter the gendered division of house-hold labor. Indeed, when the delicate system breaks down, research and anecdotal evidence suggest that it is almost always mothers who alter their professional schedules to accommodate the glitch, even when their profes-sional position and responsibilities are equal to their husbands' (Wrigley 1999; Weissbourd 1999). Likewise, the reliance on privatized solutions to providing childcare does nothing to alter onerous workplace demands regarding the length of the working day or inequities in such things as flexible schedules or the provision of subsidized childcare.

All of this is taking place parallel to the recent backlash against femi-nism and the unrelenting disciplining of women over household and childcare responsibilities in the United States, despite the many gains in gender equality. These disciplining tactics are witnessed in innumerable articles in the popular press. They address the putative dangers to chil-dren of being away from their parents for long periods, slyly suggest that if children were better cared for at home, behavioral breakdowns would not occur, or they sensationalize catastrophes involving child minders. Moreover, women consistently receive harsher punishments than do men in "failure to protect" court cases, itself an arena of broad expansion, and all manner of sources have proliferated an enduring image of women as mothers. These tactics fuel women's guilt and anxiety about not spending time with their children. Some of this guilt and anxiety is channeled in part into ensuring that the person who is there—who has usually crossed global and local gaps of inequality between the parent employers and the childcare workers—is worthy. For a growing number of parent employers, this has led to the use of spy technologies in the home.

Perhaps the most interesting upshot of these shifts in social reproduc-tion is the resurgence of the state in miniature and privatized form. If the post-Fordist, post-Keynesian state was hollowed out in terms of the provision of social reproduction, it has returned in domesticated form—under our beds. The flexing of parental and household sovereignty and the delegation of all manner of responsibility for social reproduction to the household have produced mini states (of siege). The impulse to produce a miniature state at home is appealed to and nurtured in advertisements for domestic spy and self-protection technologies and weaponry that offer such reassuring exhortations as, "Courts have ruled that government does not have a specific duty to protect individuals. ... Experience the difference of knowing you can protect yourself."[2]

In the privatized state, parents become spies. They spy on their nan-nies and on other domestic workers. Few express any ethical qualms about the practice, let alone concern for the legal implications of their acts. As one Long Island mother chillingly enthused, "When it comes to my own child, I don't care about the nanny's rights" (D.M. Katz 1998). Parents also spy on their children. When the children are young, parents are most commonly using technologies to extend the reach of their eyes and ears through the use of room and ambulatory monitors to ensure that their children are safe, but when children reach middle childhood or adolescence, the intent of the monitoring shifts to discerning whether children are being "good." New technologies allow a long arm of parental law. Some have special devices installed in their cars (often courtesy of their automobile insurance company) to monitor the speed of their teenaged drivers. After their kids have driven the family car, parents can get a readout that enables them to catch infractions that may have eluded the police. Other parents avail themselves of drug-testing kits made for domestic use. The kits come complete with instructions to parents about how to clandestinely get a lock of their child's hair. Computer surveillance is available for the completely paranoid, though most of these technologies are reportedly deployed against spouses rather than children, whose access to cyberspace is frequently censored by parent-activated filters. Nevertheless, computer surveillance technologies enable parents or partners to monitor every keystroke and thus know every addressee, every website visited, the content of every message sent, and even the user's password so that at another time they can directly enter the account. The "household state," like many larger states, is involved in surveillance and censorship and acts with little regard for inhabitants' rights to privacy, self-determination, or the presumption of innocence. Although privacy laws protect against government surveillance, there are no federal standards in the United States to protect against domestic or other forms of private spying.

In perhaps a more benign vein, parenting is also viewed as a form of community policing. Companies selling the monitoring and surveillance technologies claim to offer "innovative ways for mothers and fathers to be close to kids, but give them a sense of control and reassurance." In fact, most of these technologies enable parents and children to have a parallel existence but to feel interconnected (at least on the parents' part). Very little attention is paid in these sales pitches or the discussions around them to the experiences of contemporary children as always being watched, to say nothing of what it will mean for them to grow up taking it for granted that they are under surveillance (cf. Marx 1996).

The technologies on offer may give parents and children a sense of control and reassurance and may indeed respond to the twin plagues of anxiety and guilt. However, I argue that the problems are of a different order. It is not possible to protect children from everything—as anxious parents in the global North seem to want to do—with all the micromanagement in the world (including the children's own defiance and the stubborn fact that most of the dangers to children come from the family itself). Most significantly, the problems are social, political, and economic and so, too, must be the means to redress them. The shrunken state under our beds cannot redress the problems produced by the broad retreats from the social wage resulting from the globalization of capitalist production; by the enduring inequalities of class, race, and nation that foster lopsided domestic exchanges of money, love, and care; or by the gendered division of household labor and the unwillingness of most employees to recognize this in workplace rules that might provide for schedule flexibility, if not work-based care arrangements. All that little state can do is monitor what happens in the riven domestic field that is produced by these problems. The proliferation of child protection technologies and the broadening of surveillance across the domestic frontier mark an enormous retreat from politics. Exposing the issues that have provoked this shift provides fertile grounds for broad-based organizing and action.

Acknowledgments

Thanks to Gretchen Susi, who provided expert and speedy research assistance for this essay, and to Neil Smith, whose reading of it prompted me to strengthen my argument. Thanks especially to Philomena Mariani for encouraging me to write this and, as always, for her maverick insights on the social workings of capitalism. A version of this chapter originally appeared in the journal *Social Justice* 28, no. 3 (2001): 47–56; it is reprinted here with the journal's permission.

Notes

1. From www.securityke.com (accessed in 2001).
2. From www.protectself.com (accessed in 2001).

CHAPTER 3

Soft Surveillance

The Growth of Mandatory Volunteerism in Collecting Personal Information—"Hey Buddy Can You Spare a DNA?"

GARY T. MARX

Never underestimate the willingness of the American public to tell you about itself.

Direct-marketing executive

In Truro, Massachusetts, at the end of 2004, police politely asked all male residents to provide DNA samples to match with DNA material found at the scene of an unsolved murder. Residents were approached in a non-threatening manner (even as their license plate numbers were recorded) and asked to help solve the crime. This tactic of rounding up all the usual suspects (and then some) is still rare in the United States for historical, legal, and logistical reasons, but it is becoming more common. The Truro case illustrates expanding trends in surveillance and social control.[1]

There is increased reliance on "soft" means for collecting personal information. In criminal justice contexts these means involve some or all of the following: persuasion to gain voluntary compliance, universality, or at least increased inclusiveness in the broad net they cast, and emphasis on the needs of the community relative to the rights of the individual.

As with other new forms of surveillance and detection, the process of gathering the DNA information is quick and painless, involving a mouth swab, and is generally not felt to be invasive. This makes such requests seem harmless relative to the experience of having blood drawn, having an observer watch while a urine sample is produced for drug testing, or being patted down or undergoing a more probing physical search.

In contrast, more traditional police methods such as an arrest, a custodial interrogation, a search, a subpoena, or a traffic stop are "hard." They involve coercion and threat in seeking involuntary compliance. They may also involve a crossing of intimate personal borders, as with a strip or body cavity search done by another. In principle such means are exclusive in being restricted by law and policy to persons there are reasons to suspect, thus implicitly recognizing the liberty of the individual relative to the needs of the community.

Yet the culture and practice of social control is changing. Although hard forms of control are hardly receding, the soft forms are expanding in a variety of ways. I note several forms of this—requesting volunteers based on appeals to good citizenship or patriotism, using disingenuous communication, trading personal information for rewards and convenience, and using hidden or low-visibility information-collection techniques.

The theme of volunteering as good citizenship or patriotism can increasingly be seen in other contexts. Consider a Justice Department "Watch Your Car" program found in many states. Decals that car owners place on their vehicles serve as an invitation to police anywhere in the United States to stop the car if driven late at night. Taxicabs in some cities, beyond transmitting video images, also invite police to stop and search them without cause—presumably such searches extend to passengers as well who see the notice and choose to enter the cab.

There also appears to be an increase in federal prosecutors asking corporations under investigation to waive their attorney–client privileges, which can provide information that is not otherwise available, if at a cost of indicting only lower-level personnel. Plea bargaining shares a similar logic of coercive "volunteering," often hidden under a judicially sanctified and sanitized veneer of disguised coercion.

Another form involves disingenuous communication that seeks to create the impression that one is volunteering when that really isn't the case. Consider the following:

- the ubiquitous building signs that say, "In entering here you have agreed to be searched";
- a message from the Social Security Administration telling potential recipients, "While it is voluntary for you to furnish this

information, we may not be able to pay benefits to your spouse unless you give us the information";
- a Canadian airport announcement saying, "Notice: Security measures are being taken to observe and inspect persons. No passengers are obliged to submit to a search of persons or goods if they choose not to board our aircraft"; and
- the New York subway system automated searches by sensing machines as well as random searches by officers—potential riders need not submit, but then they may not use the subway.

The trend also involves efforts to make what legally should be a choice appear to be required. Here the assumption is that participation would be less frequent if individuals knew they had a choice. The request from law enforcement for personal information on the street, absent compelling reasons is an example. Although the law is hazy here and is changing.

The soft surveillance trend involves corporations more than government. Note the implicit bargain seen with respect to technologies of consumption in which the collection of personally identifiable (and often subsequently marketed) information is built into the very activity. We gladly, if often barely consciously, give up this information in return for the ease of buying and communicating and the seductions of frequent flier and other reward programs.

Information collection is unseen and automated (in a favored engineering goal, "the human is out of the loop").[2] It is "naturally" folded into routine activities such as driving a car or using a credit card, computer, or telephone. Such information is then used in profiling, social sorting, and risk assessment (Lyon 2003d).

Consider also those who agree to report their consumption behavior and attitudes in more detail as part of market research. A new variant goes beyond the traditional paid volunteers of the Nielsen ratings and other consumer research. Volunteers are given free samples and talking points. They seek to create buzz about new products without revealing their connection to the sponsoring business. Procter and Gamble, for example, has 240,000 volunteers in its teenage product-propaganda and diffusion network. Although many call, few are chosen (10 to 15 percent) for this highly coveted role (S. Walker 2004). These volunteer intelligence and marketing agents report on their own and others' responses to products, take surveys, and participate in focus groups.

What is at stake here isn't merely improved advertising in intensively competitive industries but a new morally ambiguous form of tattling. Regardless of whether they are compensated materially or with improved status, the providers of information to marketing research are also volunteering information on those who share their characteristics and experiences.[3] However no permission and no direct benefits flow to the mass of persons the sponsoring agency learns about. There are parallels to DNA analysis here: an individual who voluntarily offers his or her information for analysis also simultaneously offers information on family members who have not agreed to this.[4] We lack an adequate conceptual, ethical, and legal framework for considering this spillover effect from voluntary to involuntary disclosure involving third parties.

In addition to noting the differences between those who volunteer information only on themselves or on themselves and others, we can note those who offer information only on others. Another prominent form of volunteerism involves using citizens as adjuncts to law enforcement by watching others. Beyond the traditional Neighborhood Watch programs, we can note new post-9/11 forms such as a police sponsored C.A.T. EYES (Community Anti-Terrorism Training Initiative)[5] and other programs encouraging truckers, utility workers, taxi drivers, and delivery persons to report suspicious activities.

It is easier to agree to the offering of personal information when the data-collection process is automatic and hassle free and when we are compensated. Let us next consider the role of technology in potentially bypassing the need even to ask for consent or to offer rewards.

If You Don't Have to Undress, Are You Still Naked? Searching Made Easy

Many forms of voluntarism are encouraged by techniques designed to be less directly invasive. Computers scan dispersed personal records for suspicious cases, avoiding, at least initially, any direct review by a human. Similarly x-ray and scent machines search persons and goods for contraband without touching them. Inkless fingerprints can be taken without the stained thumb symbolic of the arrested person. Classified government programs are said to permit the remote reading of computers and their transmissions without the need to directly install bugging devices.

Beyond noting the ease of gathering DNA, we can consider the change from a urine drug test requiring an observer to drug tests that require a strand of hair, sweat, or saliva (see Campbell, Chapter 4, this volume). Saliva is particularly interesting. Whatever can be revealed from the analysis of blood or urine is also potentially found (although in smaller quantities) in saliva—evidence not only of disease and DNA but also of drugs taken and pregnancy. This may also be the case for detecting human odor.

The recent development of nonelectrical sensors now makes it possible to detect molecules at minute levels in saliva (Dreifus 2005).

Saliva testing is likely to offer a wonderful illustration of the creeping (or, better, galloping) expansion of personal data collection increasingly made possible by new noninvasive (or less invasive) means.[6] Surveillance creep (Marx 2005) involves both the displacement of traditional invasive means and the expansion to new areas and users. The body's protective armor must be pierced for blood to be taken. But expectorating occurs easily and frequently and is more "natural" than puncturing a vein, and it does not involve the unwanted observation required for a urine drug sample. Saliva samples can be easily and endlessly taken, and the changes charted make possible the early identification of problems.

This may offer medical diagnostic advantages to individuals who can maintain control over the content of their spit. Yet employers concerned with rising health costs, resistance to urine drug tests, and avoiding liability for the illnesses of those who work around hazardous chemicals[7] would also have a strong interest in diagnostic spitting as a condition of employment. Public decorum authorities concerned with identifying those who spit when not requested to can also use the technology (see Figure 3.1).[8]

In many of these cases, citizens are at least informed of what is going on, even if the meaning of their consent is often open to question. More troubling is the development of tactics that need not rely on the individual's consenting or even being informed, let alone receiving carrots or avoiding sticks in agreeing to cooperate. New hidden or low-visibility technologies increasingly offer the tempting possibility of bypassing awareness and thus any need for direct consent altogether.

New technologies overcome traditional barriers such as darkness or walls. Night-vision technology illuminates what darkness traditionally protected (and the technology is hidden, unlike an illuminated spotlight). Based on differential heat patterns thermal-imaging technology applied from outside can offer a rough picture of some aspects of a building's interior. There is no need for an observer to enter the space.

A person's DNA can be collected from a drinking glass or from discarded dental floss. Facial-scanning technology requires only a tiny lens. Smart machines can "smell" contraband, eliminating the need for getting a warrant or asking the sniffed for permission to invade their olfactory space or see through their clothes and luggage. Research is also being done with the goal of using human odor to identify specific persons, illness (both mental and physical), and even early pregnancy.[9] A vacuumlike device is also available that can draw the breath away from a person suspected of drunk driving, without the need to ask permission.

Figure 3.1 Sign from the British Transit Authority. (Photo courtesy of Clive Norris.)

Beyond the traditional reading of visual clues offered by facial expression, there are claims that the covert analysis of heat patterns around the eyes and of tremors in the voice and the measurement of brain wave patterns offer windows into feelings and truth telling.[10] The face still remains a tool for protecting inner feelings and thoughts, but for how long? Different issues are raised by recent improvements in the technology of face transplanting.

Individuals need not be informed that their communication devices, vehicles, wallet cards, and consumer items will have RFID (radio frequency identification) chips embedded in them with increasing frequency. These chips can be designed to be passively read from up to 30 feet away by unseen sensors.[11]

In the convoluted logic of those who justify covert (or noninformed) data collection and use, individuals "volunteer" their data by walking or driving on public streets; by entering a shopping mall; by failing to hide their faces, wear gloves, or encrypt their communication; or by choosing to use a phone, computer, or credit card. The statement of a direct marketer nicely illustrates this: "Never ever underestimate the willingness of the American public to tell you about itself. That data belongs to us! ... It isn't out there because we stole it from them. Someone gave it away and now it's out there for us to use" (personal communication).

Yes, but ...

In an environment of intense concern about crime and terrorism and with a legal framework generated in a far simpler time, these developments are hardly surprising. Democratic governments need to be reasonably effective and to maintain their legitimacy (even as research on the complex relationships between effectiveness and legitimacy is needed). Working together and sacrificing a bit of oneself for the common good, particularly in times of crisis, is hardly controversial. Relative to traditional authoritarian settings, many of these examples show respect for the person in offering notice and some degree of choice and in minimizing invasiveness.[12] Such efforts draw on the higher civic traditions of democratic participation, self-help, and community. They may also deter. Yet there is something troubling about them.

The accompanying rhetoric is often dishonest and even insulting to one's intelligence. Consider a phone company executive who, in defense of unblockable caller ID, said, "When you choose to make a phone call you are choosing to release your telephone number." In the same World Cup League of Disingenuousness is the statement of a personnel manager in a one-industry town: "We don't require anyone to take a drug test, only those who choose to work here." To be meaningful choice should imply genuine alternatives and refusal costs that are not wildly exorbitant, absent that we have trickery, double-talk, and the frequently spoiled fruit of inequitable relationships.

When we are told that for the good of the community we must voluntarily submit to searches, there is a danger of the tyranny of the communal and of turning presumptions of innocence upside down. If only the guilty need worry, why bother with a Bill of Rights and other limits on authority? There also comes a point beyond which social pressure seems unreasonable.[13] If the case for categorical information is strong, then the rules ought to require it,[14] without need of the verbal jujitsu of asking for volunteers or implying that the individual is in fact taking voluntary action in the full meaning of the term, when failure to comply has serious consequences, such as being denied a job or a benefit or appearing suspect in others' eyes.

Those who fail to volunteer can be viewed as having something to hide or as being bad citizens or uncooperative team players. The positive reasons for rejecting such requests are ignored. Yet we all have things to legitimately hide or, more proper, to selectively reveal, depending on the relationship and context. The general social value we place on sealed first-class letters, window blinds, and bathroom doors and our opposition to indiscriminant wiretapping, bugging, and informing or in giving up anonymity in public places (absent cause) are hardly driven by an interest to aid the guilty. Sealing juvenile criminal records reflects not a perverse strategy for infiltrating miscreants into adult life but rather an understanding of, and some compassion for, the mistakes of youth.

We value privacy not to protect wrongdoing but because an appropriate degree of control over personal and social information is central to our sense of self, autonomy, and material well-being, as well as it is necessary for independent group actions. A healthy, if necessarily qualified, suspicion of authority is also a factor in restricting information sought by the more powerful. As consumers and citizens, we have an interest in avoiding the manipulation, discrimination, inappropriate social sorting, and theft that can flow from combining bits of personal information that are innocuous by themselves.

Many of the new controls may seem more acceptable (or at least are less likely to be challenged) because they are hidden or built-in, less invasive relative to the traditional forms of crossing personal and physical borders. We are often complicit in their application—whether out of fear or convenience or for frequent shopper awards. Converting privacy to a commodity in which the seller receives something in return to compensate for the invasion is a clever and more defensible means of overcoming resistance.

Exchanges and less invasive searches are certainly preferable to data rip-offs and more invasive searches.[15] However, the nature of the means should not be determinative. What should matter most is the appropriateness of the collection of information and only secondarily the way that it is collected. A search is still a search regardless of how it is carried out. The issue of searches and the crossing of traditional borders between the civil and state sectors, or the self and others, involves much more than using painless, quick, inexpensive, and nonembarrassing means or "volunteering" to avoid suspicion or opportunity denial.

Other factors being equal, soft ways are to be preferred to hard, even if the control or instrumental goals of those applying the surveillance remain the same. Yet coercion at least has the virtue (if that's what it is) of letting the subject (or object) know what is happening. What we don't know can hurt us as well.

One of the most troubling aspects of recent changes is that they so often occur beneath the radar of public awareness and input. Consider the technological designs thrust on us by industrial fiat, such as caller ID (initially offered with no blocking options).

Unhappy Underlaps

Traditionally (if accidentally) there was a happy overlap between three factors that limited searches and protected personal information. The first factor was the logistics. It was not cost effective or time effective to search everyone. The second factor was the law. More invasive searches were prohibited or inadmissible, absent cause and a warrant. The third factor reflected the effrontery experienced in our culture when certain personal borders were involuntarily crossed (e.g., strip and body cavity searches and body fluid samples and, to a lesser degree, even fingerprinting).[16] Limited resources, the unpleasantness of invasive searches (for both the searched and the searcher), and the ethos of a democratic society have historically restricted searches.

These supports are being undermined by the mass media's encouragement of fear and perceptions of crises and by the seductiveness of consumption[17] concurrent with the development of inexpensive, less invasive, broad searching tools. Under these conditions one does not need a meteorologist to describe wind patterns.

The willingness to offer personal information and the fascination with the private aspects of others' lives are part of the legacy of the openness and transparency of the 1960s as we encounter the possibilities offered by the past decade's technologies. The willingness and fascination also speak to some need of the modern person (and perhaps in particular the American) to see and to be seen and to know and to be known about through ubiquitous visual and nonvisual means.

Here we see changes in a cultural strand involving the willing, even gleeful, public exposure of private information—whether in dress styles, cell phone conversations, or the mass media. Many Americans are drawn to new communications technologies like nails to a magnet, unable to resist the prurient call to watch others, but also with a near Dostoyevskian compulsion to offer information about themselves.

There can be psychological gratifications from revelation for both the voluntary revealer and the recipient of the information. This mutuality makes the topic interesting and complicated and works against a reductionist argument that knowledge always reflects the interests of those with the technology to discover.

With some revelation we see the truth in Janice Joplin's assertion that "freedom's just another word for nothing left to lose." Voluntarily offered secret information may lose its value in the sunshine. Consider the freedom from the threat of blackmail that accompanies an individual's going public with a secret, such as homosexuality or an affair. One strand of feminism views exposure of the female body and the assertion of sexuality as willful acts that, in their naturalness, demystifies and turns the viewed person into an active agent rather than the subject or object of the actions of others.

The prying and often inane TV talk and reality shows, webcams, weblogs (blogs), fans goofily waving at televised events, and videotaped conceptions, births, and last wills and testaments suggest the extent to which we have become both a performance society and a spectator society—literally from the beginning of life to the end.

Volunteering one's data and being digitally recorded and tracked is coming to be taken for granted as a means of asserting selfhood. This willful blurring of some of the lines between the public and the private self and the ready availability of technologies to transmit and receive personal data give new meaning to David Riesman and colleagues' (2001) concern with other directions.

Of course our sense of self and social participation have always depended on validation from others—on seeing ourselves in, and through, their eyes. But contemporary outlets for this are prone to induce a sense of pseudo-authenticity, an unbecoming narcissism, and a suspicious spy culture. The social functions of reticence and embarrassment and the role of withheld personal information as a currency of trust, friendship, and intimacy are greatly weakened.

The abundance of new opportunities for self-expression offered by contemporary technologies must be considered alongside the lessened control we have over information and models in distant computer systems. Data shadows or ghosts based on tangents of personal information (stripped of context) increasingly affect life chances. Individuals often have little knowledge of the existence or consequences of these databases and of how their identity is constructed or might be challenged.

This complicated issue of reducing the richness of personal and social contexts to a limited number of variables is at the core of the ability of science to predict and generalize. It is central to current ideas about economic competitiveness and risk management. The data analyst goes from known empirical cases to equivalent cases that are not directly known. Because a given case can be classified relative to a statistical model as involving a high or low risk, it is presumed to be understood and thus controllable (at least on a statistical or "probabilistic" basis). This may work fine for business or medical decisions, but civil liberties and civil rights are not based on statistical categories. They are presumed to be universally applicable, absent cause to deny them. So rationality and efficiency as ways of doing societal business increasingly clash with many of our basic Enlightenment ideas of individualism and dignity—ideas that were better articulated, and less contestable, in technologically simpler times.

There is a chilling and endless regressive quality in our drift into a society where a person has to provide ever more personal information to prove that he or she is the kind of person who does not merit even more intensive scrutiny. Here we confront the insatiable information appetite generated by scientific knowledge in a risk-adverse society. In such a society, knowing more may serve only to increase doubt and the need for more information.

Things that are "voluntarily" turned over to third parties, such as garbage or dialed telephone numbers, along with what "a person knowingly exposes to the public, even in his own home or office," such as a voice sample, handwriting sample, fingerprint, or facial appearance, are generally beyond the search restrictions of the Fourth Amendment. Efforts to protect these things (e.g., by shredding garbage or putting it in a sealed container), which clearly indicate an expectation of privacy, are not sufficient to legally guarantee it. Their exposure to the public (defined as others, rather than as a particular place) brings the risk of revelation or discovery.[18]

A central issue is of course what *exposure* means in an age of sense-enhancing (and often covertly and remotely applied) surveillance devices, which may, or may not, be widely known about or in common use. The two criteria of reasonableness offered by the landmark *Katz* case—the expectation of privacy as socially reasonable and the individual's expectations (which can be inferred from whether the individual takes actions to protect privacy and from what the individual is aware of)—are often at variance.

However my concern here is more with less visible cultural and behavioral developments than with the law. Certainly we do not lack for contemporary examples of constricted or trampled legal rights (e.g., American citizens held at Guantanamo without trial or the unwelcome elements of the PATRIOT Act). The Fourth Amendment is not what it was following the decisions of the Warren Court, particularly with respect to the exclusionary rule.[19] Yet it is still very far from what it was at the end of the eighteenth century. The overall pattern of the greater institutionalization of civil rights and civil liberties over the past century (whether involving race, gender, children, work, freedom of expression and association, or searches and lifestyles) is unlikely to be reversed. Jagged cycles rather than clean linearity will continue to characterize this turbulent history. The maximally unconstitutional Alien and Sedition Acts have not returned. Wartime restrictions (whether Lincoln's suspending of habeas corpus or limits on speech during World War II) have been lifted as calmer times returned. To be sure, the evidence of ebbs is undeniable, but, relative to the period immediately after 9/11, there are some flows as well.[20]

Other chapters in this volume give greater attention to the security theme and note how power differentials can be enhanced by recent technical developments. For the questions considered in this chapter, however, the centralizing power implications are more mixed.[21]

Certainly the more privileged have greater say in what technologies are developed and have greater access to them, as well to means to thwart them. Just because all persons radiate accessible data, it doesn't mean that data receptors are unaffected by social stratification. On balance, technical innovations are more likely to bolster, than to undermine, the established order. The developments I note can disguise a substratum of power, coercion, and inequality.

Yet some counterpoints to an unqualifiedly hegemonic perspective can also be noted. These developments suggest a paradoxical view in which the technology's spongelike absorbency is joined by its laserlike specificity—permitting both mass (nondifferentiated) and individual (highly differentiated) targeting.

Universalistic or categorical (dragnet) requests for personal information have an egalitarian, rather than an individualizing and differentiating, quality. The camera lens catches all within its province regardless of social characteristics.

The trade of personal information for consumer benefits better characterizes the more, rather than the less, privileged social groups. In addition, as with the Rodney King case and related cases, widely available, low-visibility techniques (e.g., video, audio, and audit trails) can also be used against the more powerful.

The cultural changes noted are worrisome because they are diffuse, subtle, and unseen—and they often reflect choices that, even if specious or manipulated, are difficult to challenge in a democratic society. The possibility of making a wrong choice is an inherent risk of democracy.

Individuals can use their liberty to smoke, eat rich foods, drive environmentally unfriendly cars, and watch "reality" television, as well as to volunteer personal information—whether to the government or to the commercial sector.[22] A bad law can be challenged in court or repealed. A dangerous technology can be banned, regulated, or challenged with a countertechnology. But the only way to respond to liberty-threatening choices of the kind discussed here is through dialogue and education (tools that are already disproportionately available to those supporting the current developments).

Is It Happening Here?

Contrary to the familiar Orwellian concerns about the all-knowing eyes and ears of government, recent history suggests to some observers the reverse problem—blindness, deafness, and inefficiency (e.g., the 9/11 danger known only in retrospect or the inability of 500,000 cameras in London to prevent the transit bombings, the failure of various airline passenger screening programs, wrongful convictions and the problems of some crime labs, the weakness of face-recognition technology in natural settings, and so on). In one sense there are two problems with the new surveillance technologies. One is that they don't work, and the other is that they work too well. If the first problem occurs, the technologies fail to prevent disasters, bring miscarriages of justice, and waste resources. If the second problem occurs, the technologies can further inequality and invidious social categorization and chill liberty. These twin threats are part of the enduring paradox of democratic government that must be strong enough to maintain reasonable order but not so strong as to become undemocratic.

The surveillance developments noted here are consistent with the strengthening of the neoliberal ethos of the past decade. In what might be called the "only you" theory of social control, individuals are encouraged to protect themselves and those close to them, because government can't (or won't).

The individualized strategies seen with the offering of one's own information, and information on others, grows out of noble traditions of volunteerism and individual responsibility that are central to self and social control in a democracy. Yet private solutions for social, economic, and political problems can be taken too far.

The idea of voluntary compliance and self-help valorizes increased individual choices, costs, and risks. It simultaneously weakens many social protections and programs and pays less attention to the ways the social order may produce bad choices and collective problems. The consequences of these are then left to individual and private solutions,[23] which generate a suspicious society in which paranoia is entangled with reality. This emphasis can further social neglect and the subsequent problems, leading to calls for more intensive and extensive surveillance, citizen cooperation, and privatization in social control.

There is no single answer to the questions of how the new personal-information-collection techniques ought to be viewed and what, if anything, should (or can) be done about them. From genuine to mandatory voluntarism and from open to secret data collection, the points are on continuums. We can differentiate information that is secret or unknown because an individual has discretionary control over revelation (e.g., regarding lifestyles, consumption, finances, religious and political beliefs) from information that is not revealed because a sense-enhancing technology is lacking to reveal it (e.g., traditionally being unseen in the dark or from miles away).

There are important moral differences between what can be known through the unaided senses and what can be known only through technologically enhanced senses. The moral and practical issues around the initial collection of information are distinct from its subsequent uses and protections.

Diverse settings—national security, domestic law enforcement, public order maintenance, health and welfare, commerce, banking, insurance, public and private spaces—and roles do not call for the rigid application of the same policies.

The different roles of employer–employee, merchant–consumer, landlord–renter, police–suspect, and health provider–patient involve some legitimate conflicting interests. Any practice is also likely to involve some conflict in values. Thus categorical prescreening of everyone, as against only those there is a specific reason to screen, is fair. Yet it violates other cultural standards.

We need a situational or contextual perspective that acknowledges the richness of different contexts and the multiplicity of conflicting values within and across them. In the face of the simplistic rhetoric of polarized ideologues in dangerous times, we need attention to trade-offs and to the appropriate weighing of conflicting values.[24] Given changing historical circumstances, there is no fixed golden balance point. However, the procedures for accountability and oversight so central to the founding and endurance of the country must not be weakened. Contemporary moral-panic efforts to erode these procedures need to be strenuously resisted.

It is foolish to elevate consent to an absolute, but we should not continue to slide into a world where meaningful consent is only of historical interest. At best we can hope to find a compass rather than a map and a moving equilibrium rather than a fixed point for decision making. Yet we need to rethink just what consent means when it is possible to so easily evade it. What is an individual consenting to when being in public and not shielding information that might be available to the hidden technologies?

Appreciating complexity is surely a virtue, but being immobilized by it is not. The default position should be meaningful consent, absent strong grounds for avoiding it. Consent involves participants who are fully apprised of the surveillance system's presence and potential risks and of the conditions under which it operates.[25] Consent that is obtained through deception or unreasonable or exploitative seduction or used to avoid dire consequences is hardly consent. The smile that accompanies the statement "an offer you can't refuse" reflects that understanding.

We need a principle of truth in volunteering: it is far better to say clearly, "As a condition of [entering here, working here, receiving this benefit, etc.] we require that you provide personal information." A golden rule principle ought also to apply—would the information collector be comfortable in being the subject, rather than the agent, of surveillance if the situation were reversed?[26]

We need to overcome the polite cultural tendency to acquiesce when we are inappropriately asked for personal information. We need to just say "no" when, after paying with a credit card, a cashier asks for a phone number, or when a webpage or warranty form asks for irrelevant personal information, or when a video store seeks a social security number. Offering disinformation may sometimes be appropriate. The junk mail I receive for Groucho and Karl offers a laugh and a means of tracking the erroneous information I sometimes provide to inappropriate requests.

Finally, technology needs to be seen as an opportunity rather than as only a problem. Technologies can be designed to do a better job of protecting personal information and notifying individuals when their information is being collected or has been compromised. Video monitoring systems can be designed to block out faces as their default position, and x-ray and t-ray systems can be programmed to block anatomical details.[27] E-ZPass toll collection systems can be programmed to deduct payment, while protecting the anonymity of the driver. RFID technology can build in notification by requiring that the chip make physical contact with the sensor (e.g., touching the card or item to the sensor) rather than permitting it to be read covertly at a distance. Cell phone cameras could be designed to emit a telltale sound before a picture is taken (this is required in Japan). Electronic silencers can inhibit third parties from overhearing cell phone and face-to-face conversations, and computer privacy screens can block sneaky peeks by anyone not directly in front of the screen.

From one perspective, using technology to protect one's personal information may offer legal support for an expectation of privacy. In *Kyllo v. United States,* a case involving the legality of a search warrant based on evidence from thermal-imaging technology, the dissenting judges argued that because the suspect did *not* take any actions to block the heat emissions that passed through his roof from his marijuana grow lights, he did not have an expectation of privacy. There thus is no Fourth Amendment issue, and the police action should not require a warrant.[28]

This collapsing of what can be done with what is right involves an inverted logic: once a technology becomes widely available and is well-known, responsibility for protection shifts legally (as well of course as practically) to the individual, not to those who would cross personal borders. In failing to act in response to changed circumstances beyond his or her control, the individual is seen to be making a choice and in a sense again volunteers to be searched and to accept whatever risks may be involved.

However, some responsibility must also be placed on those with the search tools as well. The goals sought and the invasiveness of the technique used need to be considered independent of any actions taken by the individual. In Europe, in contrast to the United States, greater emphasis is put on the actions of the search agent and the properties of the technology, as against the risks and rewards an individual is willing to assume.

This blame-the-victim *caveat subjectus* logic cries out for a cartoon titled, "Where will it end?" Beyond the paper shredder, which has become routine in many homes,[29] the cartoon would show a citizen protecting privacy by always wearing gloves, a mask, and perfume;[30] having a closely shaved head; talking in code and encrypting all communications; insulating home, office, and packages in thermal-image-resistant insulating material; and using only restrooms certified to be monitoring free.

In writing a prescient novel, Sinclair Lewis in 1935 ironically suggested *It Can't Happen Here*. But of course it can, and in some ways it has. In a book on undercover police practices, I considered the softening of social control in other forms beyond those discussed here.[31] In concluding that book I wrote,

> The first task of a society that would have liberty and privacy is to guard against the misuse of physical coercion by the state and private parties. The second task is to guard against the softer forms of secret and manipulative control. Because these are often subtle, indirect, invisible, diffuse and deceptive and shrouded in benign justifications, this is clearly the more difficult task. (Marx 1988)

In 2006 the hot button cultural themes of threat, civil order, and security that Lewis emphasized are in greater ascendance and have been joined by the siren calls of consumption. If our traditional notions of liberty disappear, it will not be because of a sudden coup d'état,[32] and the iron technologies of industrialization will not be the central means. Rather it will occur by accretion and with an appeal to traditional American values in a sugar- and Teflon-coated technological context of low visibility, fear, and convenience.

Acknowledgments

I am grateful to Peter Andreas, Pat Gillham, Jackie Ross, Richard Leo, John Leudsdorf, Torin Monahan, Clive Norris, Zick Rubin, and Jay Wachtel for their critical suggestions. This chapter is an expanded version of the article in *Dissent* (Winter 2005).

Notes

1. In a criminal justice context, the dragnet method illustrates some classic issues such as the tension between a standard of reasonable suspicion or probable cause and the need to solve high-profile crimes and between a presumption of innocence and of guilt, and whether the government can be trusted when it promises to destroy the DNA collected, rather than to save it in a database. There is also the pragmatic question of whether it works and under what conditions and to what degree and for what purposes; for example, with respect to the following outcomes, identification and location of the guilty for a given crime and for an unrelated crime, false positives and negatives, and a finding of nothing at all. It would be useful to contrast situations involving acquiescence to, or rejection of, voluntary requests, unsolicited volunteers, information provided as a result of a warrant, and situations in which individuals provide information under the mistaken belief that they have no choice. A review of twenty recent instances found that in the overwhelming majority of cases, DNA dragnets did not lead to success. In seven of the cases, traditional investigation methods did (Electronic Privacy Information Center 2005; see also S. Walker 2004; Chapin 2005; and Grand 2002).
2. This is the techno-fallacy of *autonomous technology* in which the hand and the assumptions of the human designer are unacknowledged. In Marx (2003a), I discuss 21 such fallacies associated with communication and surveillance technology.
3. *Volunteer* has two meanings here—first, agreeing to act without external compulsion, a kind of free will or better, within cultural and resource limits, an independent willfulness with respect to action taken. This is often, but need not be, linked to a second meaning of acting without receiving material compensation. People who participate because they are paid of course may voluntarily agree to this, but their behavior is not voluntary in the way that those who participate without direct reward is. The volunteer marketers appear to profit from seeing themselves as insiders and as members of an elite consumer group being the first to know. A distinction can be drawn between an individual offering data that permits other members of his or her group to be better manipulated à la an understanding of their demographics and attitudes and an individual offering data that stigmatize. Group stigmatization for example can apply to ethnic groups shown by DNA to have a proclivity for some illnesses (Alpert 2003).
4. The appropriate response is not to ban the individual's willful seeking of the information but to rigidly control use of the information as it might be applied (e.g., by insurance companies) to other persons to whom it refers but who have not sought it.
5. The program seeks to give "the average person terrorist indicators to watch for not race or religion" (www.cateyesprogram.com).
6. *Invasive* is a term easily thrown about in such discussions. Yet a variety of meanings can be unpacked. It can involve procedures in referring to degree of literal invasiveness by crossing a physical border of the person—here, entering into natural body orifices such as ears contrast with breaking the skin to extract a bullet. It can refer to directionality—implanting in the body may have different connotations than extracting from it. It may refer to the nature of what is discovered (information on being left- or right-handed versus having religious and political beliefs) (Marx forthcoming). The definition may depend on the kind of relationship between the parties (e.g., familial versus formal organizational). The *place* a search occurs, apart from what is searched or found, is also a factor. Thus in the *Kyllo* case, the majority held that a search of the home was inherently invasive because of where it occurred. Whether the search found heat emissions or contraceptives was irrelevant. The "where" not the "what" defined it. This relates to perceptual issues. Invasiveness can also be considered with respect to perception and subjective definitions. How do individuals view and feel about the degree of invasiveness of a given action, beyond its strictly behavioral sense involving the physical borders of the

person? Consider sexual intercourse among partners as against rape or persons who seek attention versus those who want to be left alone.

7. In such contexts the identification of early-stage pregnant employees is of particular interest.

8. The automated analysis of urine offers the same potential. A diagnostic test (routinely used in some Japanese employment contexts) requires that each time an employee enters the stall they be identified through their access card. This permits a comprehensive record of their flushed offerings over time. It is said to be of great benefit in the earlier diagnosis of health problems. On the other hand, consider, for example, the transit authority in Sheffield, England, that, as part of an antispitting campaign, distributed 3000 DNA swab kits to transportation staff. Posters proclaim "Spit It's Out" and warn persons who spit that "You can be traced and prosecuted. Even if we don't know what you look like. And your record will be on the national DNA data base. Forever." For those of another era, this is reminiscent of the grammar school teachers who threatened to add notes about misbehavior to "your permanent record."

9. Here science may come to the defense of folk prejudices, which hold that the "other" smells different.

10. Reading brain wave patterns requires attaching sensors to the head and thus an informed individual. But should the remote reading of brain waves become possible and workable, science fiction would once again become science, and another technological weakness that protected liberty would disappear. Ray Bradbury's heroes in *Fahrenheit 451* who resisted a book-burning, totalitarian regime by memorizing destroyed books would need to find alternative means.

11. The technology can require that the chip make physical contact with the sensor (e.g., touching the card to the sensor) or it can be read remotely. This nicely illustrates how technical design can have social causes and consequences. When the chip must contact the reader, the individual is of necessity aware; otherwise covert reading is possible by both the "official" reader and an uninvited thief-lurker, although with current technology this is limited to about 30 feet. The greater the distance from the chip, the more power the reader needs, and at some point this is great enough to fry the chip in the process of trying to read it. A rarely noted consequence of location technologies is their ability to identify social networks and patterns (e.g., other copresent individuals whose chips are also read and an analysis of the timing of passages). Technologies can be contrasted by whether their application requires the individual's awareness and active or passive cooperation (or at least involvement). Compare truth determination by use of the traditional polygraph attached to the individual with reading of facial signals or the analysis of word patterns. The Enron case partly relied on finding lying through the analysis of word-use patterns in e-mail. Of course in the latter cases, individuals can be informed that low-visibility techniques are being used and consent can be requested. Even when there is no formal request for permission as with being stared at, awareness may offer the possibility of deterring, challenging, or avoiding the unwanted data collection.

12. In a government context, volunteering to be searched is legal as long as police do not "convey a message that compliance with their requests is required" and refusal to volunteer cannot be used against the person (*Florida v. Bostick* 1991). Yet apart from their words and demeanor, the official status, badge, and weapon of an officer convey an alternative message. Volunteering self-incriminating information under the wrongful belief that it is legally necessary seems to violate the Fifth Amendment.

13. Consider, for example, the politicians who release their drug test records and sworn statements attesting to their marital fidelity and who challenge their opponents to do the same. Since the court in *Chandler v. Miller* (117 S.Ct. 1295, 1303 [1997]) overturned a Georgia ruling permitting drug testing of those currently holding or seeking public office, this can no longer be legally required. Social pressure and a strategic response to such a challenge is, however, another matter.

14. There also needs to be limitations on secondary use. DNA collected for law enforcement purposes is interesting in that regard. It was initially claimed that the DNA collected could be used only for identification purposes. Subsequent technical developments then made it possible to read much more of the DNA from the small sample taken, offering a broad window into the individual's genetic makeup, a factor far transcending simple identification.

15. Here I imply the ideal situation in which individuals fully understand not only what they will be receiving but also what they are giving away, how it will be used and protected, and what potential risks and secondary uses there might be. In suggesting that less invasive means of searching are preferable, we need to be mindful that these come with the threat of vastly expanding the pool of those who are searched (and, of course, as the Texas judge reportedly said, "If you hang them all you will certainly get the guilty"). Expanded nets and thinned meshes are a function of perceived threats and degrees of risk, as well as ease of application. The seemingly ever-greater ease and efficiency offered by technological means are on a collision course with traditional liberty-protecting ideas of reasonable suspicion and minimization and impracticality. They can also serve to lessen some of the personally unpleasant aspects of the search for the searcher.

16. The issue with fingerprints, beyond the symbolism in their association with criminals and a temporarily stained finger, is the absence of anonymity and the ability to link disparate records. As noted in a recent development, the dirty finger smudge problem (and reminder) has been eliminated through an inkless system.

17. See, for example, recent studies by Altheide (2002) and Glassner (2000).

18. Major Supreme Court cases here are as follows: trash—*California v. Greenwood* (1988) and *United States v. Scott* (1992); dialed telephone numbers, pen register data—*Smith v. Maryland* (1979); voice sampling—*United States v. Dinoisio* (1973); handwriting sample—*United States v. Mara* (1973).

19. Dash (2004) offers a short history of the whittling down of the exclusionary rule.

20. Note pointed congressional discussions on revising the PATRIOT Act, an explosion in state privacy laws, and the many local communities that passed resolutions in opposition to aspects of the PATRIOT Act. Of course in many ways the United States lags behind Europe, but the point is not only how far laws and policies are from the ideal but also that they are on the books and that they have a symbolic meaning and reaffirm values. In some of its actions (e.g., banking, fair credit reporting legislation, the 1986 Electronic Privacy Protection Act), Congress has implicitly legislated the ethos of the Fourth Amendment. Consider too the consciousness-raising aspects of recent legislation requiring companies that discover the electronic compromising of personal data to notify individuals and the "do not call lists."

21. Qualifications to a too-easy linkage of power and surveillance are discussed in Marx (2005).

22. Of course there are limits, such as on selling a kidney or selling one's self into slavery or waiving medical or legal liability. The recent Health Insurance Portability and Accountability Act (HIPAA) does however permit waiving of a jury trial in the event a patient has a dispute with a medical provider.

23. Katz (Chapter 2, this volume), for example, argues that the subjection of children to new surveillance tools (nanny and daycare cams, drug testing, electronic tracking, and the like) is in response to the lack of adequate social provision for the needs of children and the creation of safer public environments.

24. There is also need to analyze what is meant by trade-offs, what the empirical evidence is for concluding trade-offs are in fact present, and how focusing on one set of questions often means ignoring others (Monahan, Chapter 1, this volume). We can also identify conditions under which privacy and security are supportive or at least congruent; for example, appropriately applied, highly effective systems minimize false accusations an unnecessary searches, and the treatment of citizens with respect can enhance legitimac and cooperation with control agents.

25. The "opt-in" feature of some database systems reflects this in using the information persons who are informed and who consent.

26. These are related to 20 broad questions and related principles that I suggest (Marx 2(be asked about any collection of personal information. These involve factors suc goal appropriateness, means-ends relationships, identifying and dealing with und able unintended consequences, and reciprocity. In general the more the question be answered in a manner consistent with the underlying principles, the more legit the collection of personal information is. I prefer a contextual approach to the questions, rather than one that begins with a value that must always take prece whether this involves the rights of the individual or the needs of the community.

27. The latter would eliminate the need for same-sex monitors with its assumptions of a homogeneity regarding the sexual orientation of the watched and the watcher.

28. In this reading such a search is legal according to the Supreme Court's test established in the 1967 *Katz* case. The majority of justices, however, did not agree. On the other hand, the failure to take protective actions might also be seen to suggest that the individual expected the activity to remain private because he was unaware of high-tech means not yet widely used. He hence saw no need to take blocking actions.

29. Those not wanting to use a paper shredder might consider moving to Beverly Hills, California, where it is illegal to rummage through other's garbage left on the street.

30. However, research efforts are underway to overcome any distorting elements for human-smell essence that wearing perfume or eating garlic might disguise.

31. The means considered in this essay, along with other changes, suggest a decline in the use of domestic coercion in many spheres. Thus consider the practical disappearance of whipping, flogging, and public executions; the lesser use of capital punishment; the decline in the homicide rate and of corporal punishment in the home; and schools and programs emphasizing antibullying and the development of discussion and negotiation skills. The development of nonlethal weapons might also fit here (but as with the softening of power more generally it may come with increased use and intervention—see note 15). Nonlethal weapons are sometimes lethal. Robert Nisbet (1975) considers the softening of power in broader historical perspective, as does Foucault (1977) from a different critical perspective. Richard Leo (1992) offers a case study of the move from coercion to deception in police interrogations as the third degree largely disappeared.

32. One can also make distinctions between hard control and soft control problematic. They may share the logic of bribery, which when pushed can blur the borders between them. Thus how should we conceptualize compliance gained by the threat, but not the application, of coercion? Certainly this is hard, yet the absence of punishment or cost becomes a sort of reward, or at least an inducement. The carrot lies in avoiding the stick. In another example of blurred borders, consider the expanding number of fast-track programs that offer individuals the chance to give up personal information in return for preferential treatment, such as at airports or on toll roads (see Adey, Chapter 12, this volume; Van der Ploeg, Chapter 11, this volume). Here the potential stick of "long waits" is avoided for the carrot of "no wait," by submission to another stick—that of volunteering personal information.

CHAPTER **4**

Everyday Insecurities
The Microbehavioral Politics
of Intrusive Surveillance

NANCY D. CAMPBELL

Aggressors wage war on multiple fronts, exacting the toll of collateral damage on vulnerable populations. Wars on drugs are no different. Drugs and drug tests have operated in recent wars on drugs as both symbols and agents of the insecurities and vulnerabilities to which we are differentially subject. The rhetoric of the "drug-free" nation partakes of ritual cleansing and the power of the "clean" to expel the "dirty," an enactment that reveals the coconstitutive dependency of the one on the other.[1] Serving the symbolic goal of securing a drug-free nation, a mythical status to which the United States ever aspires and never embodies, urine testing has become the preferred technology of ritual cleansing. Proliferating everyday insecurities, drug tests inscribe the line between the "deserving poor" and the "nondeserving poor" ever more deeply. Among the rights revoked in the course of the "war on drugs" have been those many Americans hold dear: freedom of religion, association, and speech; Fourth Amendment rights to be free of unwarranted search and seizure; Fourteenth Amendment rights to due process and equal protection; patients' rights such as informed consent, privacy, and confidentiality; reproductive rights; and even property rights (Boyd 2002; Paltrow 2001). Although some revocations rise to the level of constitutional scrutiny, others represent the accumulation of everyday indignities.

Crystal Ferguson, whose appeal to the Supreme Court I examine in this article, was subjected to a drug test as a result of a protocol set up in 1989 at the height of the crack cocaine "epidemic"[2] in Charleston, South Carolina, to drug test pregnant women without their knowledge when they presented for obstetrical care at the Medicaid maternity ward of the only public hospital in the metropolitan area. Lasting until 1994, the program directly affected thirty women, who were arrested and charged with possession or distribution of a controlled substance (cocaine) or child neglect, depending on whether their pregnancies had progressed through delivery at the time of the arrest. Advocates vigorously attacked the motivations of program staff and the perceptions of "crack babies" that contributed to their motivations. They began raising constitutional questions regarding the "human research program" underway at the Medical University of South Carolina (MUSC) in 1993. Violations of personhood, privacy, and confidentiality were sometimes egregious, as advocates verified stories about women giving birth in shackles and spending their immediate postpartum hours in jail without so much as a sanitary napkin. Although pregnancy typically results in abrogations of rights and increases in social control that intensify near term (C. Daniels 1993; Paltrow 2001; D. Roberts 1997; Woliver 2002), the experience of Crystal Ferguson and other women who experienced such assaults were the result of an interlocking set of social exclusions and dehumanizing assumptions.

The MUSC program was underpinned by the routine acceptance of drug testing in the United States. Over the past two decades, drug testing has become integral not only to the U.S. workplace, but also to clinical practice, the criminal justice system, and social and human services provision. Without the development of accurate and reliable drug-testing technologies capable of withstanding challenge in the courts, drug use could not have become the basis for such extreme revocations of rights. Such indignities are rarely visited upon those who have points of access to health care other than those used by indigent people. New forms of biosurveillance are pervasive in the systems to which the poor are unevenly subject. My argument, then, is not against all drug testing but against the imposition of new bodily surveillance regimes in contexts where there is already so little regard for civil rights or social justice that being drug tested without knowledge or consent can become a matter of course.

Looking at which populations routinely undergo drug testing offers insight into the dynamics of social exclusion in the United States. For instance, drug court participants are among the most vulnerable members of U.S. society: most are under- or unemployed, and one-third do not have a high school diploma or GED.[3] "Most, if not all, drug court participants also lack the resources to find appropriate housing on the open market," yet many are subject to mandatory ineligibility and eviction laws on the basis of test results (Cooper 2003: 5). In addition, the Clinton administration's reinvention of welfare in 1996 made those convicted of drug offenses ineligible for welfare benefits in the form of cash assistance or food stamps—for life—and only eight states and the District of Columbia have opted out of these provisions (Allard 2002). "Three strikes" laws make convicted drug offenders ineligible for federal educational aid in the form of student loans, work-study, and Pell grants. Legal immigrants who are convicted on drug charges may be deported.[4] It is interesting that most if not all of these punitive provisions continue to apply even when individuals are involved in drug court programs, which are supposedly linked to drug treatment.[5] There also have been proposals and actual attempts to integrate drug testing with health care, several of which I discuss later in this chapter. Drug testing is an embodied form of surveillance developed literally to mark or tag what would otherwise be an invisible bodily state—for the purposes of leveling social consequences and differentially constituting "target" populations.

Arguing that "the new surveillance" exhibits a developing rift between virtually disembodied, "databased selves" and their "increasingly irrelevant and indigent bodies," Bart Simon suggests that we already inhabit a fantastic world of "data doubles" in which administrative processes occur independently of embodied subjects (2005: 17).[6] Data doubles come from somewhere, though, and a survey of bioassays used today suggests that new forms of "vicious embodiment" have been produced by pervasive security regimes in ways that bear distinct resemblance to older forms of embodiment. The continuing salience of race, class, and gender in determining whose bodies come under routine surveillance within security regimes suggests that it would be a mistake to discount the significance of bodily subjection through bioassays designed to surveil drug consumption practices. As casual or episodic drug use comes under increasing scrutiny, it is premature to dismiss the pervasive effects of low-intensity insecurity on everyday life. Drug test results are used to limit access to public provision, higher education, and the workplace—as well as to revoke parental rights and freedom of movement in the case of parole and probation. The microbehavioral biopolitics of intrusive surveillance contributes to the double movement between increased social control and reduced social provision so essential to neoliberal regimes. This biopolitical rationality has been enabled by the technological innovation of bioassays.

Bioassays are used to determine the strength or activity of a substance's effect on living tissue. The capacity of drug tests to serve as surveillance technologies and enable new surveillance and security routines is ambiguous when we examine the goals and assumptions of those who put testing into place. Proponents of drug testing assume that testing unimpaired workers deters drug use, enhances productivity, and reduces social costs.[7] Although few empirical studies bear out these assumptions,[8] bioassays are perceived to "work" by identifying drug users in order to discourage them from using or to encourage them into treatment. Questions not only of civil liberties but also of social justice are generated by the application of technology on the preexisting social terrain in which it is deployed. That technological artifacts have politics has come to be more widely accepted (Winner 1986), but the politics of their implementation and their work in constituting "target populations" is rarely taken into account as an aspect of technology assessment.[9] In this chapter, I explore the modes of embodiment that bioassays produce and reproduce by paying attention to the social-structural contexts within which urine tests are deployed. There has been much future-oriented discussion of the possible deleterious discriminatory effects of genetic databases and genetic profiling for insurance purposes[10] yet curiously little about mundane bioassays already in wide use within "new surveillance" regimes such as routine and ubiquitous urine testing for drugs of abuse.

Social forces and structures of belief interact with bioassay technology, regardless of the substances at issue. Although urine does not have quite the symbolic weight of blood, because urine is considered waste and blood is considered generative, there remains in drug testing the symbolic action of "taking" something against the will of another. Although some individuals are all too willing to give a sample that certifies them as "clean" and others as "dirty," others view the need to prove that they have not consumed illicit substances as an affront to their liberties in and of itself. Thus the social and economic context—the macrostructural context—in which the microbehavioral intervention takes place has a symbolic significance to the community and individual members of it. Drug testing conveys symbolic meanings of distrust, contamination, and impurity that are signaled by the colloquial term *dirty* to connote a positive toxicology screen. Such scrutiny is experienced differently by members of already vulnerable groups than by members of groups dominant in the social order. Failing to recognize this differential vulnerability to heightened scrutiny has gotten us into trouble before and likely will again until we confront the social-structural context within which ritualistic deployments of bioassays occur.

The social consequences of assumed acquiescence to intrusive surveillance have been obscured. Only social-structural approaches allow us to discern how heightened insecurity works to intensify vulnerability to scrutiny among those very groups that are already most vulnerable to negative consequences. We do not need much further empirical documentation to discern patterns in answer to the following questions: Which groups directly experience intrusive bodily surveillance on a routine basis, and which social groups do not? Whose casual consumption patterns are exempt from scrutiny or shielded from negative consequences, and whose become consequential in life-altering ways? Deployment of drug-testing technologies provides an excellent arena in which to explore these questions. Elsewhere I have examined emergent drug-testing technologies such as the sweat patch and radioimmunoassay of hair (Campbell 2004, 2005). In the remainder of this chapter, I focus on patterns of social division revealed by routine urine-testing programs, contrasting a program implemented for drug-dependent physicians with the one I described previously, in which a vulnerable population of impoverished, pregnant women of color were drug tested when they presented at a hospital for obstetrical care in what amounted to an "unreasonable search and seizure." Although Fourth Amendment protections were ultimately extended to the petitioners in *Ferguson v. City of Charleston* (2001), they were subjected to a form of "vicious embodiment" produced by mistaken assumptions that biosurveillance technologies can somehow be deployed "innocently" of the institutionalized racism and sexism deeply lodged in the practical systems of both law enforcement and clinical medicine. Bodies and bodily processes remain relevant to the administrative processes that govern our lives—and if we do not recognize that, we will be unable to ask the right kinds of questions about "the new surveillance."

Low-intensity insecurity and even the threat of surveillance induce a heightened sense of individual and collective awareness that some call "deterrence." Although the individual or subjective emotional impact of such intrusions no doubt varies, the cumulative effects of living within practical systems that are characterized by the chronic stress induced by low-intensity surveillance should be factored into the calculus of its costs. Michel Foucault set forth the study of "practical systems" as his problematic in *The Archaeology of Knowledge* (1972), defining them as a set of interlinked political rationalities that organize activity, strategy, and technology in relatively homogenous ways. "Practical systems" control material things, actions upon others,[11] and relations with oneself. "There are three levels to my analysis of power: [games of] strategic relations, techniques of governance, and states of domination" (Foucault 1994: 299). Techniques of government, the second and mediating level, refer to the governance of institutions and extra-individual relations through techniques that establish or maintain situations or states of domination. Foucault defined a situation or state of domination as one in which "an individual or social group succeeds in blocking a field of power relations, immobilizing them and preventing any reversibility of movement" by strategically blocking or freezing power relations (1994: 283). Drug-testing technology provides an example of a technique used to block, freeze, or otherwise immobilize power relations. Although drug-testing technologies differ in the extent to which they capture drug use over time, the most common one, urinalysis, offers "data" from a fixed point in time, offering no illumination of the meaningful divisions between chronic use versus episodic use, abuse versus use, or problematic consumption versus nonproblematic consumption. Drug testing always decontextualizes drug consumption or environmental exposure from social settings where it takes place. It captures an episodic occurrence frozen in time and extracted from the social context that produced it. The enduring consequences of a positive toxicology screen last far longer than the ephemeral effects of illicit drugs.

Deterrence of future drug use is the main goal behind drug testing, and the idea that deterrence works is central to the structures of belief used to justify drug testing. A recent decline of positive drug tests in military testing programs, for instance, is attributed to greater administration of tests. Most testing programs are mandated by the federal government, and many are subsidized by it. However, there was a decline or leveling off of testing programs in the 1990s due to the recognition that they are an expensive way to catch a few, relatively minor infractions.[12] Testing programs vary in form: some consist of blanket surveillance testing, others monitor compliance with mandated treatment regimes, and still others have specific sanctions tied to their results (Harrell and Kleiman 2000). Few are truly random. Indeed most are implemented in contexts structured in predictable ways, illustrated by the two types of drug-testing programs detailed later. First, however, I sketch a brief history of technological innovation in the field of medical diagnostics, which made possible the redefinition of America's long-standing, chronic drug problems as problems of casual and episodic use.[13]

Cultural Fiction: Broader Testing Will Lead to a "Drug-Free" World

The lone dissent of civil libertarians has been repeatedly dismissed as excessive paranoia that should be subordinated to the broader social goal of reducing socially problematic drug use. The U.S. government phased testing into "business as usual," despite sensible arguments to limit it to circumstances where drug use serves as a clear threat to public health and safety and less intrusive alternatives are lacking (Rothstein 1991). The first arena in which large-scale drug testing was used was when the U.S. Department of Defense faced the return of heroin-addicted veterans from Vietnam during the Nixon administration, which in 1971 turned to Jerome Jaffe, who was then running a unique multimodality drug treatment and research program in Chicago (Massing 1998: 108). Jaffe had purchased a machine to do urinalysis through the free radical assay technique, and he suggested that the machines be deployed in Vietnam so as to encourage individuals to detox themselves prior to getting on a plane to return to the States. The punishment—having to remain in Vietnam—was clear, and most, but not all, heroin-addicted veterans got the message.[14]

Workplace drug testing did not really scale up until the 1980s (Normand, Lempert, and O'Brien 1994: 178–80; Staples 2000). At first it was restricted to a few sectors where highly public accidents legitimized drug testing. The Navy implemented it in 1982 after a fatal aircraft carrier accident (MacDonald and Wells 1994). In the late 1980s federal legislative and administrative developments opened the door to widespread testing: Ronald Reagan's 1986 executive order promoting the "drug-free federal workplace"; the omnibus Anti-Drug Abuse Act (1986); enactment of guidelines for federal employee drug-testing programs; and adoption of random drug screening programs by the Department of Transportation in aviation, mass transit, trucking, and pipeline construction in 1989. The new emphasis on testing or screening contrasted to previous company approaches to dealing with alcoholism on the job,[15] which had widened to include drug addiction in the 1960s (Dickman, Emener, and Hutchison 1986: 9). However, the privatization of the drug and alcohol treatment industry created jobs for "human service change agents" looking for outlets for their skills as a result of federal funding decreases in the human and social services sector since the 1970s (Dickman, Emener, and Hutchison 1986: 9). Devolution of federal and state responsibilities for mental health created an emerging emphasis on public–private partnerships, as "public mental health agencies, alcohol/drug treatment centers and private counseling firms" saw industry as their bread and butter. Since Henry Ford, industry has taken notice of the "productivity costs" incurred by drug and alcohol use on and off the job, evolving employee assistance programs (EAPs) in response.

Just how the social and economic costs of drug and alcohol consumption are measured has been subject to many analyses, among them one from then-senator Dan Quayle, whose article "American Productivity: The Devastating Effects of Drug and Alcohol Abuse" was published in the *American Psychologist* and reprinted in Dickman, Emener, and Hutchison (1986). Quayle attributed the cause of the general productivity slowdown in the United States since World War II to the costs of drug and alcohol abuse: "The price we pay for health care, days away from work, and lost productivity as the result of addiction and alcoholism is about the same as the amount requested by the president to run the 400 programs in the Department of Health and Human Services—$70 billion. Nearly half the cost—$30.1 billion—is related to lost productivity due to employee alcohol and drug abuse" (Dickman, Emener, and Hutchison 1986: 23). The problem, according to Quayle, was widespread denial—reluctance on the part of government and business to "admit that they have people working for them who are alcohol or drug abusers. This attitude carries over to society at large—after all, who wants to admit that the spouse's social drinking or recreational drug-taking is really an addiction?" (p. 25). Because EAPs were available to only 12 percent of the U.S. workforce at the time, Quayle argued, "We need to back these initiatives [the war against drugs] with the belief that something can be done to fight these problems and the knowledge that a strong effort is needed—needed not only for social redemption but economic recovery as well" (Dickman, Emener, and Hutchison 1986: 29). Although it is rare to have the "social redemption" rationale so baldly stated, it is important to see the "drug-free" mandate as one that partakes of ritual cleansing. Drug and alcohol consumption are used to make boring and repetitive work bearable and have thus long been integral to global economic expansion: "Drugs induce or facilitate all sorts of labors that men and women, in a sober frame of mind, would ordinarily spurn" (Courtwright 2001: 144). Modernity, however, brought with it factors that shifted elite priorities toward control and regulation. Industrialization, bureaucratization, rationalization, and, above all, mechanization made it harder to absorb the social costs of what was once called "inebriety."

Workplace programs that evolved with unions have sometimes had beneficial aspirations; they cannot simply be categorized as completely unreasonable intrusion into private consumption but may sometimes be taken as evidence of corporate responsibility for employee well-being. The growth in the 1980s of EAPs stands in stark contrast to cutbacks in social provision (Stern 1988). Although critics of EAPs portray them as an "unwitting tool of big business" and even as "active participants in a conspiracy to impose more thorough social control on workers," their expansion resulted not from finer attempts at social control but from structural changes that determined how employers related to the workforce (Stern 1988: 8). The "big split in the economy [between well and poorly paying jobs] explains the contrast between the sunny optimism of EAP professionals and the grimness that grips the public welfare community" (Stern 1988: 8). Stern traced the contribution of the shift to an "information" or "knowledge-based" economy to class polarization (1988: 10). Technological change and flexible specialization placed premiums on labor force responsiveness and effectively widened the gap between winners—who get jobs with a new emphasis on quality of work-life and enhancement programs—and losers—who get abandonment, dislocation, unemployment, and under-employment. EAPs were a quality-of-life strategy undertaken mainly in unionized settings, where some collective power could be brought to bear on behalf of "sick" people. But they were a relatively confined and inactive enterprise that largely failed at seeing themselves as linked to the public sector and macroeconomic trends (Stern 1988: 21). "More often than not, EAP professionals appear to adopt management goals—profitability, cost containment, and efficiency—as their own. Rather than extending their practice to examine the organization and social origins of workers' problems, they are more likely to use their expertise to individualize and medicalize dysfunction. Practitioners have increasingly hitched their star to that of management" (Stern 1988: 21). These problems are now writ large given the flattening forces described by Thomas Friedman, who was told by one informant, "In this world, you better do it right—you don't get to pick up and move to the next town so easily. In the world of Google, your reputation will follow you and precede you on your next stop ... You don't get to spend four years getting drunk."[16] Increasingly, EAPs and other pockets of tolerance transmute into punitive mechanisms of intrusive surveillance as their goals converge with management and social control.

Another factor in the increasing implementation of drug screening and testing programs in the corporate sector has been innovation of "less invasive" and more accurate tests. Propelled by drug-free workplace legislation, the pull of the market has proved irresistible. The size and scope of the drug-testing market, which includes manufacturers, distributors, and laboratories to analyze the results, has radically expanded since the Reagan administration. The private sector soon followed the military and the governmental sector. The U.S. government remains the drug testing industry's largest and most loyal customer. No longer confined to the workplace, drug tests are now offered "direct to consumers" and are marketed especially to parents who administer the tests outside the ethical parameters of "informed consent" and with no guarantees of confidentiality. With federal subsidies, drug testing has become relatively routine in high school sports programs. It is commonplace in preemployment settings in the United States. As I mentioned previously, testing rapidly scaled up in criminal justice settings and especially diversionary arenas such as drug courts. Urine testing is used in drug and alcohol treatment settings, and it is tied to systems of sanctions in social welfare settings. "Passing" a drug test has become a commonplace activity in some economic and social sectors. Looking at where testing has become common and where it remains rare is instructive, as it reveals some of the contours of low-wage, service sector work and poverty. Although some high-wage-share jobs require testing, they remain those where public health and safety are at stake, where minors are involved, and where it can be argued that in highly limited, "exceptional circumstances" there exist "special needs, beyond the normal need for law enforcement" (*New Jersey v. T.L.O.*, 469 U.S. 325,

351, 83 L. Ed. 2d 720, 105 S. Ct. 733 [1985] and *Vernonia School Dist. 47J v. Acton*, 515 U.S. 646, 132 L. Ed. 2d 564, 115 S. Ct. 2386 [1995]). The special-needs test is a balancing test that weighs the necessary invasion of privacy against the "special needs" that warrant it. Unwarranted searches where probable cause is lacking are considered constitutional if the calculus of "special needs" tilts toward justifying the incursion.

Drug testing is likely in two circumstances—those that involve critical professions and those that involve routine matters such as preemployment screening for low-wage jobs. This difference is inscribed in the law. In *Skinner v. Railway Labor Executives' Assn* (489 U.S. 602, 617, 103 L. ed. 2d 639, 109 S. Ct. 1402 [1989]), the U.S. Supreme Court allowed the special-needs doctrine to dictate exceptions to the Fourth Amendment guarantee against unreasonable searches and seizures. Among special-needs cases granted certiorari by the U.S. Supreme Court, the court considered urine testing by the government to be a reasonable search justified either by consent or by the special-needs exception. However, the U.S. Supreme Court did not allow lower court decisions to stand when they involved nonconsensual drug testing of pregnant women in *Ferguson v. City of Charleston,* by far the most intriguing of cases involve urine testing. The outcome of the case did not necessarily head off attempts to make drug testing a routine matter in health care settings because the opinion was so circumscribed. Proposals for drug testing to become a matter of routine health care are floated by those who believe that deterrence works. For instance, a RAND Corporation document on "Drug Use and Drug Policy Futures" posed the possibility that a less intrusive testing method might "break down some of the resistance on privacy grounds" and be nearly irresistible to consumers if it could test simultaneously for other health indicators within the context of regular physical exams (Caulkins et al. 2003). The document noted, "Such a diagnostic tool might prove difficult for parents to resist." If such methods were to be linked to a program of universal health care access, they might be more desirable given the large numbers of uninsured individuals in the United States. That likelihood is slim. Instead health care may come to resemble a bodily intrusive surveillance regime, shifting "some sanctioning activity from the criminal justice system to parents, employers, coaches, and other screeners" (Caulkins et al. 2003). Were drug testing to become a routine matter of health care, procedures for confidentiality and informed consent would presumably have to evolve at a faster pace than they have thus far. However, as the large corporations who remain invested in drug testing abandon their commitments to insuring their workforce, that scenario also becomes unlikely.[17]

Cultural Fact: Diagnostic Screens Work as Intrusive Surveillance

The likelihood is that more innovative and intrusive programs will be put into place that use "diagnostic" screens to target suspected drug users. The program mentioned in the introduction was the subject of a 2001 U.S. Supreme Court opinion, which found that the city of Charleston, South Carolina, had unconstitutionally violated the rights of ten petitioners, pregnant women of color, by drug testing them without telling them on the Medicaid maternity ward of the MUSC and then calling in law enforcement to arrest and jail them. The need for a structural analysis of contexts in which economically marginalized communities of color have become subject to high rates of illicit drug use could not be clearer. Yet one striking feature of the literature on drug testing is the glaring lack of awareness about how "target populations" are constructed and reified through testing programs. There is little or no recognition that drug tests are almost always deployed by the relatively powerful against the relatively powerless—job holders rather than job seekers, administrators rather than "clients" of administrative systems, case managers rather than "cases," health care providers acting as law enforcement deputies rather than "patients." It is almost as if drug testing occurs in a vacuum of recognition of the basic underlying structural power dynamics at work in biosurveillance regimes. What is happening targets individuals from vulnerable populations, drawing them into a cycle of blame, criminalization, and recrimination that reinscribes their bodily subjection.

Civil rights concerns are consistently dismissed as somehow inappropriate in the face of the larger goal of identifying people who have used an illicit drug. However, the initial advocacy on behalf of the *Ferguson* petitioners was predicated on the notion that their civil rights were violated by the "secret screens" as part of an unethical and improper human research program. Indeed the program was suspended in January 1994 because of various agencies' responses to a complaint to the National Institutes of Health. The investigation by the federal Office of Protection from Research Risks concluded that the MUSC drug-testing program constituted a human research program conducted without appropriate institutional review board approval (Nahas 2001). Advocates did not get very far with this strategy, although it did effectively shut down the program. Although the deceptive nature of the drug tests bears resemblance to unethical research programs, the MUSC was not, after all, actually operating a scientific research program. It was operating a surveillance program evolved by law enforcement officials in conjunction with clinicians that can be considered neither routine health care nor a research program. It is best considered a conduit by which law enforcement could access arrestees with greater ease. Proponents justified their actions in terms of concern about fetal exposure to cocaine and their desire to coerce pregnant women into treatment. Let us for the moment bracket the fact that through most of the time that the testing policy was in effect, there was no drug treatment available for women in the state of South Carolina. Instead I want to contrast drug testing in the context of surveillance regimes with drug testing in the context of therapeutic regimes. My argument is not against all drug testing but against the imposition of new bodily surveillance regimes without regard for the social justice concerns involved.

Drug-testing technologies could potentially be deployed in less intrusive ways and for more beneficent reasons. Certain populations are more highly prone to problematic drug use than others—physicians, for instance, have had historically high rates because of drug exposure and availability. Programs to assist drug-impaired physicians operate quite differently from programs targeted toward, say, economically disenfranchised pregnant women or incarcerated persons. Behavioral pharmacologist Thomas Crowley described an innovative approach called "aversive contingency contracting" in which he applied the principles of operant conditioning to drug-dependent physicians by trying to ascertain what would be meaningful consequences in their social context (1984).[18]

> Drug dependence is an occupational hazard of physicians, who develop drug dependence probably more than any other profession. … the physician swims in a world of drugs, and so it's a complex issue unless the doc is willing to get out of drug use altogether. My idea was to apply one of the principles of operant conditioning to drug-dependent physicians. We set up a program in which a doc would come to me, I'd evaluate him, and then he would write a letter to the State Board of Medical Examiners, the licensing board, saying that he was a drug addict, he had relapsed, and he was surrendering his license. He would write this all out, give it to me, and then in a written contract he would tell me to collect urine from him on an agreed-upon schedule, and he would instruct me to mail the letter at any time that his urine was positive for drugs, for the specified drugs. (Author's interview with Thomas Crowley, June 2005, Orlando, Florida)

Crowley described a process in which individuals identified what they held most dear and engaged in a process that required fully informed consent, a process that was a good bit more collaborative than what happened to Crystal Ferguson, her fellow petitioners, and numerous other women who were arrested under the MUSC policy. Not only were these women arrested or threatened with arrest when they presented for obstetrical care, they were carted off to jail for the duration of their pregnancies or shortly after delivery. Their medical needs were neglected, subordinated to the interests of the criminal justice system.

The MUSC policy was in effect only in the Medicaid clinic—it was not used elsewhere in the hospital. Pregnant women who were "paying customers," in other words, were not subjected to it. Protocols described nine criteria for identifying "pregnant patients suspected of drug use": (1) no prenatal care, (2) late prenatal care (after 24 weeks gestation), (3) incomplete prenatal care, (4) abruption placentae, (5) intrauterine fetal death, (6) preterm labor "of no obvious cause," (7) intrauterine growth retardation "of no obvious cause," (8) previously known alcohol or drug abuse, and (9) unexplained congenital anomalies (*Ferguson* 2001: 4).[19] The urine of women who met even one of these criteria was tested, and the police were notified in the event of a positive toxicology screen. They then arrested the patient. Although the protocol was modified over the years that the program was in place and there were attempts to get women drug treatment referrals, these are the basic outlines of what happened to Crystal Ferguson and twenty-eight other poor, African American women from Charleston, South Carolina.[20] More detail on the implementation is available elsewhere (Roth 2002). Although being poor and African American was not one of the explicit criteria, they operated implicitly as primary criteria. Although pregnant women of color in Charleston gradually came to understand that something unusual was happening to them at the MUSC, it was the only hospital in Charleston that served women who were both poor and pregnant at a time when there were no drug treatment programs in the state.[21] Thus the policy amounted to the "use of law enforcement to coerce patients into substance abuse treatment" at an extremely vulnerable moment in their lives. As the Supreme Court decision noted, "While the ultimate goal might well have been to get the women in question into substance abuse treatment and off drugs, the immediate objective of the searches was to generate evidence for law enforcement purposes in order to reach that goal" (*Ferguson* 2001: 2). The objective was to generate evidence for the "specific purpose of incriminating these patients," and thus the Court did not group the drug tests with other blood and urine tests that are a routine part of the medical care of pregnant and postpartum women (*Ferguson* 2001: 6). Because the screening program was done in conjunction with the police rather than independent of the police, it was held to implicate the Fourth Amendment (*Ferguson* 2001: 6). Many aspects of this program have been scrutinized for their implications for social justice, access to health care, abortion and reproductive rights, and the civil rights of pregnant women. I focus on the nature of the everyday insecurities introduced by this biosurveillance regime.

Given the multiple injustices and indignities visited on the *Ferguson* petitioners, only some of which the Court addressed,[22] it may seem tendentious to focus on drug testing. The urine of pregnant women is, after all, routinely tested for signs of infection; few advocate the use of illicit drugs during pregnancy, and in fact most argue that there is a compelling state interest in deterring and treating drug use by pregnant women; and the Supreme Court did the right thing in ruling in favor of the petitioners. Why complain? The question comes down to the forms of "vicious embodiment" produced with the help of bioassays and the ways we go about responding to that state interest. Peeing in a cup, wearing a sweat patch, or handing over a strand of hair may seem like insignificant acts in the context of those whose social worlds are deeply structured by racist violence. However, these micropractices are points of ingress for a state bent on monitoring the consumption practices of its least enfranchised citizens. That anyone can now purchase and use such technologies of suspicion to conduct peer-to-peer or parent-to-child surveillance is an indicator that consumption has become a primary system of socialization, normalization, and control. Behind the appalling image of poor women of color delivering babies while shackled to hospital beds or being dragged off to jail immediately after delivery without so much as a sanitary napkin is the steady accumulation of individual, "insignificant," everyday acts of surveillance.

Conclusion: Consumption and Conscription

Drug consumption practices follow the geographic contours of the social groups to which individuals belong. Drug use patterns vary—not because of cultural differences but because drug markets are markets like any other, and thus availability varies by economic and cultural geography.[23] Contesting the "exaggeration of individual agency" involved in epidemiological explanations of poverty and disease that "blame the victim," which have taken hold especially in the United States (Farmer 1992: 221–22; Farmer 1999: 9), requires being able to discern how the macrologics of power work through even the most micrological practices. A similar structure of demand underlies markets in legal and illegal drug commodities. Capitalism works through the production and replication of the structures of demand, the facilitation of particular forms of consumption and the foreclosure of others, and the production of loyal customers. "The regulatory or disciplinary mechanisms of the market seek to control and cure the very addictions they themselves have produced" (Singer 1993: 38). Policies of prohibition divide "undisciplined" consumers, whose exchange relations take place primarily in the informal economy, from "productive" consumers, who engage in markets that require routinized, predictable, and disciplined behavior. These social and structural divisions show up in the somewhat arbitrary divisions between drug users—illicit versus licit, addiction to street drugs versus pharmaceuticals. The illogical logic of drug markets is matched by that of the treatment apparatus, which runs on "problem profits," one of the defining features of mature capitalism, that are derived from "all enterprises that exploit evolved human drives."[24] "The peculiar, vomitorious genius of modern capitalism is its ability to betray our sense with one class of products or services and then sell us another to cope with the damage so that we can go back to consuming more of what caused the problem in the first place" (Courtwright 2001: 109). "Drugs, which radiate externalities, produce far more [economic activity than soy beans and clothes driers]. They are a kind of perpetual motion machine, providing steady work for everyone from peasants to lawyers to drug historians" (Courtwright 2001: 110). The drug-testing industry is one such externality that provides steady work by constituting legitimate markets in the workplace, the health care industry, the human and social services, and the criminal justice system. Despite the illogical logic that surveillance works to deter illicit drug consumption that occurs within the contexts of structural violence, the market proceeds as if it is meeting a public need. Industry websites tout tests that are as convenient as home pregnancy tests. Employers are deluded into the misperception that greater surveillance will address productivity problems. Hospital administrators are misled into thinking that incursions into individual privacy are justified and will have a deterrent effect.

Drug policy is symptomatic of larger problems involved in governing consumption by targeting individual consumers. Problematic assumptions about demand and deterrence drive institutions away from solutions that might address the social-structural dynamics that mitigate against controlled use, harm reduction, or less socially problematic ways of using. Representations of drug problems and solutions that divert attention away from structural or macrolevel processes and toward microbehavioral modification regimes targeted toward individuals serve merely to reproduce existing "structures of demand" (Campbell 2000; Schram 2003). Such deflections secure a place for the technological innovations essential to the work of surveillance, risk assessment, and risk management in a "welfare state" that is rapidly becoming a controlled society (Lyon 2001; Garland 2001). Weeding out what is social control from what is social welfare is not the point. Instead it is time to recast the question in light of the proliferation of intrusive surveillance regimes. Why accept intrusive surveillance not only as part of the cost of doing business but also as part of institutional routines that are supposedly supportive and therapeutic? Despite protest from those who care about civil liberties, drug testing has become a mundane technology, ubiquitous in the lives of some but insignificant to the majority of those who exercise power. That it did so without robust discussion says more about the incapacity of current technology assessment for taking into account structural and cultural context than anything else.

What if technology assessment evolved to address a broader "range of identity issues, including patient identity, professional identity, and disease identity" (Wailoo 1997: 199)? Paraphrasing some of the questions that Wailoo raised about blood testing is an instructive exercise for envisioning what technology assessment could look like: What institutional relations are engendered by the technology? What economic interests are served? What interacting cultural expectations and ideologies do they embody? What diseases (or conditions) do they construct and combat? What "target populations" do they construct, and which ones do they obscure (Schneider and Ingram 1997: 102–49)? Elsewhere I have argued that "suspect technologies" join other surveillance technologies in being "especially incompatible with citizen self-determination in a democratic polity" (Campbell 2005: 394). Of suspect technologies, we should ask, Does their use reinforce or challenge current class polarizations and cultural divides? Medical anthropologist Paul Farmer has rightfully argued against analysis that foregrounds "cultural" aspects at the expense of recognizing structural violence and exaggerates individual agency (1992, 1999, 2004). There is a need not only to "bring structure back in" but also to examine the effects on "quality of life" in specific cultures and subcultures. How precisely to do so is an open question. Farmer offers the important insight that unjust, nonreciprocal research relationships that bring "First World diagnostics" but "Third World therapeutics" to those who suffer the effects of inequity are a good clue that technologies are being used in ways that cement disparities. The use of drug tests as "diagnostics" to "screen" for drug use in contexts where accessible and effective drug treatment is not widely available suggests that something else may be going on. Suggestions that this form of surveillance be routinely coupled with other health care–oriented diagnostics belie the fact that these "diagnostics" are meant to deter people by scaring or coercing them into changing their behavior despite circumstances of past and present trauma, economic disenfranchisement, and the everyday insecurities that result from "vicious embodiment." The tactic of using diagnostics for surveillance and deterrence ignores how individuals are conscripted within "structures of constraint,"[25] as well as "structures of demand." Thus a technology deployed to change structures of demand that ignores structures of constraint is futile. A diagnostic screen used to freeze a moment in time while ignoring the ongoing context of inequality and structural violence is truly useless for anything but punishment. Drug testing in nontherapeutic contexts will remain an unfair and unjust "new surveillance" scheme until the day when the poor begin drug testing the rich.

Notes

1. Tools for further reflection on the vernacular categories of "clean" and "dirty" so central to drug testing discourse can be found in Douglas (1966), which argues that social order is maintained through the regular invocation of these categories.

2. Always symptomatic of a "drug panic," the term *epidemic* fit this most localized drug problem poorly. As Philip Jenkins notes, "It is almost irrelevant whether the claims presented by the rhetoric of 'panic' are well-founded or wholly spurious: The panic itself is valuable in itself for what it suggests about the perceptions of a society as a whole, and specifically of policymakers and legislators" (Inciardi and McElrath 2004: 267, 279). See also Reinarman and Levine (1997).

3. Drug Court Clearinghouse and Technical Assistance Project. *Drug Court Survey Report* (Washington, DC: School of Public Affairs, American University, 2000).

4. The Anti-Drug Abuse Act of 1988 added an "aggravated felony" section to facilitate deportation of aliens convicted of drug trafficking. The 1996 immigration reform law also expanded the "aggravated felony" category. By 2000, more than 20,000 noncitizens were incarcerated on drug charges in the United States; only 13,000 were serving time for immigration-related crimes; and only 3,000 were serving time for other crimes. According to the former director of the U.S. Bureau of Prisons, Kathleen Hawk, most crime committed by legal and illegal immigrants is drug related. Fully 75 percent of aliens in federal U.S. prisons were convicted of drug crimes, compared to just 56 percent of incarcerated U.S. citizens. See Hawk's testimony in U.S. Congress, *Criminal Aliens: Hearings before the Subcommittee on International Law, Immigration, and Refugees of the House Committee on the Judiciary*, 103d Cong., 2d sess. 165 (1994). For an overview of this situation, see Kevin R. Johnson, *The "Huddled Masses" Myth: Immigration and Civil Rights* (Philadelphia, PA: Temple University Press, 2004).

5. For all their vaunted success in convincing people that they are a humane alternative, drug courts have not expanded access to treatment. They have instead further pressured treatment programs by bringing new arrestees into them without increasing available slots for those voluntarily seeking treatment. Questions remain as to why drug courts were scaled up so rapidly, without real cost–benefit analyses (costs were externalized in attempts to justify the rapid diffusion of drug courts) or much public discussion. A rare judge critical of drug courts argues they are "just the latest Band-Aid we have tried to apply over the deep wound of our schizophrenia about drugs. ... Drug courts themselves have become a kind of institutional narcotic upon which the entire criminal justice system is becoming increasingly dependent" (M.B. Hoffman 2000: 1441).

6. Simon argues that the shift from actual to databased selves through "dataveillance" and biometrics has altered the supervisory operations and relationships of the "new surveillance." Although not directly concerned with drug testing, he attends to "surveillance interfaces," the local, material sites where actual and databased selves meet and recognize each other (Simon 2005: 18). Simon suggests we look at surveillance interfaces as places where we can discern the effects of power.

7. For an excellent examination of the "common set of statements," what I would call a "governing mentality" (Campbell 2000), that are invoked to justify testing by those who manufacture, distribute, administer, and analyze drug tests, see Morgan (1988). Despite painstaking criticism by civil libertarians such as Morgan, who was chair of the pharmacology department at New York Medical School at the time he wrote the article, the rationale put forward for testing today remains much the same. See also the document by the American Civil Liberties Union (1999). However, justification is hardly necessary anymore, because drug testing has been widely implemented in ways that few can afford to contest.

8. A clear statement of this point can be found in the National Research Council/Institute of Medicine study edited by Jacques Normand, Richard O. Lempert, and Charles P. O'Brien,

Under the Influence? Drugs and the American Work Force (Washington, DC: National Academy Press, 1994), which repeatedly reminds readers that drug testing rarely screens for alcohol and drug use combinations that include alcohol, "the drug most associated with perceived detrimental job performance" (p. 5). This committee found "relatively low rates of alcohol and other drug abuse among the work force" and many other factors that cause performance deficiencies. The committee recommended that drug testing programs "not be viewed as a panacea for curing workplace performance problems" (p. 12). Workforce productivity problems in the United States are much broader than those that can be attributed to drug and alcohol consumption, particularly casual use.

9. There is an ongoing conversation in the policy design literature concerning the production of "target populations," as well as the misplaced concreteness of that language (Schneider and Ingram 1997).

10. DNA databases are already in use within the criminal justice system in the United States and other nations, and I do not mean to underplay the effects of these. See Troy Duster's essay and others in Lazer (2004). Most commentators make the point that the criminal justice system is structured in ways that reproduce racial bias.

11. Foucault later used the term *governmentality* (Foucault 1988; Foucault 1994: 300) to encompass the "range of practices that constitute, define, organize, and instrumentalize the strategies that individuals in their freedom can use in dealing with each other" (N. Rose 1999).

12. Social scientists have found little evidence that drug testing improves workplace productivity (Shepard and Clifton 1998), decreases drug use by students (Yamaguchi, Johnston, and O'Malley 2003), or affects the labor supply (French, Roebuck, and Alexandre 2001).

13. For an excellent critical history of drug-testing technologies and their social implications, see Zimmer and Jacobs (1992).

14. Note Robins (1973) and Robins, Davis, and Goodwin (1974) showed that most military heroin users in Vietnam succeeded in not returning to the practice once back in the States.

15. For insight into previous approaches, see *Counseling the Troubled Person in Industry*, eds. J. Fred Dickman, William G. Emener Jr., and William S. Hutchison Jr. (Springfield, IL: Charles C. Thomas, 1986), which offers the perspectives of rehabilitation counselors and social workers who trace their antecedents to AA and OAPs (Occupational Alcoholism Programs, 1939–62) developed by DuPont and Kodak in the early 1940s for skilled workers (Dickman, Emener, and Hutchison 1986: 8–9).

16. Thomas L. Friedman, *The World Is Flat: A Brief History of the Twenty-first Century* (New York: Farrar, Straus, and Giroux, 2005). The point here is that labor-capital relations have changed, thus altering the necessity of companies to respond humanely to "troubled persons," despite the ubiquitous emphasis on "wellness."

17. For instance, a high proportion of Wal-Mart workers depend on public social programs for health insurance (or choose to go without it), public housing, and food stamps because of company policies to underinsure low-wage workers (Friedman 2005: 215). Rather than insuring its workers, Wal-Mart drug tests all of its current and prospective employees except in states that prohibit such testing.

18. I interviewed Crowley on June 18, 2005, in Orlando, Florida, as part of a larger oral history project on scientific research in the addictions that was undertaken with the support of the University of Michigan Substance Abuse Research Center, the Wayne State University Center for Substance Abuse Research, and the College of Problems of Drug Dependence. For their ongoing generosity and interest in this project, I want to thank Carol Boyd, Chrys-Ellen Johanson, Sean MacCabe, and Joseph Spillane. I also want to acknowledge Jason Williams for his help with the research for this chapter.

19. A discussion of the criteria is beyond the scope of this chapter. Note, however, that number four was the only criterion directly attributable to cocaine use during pregnancy. The first three criteria had everything to do with health care access, most notably insurance. Drug-using women are generally reluctant to seek health care given the punitive climate in which their illegal practices would be exposed. The amicus briefs were very clear on this latter point, seeking to document a "deterrence" effect, and state legislatures, with the notable exception of South Carolina, took this claim seriously during debates on mandatory reporting laws.

20. The one white arrestee had an African American boyfriend, a fact recorded by the nurse, Shirley Brown, who was integral to the implementation of the program and whose racist motives were fairly evident in the documents pertaining to the case and the publicity surrounding it (Roth 2002: 151; D. Roberts 1997: 175).
21. According to Roth, there were no residential drug treatment programs in South Carolina for women (much less pregnant women who encounter liability concerns when they seek treatment) until the spring of 1992. Not until November 1994 did a six-bed facility open in Charleston. Barriers that deny clients access to drug treatment remain high because of the kinds of restrictions and regulatory requirements that agencies are under.
22. Nahas (2001) contends that the Court performed a thin, "threshold analysis," circumscribing its opinion so narrowly that it simply could not comment on the implications of the case for privacy, due process, or reproductive rights.
23. There is no better example of this than crack cocaine, the drug at issue in *Ferguson v. City of Charleston*, which was really available only in poor, urban communities of color despite evidence of use across class and race categories (Chasnoff 1990). The national debate over maternal crack cocaine use was a quarrel over allocation of health care resources to "boarder babies," constructed as "surplus" in the context of a crisis in urban social reproduction (Campbell 2000: 185–87). During the debate, policy makers voiced their fears that mothers and grandmothers were no longer fit caregivers just when the costs of caring for "drug-exposed babies" escalated. In a 1989 hearing before the House Select Committee on Children, Youth, and Families aptly titled *Born Hooked: Confronting the Impact of Perinatal Substance Abuse*, Haynes Rice, director of Howard University Hospital, stated that neonatal units overcrowded with the babies of poor women—"not the most wantable product"—directly threatened "wanted" children (U.S. Congress 1989: 121). Poor women were depicted as absorbing more than their fair share of public health care resources, as their babies displaced the "normal deliveries" of middle-class mothers in urban hospitals. Although the fact that the MUSC implemented the program it did was no accident given the stated motivations of all of the players, it is perhaps more surprising that more urban hospitals that lay at the local epicenters of the late twentieth-century crack cocaine crisis did not go that route.
24. Courtwright (2001) argues that fast food consumption, "like drug commerce, [has] a transcultural biological foundation" (pp. 108–109). Just as the field of science and technology studies has been critical of biological and technological determinism, we should critically evaluate the meaning we attribute to such a claim. There may well be a physiological, neurobiological, or biochemical component to consumption, but the questions then become what social forms of consumption are encouraged or discouraged; how "scientific" evidence is adduced to reinforce or destabilize those socially prescribed forms; and what are the politics and policies by which they are enforced.
25. Feminist economist Nancy Folbre's analytic framework for thinking about how gender works can be found in *Who Pays for the Kids: Gender as a Structure of Constraint* (New York: Routledge, 1987).

CHAPTER 5

Indoor Positioning and Digital Management

Emerging Surveillance Regimes in Hospitals

JILL A. FISHER

Not all surveillance is intended as such. In spite of intentions, the valence of some technological systems toward surveillance should not be underestimated. Within the domain of health care, there has been an increased emphasis on the use of information and communication technologies to streamline processes by centralizing patients' records, locating medical equipment, and tracking hospital staff and patients. Although these changes are often couched in terms of improving patient care, the direct benefits to patients are often considered too "soft" to measure compared to a "hard" economic outcome like hospitals' return on investment. What is rarely mentioned—and then only in the most guarded terms—is the tendency of these technologies to function as surveillance systems that monitor the activities of patients and staff, particularly nurses.

In this essay, I examine the emergence of radio frequency identification (RFID) as one such technology within hospital settings. First, I describe the technology and its applications outside of and within health care. Next, I examine the implications of RFID technological systems on existing hospital infrastructures, paying particular attention to their effects on existing divisions of labor. Finally, to highlight the politics of surveillance, I analyze the intersection between discourses of "indoor positioning" and "workflow management." The argument here is that the deployment of these technological systems is reflective of broader trends in managerial cultures. As such, the operations of power within these systems must be examined both as local and specific and as global and contingent.

A Technological "Solution" Looking for a Health Care Problem?

Although RFID technologies have historically been associated with military uses (Landt and Catlin 2001), they have thrived within manufacturing and distribution industries. RFIDs are classified as "automatic identification" technologies that are used primarily for "data capture." What this means is that once equipped with RFID systems, items that are tagged with RFIDs can be counted, tracked, and processed as they pass by an RFID reader (also called "interrogators" or "scanners"). These systems are considered far superior to their predecessors like barcodes or manual methods of collecting data because they are not optically read (Zhekun, Gadh, and Prabhu 2004). For example, barcodes require a direct line of sight, so that the reader must be placed directly against or near the barcode. Although this is an effective technology, it is considered especially vulnerable to conditions: barcodes can become dirty, tear, and fail to work. In contrast, RFID tags can be read regardless of most conditions because they can be read without a direct line of sight as long as they pass through or near a reader. In industries such as manufacturing and distribution, the development of low-cost RFID technologies often referred to as "smart labels" are said to increase knowledge within supply-chain management (Brewer, Sloan, and Landers 1999; d'Hont 2002).[1]

The economics of this technology explain its recent surge in sales and the interest of manufacturers, distributors, and retailers to implement RFID systems. What is special about RFID for those wishing to maximize its value is the facility with which it fits within global systems of production and consumption. Given the emphasis on flexibility within discourses and regimes of economic globalization, RFID technologies enable post-Fordist forms of production, most notably just-in-time manufacturing because distribution and retail companies are better able to monitor their inventories as they flow across borders and spaces. Moreover, these technological systems promise to bring the flexibility of production to the retailers. Through the development of RFID systems to track not only the number of products in retailers' inventories but also the number of those products on the shelves, the goal becomes the creation of just-in-time retail environments to complement and work in conjunction with just-in-time production (E. Hess 2003).

Although most advanced levels of retail uses of RFID systems have not yet been actualized, Wal-Mart has become a leader in promoting RFID implementation from manufacturing to product sales. In a move to increase the use of this technology, Wal-Mart required their top 100 suppliers to tag all case and pallet shipments with RFID. This mandate went into effect in January 2005, and its goal for Wal-Mart was to improve distribution of products to the retail stores from their own warehouses. According to early studies of the efficacy of these systems, Wal-Mart reports that stores are better able to keep products in stock and on the shelves and to speed up the process of replenishing out-of-stock items (Malone 2005). In spite of Wal-Mart's support for RFID, few other retailers have similarly begun making demands of suppliers to tag their shipments.

What is interesting is that retailers experience more financial savings and gains through the deployment of RFID than do manufacturers. As a result, without the pressure of their retailers, many manufacturers have not begun integrating RFID to the extent that had been projected. According to one industry analyst, the RFID industry "continues to over-promise and under-deliver," reporting that the developments in RFID technology have been slower than promised, the supply of existing technology has not caught up with the demand, and the cost of the tags has remained high (Roberti 2005). In other words, the demand by retailers like Wal-Mart for suppliers to use RFID passes on the cost of implementation while retailers benefit from the cost saving that comes with these systems. The case of Wal-Mart, and its positive experiences with RFID, is important because it has led to increased publicity for these systems over the past few years (Murphy 2003). Given the perceived benefits of the use of RFID in retail, the technology companies and other industries began to speculate about the transformative value RFID systems could have for organizations ranging from education to health care (Stanford 2003).

Within health care in particular, the impetus for integrating RFID systems into hospitals has been enabled further by federally mandated initiatives. In April 2004, President Bush issued an executive order calling for the incorporation of health information technology into all medical practices nationwide and the creation of a National Health Information Technology Coordinator to oversee the process.[2] In May 2005, the U.S. Department of Health and Human Services issued a complementary report calling for government partnerships with private technology companies to accelerate the process of developing health information technologies (Lewin Group 2005). These policy positions are representative of a larger, ongoing shift toward information technology systems in public, private, and nonprofit sectors (Monahan 2005a).

The transition of RFID systems from manufacturing to health care has not been as seamless as hospitals and technology companies had hoped. The implementation of these systems is seen as a potential solution for the clinical problems that many hospitals are facing, yet critics wonder if RFIDs are solutions looking for a problem (Greene 2004, hospital representative, personal communication). On one hand, these systems do not adapt easily to hospital settings because the infrastructure of hospitals—in terms of space, equipment, personnel, and patients—is much more complicated than factory or warehouse settings (Ostbye et al. 2003). On the other hand, these systems promise to decrease the operating expenses of already cash-strapped hospitals by increasing workflow and asset management (Calvaneso 1999). Although RFID has the potential to provide a robust return on investment for hospitals, what is much less clear, however, is how well these technologies can improve health care delivery, particularly without creating new burdens on overworked clinical staff.

As for their actual uses within hospitals, RFID systems allow for the electronic tagging of hospital assets, inventory, personnel, and patients. Essentially, the RFID systems work by placing unique electronic identifiers on *items* (in the form of stickers embedded with RFID chips) or on *people* (in the form of bracelets or badges embedded with RFID chips). Once "tagged," items and people can be identified, tracked, and managed through a centralized database. Many hospitals have begun to adopt RFID systems with the goal of locating pieces of equipment when medical staff needs them. This serves two stated purposes. First, medical staff, especially nurses, can spend less time "hunting and gathering" equipment that they need and spend more time providing direct patient care (McCarthy 2004). Second, hospitals can more efficiently utilize the equipment they have and lower expenses on equipment rental and purchasing (Glabman 2004).

Other hospitals have begun to adopt RFIDs for patient and personnel identification and location purposes (U.S. Medicine Institute for Health Studies 2004). For example, RFIDs have been embedded in patient bracelets so that medical staff can electronically identify patients before surgery and before administering medications and blood transfusions. In addition, these systems have been implemented to locate where patients are and to collect data on patients' movements through hospital services. Similarly, medical staff members have been given RFID tags on badges to collect data on workflow to find inefficiencies in current hospital operations. These latter types of systems have primarily been implemented in emergency departments and surgical centers, places where there are large volumes of patients and heightened risks of medical error.

Thus, RFID systems are thought to offer great promise for increased efficiency and cost savings in hospital settings, but little empirical evidence exists on what the implications of these systems are on existing infrastructures, including staff practices and procedures. Existing literature on hospital uses of RFIDs touts the potential for heightened patient safety (Neil 2005; Jossi 2004), better tracking of drug supplies (Young 2004), and real-time management of hospital assets (S. Davis 2004; C. Becker 2004). Other studies of medical RFIDs highlight the complexity of integrating multiple technical systems when so few of them possess interoperable capabilities (Perrin and Simpson 2004)—this is in part due to the proprietary nature of most information technologies. A larger constraint placed on hospitals is the lack of financial resources and technical staff necessary to implement even basic health information technologies to meet the requirements of federal regulations, let alone more specialized RFID systems (Office of Inspector General 2003).

Implications of RFID Systems for Health Care Workers

In an era of information management and audit culture (Strathern 2000), RFID is a valuable information technology because of its ability to collect data in real time. Its application within hospitals can be understood within the domain of "workflow management" and the attempt to make hospital processes more efficient (U.S. Medicine Institute for Health Studies 2004). Given this particular mode of use, it is important to understand the organizational and social effects of this technology on health care workers. This section describes specific RFID implementation projects to highlight the effects of these systems on hospital employees.

The data that follow were collected in the summer of 2005 and constitute part of a pilot study on the implementation of RFID systems in hospitals. The methods for this initial project consisted of participant-observation at an industry conference that largely served to sell RFID systems to the hospital administrations and representatives who attended. I also identified the major RFID hardware and software companies that were directly marketing their products to hospitals. This involved speaking to representatives at the industry conference, conducting informal phone interviews, and reading through materials on companies' websites (particularly press releases). In addition, I conducted several informal interviews with representatives of hospitals that I identified from the Internet as having installed or being in the process of installing RFID systems. Although this preliminary project was not highly systematic, it provided a good sense of the ways in which the technology companies and hospitals viewed this emerging technology. I do not name the hospitals I describe, and although many of these organizations can be identified fairly easily on the Internet, I want to draw the reader's attention to trends for RFID use in hospitals rather than to which hospitals are using the technology and for what purpose.

At the end of 2004, a large university hospital deployed a partial RFID system to track equipment within their surgery department, consisting of more than thirty operating rooms, pre- and postoperative care units, and equipment storage rooms. According to a Radianse press release, the installation of what this technology company has dubbed its "indoor positioning system" at the hospital was meant "to help staff prepare for procedures by providing the real-time location of necessary medical equipment, devices and accessories. The use of a Radianse [indoor positioning system] is expected to save time and increase clinician satisfaction and productivity while reducing asset shrinkage and the need for excess rentals or repurchases" (Radianse 2005).

From the hospital administrators' point of view, an RFID system was an attractive solution to cutting down costs associated with hospital equipment by being better able to use a smaller number of medical tools and machines. RFID technology companies describe one problem that has been identified with equipment as "hoarding" by nurses of items that they frequently use (Reid 2004). In this view of hospital function, a small number of nurses stockpile equipment so that they know where those items are when they need them, and this results in other nurses (and—in the narratives—not infrequently doctors) being unable to find the items they need when they need them. The administrators anticipated not only that this system would have an economic benefit for the hospital, but also that the system would increase nurse satisfaction because they would spend less time looking for equipment.

After installation, the technology worked just as Radianse had promised. The software identified the location of the equipment that had been tagged with RFIDs within the areas of the hospital equipped with readers. Yet in spite of the success of the technological elements of the system, the hospital could hardly declare the implementation of the system an unqualified success. What the administrators had not anticipated was the huge resistance to the RFID system on the part of the nursing staff. Rather than giving the expected response of gratitude, the nurses directly sabotaged the system by removing and often destroying the RFID tags attached to equipment. Moreover, the hospital had not envisioned a process for how the technology would be used. For instance, it was unclear whose responsibility retrieving equipment should be, and it was even more ambiguous who should be part of the support staff to ensure tags are replaced, missing equipment is investigated, and reports are written. The problems with the system were based not on the efficacy of the technology but on the material infrastructure and receptivity of personnel.

According to a hospital representative (personal communication) who was quite frank about the mistakes that the hospital has made with the installation and use of the RFID system, the root of their problems stemmed from the hospital's desire to have the newest, most advanced technology. The technological imperative in information management preceded careful thought about the goals, necessary infrastructure, and staff acceptance of the technology. As a result, there were widespread misunderstandings about the technology and what types of data it was collecting. Many of the nurses referred to the system as "big brother." To disabuse nurses of the notion that the RFIDs were minicameras, the administration scheduled what it perceived as an overdue training course to educate nurses about the technology and its function within the hospital.

In spite of the administration's attempt to quell nurses' resistance to the system, the training session did little to change their reception of the technology. The information about the RFIDs may have mitigated their suspicion of the system, but it resulted in the nurses' perceiving the technology as "offensive" (personal communication). Even though its capacity to surveil individuals is not as direct as many of the nurses had at first imagined, the system has a disciplinary valence for nurses. Because the equipment is being tracked and monitored by the RFID system, nurses could no longer claim equipment as their own, even if this previous system worked better for them than the indoor positioning system. The RFID technology has the effect of surveilling the practices of nurses in the aggregate even if individuals cannot be specifically identified. The nurses' resistance to this technological system can be understood in terms of the work intensification that seemed to accompany its implementation. Within the context of understaffed hospitals and overworked nurses, the assumption by many nurses was that the RFID system might increase their workload and that it could not reduce their work burden in any significant way.

Examining the technology within its use context, it becomes apparent that the technological system is ultimately more about the people using the medical equipment than it is about the items being tracked by RFID. The problem is not that equipment disappears of its own accord but that those using it are perceived as not sharing it effectively. This framing applies equally to nurses who are intentionally hoarding equipment as it does to the more common occurrence of equipment being left in the last place that it is used (and therefore making it difficult for staff to know where that use took place). From the administration's economic perspective, the installation of the system was seen as a better alternative than outfitting each room with all the necessary medical equipment. This was the case because the goal was not so much about making sure the equipment was readily available when needed but rather to save money by identifying the minimum number of each piece of equipment that was necessary for the hospital to run efficiently.

If RFID systems that track equipment have disciplinary effects on people, what then are the effects of RFID systems that track the people themselves? When RFID is used to locate people within hospitals, it can be used to different effects depending on whether it is patients or personnel, or both, who are tagged and to what extent the hospital is equipped with scanners to locate those individuals. These systems range from universal coverage at hospitals to the monitoring of relatively small areas such as emergency rooms or surgical wards. The next examples serve to illustrate some of the implications of indoor positioning with the purpose of tracking people.

When patients are tagged with RFID, it is often so that individuals do not get "lost" within the hospital or incorrectly identified during medical procedures. The technology can be embedded innocuously in hospital identification bracelets or can be a more complex plastic badge that has buttons that are programmable by the hospital for various functions and then worn by patients. It can now even be implanted in patients' bodies.[3] Part of the logic of using indoor positioning to track patients is to know where they are at any given moment and often to know how long they spent waiting in various hospital departments. Several large urban hospitals that implemented this type of system explained that before its installation, patients would be "lost" because of communication breakdowns between units. As an example, a patient may be taken to radiology, but the floor nurses may not be informed. Similarly, patients can get "stuck" in departments when they are caught between shifts, and no one knows to return them to their rooms. Other hospitals have mobilized RFID to verify the identity of patients before dispensing medications, conducting blood transfusions, and performing surgery. This latter function of linking the identity of the individual to the RFID tag is particularly concerned with reducing the number of medical errors that occur within hospitals.

In a different type of tagging patients with RFIDs, one large urban hospital has implemented the technology not to identify individual patients per se but to streamline hospital processes. For example, the administrators at this hospital argued that nurses were not notifying housekeeping as soon as patients were discharged to prepare the rooms and beds for newly admitted patients. From the perspective of nurses, this is often seen as a strategy to have a temporarily lighter patient load in their overburdened schedule (due to a nursing shortage and understaffing at hospitals). From the perspective of administrators, this delay costs the hospital money because the beds are empty. An RFID tag embedded within the patient identification bracelet was programmed to send a message to housekeeping when the bracelet was cut at discharge. In this case, the technology was designed to circumvent nurses altogether in the process of preparing rooms for new patients. The hospital reported, however, that nurses responded by "forgetting" to cut the bracelets (either by sending patients home wearing them or even by slipping them off patients' wrists intact).

In another example of using RFID to streamline hospital procedures, a large rural hospital implemented the technology in its surgical department. The hospital was interested in using RFID to collect data about its current practices to understand how and why bottlenecks occur and to build solutions from its own data to establish (and evaluate) better practices. To do so, the hospital implemented a full indoor positioning system to track equipment and people. Patients, nurses, and physicians are tracked within the system by the RFID badges they wear. More than using RFID as just a positioning system, however, this hospital uses it to capture time data for its complementary software system. By measuring how long patients are in particular locations in the surgical department, how long specific elements of procedures take, and which personnel are present at each stage of the process from registration to discharge, the hospital aims to make all of these processes more efficient for both the staff and the patients. Other features of the system include an electronic white board with real-time information about the status of each patient and a waiting room terminal from which people waiting for patients in surgery can receive information about their progress.

Unlike the staffs in most other hospitals, the primary advocate of the RFID system at this hospital was an administrator with a background in nursing. This led to several unique features of the system. First, the staff members in the surgical department were included in the design and implementation of the system so that it would be better suited to its users and more sensitive to the specific functions of their hospital and their unit in particular.[4] In addition, the staff members' RFID badges were programmed with a privacy button, so that they could opt to be "invisible" within the system if and when they so desired. One of the rationales for this was to make staff breaks more formal within the system (particularly because of the system's data collecting function) and to give staff members a sense of control over the technology's surveillance of their activities. Finally, as a result of her experience as a nurse, this administrator recognized that one of the most common delays in the operating room is due to physicians' absence or tardiness. She observed that physicians can "disappear" in various parts of the hospital, and surgeries are often delayed as a result. From her perspective, the benefits of the indoor positioning system far outweighed the pager system that they had previously relied on. When the exact location of physicians can be pinpointed through RFID and their time to respond can be measured, she argued, physicians have more incentive to show up to the operating rooms on time or more quickly after a page.

In these examples of RFID systems implemented in hospital settings, it is unclear if the technology is providing a solution to health care problems. On one hand, it can be said that RFID does indeed offer a technological fix, as in the example of equipment tracking. In these cases, hospitals have limited budgets and limited equipment, and indoor positioning can potentially aid in the efficiency of use of scarce resources within busy departments. On the other hand, however, the more complex indoor positioning systems that are tracking the movements and activities of people, whether patients or staff, do not seem to be addressing any particular problem that would be identified by hospital personnel or patients. Instead, these systems are creating modes of digital management to collect increasingly specific data on hospital practices and to increase the accountability of personnel. In other words, the technological systems are predisposed to disciplinary or social control uses within these specific settings.

Depoliticization of Surveillance

In their own understanding of the data being produced through indoor positioning systems, hospital and technology company representatives describe the results as "workflow management." I understand the term *workflow management* to be reflective of the insertion of new modes of scientific management or neo-Taylorism into the governing rationale of organizations. Rather than focusing on the broader organization of work, workflow management tends to individualize processes by looking for inefficiencies that are created through staff practices. The management goal becomes the creation of standard operating procedures and best practices that personnel, particularly nurses and support staff in hospitals, are compelled to follow.

Any mention of surveillance is deflected by discussions about the stated purpose of these systems, which is to create more efficient processes, not to monitor individuals within the systems. In a rhetorical move, surveillance fears are discounted because they are associated with individuals, not groups. Within this technological discourse, surveillance is positioned as irrelevant within the stated aim of organizational change. By reframing the actions of participants within the system as "data," the tracking of those actions is artificially delinked from the politically charged realm of surveillance and the contextually complicated social and material spaces of hospitals. Moreover, it should be noted that surveillance is further discounted in these settings because the systems are not visual systems employing optical modes of supervision or examination (and they are only rarely linked to closed-circuit TV security systems). Because the politics of surveillance are so intimately linked with visibility, indoor positioning systems can be presented as "simply" ubiquitous, disembodied radio waves that are somehow separate from the human actions they are capturing.

The distinction between and separation of workflow management and surveillance is dangerous because it has the potential to leave the individuals within the system exposed to exploitation and abuse. When they are told that they are not being watched or that the individual-level data does not matter, the importance of the implications of group-level surveillance is undermined, whether those groups are constituted by patients, doctors, nurses, or other hospital personnel. The data collected and the systems themselves have real implications for the policies and decisions that will be made regarding those groups or the broader organization. The effects can range from changes in how work is distributed, how accountability for mistakes is determined, and how budgets should be allocated. Surveillance is about control; if the RFID systems can monitor groups or flows to regulate practices, then social control and thus surveillance are occurring.

Although RFID and indoor position systems may indeed prove invaluable in health care settings such as hospitals, it is important to understand the politics of the technologies and anticipate the types of outcomes that are produced as a result. RFID may indeed be found to have an extraordinary ability to reduce medical errors. When the goals and aims of health care are not clearly defined in the development and implementation of the technology, however, the capabilities—and hence the valence—of the technology have precedence in defining the form and function of the systems. The technology is underdetermined and shapes itself to the existing institutional inequalities within particular hospitals and health care systems more generally. Denying the surveillance functions and potentials of these systems may artificially depoliticize them, but it does not make the participants any less observed or controlled.

Notes

1. It is important to mention that there are different types of RFID technology. There are two primary types: active and passive. The difference between the two is whether the RFID has its own battery source. Active RFIDs have a miniature battery that enables them to actively emit radio frequencies to the system, whereas passive RFIDs do not have their own source of power and must be activated through the use of "reader" devices (U.S. Department of Commerce 2005; Monahan 2006).
2. Presidential Executive Order 13335 (Bush 2004).
3. An implantable RFID chip was approved by the U.S. Food and Drug Administration for human use in October 2004. As of this writing, it is currently being used in two large hospitals in the United States and in several hospitals in other parts of the world. According to a press release in December 2005 by the technology company VeriChip, the company

has agreements from 65 other medical facilities to begin implanting chips in patients in the near future. The idea behind an RFID implant is that patients can carry their medical records (or, more accurately, an identifier to access their records) with them wherever they go.

4. This type of involvement of the end users can be considered "participatory design."

CHAPTER 6

Technologies of Citizenship
Surveillance and Political Learning in the Welfare System

VIRGINIA EUBANKS

Virginia Eubanks (VE): Since you've been working with data entry lately, has it made you think any more about how DSS [the Department of Social Services] uses information systems?

Amanda Demers (AD): Just how *easy* it is to get the information. Who knows who has access. And who knows who I know back there … Who knows what kind of information they have? … Because they have your social security number, your birthday, your mother's name, your father's name, your birth certificate, your social security card, your picture. Everything. They can ruin your life. Who knows? But at the same time, you have to keep the faith in them, that that won't happen.

VE: Are you able to look at your [computerized] file at DSS?

AD: I'm sure, if I asked them. But when you go to the window and you tell them you want to see your worker—it doesn't matter for what— they ask for your case number or your social security number. I never remember my case number, so I always tell them my social security number. You hear a million social security numbers a day at DSS. Who's to know that you're not going to remember mine? When they punch it in, all my information comes up. I can look through the glass and see what my previous addresses were. All they have to do is get your social security number and they're in there.

VE: It's interesting how computers become the face of the system ...

AD: Yeah! That's just what it is, too—that screen behind the glass—all you have to do is tell them your numbers. They're going to stick a chip in us soon. [laughter] For real. They'll just make you stick your hand through the glass, and they'll scan you ...

VE: You and I should write a science fiction book!

AD: For real, though. It's happening. And it's not so much fiction ... it will definitely happen. My mother says about immunizations—they used to just line us up and poke us, poke us, poke us. Now they're going to poke us with some chips. They're going to know *everything*. (Interview with Amanda Demers, February 2, 2004)

Introduction: Popular Technology

As Amanda Demers argues above, surveillance of low-income women in the United States is nothing new, though the techniques may have changed. *Practically,* being lined up and "poked" for immunizations is not unlike having an embedded microchip scanned at the welfare office. Low-income people's role as test populations for technologies of state surveillance and control is no innovation. From techniques of reproductive sterilization to methods of industrial psychology, the canaries in the coal mine of technological "progress" have routinely been the poor and oppressed. *Conceptually,* computerized information systems in wide use by departments of social service are not very different from invasive home visits by caseworkers, extensive (though narrowly focused) case records, or evaluations in workhouses by "overseers of the poor" (Gilliom 2001; Tice 1998; Piven and Cloward 1971). *Politically,* the purposes of surveying the poor have largely stayed constant for three centuries: containment of alleged social contagion, evaluation of moral suitability for inclusion in public life and its benefits, and suppression of working people's resistance and collective power.

So what is new about surveillance technologies in the welfare office? In this chapter, I offer evidence that women receiving public benefits in a small city in upstate New York perceive significant—and troubling—differences. First, information technology (IT) has facilitated an intensification of surveillance and discipline in the social service system. Welfare "innovations" like electronic benefits transfer cards make possible more precise tracking and monitoring of client behavior. These technologies also act to significantly limit clients' autonomy, opportunity, and mobility: their ability to meet their needs in their own ways. Second, the system seems increasingly opaque, unpredictable, and arbitrary. The rapid sharing of databased information between agencies lends credence to clients' fears that they are trapped in a system where every detail of their lives is known and freely shared among powerful players who do not have their best interests at heart. Rules for information gathering, sharing, and retrieving are obscure, and mechanisms ensuring accountability are rare. Finally, IT systems and the specialized expertise that sustains them extract and fragment the knowledge of social service clients and workers alike, misrepresenting the lives of people they seek to efficiently describe. The rigid architectures of new technologies of information storage and retrieval do not allow for contextual information—the lived experience, struggles, purposes, and motives of women doing the best they can to survive and raise their children with dignity. Though the women I interviewed, and worked with in popular technology workshops and other public events, often describe these problems under the general rubric of "privacy concerns," I argue that their concerns are less about privacy and more about power, oppression, and autonomy.

I seek to make a second argument, as well. In his insightful introduction to this volume, Torin Monahan suggests that many scholars are asking the wrong questions about surveillance and security because they fail to recognize that technologies operate not only as tools, but also as creators of social worlds. Among the *right* questions to ask about surveillance, he argues, is "What social relations are produced by surveillance systems?" In this chapter, I seek to answer a corollary question: "What kind of social world (and what sort of citizen) do surveillance technologies (re)produce when they are deployed in the social service system?" I provide empirical evidence that ITs play a considerable role in reproducing power assymetries and constructing manageable subjects for governance regimes. I argue that new ITs provide a solidified, artifactual form of what Barbara Cruikshank (1999) calls *technologies of citizenship*. That is, in addition to providing new forms of discipline and control, interaction with IT serves as a site of *political learning* for low-income women—both those who are classified as "users" and those often classified as "nonusers"—teaching lessons about their comparative social worth, competence, and opportunities. Therefore, as citizenship activities and modalities (such as voting or welfare benefits receipt) are increasingly routed through complicated information systems, it becomes imperative to think about "high-tech equity" as a question of critical technological citizenship (rather than formulating policy problems as lack of access or technical skill).

These insights are the outcome of four years of participatory action research with a group of women called Women at the YWCA Making Social Movements (WYMSM).[1] We set out to construct and sustain a sociotechnical infrastructure to support technology training through participatory programs that emphasize peer education and the political and economic context of knowledge work, technological design, and political decision making. We conducted this work through a "community–university partnership" with the Sally Catlin Women's Resource Center and, later, designed and developed its associated Technology Lab. Both are housed in the YWCA of Troy-Cohoes, a residential facility for 90 highly resourceful women living in transitional circumstances and seeking to craft the lives they want for themselves. Executive director Pat Dinkelaker once described the organization as "technologically poor but curious." But the YWCA has historically provided technical training opportunities for women attempting to access employment in the various "high-tech" industries in the Collar City of their time: from collar and cuff stitching and laundering in the 1890s to nursing, food preparation, and data entry today.

Participants often came to programs having directly experienced the extractive functions of large-scale technological systems in the workplace, health care settings, or the social and human services sector. Furthermore, they understood themselves to be "canaries in the coal mine" of high-tech disciplinary systems, expressing great concern that they were being used as test populations for technologies that would be integrated into the everyday lives of middle-class citizens. Rather than read our collaborators' critical ambivalence toward technology as a sign of resistance or fear—as an individual deficit to be overcome—we recognized it as a sign of incipient analysis. Experiences of the disconnect between the powerful symbolism of IT as an engine of social and economic progress and low-income women's lived experiences of computers as the face and the heart of "the system" formed the basis for constructing nonextractive relationships and generating structural analyses with participants. Instead of allowing the ruling relations to extract people's activities and "subject them to technological and technical specialization, elaboration, differentiation, and objectification" (D. Smith 1999: 77), we used participants' insights about their own experiences with technological extraction and subjection as the basis for producing a collective social diagnosis of what might need to change for IT to become an empowering "popular technology" (Campbell and Eubanks 2004).

Extractive Technologies of State

To better understand the context in which low-income women come into contact with IT, I sought in thirty interviews conducted in 2003 and 2004 to answer the question "What lessons about politics, government, and citizenship are my collaborators learning from social service information systems?" Rather than being "information poor" in any simple way, participants in popular technology education programs at the YWCA had copious direct experience with large-scale bureaucratic IT systems. My collaborators provided extremely articulate and astute critiques of the ways that IT is deployed within the social service system to limit their dignity, freedom, and opportunities. In many of my collaborators' views, IT is one thread that binds together with the local department of social services (DSS) and broader socioeconomic strands of injustice to create a net of constraint they commonly refer to as "the system." Because of this, it is often difficult to separate views about the DSS, racism, poverty, or sexism—more generally—from views on ITs and computers specifically. The insight that IT, the DSS, and structural inequality combine to create a system of disempowerment proved enormously productive for our collaborative educational processes, both in conversation and in collaborative project design.[2] This was particularly the case when we reexamined what is often misread as adult women's "reluctance" or "inability" to engage with technological training and when we puzzled through participants' resistance to viewing IT as a tool for social change and justice.

In interviews, public events, popular education programs, and design workshops, my collaborators expressed concerns about the ways in which IT provides a means to more efficient control within the social service system. Their concerns fell into three broad categories:

1. IT is being used to build an increasingly invasive and disciplinary system of citizen control. Rather than discouraging fraud or increasing efficiency, IT largely serves to track and monitor individuals' behavior. Technological "innovations" act to limit clients' opportunity and mobility.
2. This system is increasingly opaque, unpredictable, and arbitrary to its "clients." Rules for information gathering, sharing, and retrieving are obscure, and mechanisms ensuring accountability are rare.
3. IT systems and the specialized expertise that sustain them extract and fragment the knowledge of social service "clients" and workers alike, misrepresenting the lives of people they seek to describe. Rigid IT architectures shear away context and limit the possibility of attaining a holistic viewpoint or critical coherence.

Such critical concerns are rarely aired, much less addressed, in technology training, but my collaborators' insights in popular technology programs helped us start connecting technological literacy to macrolevel political and collaborative analysis of women's economic and social position. My collaborators often perceived IT as threatening, intimidating, and extractive not because of technique, hardware, or software but because of how personal information is used against them in the bureaucratic information systems to which they are subjected. They draw a realistic sense of threat and negative valence from these experiences, attributing an invidious agency to the technology. Cuemi Gibson argued,

> The computers find out who you are, too, because I'm sure when they put your name and your social security number in there that everything comes down. That's my experience with SSI [Social Security Insurance]. Here you go—all the way into the system now. Every part of your life, everything about you, is available. And I learned that in the military. That my name meant nothing. My social security number became me—that was offensive to me ... When I was in the military, and they ran my name ... like when you talk over the phone and they ask you your mother's maiden name. The system—that person that you're talking to—knows everything about you. Knows more about you than you know about them, and that's not a fair game. (Gibson 2003)

This perception of IT as threatening and invasive is perfectly reasonable and cannot be attributed to simple fear of technology or resistance to change. Gibson's intuitions about the role of IT systems in the DSS were more than adequately confirmed by the experiences of other women in the YWCA community.

Tracking and Monitoring Behavior

Other participants expressed concerns that recent innovations in social service technology—the distribution of benefits on ATM-like (electronic benefits transfer) cards, for example—facilitate more precise tracking and monitoring of client behavior. The "benefits card" was purportedly introduced to minimize welfare fraud and reduce the social stigma of food stamps. As Meredith Vary explained, "There's a card like an ATM card, so you can scan it at the credit card thing at Price Chopper ... They don't give you the little books of food stamps anymore—it's a little credit card. [They changed that] because people were selling their food stamps to drug dealers, [but] people still do it all the time. They just take their drug dealer grocery shopping with them" (Vary 2003). Amanda Demers concurred, "Right. They did it to prevent people selling their food stamps and stuff.

But they can still sell their food stamps! ... I give my card to my mother all the time—so if she needs anything, she can just go get it—if that's what they're trying to prevent, they didn't find the solution" (Demers 2004). In my collaborators' estimation, the benefits card is a remarkably ineffective method for curtailing fraud. Women I talked to suspected that the elimination of fraud was just a cover story for the cards' actual purpose: tracking welfare recipients' movements and purchases. Amanda went on to explain, "I think [it's for] tracking, because there's not only food stamps on the card, you get cash, too. Like me, my baby-sitting money comes on my card—I give my card to my baby-sitter, have her take it all off. She ended up going to the mall, and she's swiping it and swiping it. So [the next time I had an appointment at] DSS, they asked me, 'Why is your money being taken out like this?' ... [or if] I was to go to the corner store and spend $80 in food stamps, they're going to ask me why. ... Stuff like that—they use these cards as a tracking device. That's what it is" (Demers 2004).

Limiting Options and Mobility

Concerns about lack of privacy and agency abuse of information keep many people from collecting their entitlements. As Cuemi Gibson argued, "A lot of people won't go to DSS because of the privacy aspect—the information aspect—of it. 'You all know who I am and everything I do!' And you only allow me $290 [a month] and then won't let anyone live with me. Why can't I have a roommate? This money—you're saying it's mine, but you're monitoring what I'm doing with it. That's not fair!" (Gibson 2003). Therefore, in a very real way, IT supports a system that limits the options and the freedom of low-income people. It can keep people from attaining the support to which they are entitled by law. It also constrains clients' behavior in more subtle ways: because benefits are now distributed on cards, clients are unable to shop at small local stores and farmers' markets, which lack card readers. Their benefits cards (like many food pantries) limit their nutritional choices and act as tacit endorsements of more expensive and less-accessible (suburban) chain stores.

Lack of Transparency

The opacity and complexity of IT systems, and the social service system rules, cause further problems. Rebecca Cusack explained,

> It just seems like from person to person the rules fluctuate. I don't see consistent anything. 'Cause I look at me and Miranda. She is pregnant and I'm pregnant but they won't give her cash assistance. They won't help her out. She gets the food stamps ... I don't understand any of it. I don't know if [rules] in the computer [determine if] people

get denied, and that's how they do it, or what their basis for accepting and not accepting are ... [At DSS] they write their notes and then they disappear, and then they are like 'All right give us a week.' Do they just look at it and are like 'OK, data, data, data'? Or is like fields on the computer screen you have to enter, and then the computer goes through all the rules that it has been programmed with, and [then it] says 'Accepted' or 'Denied'? How is it based? Because it makes no sense to me ... I get my $139 of food stamps. I get my $62 every two weeks. Yet Miranda doesn't. From one person to another it just switches ... [VE: "It seems just like a random lottery."] You get the special prize. You get money. (Cusack 2003)

The feeling of arbitrariness is intensified when benefits are electronically distributed. It seems like magic, participants explained, benefits just turning up on or disappearing from your ATM card. Amanda Demers laughed and said that it seems like her phone number receives her benefits, not her. Cusack remarked, "The food stamps and all that. They put them on your card on certain days. I would die to find out how to be the first day or the second day. I have to wait until the 8th and I can't wait until the 8th. It is too far away. I'm like starving—I want some food" (Cusack 2003). Meredith Vary considered the effect these issues have on women's relationship to technology: "I know that a lot of people get mad at the computers at social services, because sometimes they won't put their food stamps on their card on time, or their cash benefits. So they are calling DSS all the time, asking 'Where is my money?' And they may have no food. I know a lot of people get really mad about that" (Vary 2003).

Undisclosed Information Sharing (Information Abuse)

Agencies often share databased information among themselves without informing clients, which lends credence to the idea that IT creates an all-pervasive system of control and constraint. IT, Cuemi Gibson argued, "is monitoring what I'm doing ... and [agencies] swap information about you, and make you sign forms releasing your rights to confidentiality. And you're not told you can amend that. Or that you can get that information back" (Gibson 2003). YWCA staff member Liz Girolami also expressed concerns about inappropriate information sharing: "A lot of women ... face that at the public housing authority. They can't get in [to public housing] because of something [in their past] ... The crazy thing is that [the housing authority] is not supposed to be able to look at records from when you are a teenager, but they find out" (Girolami 2003).

Information Slavery

The effects of IT surveillance are further differentiated by race and gender. For some, particularly African American women, it seems that IT is deployed in ways that collude with the social justice system to create a new kind of slavery. As Zianaveva Raitano argued, "The whole conception of this information highway is maybe some kind of mental slavery ... Technology can just enslave somebody. It sometimes seems like a sinister tool" (Raitano 2003: 17.3). Cuemi Gibson asked, "If you got all that information about me in the system, why can't you find me my reparations? Where's my money, man? *I know I was a slave!*" (Gibson 2003). Gender is a significant issue as well. One of the reasons she failed to engage with technology at an early age, Gibson explained, was that she saw learning technology only as a route to serving others, particularly men. "When I went to school, I was a tomboy, and I saw the girls who learned technology, like typing, were learning it to serve other people—to be a secretary or whatever—and that wasn't working for me, either. Like technology was only clerical. I didn't see the other part of it. And my lifestyle was not going to allow me to wait on a man to work" (Gibson 2003).

Extraction and Fragmentation of Knowledge

Information plays a complex role in women's poverty and the state's response to their demands. Complex disciplinary technologies collect and manage enormous amounts of data on low-income women (and men). Still, my collaborators did not reject the idea of "information poverty" outright, arguing that there are important informational resources to which they still lack access. In my July 2003 interview with WYMSM member Cuemi Gibson, I explained some of the ways that the concept of "information poverty" was being used in public policy and asked for her reflections. She linked her complicated relationship with information and ITs to her continuing experiences with racial injustice:

Virginia Eubanks (VE): Is the problem that poor folks are information poor? What do you think?

Cuemi Gibson (CG): Well, yes, because we don't know our roots. We never did. We never were allowed to. Basically, I can't know who I am or where I'm from because our race was scattered. Honestly. When I was growing up, my fore-parents didn't know how to read or write, so we didn't have a head start in that, Virginia.

VE: But if poor people are information poor, why does it take two and a half hours to fill out DSS intake forms?

CG: Because of the kind of information they're looking for. I recently got my file from [a local agency]. People of color don't know that you can take back your information. They don't tell you a lot of things. If you don't have an education, it's hard for you to know how to seek out [even your own] information.

   We were taught to believe that white people are powerful. In the King James version of the Bible, the word "master" is in there more than any other word. And that's where our fore-parents were fooled. My aunt used to say, "Don't fight people, Cuemi." Because they thought it was threatening. Because of their fore-parents' experiences with white people. So the information that we had—our fore-parents wouldn't speak it. They were afraid—afraid to confront white people. So when you say information poor, that's from history … and add to that that most people of color are only getting a seventh grade education, so we have two generations of people who are walking around functionally illiterate.

VE: Is it as much a question of feeling that you lack control over info?

CG: Yeah. People are systematically abused. … Like CPS [Child Protective Services] has so much information on families. That's overwhelming, because they're not searching for anything positive. (Gibson 2003)

Gibson pointed out that it's not lack of information that matters—it's *control* over information. For African American people, she argued, it is risky either to volunteer or to withhold information. She explained that in the case of communicating with social service agencies, it is dangerous to *withhold* information: "With [a local drug rehabilitation agency] when you say 'I don't know, I don't know,' it works against you because they think you're trying to bullshit them. So they automatically take you for a piss test. And if you fail, your welfare income is denied. *So if you refuse them information you lose your income*" (Gibson 2003; emphasis mine). On the other hand, it is also dangerous to *volunteer* information, particularly with the police. She explained that letting police know that you are aware of your rights as a citizen can escalate an already tense situation. In our interview, I asked if she felt that her being in control of her own information made her seem like a troublemaker to the police. She responded, "Absolutely. Because I'm a black woman." Though she acknowledged that sometimes withholding information could be an expression of power, she insisted that "the less information I have, the more power they have" (Gibson 2003).

Loss of Context

It is not only social service clients who sometimes feel trapped by the dictates of IT systems. ITs sometimes work against the best intentions of social service workers. An interviewee related a story about a job she had doing data entry for a contractor who was developing a tracking system for young people in the public educational system. The frustration that finally drove her to quit the job was that the architecture of the database didn't allow social service workers to include narrative information about the context of kids' behavior. Simply, the system tracked each student's "success" or "failure" in a number of different programs. There was no place in the system to account for the (sometimes pages of) contextual information written in case reports by social workers. YWCA community member Barbara Ann Ryan had a similar experience in the mental health system: "When you go into the mental health world there is this standard test which is called the 500 questions test. ... This has been one of the fundamental pieces of diagnosing people for a long time. So [I went to take it], and this guy just transferred it to a computer program. ... He was [so] completely overcome with delight that he could make this computer program ... [that] he wasn't listening to me. I was so humiliated. He wasn't trying to help me figure out what I was dealing with. He was totally focused on his computer program" (B.A. Ryan 2003). The problem, as these two community members saw it, has to do with what is interpreted as "signal" and what is interpreted as "noise" in an informational system. So what matters is not necessarily the information that state services clients or patients *have* but rather what is left out, how the structure of technological systems erase the embodied contexts and knowledge of the people described in them.

Lack of Critical Coherence

My collaborators defined the problem as less the lack of information and more the fragmenting and "specialization" of knowledge—facilitated by IT—that leads to the elimination of more holistic (and critical) views of the world. Barbara Ann continued,

> People are losing something ultimately that relates to reason, to a lack of cause and effect, which ultimately leads to justice ... [The problem] with digitally related information ... is that there is information that is known [but not used] ... That guy that wrote *Rent*, [there was an x-ray taken in the emergency room of a NYC hospital] showing this hole in [the] major vein in [his] chest—[a] rupture for 7 inches. It showed on an x-ray ... and they told him that he had food poisoning, and they told him to go home. Twice. And he died on the

kitchen floor … It's like famine. There are tons of food; it just doesn't get where it needs to go. (B.A. Ryan 2003)

What is missing, she argues, is not information but an overview, "the whole picture." In this insight, Barbara Ann echoes Paulo Freire (Freire 1973, 1997, 1998). For Freire, critical literacy takes as its goal a movement toward more coherent understandings of the world. Therefore, specialist knowledge has low coherence and little criticality. Critical literacy, on the other hand, fosters linkages between "self-contained areas of expertise" and the "social and political realities" that frame people's understandings and their integration of their ideas and artifacts into the world.

It would not surprise Freire, then, that the participants who persisted the longest and appeared to gain the most from popular technology programs often had the most negative valence toward technology at the beginning and would have resisted more strenuously had we assumed that IT was an unmitigated social good. Though we must acknowledge and honor low-income women's critical ambivalence in the face of IT, technological citizenship is an increasingly important mode of participation in public life. Popular technology programs at the YWCA turned women's insights about the place of technology in their lives "inside out," using them as a starting point for shared inquiry and political intervention. Turning negative experiences that could be considered barriers to learning into resources for critical engagement functioned to considerably alter women's relationship to technology. But to understand the particular impact of IT on the experience of citizenship by low-income women, we must in addition consider that technology offers a site of *political learning* and a means of structuring political possibility.

Political Learning in "the System"

Langdon Winner, in his generative 1977 work *Autonomous Technology,* defines technology as a wide range of activities and artifacts that form an emerging technical-political system. His definition of technology includes not just the physical devices (which he calls "technic") but also the activities—skills, methods, procedures and routines, or techniques—and varieties of social organizations: factories, workshops, bureaucracies, armies, and research and development teams (Winner 1977: 12). Furthermore, Winner points out that technological artifacts, being the result of human conscious and subconscious design, necessarily embody specific forms of power and authority that encourage certain attitudes and values and discourage others. That is, technological artifacts have politics (Winner 1986: 19). He writes,

Technology in a true sense is legislation ... technical forms do, to a large extent, shape the basic pattern and content of human activity in our time. Thus, politics becomes (among other things) an active encounter with the specific forms and processes contained in technology ... technology itself is a political phenomenon ... modern technics, much more than politics as conventionally understood, now legislates the conditions of human existence. (Winner 1986: 323)

Rejecting a utilitarian-pluralist approach to technology decision making that sees technology as "only problematic in the sense that it ... requires legislation," Winner argues,

New technologies are institutional structures within an evolving constitution that gives shape to a new polity, the technopolis in which we do increasingly live. For the most part, this constitution still evolves with little public scrutiny or debate. Shielded by the conviction that technology is neutral and tool-like, a whole new order is built—piecemeal, step by step, with the parts and pieces linked together in novel ways—without the slightest public awareness or opportunity to dispute the character of the changes underway. (Winner 1986: 323–24)

As Lawrence Lessig (1999) argues, the onset of the "information age" has sped this tendency, though the ability of IT systems to centralize power and control has been obscured by cyberlibertarian fervor. In *Code,* Lessig describes the Internet as "an exploding space of social control" where "control is coded, by commerce, with the backing of the government" (Lessig 1999: ix–x), often by default—without democratic deliberation. Like Winner, Lessig calls for an expansion of our understandings of how regulation and other forms of political life are constituted through the architectures of our technological artifacts. He urges IT users and designers to condemn the falsehood that cyberspace can regulate itself and to consciously create a world where freedom can flourish (through politico-technical interventions such as open code systems). He writes,

We build liberty, that is, as our founders did, by setting society upon a certain constitution. But by "constitution" I don't mean a legal text ... I mean an architecture ... that structures and constrains social and legal power, to the end of protecting fundamental values—principles and ideals that reach beyond the compromises of ordinary politics. Constitutions in this sense are built, they are not found ... As our framers learned ... we have every reason to believe that cyberspace, left to itself, will not fulfill the promise of freedom. Left to itself, cyberspace will become a perfect tool of control. (Lessig 1999: 6)

Like Winner, Lessig argues that we can create a cyberspace that protects our values or we can build (or, worse, simply allow through our inaction) a cyberspace that permits those values to disappear. Different technological architectures embed different values, and these architectures are not found but built. Winner and Lessig underscore the importance of actively choosing the kind of technosocial worlds we want to inhabit.

The historicity and openness of Winner's and Lessig's accounts of the technosocial order are essential, particularly in a culture that ascribes such autonomous agency to technology. However, both authors obliquely or directly accuse the public—excluding a few radical organic farmers and open-source software coders—of apathy, political powerlessness, submissiveness, even complicity. Winner argues that (most) Americans' relationship to technologies of control is characterized by somnambulism; Lessig argues that "too many believe that liberty will take care of itself" (Lessig 1999: 58). But my collaborators readily recognized the "architectures of identification" that Lessig describes, in both their online and offline forms, narrating the ways that IT systems are used within existing structures of political constraint to track and shape their behavior. In interviews, public forums, and design workshops, my collaborators articulated sophisticated critiques of how IT is being used in increasingly disciplinary ways and made reasonable predictions as to the coming impacts of the new "information age" on their lives and livelihoods. I have described these kinds of insights as leading to a critical ambivalence about technology in general and technological training opportunities in particular. Low-income women disproportionately bear the negative effects of the "information economy," so that the positive cultural symbolism of IT is continually subverted and deferred—their empirical experiences don't match the powerful promise they nevertheless see in the technology. This creates a critical ambivalence with both resistant and defeatist edges.

This (perfectly reasonable) ambivalence is too often misinterpreted as irrationality, reluctance, ignorance, fear, or apathy. But low-income women are considerably more technologically aware and involved than many scholars and policy makers assume or report. In addition, many low-income women's primary point of interaction with IT is as subjects of social service information systems. This is a crucial form of engagement with IT. These interactions teach women lessons about their role as client-citizens in a new informational order and therefore provide the most direct and compelling illustration of how IT acts as a technology of citizenship. Low-income women's client status and interactions with the social service bureaucracy comprise an important part of their statist political experiences. Joe Soss argues that social assistance programs provide many beneficiaries with their most direct exposure to formal political institutions and are therefore sites for adult political participation and learning. "These programs," Soss argues, "provide the handiest and most reliable points of reference [for thinking about governance] ... Program designs not only communicate information about client status and agency decision making but also teach lessons about citizenship status and government" (Soss 1999: 376). Citizenship, then, is a relationship learned in context, differentially available to women according to their institutional positioning (a different form of client-citizenship is, for example, available to women on Temporary Aid to Needy Families [TANF] than to women on Social Security Disability Insurance [SSDI]).

As Soss points out, being an Aid to Families with Dependent Children (AFDC, now TANF) recipient "reduces the odds that a person will vote to slightly less than half of what it would have been otherwise" (Soss 1999: 364), even if other demographic characteristics are held constant. In confirmation of Barbara Nelson's (1984) arguments about the effects of the two-tiered benefit system, Soss notes that SSDI recipients, on the other hand, are just as politically active as the rest of the citizenry. For Soss, this is a clear indication that there is a unique relationship between participation in means-tested social service programs and participation in other formal mechanisms of governance. In fifty in-depth interviews with AFDC and SSDI recipients, Soss found that, through their program experiences, AFDC clients came to see agency decision making as an autonomous and unresponsive process, unconstrained by formal rules. They also saw their degraded status as beneficiaries as putting them in a position where asserting their grievances—even in situations with profound effects on their families and themselves—is both unprofitable and unwise. In addition, his respondents saw the welfare office not as a part of government but as a *microcosm* of government, so that "lessons learned about speaking up at the agency spill over into other forms of political demand making" (Soss 1999: 367–68). He writes,

> As clients participate in welfare programs, they learn lessons about how citizens and governments relate, and these lessons have political consequences beyond the domain of welfare agencies. Program designs structure clients' experiences in ways that shape their beliefs about the effectiveness of asserting themselves at the welfare agency. Because clients associate the agency with government as a whole, these program-specific beliefs, in turn, become the basis for broader orientations toward government and political action. (Soss 1999: 364)

These orientations toward government and political action stemmed not, Soss finds, from clients' low estimation of their own political capacity but rather from their estimation of the efficacy of making political demands.

His respondents perceived themselves as quite politically astute, echoing Nelson's arguments that AFDC participation is a particularly challenging and demanding relationship with the government, and questioned whether Soss would be able to understand its complicated demands and irrational rules well enough to complete his article.

Technologies of Citizenship

The concerns low-income women express about the effect of IT on their lives may be counterintuitive for some readers. Isn't *increased* transparency the great promise of flexible, decentralized information systems? Don't digital technologies like the cell phone and the laptop *facilitate* mobility and multiply opportunities? It depends on who you are and on the context in which you most commonly encounter it. Different target "users" of (or, more exactly, different targets for) technology, like different target populations for public policy, receive quite different messages. There are strong pressures for public officials and IT designers to provide beneficial policy and systems to enable greater flexibility, transparency, and mobility for powerful, positively constructed target populations. Similarly, there are strong pressures to provide negatively constructed target populations—such as TANF recipients—with policy and IT systems that fragment knowledge, demobilize collective thinking and action, monitor and discipline behavior, and obscure the operation of bureaucratic systems (Schneider and Ingram 1993). The differential construction of target populations for IT systems, as for public policy, teaches lessons about competence, value, and personal worth.

The social service system provides many low-income women with their most direct exposure to high-tech information systems. They therefore provide the most common form of "technology training" that these women receive. Through their program experiences, many of my collaborators learned to see the deployment of information systems as an invasive, autonomous, and unresponsive process, unconstrained by formal rules and unconcerned with transparency of process. Their degraded status in the system puts them in a position where controlling their own information—whether choosing to volunteer or to withhold it—is difficult and potentially dangerous. Finally, participants saw IT not as simply a tool of government but as a microcosm of government—technology, for them, is the face of the system. Therefore, to modify Soss's argument, I conclude that lessons learned by interacting with IT at social service agencies spill over into (1) other forms of technological engagement and (2) other forms of political demand making.

Rather than being technologically unaware or apathetic, participants at the YWCA explicitly recognized their role as a test population for technologies of control. In addition, they expressed real concern that the techniques and technologies used to regulate their behavior in the social service system would eventually be used on the population at large. Amanda Demers, for example, explained that rich people were too insulated and naive to understand that the technologies that were tested at the DSS would eventually be used on them. Women at the YWCA often saw themselves as "canaries in the coal mine" and therefore felt a high level of responsibility for political action and education of the general public. The women I worked with in my four years at the YWCA were far more aware of the relationship between IT and political systems of control than most readers of Lessig and Winner might assume. For many of my collaborators, however, participation in technological systems—like participation in social service institutions—has proved both dangerous and ineffectual, and these institutions produce certain forms of citizenship (like client-citizen) that serve disciplinary and punitive functions. But critical ambivalence should not be confused with informational or technological poverty. To the contrary, in many cases, *low-income women have had too much interaction and too intimate a relationship with ITs.* The challenge of popular technology workshops is to turn these experiences into resources for—rather than barriers to—learning and engagement.

Different technologies of citizenship—social service programs and information systems—produce differential forms of citizenship. Soss finds that SSDI recipients (who do not experience casework relationships or an ongoing need to prove their eligibility for assistance) have generally positive experiences with the social service system, and their ideas about political participation were largely unchanged by those experiences. In addition, Soss found that participation in more democratic programs like Head Start mitigated or superseded the demobilizing effects of AFDC. Soss concludes,

> More participatory program design encourages more positive orientations toward political involvement. Head Start provides clients with evidence that participation can be effective and fulfilling. From the perspective of participatory theory, it is not surprising that these experiences have spill-over effects. "The taste for participation is whetted by participation." (Soss 1999: 374)

As Winner reminds us, "Different ideas of social and political life entail different technologies for their realization. One can create systems of production, energy, transportation, information handling, and so forth that are compatible with the growth of autonomous, self-determining individuals in a democratic polity. Or one can build, perhaps unwittingly, technical forms that are incompatible with this end and then wonder how things went strangely wrong" (Winner 1979: 460).

This hope—building technological artifacts and infrastructure that are compatible with autonomy, self-determination, and democracy—has animated the creation of a collaborative response to these issues. The Popular Technology Workshops[3] use popular education methods to create spaces in which low-income people can define and engage the injustices of the high-tech global economy. In annual three-day intensive workshops and monthly Saturday Schools, we explore local social and economic justice issues and provide networking, media, and organizing training for concerned community members. We are driven by the belief that ordinary people have the ability and the right to create their own tools to promote economic, political, social, and cultural democracy. The first workshop, "Our Knowledge, Our Power: Surviving Welfare," held in July 2005, brought together seven diverse women to discuss the promise and problems of public assistance in the Capital Region. The workshop included three sessions of intense facilitated discussion, two "tech tools trainings" (microradio for social organizing and video documentation), several lively meals, and a small dance party.

Summer workshop participants suggested tackling three major issues in this year's Saturday Schools: the relationship between caseworkers and clients, the welfare system's inability to provide for true self-sufficiency, and—not surprising—the violation of recipient's privacy rights. Members of the group even produced a short public service video called *Watching Me*, which opens with women reciting a litany of abuses: "He watches my every move," "He only lets me spend the money the way *he* says," "She doesn't like my friends," "He threatens to take my children away." Then the hook: "Do you think I'm talking about my boyfriend, my lover, my husband?" they ask. "No. I'm talking about my caseworker." It is our hope that focusing on the broader and more vital issue of critical technological citizenship as the goal of technology education and advocacy—rather than simple access or technical skill—opens up avenues like this for welfare moms' voices to be heard and to create IT policy as if low-income women mattered.

Acknowledgments

This work would have been inconceivable without the remarkable generosity and resourcefulness of the women of the YWCA of Troy-Cohoes community. I especially want to thank our research collaborators in WYMSM—past, present, and future—including Nancy D. Campbell, Jessica Constantine, Josephine Gay, Cuemi Gibson, Ruth Delgado Gutzman,

Cosandra Jennings, Chitsunge Mapondera, Patty Marshall, Christine Nealon, Zianaveva Raitano, Jennifer Rose, and Julia Soto Lebentritt. Special thanks to Isaac and Mark, who kept us smiling through long afternoon meetings. This research was funded, in part, by a HUD Community Outreach Partnership (COPC) grant and a National Science Foundation dissertation improvement grant (NSF No. 0322525). I owe a debt of gratitude to Anne Bink and Jessica McNamara, graduate students in the Department of Women's Studies at the Univeristy at Albany, SUNY, for their research and organizing support.

Notes

1. WYMSM consisted of Nancy D. Campbell, Jessica Constantine, Josephine Gay, Cuemi Gibson, Ruth Delgado Gutzman, Cosandra Jennings, Chitsunge Mapondera, Patty Marshall, Christine Nealon, Zianaveva Raitano, Jennifer Rose, Julia Soto Lebentritt, and me.
2. This experience tends to support the claims of Freire, Horton, and other popular educators, who insist that radical, "problem-posing" education truly starts when facilitators reflect back to participants the *contradictions* that shape their lives for analysis and action. I argue, therefore, that my collaborators' critical ambivalence in the face of technology is a sign of incipient analysis rather than apathy, fear, or ignorance.
3. See http://www.populartechnology.org.

CHAPTER 7

The Surveillance Curriculum
Risk Management and Social Control in the Neoliberal School

TORIN MONAHAN

On the morning of April 20, 1999, two students walked into Columbine High School in Littleton, Colorado, and opened fire. Armed with shotguns, a rifle, a handgun, and homemade bombs, Eric Harris, age eighteen, and Dylan Klebold, age seventeen, went on a forty-nine minute shooting spree that resulted in the death of fifteen people, including a teacher and the two shooters (who committed suicide), and the injury of twenty-three others (CNN 2000). The activities of Harris and Klebold that day were caught on video surveillance and broadcasted across the major television networks, despite protests from students' parents and school officials (BBC 1999). It is ironic that although the school's surveillance system and an on-site, armed security guard were unable to prevent the killings at Columbine, the terrifying shooting has become a key reference point in justifying increased surveillance and security systems in schools throughout the United States.

This chapter questions the rise of high-tech surveillance systems in public schools and argues that debates over student safety, although important, tend to obscure deeper changes in social relations brought about by surveillance and security regimes. After all, schools continue to be some of the absolutely safest places for youth: with a one in two million chance of dying a violent death in school, "students are safer at school than they are in their own communities, in cars, and even in their own homes" (American Civil Liberties Union [ACLU] 2001). But one would be hard-pressed to believe this fact, given the increased media attention to school violence and the continuing investment of millions of dollars in school surveillance equipment. What might be even more surprising is that independent evaluations of video surveillance systems have found them to be entirely ineffectual at preventing violent crimes (Armitage 2002; Rice-Oxley 2004; Ditton et al. 1999), yet these systems continue to be funded at a record rate.

To say that surveillance systems are ineffectual at preventing violent crimes, however, does not imply that they are without effects. The most profound results from surveillance in schools may be the integration of law enforcement functions into the everyday practices of individuals at schools and the subsequent rise of a culture of control that supplants other social or educational missions of public education. Currently, more than 75 percent of all new schools are being equipped with video surveillance systems (Dillon 2003), and school districts are lobbying for funds from federal and state governments and from the private sector for surveillance in older schools. The most common school surveillance devices are digital or analog cameras for video recording, but others include metal detectors, ID cards, Internet tracking, biometrics, transparent lockers and book bags, electronic gates, and two-way radios.

Thus far, except for words of caution from civil liberties groups, there has been almost no inquiry into the kinds of relationships being produced from this new amalgam of high-tech industry, law enforcement, and public education. By examining several recent high-profile cases, this chapter begins to probe these emergent relations and their wider implications. The argument advanced here is that surveillance systems operate as extensions of the neoliberal state, carving out new markets for high-tech companies and integrating police functions into the social worlds of public education. Neoliberalism, as discussed here, is characterized by a simultaneous retreat from social programs and an advancement of social control over the public (Bourdieu 1998; Monahan 2005a; Katz, Chapter 2, this volume). The mass media advance this process by presenting students as either victims or criminals who can be protected or controlled, respectively, by surveillance systems. As a result, criminalization and victimization may become the primary experiences for students in public education.

The Hummingbird's Song: Biometrics in Public Schools

In late 2003, the sheriff's department of Maricopa County, Arizona, installed a face-recognition surveillance system at the Royal Palm Middle School in Phoenix. As with other biometric systems, such as those based on fingerprinting or retinal scans, the primary objective is not to track the movements or activities of people but instead to identify them (Van der Ploeg 1999a). Specifically, the data from face scans at the middle school are transmitted straight to the sheriff's department for immediate, automated comparison with national databases of sex offenders, child abductors, and missing children. Should a positive match be found, the sheriff will dispatch officers to the school site, bypassing administrators and teachers, effectively removing school representatives from the intervention process.

As with most schools, Royal Palm Middle School has had no previous (reported) problems with sex offenders, child abductors, or missing children. What, then, are the reasons behind this seemingly sudden and extreme move? The impulse for this system originated with a $350,000 donation of equipment to the sheriff's department by Hummingbird Defense Systems, Inc., a security technology company in Phoenix (Kossan 2003). This donated equipment was earmarked for "pilot programs," presumably to test the efficacy of the systems but also to locate new markets for biometric security systems designed by the company. According to one news source, the "Sheriff's Office and Hummingbird's CEO concocted the idea of using the technology in schools" (Brown 2004). The sheriff, leveraging much more clout than any single high-tech company could on its own, persuaded the superintendent and school board to allow the system to be implemented, on a trial basis, in the school district.[1] And whereas local news stories framed this donation as a "gift" to the schools, press releases from the company's partners put an entirely different spin on the relationship:

> Hummingbird's CEO Steve Greschner said, "This is a great application of technology and a great opportunity to help make schools a safer place for our children. The system is deployed on a school by school basis and should generate recurring revenue of approximately $350,000.00 (USD) per year for Acsys Biometrics." (Acsys Biometrics 2004)

The press release states quite clearly that the company's goal is to insert these systems into all schools within Maricopa County, not to have Royal Palm Middle School serve as an isolated test case (Acsys Biometrics 2004).

Hummingbird Defense Systems, Inc., is not alone in cultivating or capitalizing on new public markets for security systems post-9/11. In 2002 the industry for biometric systems was already huge, with gross sales in the United States expected "to grow from $400 million in 2000 to $1.9 billion in 2005" (Nieto, Johnston-Dodds, and Simmons 2002: 8). In 2004 the U.S. Department of Homeland Security blew that projection out of the water by awarding a 10-year contract of up to $10 billion to the private company Accenture for biometric systems at U.S. ports of entry (Lichtblau and Markoff 2004). A total of $250 billion in U.S. tax dollars has been spent

Figure 7.1 Hummingbird Security. (Courtesy of Hummingbird Defense Systems, Inc.)

on airline security alone since 9/11 (Mother Jones 2005). Thus, the larger context of public security systems is vast. One can learn much about the assumptions driving surveillance regimes in public schools and beyond by attending to the discourses employed by surveillance and security companies such as Hummingbird.

Hummingbird's website presents the quest for security as a dangerous war against unknown assailants or terrorists. The "solutions" they provide to their potential clients are explicitly militaristic "command and control systems" developed in government laboratories:

> Security technology, specifically command and control systems and environments, have been developed and operated in federal and national government laboratories and environments for the past 10 years. It is this sophisticated and critical-level technology that is now being brought to the commercial business industry. (Hummingbird Defense Systems, Inc., 2004)

Graphic illustrations on the website depict a centralized environment of surveillance and identification subsystems, networking infrastructures, and alerting mechanisms orbiting around the command and control center of servers and software that run the system. Should one get the impression that such a centralized system is cumbersome or labor intensive, Hummingbird assures clients that their solutions are entirely "flexible" and labor saving, requiring only one operator to manage the entire system and deflect threats in real time (Hummingbird Defense Systems, Inc., 2004).

The intended message is clear: security is achieved through militaristic technical systems of automation, standardization, and centralization. Whether the client is a school, a corporation, or the military, the same command and control systems will provide solutions to its security problems.

Hummingbird's argument gains rhetorical force by erasing the social world from its flowchart representation of reality; the mission of "security" is the same even if the threats are wildly divergent across contexts of use or if the threats are entirely manufactured. Indeed, security is something that is never operationalized—it is, instead, assumed to be a universal value and a good that is beyond question. But it is worth asking what happens to the social functions and climates of public schools when they are perceived as urban outposts in need of military-grade protections.

Surveillance systems of the sort designed by Hummingbird and implemented by the Maricopa County sheriff's department signal one dimension of the growing culture of control in public education. In this case, the systems promise to manage a range of risks: the risk that a child molester or abductor will be circulating among schoolchildren without anyone's awareness, the risk that *your* child might be abducted or molested, the risk that an abducted child will never be found, the risk that police will not arrive to the scene in time. All these "risks" are really "fears" that were vague or nonexistent prior to the introduction of the systems and the subsequent media coverage and public conversation. By means of this process of fear cultivation, the surveillance systems become "necessary" interventions, worth any cost, inconvenience, or more profound alteration of educational environments. As the sheriff avers, "If it works one time, locates one missing child or saves a child from a sexual attack, I feel it's worth it" (Rushlo 2003).

In the networks of control being established in Phoenix schools and elsewhere, law enforcement personnel are absorbing more power over school operations, especially those operations concerning risk management and student discipline. Many schools have on-site armed police personnel—typically called school resource officers (SROs)—who handle disciplinary matters, develop relationships with students, and often garner more fear and respect from students than do teachers or principals (McDaniel 2001; Brotherton 1996). Students' ambivalent relationships with SROs are well grounded, because with the advent of zero tolerance policies for drugs or violence at schools, SROs become the primary agents for funneling students into the criminal justice system. Public education and criminal justice systems are overlapping in many places and are initiating youth into disciplinary relationships with the state (Kupchik and Monahan forthcoming). In this context, for schools without SROs, surveillance systems like Hummingbird's give police an open invitation to charge into schools whenever they suspect a positive match, even though face-recognition systems are notorious for delivering false positives (Garfinkel 2002). But because police or security personnel are already present at many school sites,[2] the surveillance system functions as one more hardwired justification for police presence, interaction, and intervention with public education.

Scopophilia and SWAT in Public Schools

Students arriving at Stratford High School in Goose Creek, South Carolina, early on November 5, 2003, were met with an unforgettable experience. As they were socializing in the hallways, stashing lunches and books in their lockers, and using the restrooms before class, teams of uniformed police officers stormed into the building with guns drawn. Seemingly coming from nowhere, the police bore down on students in a SWAT-style paramilitary raid, yelling, "Get on the ground! Get on the ground! Hands on your head, hands on your head, do you understand?" (Associated Press 2003). Students who did not immediately comply were forced down at gunpoint, and plastic ties (similar to those used by police on protesters or by U.S. troops on prisoners in Iraq) were cinched tightly around their wrists behind their backs. Next, a menacing police dog was led down the hallway, barking and grabbing and shaking students' bags with its mouth and periodically jumping as it passed just inches from students' heads in its search for illegal drugs.[3] No drugs were found. Yet as officers left, they threatened students with a repeat of that morning's assault: "If you're an innocent bystander to what has transpired here today, you can thank those people that are bringing dope into this school. Every time we think there's dope in this school, we're going to be coming up here to deal with it, and this is one of the ways we can deal with it" (Associated Press 2003).

This entire event was captured on the school's elaborate video surveillance system and later broadcasted across local and national television news stations. As seen in the school's video playback, one of the officers was brandishing a video camera instead of a gun, recording the scene from yet another perspective. Afterward, the principal gave several media interviews from his office, where he proudly displayed five of his video monitors (each divided into sixteen frames, one per camera), played back the scene of the police raid, and narrated it, seemingly without any compunction or concern that his recorded words might later be used against him in court. But the surveillance system, it turns out, was not simply an objective observer to what happened that day; it helped motivate the raid, because the principal—although he could not see it, and perhaps *because* he could not see it—was certain that somewhere, somehow, students were evading the system to sell large quantities of illegal drugs at the school (Mizzell 2003).

The media broadcasts of the raid solidified the event for the community, becoming a tangible reference point for parents in their anger and outrage.

The principal responded to the public by both defending the actions of the police and distancing himself from them: "I have to defend all the trained professionals. If that's how they've been trained and been instructed on what to do. Yes, it was a situation. This was real" (Mizzell 2003). Yet this attempt to separate himself from the police and their training rings somewhat false, because he was the one who planned the raid with the officers, hiding them in closets, offices, and under stairwells so that they could descend stealthily and rapidly on the students (ACLU 2003a). The principal also adopted a hands-on approach of walking the hallways with the police and instructing them to restrain certain black students with plastic ties and subject them to extra scrutiny—orders that the police willingly obeyed (Lewin 2003; ACLU 2003b).

Soon after the raid, the ACLU filed a lawsuit on behalf of 20 of the students, claiming that the police and school officials violated these students' constitutional rights to be safeguarded against unreasonable search and seizure:

> By deploying uniformed police officers with their firearms drawn in the school, by allowing these officers to threaten plaintiffs with a large and aggressive police dog, and by searching the persons and property of the plaintiffs and other students, the defendants terrorized the students and betrayed the promise of a safe, secure learning environment. (ACLU 2003a)

The community was not soothed by the fact that the police accosted a disproportionate number of black students during the event. According to one report, "While Black students make up less than a quarter of the 2,700 students at Stratford High School, two-thirds of the 107 students caught up in the sweep were Black" (*San Francisco Bay View* 2004). On December 16, 2003, Reverend Jesse Jackson traveled to the school's county to participate in public protests against the aggressive and discriminatory tactics used by police in the drug search.

The school's surveillance system plays an interesting and complex role in this story. Yes, it fostered public awareness about the extreme tactics used on students, most of whom were minors. But it also seems to have facilitated a profound disconnect between the principal and the students under his care in the first place. The surveillance system contributed to the principal's paranoia about illicit activities occurring somewhere *outside* of his almost ubiquitous field of vision yet *inside* the protected territory under his watch. Holed up in his office, cycling through all the video feeds like a cross between a security guard in a war-zone bunker and a channel surfer at home in his living room, he was able to demonize the students and see them as dangerous criminal threats rather than as young people. The video terminals filtered reality in an extremely underdetermined way, inviting him to weave any narrative or impose any biases that he pleased. As he watched the playback on his monitor, he explained to one interviewer that the reason the dogs did not find any drugs was that the students had already dumped them, and the reason why other students did not arrive with drugs was that they received cell-phone tips from others (ACLU 2003b). Because these (and other) constructed "facts" find no representation in the surveillance monitors, they paradoxically become all the more true for the observer—the cameras do not prove otherwise.

Surveillance systems may not directly create prejudice or fear, but they tend to cultivate extreme voyeuristic impulses (scopophilia) that enforce divisions between subjects and objects and amplify the base qualities of those doing the watching. For example, from 2002 to 2003, administrators at a public middle school in Tennessee illegally used video surveillance to monitor students in locker rooms (Dillon 2003). Records from Internet service providers show that the saved digital recordings, mostly of girls, were accessed 98 times through the Internet at all hours of the night and from multiple states (Riley 2003; National Consumer Coalition 2003). In the example of the police raid at Stratford High School, students under surveillance were marked as criminals in advance, and this encouraged police to adopt paramilitary tactics appropriate to dealing with extreme threats. When no drugs were found, the students were not vindicated but still perceived as criminals; they just happened to be clever enough to evade the system, this time. But even if drugs had been found, the discovery would not have justified the means employed, the assumption of student guilt, or the absence of genuine social relations between administrators and students.

Taking the Media to School

Would that the media were neutral parties in the ongoing transformation of schools into fertile sites for police intervention and profitable markets for private companies.[4] But there is nothing impartial and little factual about news reporting on violence in schools. When shootings such as those at Columbine occur, media outlets such as CNN provide 24-hour coverage, and school violence is declared to be a widespread "epidemic" that demands that policy makers immediately make schools safer. Video surveillance fuels this perception and desire by allowing for continual playback of "real" events, casting all viewers as on-site witnesses, complicit in the events and guilty for their own inaction. Every rebroadcast accretes upon the last, further reinforcing the belief in a widespread "pattern of violence" until the epidemic is taken as truth and fear sets in.

The statistics on school violence tell another story. Contrary to media-generated popular perceptions, violence in schools has steadily *decreased* over the past decade, creating a discernable trend toward safer schools (Lawrence and Mueller 2003). In 1992–93, there were 42 student homicides on school premises throughout the United States, but after steady decline, that figure reached 4 student homicides in 2002–2003 (Youth Violence Project 2003).[5] Serious violent crimes (i.e., rape, sexual assault, aggravated assault, or robbery) also have diminished, starting at 10 per 1,000 in 1992, peaking at 13 per 1,000 in 1994, and dropping to 6 per 1,000 in 2001 (DeVoe et al. 2003). And even before the Columbine shooting and the subsequent rush to equip schools with metal detectors, of which only 1 percent of schools currently use (Chandler 2004), gun possession by students had dropped from 6 percent in 1993–94 to 3.8 percent in 1997–98 (Burns and Crawford 1999). Considering that school populations have increased by 19 percent over roughly the same period of time, from 45.4 million in 1988 to 53.9 million in 2001 (Hussar and Gerald 2003), the few occurrences of school violence can hardly be equated with an epidemic of any sort. In fact, school violence does not appear to be a pressing problem at all when compared to the 2,000 to 3,000 children killed each year by parents or guardians (Burns and Crawford 1999). Just as an unjustified fear of increasing crime pushes people into gated communities (Low 2003), this "phantom epidemic" of school violence (Best 2002) nonetheless generates fear-inspired social practices that aggravate social inequalities and arguably give rise to even greater fear of others, whether in schools or in neighborhoods.

The culture of fear generated by the media spills over into a culture of control in schools. When news media continually return to the motif of school violence, they effectively fuse fear with the topic, such that "school violence" elicits an emotional response apart from its specific circumstances or degree of magnitude.[6] Surveillance equipment is one material and symbolic manifestation of this reactionary culture of control that infiltrates social worlds and structures social relations. Not only does surveillance in schools produce a demand for even more surveillance, as with the Columbine case or other high-profile events caught on video, but it also provides a rationale and responsibility for police to involve themselves as agents of discipline and control within schools.

The culture of control produces so-called "victims" and "criminals" and imposes these identities on students, as was seen with the two examples of surveillance in schools presented previously. In the process, school practices mutate into those of risk management. When students are constructed as victims, the radical interventions for the protection of their bodies and for the protection of school districts from liability are seemingly justified. Victimhood, in other words, serves as the motivating logic for the advancement of systems of control in public education. The reason for this is that the production of students as victims—who are "innocent children" or "kids"—engenders moral outrage on a far greater scale than stories about the victimization of the general public by young delinquents or gang members. Childhood is a sacred state, one that society demands be protected by public institutions, until the "children" become "criminals," at which point they are tossed into a moral abyss, perceived as somehow less than human but increasingly held accountable as adults.[7]

Although victimhood is a risk that demands mitigation, (potential) criminals must also be managed (Lyon 2001). Surveillance regimes in schools, police in schools, and zero tolerance laws are overlapping and complementary mechanisms for risk management and the advancement of the culture of control (Kupchik and Monahan forthcoming). As Henry Giroux expounds, these mechanisms "signify a shift away from treating the body as a social investment (i.e., rehabilitation) to viewing it as a threat to security, demanding control, surveillance, and punishment" (cited in T. Lewis 2003: 348). The cultivation and imposition of criminal identities are as important as the identities of victimhood to the perpetuation of the system. Public education depends on victims and criminals, potential or actual, to justify its risk management functions, which enmesh industry interests and police actions with educational institutions. The media eagerly meet this need for victims and criminals by manufacturing them and/or elevating them to epidemic proportions in the public imagination. Such media reports are influential in shaping public opinion and policy agendas, whereby policy makers and law enforcement agents feel compelled to respond to the public's augmented concerns about school safety.

The media's production of fear, then, acquires force by transforming particular and idiosyncratic events into universal and absolute threats. Random acts of school violence are presented as evidence of widespread social chaos and moral decay, and the perpetrators of these crimes are viewed as enemies of the social order or the very fabric of society. In this way, "moral panic" is cultivated (Burns and Crawford 1999), increasing both the stakes of any response and the demand for harsh retaliation, because failure to win decisively the battle against criminals (or terrorists) means nothing less than the demise of civilization. The framing of the debate along these lines should not be seen as specific to school violence; instead, it is the dominant rhetorical modality for repressive social control within neoliberal states and for imperial practices beyond them (Garland 2001; Wacquant 2001; Winner 2004). Discourses of routine exceptional events that carry universal importance (such as police actions in foreign countries) are the contemporary colonizing agents of global capital (Hardt and Negri 2000; Agamben 2000, 2005).

The phrase "taking the media to school" might imply teaching them the real data on school violence or the negative effects of irresponsible reporting, but the larger problem is that the media are already involved with schools and are thoroughly invested in the image of schools that they project. Just as high-tech surveillance companies stand to profit handsomely from the so-called epidemic of school violence or from hypothetical threats to students, so too does the media thrive on fear and control in schools. The media oversaturation of rare school shootings, for instance, attests to the profitability of hyping fear to boost ratings (Burns and Crawford 1999). More often than not, what should be local interest stories about random occurrences of school violence are exported to national or international media audiences, further reinforcing public perceptions that the situation is out of control.

Footage from video surveillance makes some of the best fear-generating news possible. Whether of the shooters at Columbine, the killers of young Jamie Bulger in England,[8] the police beating Rodney King, or the police terrorizing students in Stratford High School in South Carolina, video recordings concurrently personalize and universalize threats. They animate the scenes, providing unclear visual representations that invite replay for further investigation or analysis. The lack of visual quality testifies to the "reality" of the recordings and lures viewers into the scenes, positioning them as agents charged with deciphering the ambiguous text. Replaying surveillance footage or exporting it to other media markets connotes widespread manifestation of the events depicted, where the viewing activity is inflected with the unspoken insinuation that for every event caught on tape, there must be many more not captured. Finally, surveillance footage whets voyeuristic appetites that both shame and titillate viewers, creating a hunger for even more recordings, and thus more surveillance systems, throughout public life.

The media's relationship to the surveillance industry runs deeper than a simple interest in television ratings, however. Because media corporations are megalithic conglomerates with financial ties to many industries, it should not be surprising that they or their sister companies produce surveillance equipment. Although the terrain of corporate mergers and partnerships fluctuates constantly and is therefore difficult to pin down, connections among media and electronics corporations persist, even as the companies' names or owners change. For instance, General Electric presently owns MSNBC, and they produce, in addition to military munitions, an entire line of surveillance technologies for public and private sectors (Think & Ask 2002; General Electric 2004). As another example,

General Motors owns Hughes Electronics Corp., which owns DirectTV; and the AOL TimeWarner CNN conglomerate is in partnership with General Motors, Hughes, Philips Electronics, and Raytheon (Regan 2001; Williams 2001; Global Security 2002). Philips produces surveillance equipment of all sorts, from video to radio frequency identification systems, and Raytheon manufactures high-grade surveillance devices, such as thermal-imaging equipment for police, military, or border-control use (Philips 2004; BurleCCTV 2004; Raytheon 2004). These links between media corporations and the surveillance and military industries are just the tip of the iceberg and are worthy of further research, but they do suggest media interest in developing the portfolios of parent companies and corporate partners. And unfortunately media companies have demonstrated a track record of unabashedly promoting products within their corporate families or shielding their partners from public criticism (Jackson and Hart 2002).

This section has argued that the media are complicit in the unfolding of surveillance regimes and cultures of control in public education. By cultivating fear of school violence, presenting students as victims or criminals, airing surveillance video recordings, and (perhaps unintentionally) promoting the use of surveillance equipment in schools, the media celebrate technological fixes to social problems while ignoring the social relations being produced by those purported fixes. Above all, the media portrayal of school violence as an epidemic supports institutional criminalization of students while effectively diverting attention away from root causes of crime, such as gross inequality, whether in schools or in society at large.

Conclusion

The cases of surveillance in schools presented here illustrate two possible configurations of social relations and material embodiments in the neoliberal state. As Cindi Katz (Chapter 2, this volume) writes about surveillance devices in the child protection industry, the simultaneous elimination of the social wage and rise in social control aggravate inequalities and reinforce fears about others. One result is the displacement of responsibility for care of children (and students) onto individuals, families, and private service companies who promise to meet the social and emotional needs of those who can afford them, whereas others must struggle without much assistance from the state or from employers. Historically, public education has been an institution of social welfare and control, providing civic education for citizens while socializing them into mainstream norms and relations. In this neoliberal climate, public education is a tense and unstable enterprise, rife with new contradictions over obligations to educate and control students with diminishing public resources and for labor markets with fewer viable opportunities. As this chapter has shown, law enforcement and technological encroachments into public education may make victimization and criminalization the primary educational experiences for students in the system.

Even within the stigmatized worlds of public education, however, neoliberalism finds varied and unique expressions as it is mediated by local places and cultures. In Royal Palm Middle School in Phoenix, police and media discourses situate danger and risk outside of the school grounds; biometric surveillance devices serve as high-tech fortification against potentially malicious others in the community at large. Embedded in this rhetoric is the notion that even though these others may look and act like anyone else, should they attempt to infiltrate the school, the face-recognition system will pierce their disguises of normalcy, fix their identities, and initiate a rapid-response law enforcement intervention. Because the school has no reported history of internal crime or verified external threats, social control and police authority are justified in reference to vague and implausible—yet frightening—threats of child abduction. Students are constructed as (potential) victims, and the school becomes a material and metaphorical extension of the private gated communities prevalent in the region. But unlike private communities where individuals willingly sacrifice freedoms and submit to increased scrutiny at their own expense, the social and financial burden of school-based security regimes is placed squarely on the public's shoulders.

In Stratford High School in South Carolina, by contrast, the principal and police construct the criminal threat as internal to the school site. Video surveillance systems actively monitor students in an attempt to collect evidence of criminal activities and then use this intelligence to guide targeted attacks against individuals perceived as delinquents. The surveillance system is employed with the purpose of mitigating risks and controlling the student population; as with police on campus or with gates around schools, surveillance is but one tool for containing (and potentially neutralizing) threats within schools so that they do not overflow into surrounding communities. In this scenario, students—especially black students—are constructed as always-already criminals. This interpretation is supported by the principal's insistence that the students must have cleverly evaded the drug raid. They were not innocent; they were just lucky. If students are seen as criminals and as threats to society, then the effective operation of the school system, beyond containment, is to socialize students to police abuse and escort them into the criminal justice system.

Surveillance regimes in most schools, however, operate somewhere between these two poles of victimization and criminalization. In ethnographic research I conducted with Los Angeles public schools from 2000 to 2001, discourses of security from outside threats prevailed (Monahan 2005a). All the fences with barbed wire, locked gates, student and visitor checkpoints, video cameras, metal detectors, and police presence on school sites were described as necessary insulation against the criminal and gang activity outside. Whereas the *discourses* emphasized outside risks, the *practices* were those of prisonlike containment of poor minority students. It is shocking that it did not seem to matter to most teachers or administrators that students would roam the school grounds all day without ever stepping foot inside a classroom; as long as students were not on the streets, the public education system had fulfilled its social duty. Thus, students were seen as both potential victims and potential criminals, and the two interpretations blurred without any apparent dissonance on the part of school personnel. Either way, the systems of monitoring and control were never called into question.

In most discussions about surveillance in schools, what goes unasked are questions about how emerging relationships among public schools, private technology companies, and the police connect with the larger political economy. One obvious answer is that the implementation of surveillance equipment in schools effectively transfers enormous amounts of sorely needed financial resources from the public education system into the private sector (a similar argument could be made for putting computers in schools). But unlike contentious political movements to privatize public education or establish voucher systems, this transfer of capital occurs under the political radar screen. It meets many of the goals of privatization without the political backlash. It is not a coincidence that the imperative for security systems in schools is propelled by the mass media, who stand to profit both directly and indirectly from this development. Furthermore, inequality drives the neoliberal system, producing both fear of others and individual desires to accumulate capital. Fears can be assuaged temporarily through investment in surveillance systems, and these systems, in turn, feed those fears, as was seen with the biometrics example in Royal Palm Middle School in Phoenix. The criminalization and containment of students serve a dual purpose of safeguarding capital from the marginalized and dispossessed in society while also producing a vast and growing criminal base to justify further social exclusion and inequality (Reiman 2000).

The surveillance systems discussed here shape identity constructions and social interactions. In other words, they produce social relations. In a sense, students have to be seen as victims to justify biometric systems that are tied in with the sheriff's department, and students have to be seen as criminals to warrant the extreme scrutiny of omnipresent monitoring with video surveillance. But the systems, once in place, also invite these constructions of students and resist other uses or interpretations. With the biometric system at Royal Palm Middle School, the very presence of the technology conjured fears in parents that were previously remote or nonexistent. And the deployment of surveillance cameras throughout Stratford High School facilitated the principal's social disconnect from students, allowing him to isolate himself in his office and stoke prejudices and fears that would likely be kept in check if he were interacting and socializing directly with students. These surveillance systems engender identity constructions of students that appear radically different: either victims or criminals. But what these constructions share is a view of students as passive, as individuals whose identities are prescripted.

A more empowering role for students would be that of "agents" who are active in their own identity formation. Of course, students are already agents, but the systems being deployed offer very little support for identities outside the dominant binary of victim–criminal. Instead, all student actions are filtered through this conceptual lens by authorities and by the media, and students adapt accordingly to these roles. A corrective to this situation would be to recognize students' agency, accommodate multiple student identities, and provide avenues for students to participate in structuring the material, social, and symbolic conditions of their lives. It could be, however, that modern surveillance regimes preclude these possibilities or that the control society—which they are expressions of—has effectively colonized the lifeworld of the body. To allow individual and communal expressions of agency and equality to flourish may require a radical reconfiguration of surveillance regimes and the neoliberal state.

Acknowledgments

I want to thank David Altheide, Aaron Kupchik, and Jill A. Fisher for their helpful comments on this chapter.

Notes

1. This is the same sheriff—Sheriff Joe Arpaio—who is infamous for his humiliating and dehumanizing treatment of inmates and others under his jurisdiction. Some of his highlights to date include "jail cam," an Internet camera for broadcasting live images from the county detention center (Lynch 2004), and "tent city," where inmates are relocated to un-air-conditioned tents in the sweltering Arizona desert, required to pay for their meals, and forced to dress in pink underwear (Hill 1999).

2. In a 1996–97 survey of U.S. public schools, 39 percent of high schools with 1,000 or more students reported the presence of full-time police officers on campus (Heaviside et al. 1998). That figure has likely increased dramatically since that time.

3. Whether or not the suspects were minors, this use of a police dog is in violation of the Goose Creek Police Department's policy on detecting illegal drugs. The policy states, "Only after the on-scene supervisor has cleared the area of all personnel will the canine enter and conduct an illegal narcotics detection" (cited in Associated Press 2003).

4. The view of public education as a market is nothing new, of course, as can be seen clearly with widespread advertising and the sale of branded products on school grounds. This trend is epitomized perhaps by Channel One, a news program with paid advertisements that is beamed into more than 10,000 schools by satellite, especially into relatively poorer school districts (Bromley 1998). What I am drawing attention to here are some of the ways that the insertion of these market logics into educational domains produces new subject positions and institutional relations. See Monahan (2004) for focused attention on the role of information technologies, more generally, in the ongoing commodification of public education.

5. These figures account only for homicides of minors on school premises and do not include death by suicide.

6. See Altheide (2002, 2006), Glassner (2000), and Furedi (2005) for treatments of media-constructed fear more generally.

7. See Kupchik (2006) for a superb comparative analysis of children prosecuted as adults in both juvenile and criminal courts.

8. See Chapter 1 of this volume for a discussion of video surveillance and the Jamie Bulger case in England.

CHAPTER 8

"Don't Be Low Hanging Fruit"

Identity Theft as Moral Panic

SIMON A. COLE AND HENRY N. PONTELL

Introduction

If asked to think of a crime that implicates the issues of surveillance and security, most Americans would probably mention the apocalyptic specter of terrorism before the quotidian crime of identity theft. And yet it is identity theft, not terrorism, that over the past decade has rocketed from being a virtually nonexistent offense category to becoming "the fastest growing crime in America."

The study of identity theft provides a new window from which to view processes of deviance and social control. The most sophisticated analyses of privacy, surveillance, and control tend to focus on state and organizational intrusions into individual privacy. Discussions of terrorism, for example, tend to focus on state surveillance as a cost that the citizens pay in exchange for (supposedly) enhanced security. Surveillance engenders security, and citizens can have security in proportion to their willingness to sacrifice privacy.

An analysis of contemporary discourse surrounding the seemingly mundane crime of identity theft raises rather different issues of surveillance and security than would an analysis that takes terrorism as its starting point. Identity theft embodies a form of surveillance for its own ends that appears increasingly immune from traditional means of control: that used by criminals to commit offenses through identity fraud. Surveillance by criminals also attempts to break through personal borders by exploiting weaknesses in current systems of privacy control. In this sense, criminal surveillance by identity thieves represents yet another form of "casing the joint." Surveillance by other citizens with malicious intent engenders not better security but insecurity. The citizen's response to fear of identity theft—calls for state protection from criminal behavior—amounts to a call for increased privacy, increased security, and increased state surveillance and regulation. The citizen proposes not to sacrifice privacy in exchange for surveillance but instead to receive privacy-enhancing surveillance. This, as we shall see, has the odd effect of producing citizen demands for surveillance to protect individual privacy. Thus, a possible latent function of what we call the "identity theft panic" may be to gull the public into demanding a host of oppressive surveillance technologies that it would otherwise resist.

What is even more curious is that state and corporate actors, typically conceived in surveillance and security discourse as insatiable Orwellian actors intent on extending their surveillance capabilities as far as possible, are strangely resistant to citizens calls for greater surveillance, regulation, and control. Instead, these actors have sought to portray the protection of individual "identities" as the sole responsibility of each individual. In this chapter, we argue that the contemporary "panic" discourse surrounding identity theft is an example of "soft" surveillance, in which individuals are encouraged, or even required, to take responsibility for their own protection. As Marx notes,

> The surveillance developments noted here are consistent with the strengthening of the neoliberal ethos of the past decade. In what might be called the "only you" theory of social control, individuals are encouraged to protect themselves and those close to them, because government can't (or won't). (Chapter 3, this volume)

Narratives of Identity Theft

The phrase "identity theft" generates no results in a search of Newsbank for 1994 but thousands of hits after 2000. It is not an exaggeration to say that we are experiencing an identity theft panic, akin to other moral panics (Jenkins 1998; Cohen 1972; Goode and Ben-Yehuda 1994). As Poster notes, "Everyone in the United States now knows about identity theft and probably has some degree of fear and insecurity because of it. People know about it and are anxious about it not necessarily because they have directly experienced identity theft but because the media have relentlessly informed them about it" (Poster 2006: 94). Americans, including university professors, appear to be obsessed with the phenomenon. For example, at a recent university-based symposium on "Human Rights, Technology, and the Humanities," the conversation quickly and inexorably narrowed from the human rights of the world's people to the credit ratings of Americans.[1]

Media accounts typically begin with a sample horror story in which a person becomes aware of having been victimized, cancels his or her credit cards, and then experiences the now-familiar Kafkaseque dilemma of trying to restore his or her financial identity in the twenty-first-century economy. Experts comment on the seeming helplessness of consumers, financial institutions, and governments to stem the rising tide of identity theft. Their message is akin to trying to bail out a sinking ship with an eyedropper. They bemoan the lack of security regarding personal information in society, and blame is apportioned, usually to credit card companies and other businesses and government entities that collect and hold such data. A second genre of stories concerns mass identity thefts. These stories report not individual consequences of identity theft but rather the theft or loss of personal and financial information of thousands of individuals. Typically, this identity information is stolen from databases maintained by educational institutions, banks, credit reporting agencies, or related businesses (Connell 2004; Menn 2005a; Colker and Menn 2005). In 2005 alone at least 96 security breaches occurred through August, affecting nearly 56 million Americans (Identity Theft Resource Center 2005). Moreover, in June 2005 it was reported that hackers had breached a network that handles merchant transactions, resulting in the loss of 40 million credit card numbers (Menn 2005b).

Identity theft is now widely described as the "fastest growing crime in America." This is a remarkable claim, one that we will examine more closely in this chapter. But more to the point here, why and how identity theft has come to command so much attention as a social problem—especially in an age of such folk devils as terrorists and sexually violent predators—remains a significant sociological question. In the first place, it is a rather odd thing to think an "identity" is possible to "steal," in that it is generally thought to be something that inheres in an individual and, therefore, is nontransferable (Poster 2006). Although there is the unusual circumstance when identity thieves steal large sums of money and wreak major financial and personal havoc on their victims, in other cases the financial burden is rather modest, inasmuch as identity theft involves the misuse of existing, or the creation of new, credit cards. Because credit card companies are—at least at this point in time—obliged from the point of view of maintaining customer relations to cushion the financial blow of identity theft, retailers absorb a significant portion of the actual losses. A curious attribute of identity theft is that financial displacement from victim to thief is usually the least destructive—and, in many cases, the least expensive—aspect of victimization. The true damage and real victimization lies in the sense of personal violation, psychological trauma, possible medical care, family issues, and other ill effects, which of course include the time and expense involved in trying to restore one's financial identity. Identity theft is, in this sense, a second-order crime; the value of the object stolen (identity) is generally far less than the value of goods whose security is endangered by the theft (bank accounts, credit rating, etc.). Identity theft is thus analogous to the theft of a key. The key itself is not particularly valuable, but the theft engenders insecurity disproportionate to the value of the key, which entails further costs (i.e., changing the locks). Well before this age of identity theft, middle-class Americans were familiar with the sensation, upon losing—or thinking they had lost—their wallet, that the lost cash was the least significant loss. Credit and identification cards constituted the far greater loss, in part because they can give access to things of greater value, such as bank or credit accounts, and in part because of the inconvenience of replacement. Indeed, many persons recognize the sensation of being—or imagining that they would be—*grateful* for the return of a wallet with only the cash removed.

In identity theft narratives, it is the *repairing* of identities and credit that constitutes the true horror of identity theft. This is a consequence not only of the theft or the thief but also of the indispensability of credit and bureaucratic identity in modern society. The personal damage resulting from identity theft is attributable not only to the perpetrator but to the appallingly Byzantine nature of banking, credit, and financial citizenship in the early twenty-first century. Many victims of identity theft, as with the theft of a wallet, would gladly give up the lost money to avoid the amount of labor they report is required for repairing their identities (Pontell and Tosouni 2005).

Identity theft, then, is clearly not the sort of crime that citizens generally think of when they think about "the crime problem." It is nonviolent and generally involves modest sums of money and in some cases no direct financial loss to the victim at all. Identity theft hews close to the border between crime and mere inconvenience, making it an unlikely issue to suddenly surface as an acute social problem. In contrast, for example, the public, the media, and some academics do not even consider white-collar crime as part of the "crime problem," even though its known objective harm far surpasses that due to street crime. As one commentator noted in regard to identity theft, "You have this seemingly low-level crime that, cumulatively is a national crisis" (O'Harrow 2003).

Narratives of identity theft emphasize connections with more canonical categories of crime and echo thematic elements from those categories. One example is the relationship between identity theft and methamphetamine, thus enrolling identity theft in the much broader narrative of drug crimes. At a recent identity theft presentation held at a major university, students were told that identity theft had surpassed Columbian drug cartels as "the number one crime problem in the United States" (UC, Irvine Police Department et al. 2004). Not satisfied merely with the usual connection between theft and drug use—users needing money to feed their habits—the identity theft panic actually posits a functional relationship between methamphetamine, America's current problem drug, and identity theft. According to a federal prosecutor, "The meth user tends to be more prone to this type of behavior than other drug users" (Mihm 2003: 46; Schabner 2004). Meth heads, it is said, are the perfect identity thieves: they are able to stay awake long hours at a stretch and willing to accurately perform tedious bookkeeping and technical tasks: "To a person on meth, tasks that might otherwise seem boring—like sorting thousands of tax forms or reconstructing shredded patient records—are said to become oddly enthralling. Meth could turn slackers into hyper-efficient paper pushers" (Mihm 2003: 46).

Identity theft narratives also draw on traditional themes of "good guys" and "bad guys" common in contemporary crime discourse. For example, the subtitle of the university campus "I.D. Theft" event was "How Bad People Get Good Credit." The tagline represents a conflation of moral judgment with a financial and actuarial one. It implies that people with credit are necessarily "good" and that those without it are necessarily "bad," which, in both cases, is not necessarily true.

Narratives also connect identity theft and violent offenses, which feature most prominently in the public's notion of "crime." Identity theft has been linked to terrorism, as in the case of Ahmed Ressam, who was convicted for plotting to blow up the Los Angeles airport. Ressam and his accomplices were reported to engage in identity theft to fund their activities (Browning and Graves 2002; Lighty and Gibson 2001). In other cases, identity theft is linked directly to murder. At the campus event, police officers used a PowerPoint presentation to discuss the case of Demorris Andy Hunter, a convicted murderer turned identity thief who allegedly went on to kill two people. Thus, identity theft is no longer just about unauthorized purchases that credit card companies reimburse or, even more importantly, one's credit rating; it is a matter of life and death.

Identity theft narratives also draw on other familiar elements of traditional crime narratives, such as racial anxiety. For example, during their campus presentation, police officers showed a slide of Demorris Andy

Hunter and Michael Berry (see Figure 8.1). Michael Berry, the police officers noted, is a Washington, D.C., political operative with an excellent
credit history. Demorris Hunter is a convicted murderer and identity thief
who lived in Orlando, Florida, and South-Central Los Angeles. Both men
pictured obtained identity documents and credit as Michael Berry. Which
one, the officers asked, is the real Michael Berry?

It might have been anticipated that the students were going to be taught a
lesson about the fallibility of their assumptions regarding race and appearance of respectability and that they were going to be told that, in fact, the
African American with the shaved head was the victim and the white man
in the suit was the criminal. This would have conformed to the stereotype
of the identity thief as a white-collar (and thus white) criminal, a descen-
dant of the con artist (hence the suit), and somewhat of a computer geek.

This was, in fact, wrong. Demorris Hunter is the man on the right. The
narrative resurrected the same racial stereotypes that characterize popular
notions of violent crime: black, working-class perpetrators and white privileged victims. The notion of "criminal identity theft," described later, further
solidifies the relationship between identity theft and conventional crime.

Figure 8.1 Michael Berry and Demorris Andy Hunter.

Theoretical Approach

Although identity theft is undoubtedly real, it is also the case, from a sociological viewpoint, that its construction as a social problem remains troubling. That is, its portrayal in the media, by the government, and by law enforcement agencies may not represent the true nature or causes of the phenomenon. The problem of identity theft has been constructed rather rapidly, over a remarkably short period of time (Poster 2006). We draw on the literatures concerning the construction of social problems and moral panics to explore the construction of identity theft (Jenkins 1998; Cohen 1972; Goode and Ben-Yehuda 1994). Crime, like other social problems, is both "real" and socially constructed (Jenness and Grattet 2001; Rafter 1990; Best 1999; Holstein and Miller 2003). That is, incidents of identity theft certainly do occur. People are victimized, property is involuntarily reassigned, and harm is done.

At the same time, however, those behaviors considered to be criminal do not exist in natural categories (H.S. Becker 1963). Rather, criminalization can involve numerous processes related to social movements, triggering events, the media, interorganizational conflicts, and the state (Jenness 2004). The case of the criminalization of identity theft appears to most closely resemble that of computer crime, in that many of the activities it covers are not new crimes and that the media and individual crusaders, rather than a grassroots movement, were the main forces in new legislation (Hollinger and Lanza-Kaduce 1988). Moreover, the number of crimes involving identity theft being reported to local, state, and federal agencies has grown dramatically in recent years, straining their organizational capacities to respond. Law enforcement agencies have thus been pushed into the forefront of efforts to both define the situation and help remedy the problem.

Similarly, moral panics can also concern real victimizations and real social problems, but the panic, as expressed in the media and popular consciousness, is disproportionate to the harm that actually exists. Such concern may also be misplaced in terms of identifying the true nature and causes of the problem at hand. The current discourse concerning identity theft bears many of the characteristics of a moral panic. It may therefore be characterized as an "identity theft panic" without denying that identity theft is indeed a significant social problem.

Identity theft as a crime category encompasses offenses both old and new. On one hand, it is related to and facilitates new crimes, made possible by technological advances (principally the networked computer) and new financial and social arrangements that include large amounts of personal information that are stored in a variety of public and private databases (e.g., online banking, the proliferation of credit, e-business records, etc.). Legally, identity theft dates only from the Identity Theft and Assumption Deterrence Act of 1998. This combination of new technology and new finance has increased the value of "identities"—that is, of sufficient information about a real or fictitious individual's personal and financial information, so that a claim to be that individual will be corroborated by information stored in various databases, thus persuading a financial institution to extend credit and release funds to the claimant. At the same time, new technology and financial arrangements have facilitated the theft of those highly valued identities through such practices as hacking into large databases.

On the other hand, in the midst of what could be construed as an identity theft panic, the term *identity theft* is being used to describe a wide variety of offenses such as check and card frauds, financial crimes, counterfeiting, forgery, auto thefts using false documentation, trafficking in human beings, and terrorism, all of which existed as established crime categories prior to the diffusion of the term *identity theft*.

In reviewing the current literature on identity theft, Newman and McNally cite the importance of victimization issues in the creation of the new crime category in federal law:

It is clear that these identity theft-related crimes are not new crimes at all, but rather are old crimes enhanced by the use of, or theft of, stolen identities. However it is our assessment that the federal law derives not so much from those old crimes, but from the wide publicity in the late 1990s of victims of identity theft. These were victims who were repeatedly victimized over a period of time from months to sometimes years and who were unable to get back their identities or were unable to convince credit issuing and reporting authorities of their loss. The publicity gave rise to a series of Congressional hearings, which eventually resulted in the Identity Theft Act of 1998. (G.R. Newman and McNally 2005: 5)

Some criminologists argue that *identity theft* is a less useful and comprehensive term than *identity fraud* and see the former as a subcategory of the latter (Pontell 2003; G.R. Newman and McNally 2005). Many of the behaviors now termed identity theft are simply age-old scams, swindles, and confidence games that are mass perpetrated by the use of new technology. To the extent that this is the case, identity theft is not a new crime at all but rather a means to enact older crimes that is both made possible and enhanced by available technology and corresponding cultural lags regarding the potential misuse of that technology.

Thus, the characterization of identity theft as "the fastest growing crime in America" is the product of both these processes: the stimulation of new criminal activity through opportunities created by new technology and new financial arrangements, and the recategorization of existing criminal behavior under a new label. The much-ballyhooed rapid growth of identity theft, therefore, reflects several things: increased criminal activity, increased reporting by victims, and the plundering of other crime categories.

The Crime of Identify Theft

In describing an identity theft panic, we by no means deny the reality of the phenomenon. Identity theft entails three main categories of offenses (Caponetto 2004). The first category, *financial identity theft,* entails the use of personal identifying information, primarily a Social Security number, to establish new credit lines in the name of the victim, such as telephone service, credit cards, and loans, and to buy merchandise and lease cars or apartments. The second category involves *criminal identity theft,* where an offender offers law enforcement another's identifying information in place of his or her own (California Department of Consumer Affairs 2003). The third major type of identity theft is *identity cloning,* where imposters use a victim's personal information to establish a new life. This crime may also include financial and criminal identity theft as well, and the people engaged in it can include undocumented immigrants, wanted felons, those trying to avoid child support payments, individuals escaping from abusive situations, and those who wish to leave behind a poor work or financial history. Imposters can also engage in identity cloning to file for bankruptcy on merchandise purchases while using another's personal information (California Department of Consumer Affairs 2003). Most attention, however, focuses on the first category of identity theft, where it is used primarily to commit financial fraud.

Financial Fraud and Identity Fraud

Financial frauds have been part of the economic crime landscape for many years. Since the classic writings of Donald Cressey on embezzlement (Cressey 1953) and Edwin Lemert on check forgers (Lemert 1958), new financial frauds have emerged, including bank frauds, credit card frauds, computer-assisted thefts, and securities fraud, among others (Rosoff, Pontell, and Tillman 2004). Financial fraud also played a significant role in the savings and loan crisis of the 1980s, where organizational crimes committed by controlling insiders resulted in the insolvencies of financial institutions (Calavita, Pontell, and Tillman 1997). Moreover, the recent corporate and accounting scandals in the United States, which comprise the most costly set of financial frauds in history, show how little was learned from the savings and loan crisis in terms of the genesis and control of financial fraud, the sheer amount of which has ravaged the American economy as well as worldwide markets.

With the rise of the Internet, new crimes, such as auction fraud and online banking fraud, have begun to wreak economic havoc on consumers and the e-commerce system. The proliferation of electronic means for personal banking has opened new doors for fraud, with losses easily surpassing those of traditional forms of property crimes. One recent major survey found that more than 4 million consumers were victimized by checking account takeovers during the past few years, with half that number saying the thefts had occurred within the past twelve months, indicating a sharp increase in the activity (Sullivan 2004). Consumers reported an average loss per incident of $1,200, making the total losses higher than $2 billion for the year. Although there has been a dramatic increase in the abuse of checking accounts online, no fraud detection solutions currently exist. Simply put, the computer has done for financial fraud what the microwave has done for popcorn.

There is no question that financial fraud is a major problem in the United States and throughout the world. It has recently merged with identity fraud, which has been called the fastest growing crime in America. Identity theft, where a known person's identity is stolen, has morphed into a larger category of criminal offenses. Identity fraud includes those crimes where a person's identity is stolen or a fictitious identity is created to engage in criminal acts. Many older forms of crime are possible only through identity theft, such as credit card fraud, which is the largest reported category of such offenses. Criminals, however, have increasingly taken advantage of technological advances to employ electronic means of theft using another's identity (Grabosky et al. 2001; O'Brien 2004). Many of these scams have been noted as lower level frauds, committed by organized crime rings and individual criminals. The cumulative effects, however, are quite large. In addition to significant financial losses is the resulting personal trauma of victims, who can spend months or years reestablishing their economic identities.

Although the types of financial frauds that criminals can engage in seem endless, there are also numerous means by which they can obtain personal information to commit these crimes. These means include stealing wallets and purses, which contain identifying information; stealing mail, including tax, banking, and credit card information; diverting mail to a new location by filing change of address forms at the post office; rummaging through trash for personal information (also known as "dumpster diving"); fraudulently obtaining credit reports; finding personal information in one's home; using personal information shared on the Internet; obtaining personal information from e-mail by posing as a legitimate organization (also known as "phishing"); and obtaining information from the workplace by bribing employees, stealing it if they are an employee, and hacking into databases (also known as "business record theft") (Grabosky et al. 2001).

Phishing e-mail is one of the more widely used tricks to deceive customers into giving away their personal information. The biggest danger posed by this relatively new form of identity theft is that by stealing the identity of an organization, a thief can obtain the personal information of numerous individuals who may then be victimized. It literally constitutes identity theft (of a company) to engage in identity theft (of individuals). Phishing has thus exponentially increased the ability of thieves to engage in identity fraud.

Banks are currently overwhelmed by customer service calls because of such thefts. Trojan horse programs and key loggers are also used to steal passwords and account information (Sullivan 2004). These can be installed on users' home computers through e-mail that contain viruses. Persons who do their online banking in places such as Internet cafes are also likely to be affected by such surveillance programs. Online bill paying and bank management practices also currently leave users prey to online criminals who can tap into their accounts. In most cases consumers are refunded the lost funds, but only within a 60-day window (Sullivan 2004).

The Growth of Financial Identity Frauds

To put this growth of personal financial identity frauds in perspective, consider that the U.S. Federal Trade Commission reported more than 27 million victims of identity theft in the past five years. This is expected to grow to almost one in four citizens in the near future. One account notes,

> The F.T.C. said 27.3 million Americans had their identities stolen from April 1998 to April 2003—with more than a third of them, or 9.9 million, victimized in the last 12 months of that period alone. The crimes ranged from the theft of a credit card number to more elaborate identity thefts used to secure loans. During those 12 months, the report said, businesses and financial institutions suffered about $48 billion in losses because of identity theft, and victimized consumers paid more than $5 billion in out-of-pocket expenses to regain their financial identities. (O'Brien 2004: 5)

Moreover, the Federal Trade Commission survey found that "only 50% of all victims knew how their personal information was stolen—the other 50% still have no idea" (O'Brien 2004: 5).

Financial identity fraud has an increasingly international component as well. The FBI reports that many identity thefts and cyber crimes that occur in the United States originate in other countries, including Russia, Romania, and West Africa. The Federal Deposit Insurance Corporation, a leading bank regulator, warned in June 2004 that increased corporate outsourcing of call-center tasks and other jobs overseas had also increased the risk of identity theft for Americans, whose personal and financial information was now "outsourced" as well (O'Brien 2004).

Contrary to many media and law enforcement depictions, however, identity fraud does not generally appear to constitute what most criminologists who study such issues define as white-collar crime. For example, many financial crimes enacted through identity fraud are the work of con artists and organized crime rings, where offenders possess *no legitimate occupational status*, which is a defining element of white-collar crime. With the exception of insider frauds committed by employees who use or sell personal data kept by their companies and organizations (one form of "business record theft"), identity frauds are not traditional white-collar crimes. Yet they are usually financial in nature and, like more complex white-collar crimes, can sometimes leave an extensive paper (or, increasingly, electronic) trail for investigators. Other than these elements, however, identity fraud can be considered anything but a "white-collar crime." Financial identity frauds are certainly *economic crimes* in that they entail monetary loss, but most of them do not involve relatively high-status offenders or persons in legitimate occupational or organizational roles, other than perhaps lower level employees who can be participants in organized criminal activities.

One report, for example, documents the investigation of two identity fraud rings between 1999 and 2001 in Queens, New York, known as the "Nigerian Express," and another in Detroit, Michigan (K. Davis 2001). These rings resemble many others, in that they are multitiered and organized and contain a number of participants, from main conspirators, information gatherers or "data miners," "runners," and legitimate accomplices, many of whose role within the ring is played out well before a single purchase is made or actual cash is obtained.

First, identity information is collected, and not always from victims who are careless with their personal data, as the Federal Trade Commission, police investigators, and other entities seem to imply when they offer victim-based tips, such as warning citizens not to carry a Social Security card or to give out personal identification numbers. That is, *there is virtually nothing that consumers can do when employees of credit card companies, retail establishments, and other companies disclose their information.* In the Detroit case, three of the twenty people arrested were customer service representatives of American Express who sold customer names, addresses, telephone numbers, credit card expiration dates, and Social

Security numbers for a few hundred dollars. In addition, in both Queens and Detroit, large files containing mortgage and video store applications and other paper items containing enough information for victimization were seized. The information necessary for financial identity fraud can be obtained by fraud ring members whose work positions give them access to sensitive information or by recruitment of holders of these positions, such as customer service representatives and data entry clerks. Perpetrators who possess such information can travel with it from city to city for years, knowing that much of it is still valuable on the street.

Buyers of stolen information can be savvy and selective. The most sophisticated ones will know by the first four numbers on a credit card who the issuer is and their policies and will decide whether to purchase the information. It has been reported that the current supply of such information is so great that prices are depressed. Identities that were bought at $25 or more a few years ago can now be obtained for $15 or less.

With this principal information, more data collection begins. Files, often kept on computers, store essential pieces of identities. "Information specialists" fill in the gaps when information is incomplete. With just a name and Social Security number, a specialist can order a copy of a victim's credit report and obtain information on open credit lines. Credit card personal identification numbers can then be accessed, addresses changed to reroute billings to fraudulent addresses, and multiple users added to an existing account. A mother's maiden name can be obtained through contact with a vital-records bureau. The final financial transactions usually occur through runners, who purchase expensive electronics that are then sold to another retailer willing them for about half the real value. Runners are paid about 10 percent of the profit earned by ringleaders. The other players in the ring (e.g., fake identification makers and addressees who allow delivery of items to their home) are paid in similar fashion. In addition to item purchases, runners can also be assigned to make large ATM and credit card cash advance transactions (K. Davis 2001).

In terms of the rapidly escalating numbers of identity thefts, it appears that organized criminal activity plays as much if not much more of a role than does traditional white-collar crime. Identity thefts that are solely economic in nature are hidden for some period of time before victimization is realized, are more complex than common crimes, and involve proportionately more enforcement resources to successfully investigate and prosecute offenders. These thefts certainly share features characteristic of many white-collar crimes. Yet they appear to represent only hybrid forms of such offenses when involving those in legitimate occupational roles who are enlisted by organized crime groups. They could be more accurately classified as economic crimes when such participation is absent.

Distinctive Aspects of the Identity Theft Panic

The identity theft panic is consistent with features present in other moral panics, which include an intense and widespread feeling on the part of the public that something is terribly wrong in society. Whether it is a moral failure on the part of a specific group, some subpopulation that has been defined as an "enemy," or simply a "folk devil" doesn't matter. What is important is that a new category of persons has been made deviant and a new category of deviance has been created. In this sense, the social construction of identity theft is not very different from the social construction of wilding, freeway violence, acquaintance rape, hate crime, or stalking. In some cases such as drug use, the category of deviance may have existed for some time, but the rapid escalation and intensity of public reactions to it in a given period of time, regardless of its objective threat to society, is indicative of a moral panic.

Goode and Ben-Yehuda note that moral panics, although overlapping with the general phenomena of social problems, also differ from them in significant ways. In episodes of moral panic, persons become "intensely concerned about a particular issue or perceived threat—which, as measured by concrete indicators, turns out not to be especially damaging—and have assembled, and taken action, to remedy the problem" (Goode and Ben-Yehuda 1994: 4).

Moreover, they argue that in contrast to moral crusades, moral panics imply that general concern and fear are not simply a product of the magnitude of the actual threat and "therefore that the steps taken to protect society from that threat may be somewhat misplaced" (Goode and Ben-Yehuda 1994: 20). The handling of events by the press is characterized by exaggerated attention, reports of sensational events, distortion based on incomplete information, and stereotypes. Given that this myth-making (which is a given characteristic of all societies at all times) is especially rapid, the "given myth is especially likely to be believed on relatively little evidence" (Goode and Ben-Yehuda 1994: 25). The public must have some latent potential to react to the given issue at hand, and some raw material must exist from which a media campaign can be built. Law enforcement is called on to deal with the "clear and present danger," ties between agencies and police forces are strengthened, and efforts are made to broaden the scope of enforcement as "new situations need new remedies" (Goode and Ben-Yehuda 1994: 27). Politicians and other groups align themselves against the folk devil and on the side of good, "which is not at all difficult since the target they picked hardly existed in the first place" (Goode and Ben-Yehuda 1994: 28).

However, the construction of identity theft seems to differ from other new crime categories in at least two significant ways. First, the identity theft panic has not simply been a product of grassroots interest groups mobilizing to convince the authorities of the seriousness of the crime. Law enforcement and banks appear to have played as active a role as victims in promoting public awareness of identity theft, perhaps because identity theft victims are qualitatively different from most other crime victims in that they share victimization with credit card companies, retailers, banks, and other organizations. This seems consistent with the construction of other high-tech, white-collar crimes. For example, computer crime was criminalized without "significant interest group involvement" or pressure from "moral entrepreneurs" (Hollinger and Lanza-Kaduce 1988; H.S. Becker 1963).

Second, the discourse surrounding the identity theft panic has focused more on prevention in general—and, specifically, on *individualized* rather than *systemic* prevention—than has been the case with the construction of other new crimes. Public education concerning any crime generally includes a mix of systemic and specific issues, calls for systemic action, and advice for individualized prevention. For example, a "Take Back the Night" rally might include calls for systemic solutions such as rape shield laws, better campus lighting, crackdowns on sexual harassment, more sensitive treatment of sexual assault victims, and individual safety tips such as "don't walk alone" and "use the campus safety escort service." The discourse on identity theft, however, appears to tilt more toward individual prevention. Systemic solutions, entailing more effective prevention and a higher degree of regulation of personal information in the private and public sectors, are hastily dismissed as impractical or impossible, and the emphasis quickly turns toward teaching individuals to avoid victimization.

The aforementioned campus event illustrates these features of identity theft discourse. The posters that festooned our campus invited students to attend an evening presentation on the "Fastest Growing Crime in America!" (see Figure 8.2). The event was sponsored by the campus police, the local police, the district attorney's office, the United States Postal Service, and Citibank.

The speakers and handouts cited alarming figures. An identity theft occurs every 79 seconds. Nearly 10 million people had been victims of identity theft in the past year, and 27 million had been victimized in the past five years. That amounted to approximately one in ten Americans having been victims of identify theft. In a single year, businesses and financial institutions lost $48 billion to identity theft, and individual victims lost $5 billion.

Figure 8.2 Identity theft: The "Fastest Growing Crime in America!" (Courtesy of the University of California at Irvine.)

The promotional tone of the event was striking. (Consider the curious characterization of the crime as "popular.") These were not law enforcement officials who had finally been worn down by feminist agitation to hold a forum concerning women's safety on campus. The initiative for the event derived from law enforcement and the banking industry and not directly from a grassroots movement or victims.

Almost no attention at the event was devoted to systemic solutions to the problem of identity theft. What little discussion there was surrounded issues that were presented as hopeless. For example, it was noted (correctly) that many identity theft problems are created by the use of insecure and nonprivate information, principally Social Security numbers as de facto passwords, by banks, utilities, and even government agencies. It was also noted (correctly) that use of the Social Security number for identification is against the law; it violates specific provisions of the Social Security Act. But this information was presented as an amusing example of the nonenforcement of laws. No one seriously suggested enforcing this law.

Instead, the event was heavy on individualistic advice. Students were advised to purchase shredders, to avoid using unlocked mailboxes, not to carry their Social Security card in their wallets, not to conduct commerce over the Internet, and so on (United States Postal Service 2005). The overall message of the event was that systemic solutions were not possible; the fastest growing crime in America could not be stopped. The advice overwhelmingly focused on how the audience members could make themselves less attractive targets for identity thieves. The idea was not to stop identity thefts but rather to create more savvy audience members and help them to avoid becoming victims. To quote one of the speakers, "Don't be low hanging fruit. Let it happen to someone else."

This general attitude is consistent with media narratives of identity theft. Almost inevitably, they end with recommendations as to how individuals can avoid becoming victims, with titles such as "How to Protect Yourself" (Bergman and Rummel 2004; McGeehan 2004; O'Harrow 2003). It is this last phase of the narrative that is particularly interesting—and unusual. Media accounts of murder and robbery, for example, are not generally followed by a set of bullet-point recommendations for how the reader or viewer can avoid becoming a victim. Again, sexual assault provides a good comparison. Although it is true that the discourse that helped raise awareness of rape was also often accompanied by educational "safety tips" teaching women how to avoid becoming victims of sexual assault, the prescription plays an even greater role in discourse on identity theft. Media accounts of identity theft can easily be viewed as a hybrid mixture of classic crime stories and lifestyle stories, in which the story ends with handy tips for instituting positive changes in one's daily routine. In popular depictions of identity theft, prevention is not an afterthought but an essential part of the construction of the crime. At least as much time is devoted to prevention as there is to discussing etiology, the scope of the problem, and enforcement. Responsible consumers who followed the media's advice in preventing identify theft would purchase a shredder, destroy all personal records, never use a mailbox that was not physically secure, obtain a credit report at least annually—consumers are now advised that by staggering their requests to each of the three major credit reporting agencies, they can obtain a report every four months (Associated Press 2005)—never exchange financial information over the telephone or Internet, and never carry their Social Security card, among other necessary preventative actions. The characterization of consumers who enact these prophylactic measures as virtuous is palpable in most media narratives of identity theft.[2]

Needless to say, this is a rather daunting proposition for most citizens. Does the law enforcement community really feel that a shredder is now a necessary accoutrement of responsible citizenship? Do they really expect shredders to become standard appliances in every household in the

United States? And, why, one might ask, is the United States Postal Service advocating the disuse of mailboxes?

The overall prevention message is that identity theft is too widespread, technically complicated, low stakes, and diffuse to ever be eradicated or even policed effectively (Pugh 2005; Zeller 2005). "Smaller cases are sometimes ignored or delayed until they can be bundled into high-profile, high-impact prosecutions" (O'Brien 2004: 5). Therefore, "the solution" offered to the consumer is to become a less vulnerable target than one's neighbor; in other words, *let it happen to someone else.*

Again, the construction of sexual assault offers a useful counterexample. Imagine even the most poorly sensitized law enforcement official using the phrase "Don't be low hanging fruit" in the context of rape prevention. This blaming the victim mentality would be rightfully condemned, and certainly no enforcement policy based on the idea of "letting it happen to someone else" would ever be acceptable.

Identity Theft: An Interpretation

Moral panic theory posits three general causal explanations for the phenomenon. The grassroots theory suggests that the panic arises from the populace, perhaps from actual incidents, but then generates disproportionate concern. This does not seem to fit the current case very well. Individuals victimized by identity theft are rather isolated and diffuse. Although some progress has been made in organizing and networking victims of identity theft, there is no major social movement; identity theft victim groups are still in early stages of organization and collective influence. Rather, it appears that other social institutions such as law enforcement agencies, governments, and banks are entrepreneurially promoting the identify theft problem. Unlike traditional moral entrepreneurs, the government and corporate institutions—law enforcement, banks, and the U.S. Postal Service—are promoting the crime.

The elite engineered model suggests that the panic is created by social elites in the interest of perpetuating their social position, perhaps by distracting the less privileged. There is some plausibility to this theory. Certainly, the identity theft panic could be characterized as a distraction, from any number of seemingly more dire social problems or from more closely associated but more complex social problems, related, for example, to the credit industry, the use and sale of identifying information, the regulation of databases with identity information, and technological advances and gaps that affect traditional notions of personal identity. The credit card industry is now the most lucrative sector in U.S. banking, comprising an industry in its own right, and the American populace is carrying what most experts agree is a dangerous amount of debt (Poon 2005). And, of course, some of the credit card industry's tactics and policies are considered by many to be predatory and morally offensive (Bergman and Rummel 2004; McGeehan 2004). Moreover, it can be claimed that the identity theft panic distracts from the essential problems of authentication and, more generally, the protection and use of identity information in business and government.

The relationship between identity theft and surveillance technologies is complex. On one hand, technologies related to surveillance are implicated in the creation of the problem, such as computer networks, large databases, and the thriving market in individualized personal information. In this sense, identity theft might be expected to provoke a libertarian response hostile to Orwellian surveillance technology. But when we consider the available technological fixes for identity theft, the picture becomes more complex. Some potential solutions, such as encryption, are indeed libertarian. But others are decidedly not. For example, biometrics, or the linking of archived personal information to the physical body, is frequently cited as a solution—sometimes as the only solution—to the identity theft crisis. The California Department of Consumer Affairs recommends that victims of "criminal" identity theft voluntarily have their fingerprints electronically scanned at their local police department or sheriff's office (California Department of Consumer Affairs 2003). This may be perfectly sound advice, but Americans have long resisted extending the scope of fingerprinting beyond criminals and other special populations to "law-abiding" citizens (Cole 2001). It is interesting to see how easily this barrier may be breached. It is certainly true that archived information that can be accessed only through biometrics can be less easily liberated from its owner than when it is accessed through information that can be coerced, stolen, or simply is (like the Social Security number) de facto public knowledge.[3] The elite engineered model might predict, therefore, that the identity theft panic will induce the public to clamor for the very Orwellian surveillance technologies, such as biometrics, that will eventually enslave them. Gary Marx, for example, notes:

> The study of privacy and secrecy overlaps the study [of] deviance and social control. In many settings privacy and surveillance are different sides of the same nickel. Privacy can serve as a nullification mechanism for the power offered by surveillance. Surveillance seeks to eliminate privacy in order to determine normative compliance or to influence the individual or for its own ends as with voyeurism. (Marx 2003b: 370)

Finally, the interest group theory suggests that some social group profits by a moral panic. As indicated earlier, suspicion naturally falls on the credit card industry. Indeed, in the "experts" stage of identity theft narratives, a common theme is to blame the credit card companies for having created the problem of insecure identities linked to large lines of credit in the first place. Indeed, privacy pundits have located a fundamental cause of the identity theft problem in the banking industry's failure to appreciate the difference between a *name* and a *password*. As Brin cogently explains, the Social Security number is a name that nearly every American public and private information bureaucracy treats as if it were a secure password (Brin 1998; Garfinkel 2000). The same may be said for birthdays, mothers' maiden names, and so on.

It also has been suggested that the identity theft panic serves to stimulate demand for secondary markets for "protection" against identity theft, protection that is of questionable value both in terms of preventive effectiveness and in terms of making good on promised remuneration (Marx, Chapter 3, this volume). In this account, credit card companies created the identity theft problem and are now profiting from it through the sale of secondary protection. And, protection is only one of a host of secondary services, such as restoration of credit services and the sale of "secure" credit cards (Menn 2005c; Colker 2005; Associated Press 2005).

Thus, we are positing an interest group explanation for identity theft, but the interest concerns not so much the construction of crime as the construction of responsibility. The outcome of the identity theft crisis is an abandonment of responsibility for the problem among those institutions with the power to combat it at a systemic level. Instead, the problem is constructed as an individualized and privatized one in which citizens bear responsibility for the security of their own identities. It should be noted, of course, that this is a far more daunting prospect than the securing of one's person or physical property, in that one's identity is more amorphous and socially constructed and that information that relates to it is *stored* in remote government and private databases not under the individual's control.

The overarching effect of the identity theft panic is less one of propagating fear, as in the classic case of moral panics, as it is of creating self-blame and pushing the problem downward. In this sense it directly corresponds to Ryan's classic conceptualization of "blaming the victim" (W. Ryan 1976). Unlike other crime panics, which are used to justify stricter law enforcement measures and tighter surveillance, the identity theft panic does not necessarily serve to justify augmenting law enforcement. The discourse is rather one in which law enforcement appears helpless and overwhelmed with these and other matters, and responsibility for prevention lies with the citizen. The effect of the panic, then, is to create "newly disciplined" citizens, diligently performing prophylactic tasks such as shredding documents and delivering their utility bills directly to the post office to compensate for information insecurities left unaddressed by government or financial institutions. Moreover, because the discourse is less about stopping victimization than it is about learning how to make one's neighbor more likely to be the victim than oneself (bringing to mind the old joke "I don't need to run faster than the mountain lion, just faster than the guy next to me"), we are left with a sort of neo-Darwinian struggle—a metaphor for which the ecological imagery of the phrase "Don't be low hanging fruit" seems particularly apt—for creditworthiness in which "only the shredders survive."

When consumers inevitably fail to enact all these daunting measures, they will be prone to blame themselves for identity theft. If, therefore, we are to explain the seemingly curious entrepreneurial promotion of identify theft by the very institutions that are likely to be blamed for failing to control the problem, we suggest that it may be an effort to preemptively lay the groundwork for the public to accept responsibility for the prevention and even enforcement of this new crime, or in essence to decriminalize, or at least privatize, identity theft. In other words, the panic seeks in the name of "education" to get the public to accept responsibility for a crime that government and law enforcement seem to have little interest in, or capacity for, tackling. And even if they claim to be genuinely concerned, all available evidence clearly indicates that they continue to be extremely slow on the uptake, especially regarding what they have characterized as the fastest growing crime in America.

Conclusion

The lack of an integrated plan on the part of government and the business community to deal with the rise in reported cases of identity fraud remains a central problem. Despite increased penalties, criminals generally have little to fear from such sanctions, as agencies are swamped with cases that are inherently costly and time-consuming to investigate, which is a characteristic shared by identity fraud and white-collar crime. That identity frauds can involve financial fraud, or that some are committed with the assistance of organizational insiders who have access to personal data, does not make identity fraud a white-collar crime. Not recognizing this can lead to misguided policies and neglect of the core problems associated with identity fraud, which revolve around issues of what constitutes privacy and the adequate protection of personal information. The current practices of companies that store and use personal information also require a standard of regulation commensurate with the potential for the misuse or theft of persons' identities. New technologies providing coordinated mechanisms to ensure authentication of a person's identity in financial transactions need to be developed and applied to ensure consumer safety. The central structural problem that remains to be reconciled is that the values of the free market, which encourage financial transactions such as buying on credit and using new forms of electronic banking, currently take precedence over, and are generally at odds with, mechanisms that would increase privacy and the protection of personal information and prevent many forms of identity fraud. Official responses that encourage citizens to guard their information more carefully can be effective only as part of a fully integrated plan; making it the centerpiece can easily lead citizens to neglect the fact that their personal information is not entirely in their control.

As we have attempted to show, the emphasis on individual responsibility in social control responses and in official narratives of identity theft represents a case of the cure being worse than the disease. Linda Foley, a leading identity theft consumer advocate notes, "We've created a victim population that is self-blaming. Most of these problems start with companies that are too loose with consumer and employee information" (O'Brien 2004: 5). Thus, in neglecting the larger social reality of identity fraud, such narratives allow systemic problems related to such crimes to remain unaddressed, which increases the likelihood that the problem will become worse and that a fearful public will support even greater surveillance in the hope of rectifying it. Thus, the resulting "irony of control," to use Marx's phrase (Marx 1981), produced by such official narratives based on individual responsibility is further erosion of privacy and diminished personal control of one's identity information.

> The idea of voluntary compliance and self-help valorizes increased individual choices, costs, and risks. It simultaneously weakens many social protections and programs and pays less attention to the ways the social order may produce bad choices and collective problems. The consequences of these are then left to individual and private solutions, which generate a suspicious society in which paranoia is entangled with reality. This emphasis can further social neglect and the subsequent problems, leading to calls for more intensive and extensive surveillance, citizen cooperation, and privatization in social control. (Marx, Chapter 3, this volume)

Katz (Chapter 2, this volume) provides an example of this, showing that the subjection of children to new surveillance tools (nanny and daycare cams, drug tests, electronic tracking, and the like) is a response to the lack of adequate social provision for the needs of children and the creation of safer public environments.

Etzioni and others observe that the prevailing compromise between libertarianism and authoritarianism has resulted in a lose–lose proposition (Etzioni 1999: 131). The insecurity of consumer information neither protects citizens' privacy effectively nor gives them the benefits of a secure government-run identification system. The current identity theft panic is less likely to change this situation than it is to focus blame on individual victims when crime ultimately occurs.

Notes

1. We are grateful to Tom Cohen for making this point.
2. For example, "Dr. Kenneth Wasserman ... considers himself a conscientious consumer. He never shops on the Web, keeps his Social Security card at home, and refuses to use online banking" (Zeller 2005: B3).
3. Of course, some biometric information can be forcibly liberated from its owners as well, though less easily so, leading to all sorts of gruesome science fiction—and real-life—scenarios (Kent 2005).

CHAPTER 9

Cop Watching in the Downtown Eastside

Exploring the Use of (Counter)Surveillance as a Tool of Resistance

LAURA HUEY, KEVIN WALBY, AND AARON DOYLE

Monitoring by electronic and televisual means is an increasingly significant mode of governance. Surveillance, the collation and storage of information concerning a subject population and the direct supervision of that population's conduct, is usually conceptualized as an activity engaged in by elites for purposes of controlling subordinate social classes. Indeed, the usual understanding of the term *surveillance* is of an omnipresent, omnipotent, and centralized political apparatus keeping tabs on its citizens. In the present work, however, we are concerned with the more generalized, dispersed, and overlapping practices of social monitoring made possible by the proliferation of information and communication technologies in the early twenty-first century. The mass production of camcorders, cell phone cams, spy cams, and other monitoring and recording devices has, for better or for worse, put in the hands of anyone who can afford it the means of televisual surveillance.

This chapter is about the politics of surveillance and, more specifically, about the politics of resisting organizational forms of power through surveillance activities. We ask if it is possible or desirable to "reverse the gaze," so to speak. Our inquiry concerns the increasingly popular activity of "cop watching." In North America many volunteer-based Cop Watch groups have begun to organize for the purposes of "policing the police."

Although our list is hardly comprehensive, we note that Cop Watch groups have sprung up in Austin, Berkeley, Cincinnati, Denver, Eugene, Houston, Los Angeles, New York, Oakland, Phoenix, Portland, San Diego, San Jose, Santa Cruz, Seattle, Toronto, and Vancouver, among other cities.

Through the monitoring of on-duty police behavior, Cop Watch groups attempt to decrease police misconduct and brutality, which their members see as all too often directed against society's most vulnerable populations. These grassroots groups want police to be held accountable for their behavior, and they ultimately desire the realization of a reimagined relationship between police authorities and the communities they serve. Most Cop Watch groups are against all forms of oppression and are particularly concerned with racialized profiling. Cop Watch tactics often involve the use of video surveillance equipment, offering training sessions and literature on how to properly use video surveillance equipment for monitoring police. The most obvious example used to dramatize the ostensible potential of cop watching is that of George Holliday's videotaping of the Rodney King beating. The following is posted on the Phoenix, Arizona, Cop Watch website:

> As the Los Angeles police beat Rodney King over sixty times, one citizen with a video camera taped the whole event. Without that camera, the assault on King would have never been exposed and he would have been just another victim of anonymous police brutality.

In the pages that follow, we analyze the Cop Watch phenomenon in light of two competing views of the use of surveillance. Cop Watch members see their work as promoting democratic accountability of a state institution that has tremendous power in the lives of marginalized citizens. This conceptualization of their work can be characterized as *sousveillance*—a term coined by Steve Mann (2004a) to describe the use of surveillance technologies and tactics by the lower classes for the purposes of increasing equality through making public the hidden workings of powerful institutions and groups. The work of Gary Marx and other surveillance scholars, however, provides a second framework for assessing the Cop Watch phenomenon: as ultimately antidemocratic and thus as a reproduction of the hegemonic values that Cop Watch members claim to be at odds with. When the politics of resisting organizational forms of power through countersurveillance activities bump up against the complicated goings-on associated with organizing dissent, the unintended result can be the undermining of democratic principles through the very means by which the movement intends to rescue them. It is interesting that in the recent explosion of books and articles on social monitoring, with the notable exception of Monahan (forthcoming), very little is found that analyzes any kind of surveillance as a resistance tool. Countersurveillance as dissent is a relatively diminutive theme of study in the emergent body of literature coming to be known as "surveillance studies."

This chapter is presented in four parts. First, we share the methods by which we collected the data discussed in this chapter. Second, we offer a more thorough discussion of the activity of cop watching, with a particular focus on a Cop Watch group in Vancouver, Canada. Third, we analyze the phenomena of cop watching by using two divergent theoretical perspectives: one that sees countersurveillance as progressive and leveling of surveillance hierarchies, and another that is resistant to increasing surveillance because of its potential antidemocratic essence. Finally, we conclude with a discussion of the implications of using video surveillance equipment and other surveillance devices for confronting bureaucracies and resisting authoritative organizations such as police agencies.

Method of Inquiry

The present work is informed by data drawn from two larger ethnographic studies of public and private policing in Vancouver's Downtown Eastside (DTES). To provide some context for understanding the urban space in which Vancouver's Cop Watch program operates, we note that Vancouver's DTES is a community of approximately sixteen thousand residents with the lowest socioeconomic status of any urban area in Canada (Lees 1998; City of Vancouver 2001; MacPherson 2001). Although much of the media and public discourse on the DTES has focused on the site as a skid-row district, it is home to a diverse population that includes lower-working-class families, individuals, and groups of varying ethnic backgrounds; the homeless; local artisans and writers; the mentally ill; community activists; and a variety of other groups.

The site's reputation as a skid-row district began in the 1950s and 1960s when the site was associated with chronic alcoholism—in 1960 it was estimated that the area housed a core population of some six hundred chronic alcoholics (Obe 1960). Heroin became increasingly popular in Vancouver throughout the late 1960s and 1970s, with much of the drug trade activity contained within this particular neighbourhood (Vancouver Police Department 1977). With the introduction of crack cocaine in the 1980s came a well-established open-air drug market throughout the DTES, with much of the drug activity centered at the intersection of Main and Hastings (MacPherson 2001; Huey 2005). Throughout the 1990s and early 2000s, the DTES has been subjected to various policing campaigns centered on breaking up the drug and other illegal markets that fuel much of the area's informal economy. These periodic police crackdowns have angered some local residents and launched protests from activists from both within and outside the community. From these protests has spawned a local Cop Watch movement.

Our interest in the Cop Watch phenomenon began when, during the course of performing research for a study instigated by a local community group on the use of private security in the DTES, one of the authors learned of the existence of a Cop Watch program operating within the DTES. Interest piqued, she subsequently interviewed the program's founders and some of its members, joined the organization's mailing list, and spoke with several of its critics.

The interview data that we use here are extracted from some of the ninety-five interviews conducted in Vancouver for the two larger field studies. Interview participants include Cop Watch members, police officers of varying ranks, members of local community groups, and residents of the DTES.[1] When we quote interviewees, we refer to them as members of a given category; we adduce additional information about the participants but only when doing so does not compromise their anonymity.

We also collected relevant textual materials, including a version of the Vancouver Cop Watch manual, various related street posters, newspaper articles, and Cop Watch Internet bulletins and postings. In all, we amassed several file folders of material documenting various incarnations of the Cop Watch program.

Cop Watching

Gotta catch them pigz on film! (e-mail posting to a Cop Watch group, 2003)

In the summer of 2002, local activists in Vancouver's DTES founded a Cop Watch program. The articulated purpose of this program is as follows: "By observing, recording and documenting police abuses we hold them accountable and send a message that we will not tolerate the systematic harassment and routine physical assaults on poor and marginalized people which has unfortunately become a tool of the police trade" (Cop Watch report, November 24, 2003). Modeling their activities on similar programs in the United States and Canada, Cop Watch volunteers organize street patrols to observe and document instances of perceived police violations of citizens' rights and of harassment and brutality and to help victims of abuse to complain about their treatment.

The basis of Cop Watch work is participation in "witnessing shifts." Witnessing shifts require volunteers to walk through the streets and alleys of the DTES, following police officers and recording police behaviors on Cop

Watch forms or videotape. Depending on volunteer availability, shifts are scheduled for once or twice a month, typically operating at night, from 10 p.m. to 2 a.m. (Hui 2003). Volunteer coordinators communicate with volunteers through an e-mail Listserv, and shifts are sometimes organized through e-mail calls for participation. Interested volunteers are invited to contact a coordinator for information. For security reasons, details concerning the times and dates of future patrols are not posted on the Listserv.

While on patrols, volunteers observe police interactions with local residents from a distance of approximately twenty feet (Hui 2003). Volunteers are advised not to interfere with police or to initiate or escalate any aggressive contact with police. As a program member explains of their tactics,

> The basic premise behind [cop watching is] to try to get people in the community, not to intervene, not going up and directly confronting the police while it was happening, because we didn't want to exacerbate the situation and have the police come down on the individual harder, but just to watch what was happening and to record any breaches of [police] professional codes of conduct.

Witnesses who observe what they perceive to be abuses of police powers or authority fill out internal incident reports to document their findings. Interactions recorded include

> things like, everything from police mistaking a person's identity and pushing his head up against the wall so that his glasses went flying up the street. And when he went to go and complain to the police department, the police eventually figured out that he was the wrong guy. When he went to the police department to file a complaint they said, "Well, we'll pay for your glasses, but you have to sign this thing saying you won't file a complaint." So everything from that to where there was a whole process involved, to someone using drugs getting strip-searched in the middle of the winter. Female by a male cop. (Cop Watch member, interview)

We asked a participant in the program about the purpose of these reports. Her response was, "It was more just for like if someone was ever to look back reflectively ... it never would hold water legally."

Patrol volunteers carry "rights cards" and affidavit pamphlets. Rights cards, produced by a local legal activist organization, inform residents of their legal rights when dealing with the police. Individuals who wish to file a complaint concerning problematic police behavior, such as discriminatory treatment, verbal harassment, or physical abuse, can lodge a complaint with either the police department or the Office of the Police Complaint Commission. Members of the force's internal affairs division then investigate complaints. Affidavit pamphlets, however, advise residents on an alternative process: filing a complaint with an activist organization that promises to pursue complaints on the behalf of complainants. Formal complaints by citizens against police have quite an uneven history in general and in Vancouver in particular (Doyle 2003: 102), which has led to extensive debate about whether it is appropriate for police to police themselves (e.g., G. Smith 2004). Contemporaneous with the beginning of the Cop Watch patrols was a local affidavit campaign launched by the PIVOT Legal Society, one of the founding organizations of Cop Watch. Although we are unaware of any of the outcomes of any of the affidavits filed by Cop Watch members or those individuals encountered on patrols, the campaign did lead to the release of a report titled "To Serve and Protect" (2002), which laid out fifty allegations of police abuse and wrongdoing. At this time of writing, a Royal Canadian Mounted Police report has substantiated eight of the allegations (M. Roberts 2005; J. Graham 2005); however, the Vancouver Police Department's chief constable Jamie Graham (2005), subsequently claimed, "There was not a single case of criminal activity by a Vancouver police officer." In 2005, following increasing pressure on the government to respond to several high-profile incidents involving the Vancouver Police Department, the provincial attorney general ordered an independent audit of all British Columbia municipal police forces, including the Vancouver Police Department.

Another possibility is for Cop Watch members to release videotaped footage to the news media, as with the Rodney King video and a number of lesser known examples (Doyle 2003: 74–75). However, it is not simply the case that "seeing is believing" with home video of police activity, and there is often a complex politics of interpretation when it is given to the media (Doyle 2003: 78–80). Even so, police pay close attention to the cameras as a potential source of trouble, as we discuss later.

Although all Cop Watch members participate in basic surveillance of the streets, designated volunteers are specially trained in the use of video camera equipment to record police activities. The camera used has a zoom function, takes still pictures, uses infrared to capture night activity, and can download streams of images onto the Internet. Images captured on tape are sometimes organized through a narrative delivered by an experienced Cop Watch member:

> You'd have like another junkie, he'd be in the next street and watching, and they'd be kind of narrating how this would be going. They'd be like, "If [we] weren't there that guy's head would be under his foot right now. Arm behind his back. He would never say that." But the cop would be like "You're under arrest for possession of. You will be

given the opportunity to contact a lawyer. Do you understand that you are under arrest?" (Cop Watch participant, interview)

The Vancouver Cop Watch manual also offers a number of useful instructions to Cop Watch and would-be Cop Watch members:

- Do not film criminal conduct if you see any. Focus on the police.
- Try not to record yourself getting into arguments with the police. Good footage of an event with a hostile commentary from the videographer is not as useful. Try to let the situation speak for itself. Let the other group members do the talking if it is necessary.
- Keep the strap around your neck when you are filming for safety's sake.
- When you are done using the camera, take the battery out so that it does not run down.
- Be sure to press the button that gives the date and time on the screen.
- Do not let the sun shine directly into the lens. Do not put the camera at undue risk of being confiscated. Back off if necessary.

Of concern to Cop Watch participants is the potential for their video surveillance footage to be confiscated by police. In response to these fears, program participants have developed methods of retaining possession of their tapes in the event that police should attempt to seize them. A Cop Watch member explains, "We had our method, which was that if we had a tape and the camera was supposed to get seized we had somebody in the group that the tape would get handed off to ... I think the plan we had was that the tape would get handed off and thrown in a mailbox or hidden somewhere immediately."

Although there is no evidence to support the fears of Cop Watch participants that police officers will "jack" their surveillants to recover potentially incriminating tape, in a controversial, somewhat parallel incident, Vancouver police did confiscate all the footage taken by three local television stations of the so-called Stanley Cup riot in June 1994, using it to help lay 300 criminal charges (Doyle 2003: 108).

Vancouver police officers have been clear in expressing frustration over the Cop Watch program and what they perceive to be its members' anti-police values. One veteran police officer described in the following terms what he sees as the program's impact on policing in the DTES:

The politics are fierce. And there is really very little thanks. That's what most guys I hear from ... they get shit upon by everybody so, to some extent guys are even pulling back from their doing their jobs, thinking why are they going to get into a scuffle arresting a guy, when there's somebody across the street videotaping with a camera.

Another veteran cop from Vancouver's DTES recently published an editorial piece in which he detailed similar observations in relation to Cop Watch's purpose and style:

> Activists are now cruising Downtown Eastside streets, looking for conflict with the law. Police checks are often interrupted, with activists stepping between an officer and a person being checked, demanding to inform the subject of his rights. They'll reach out to hand the subject something, claiming it contains legal advice. Every officer is trained to establish a safety perimeter in such moments. Anything could be handed to a subject being checked—a razor, a handcuff key, a gun. The activist will be warned. The return tone will usually be that of someone looking for a fight. And yes, all too often we'll see we're being set up, that it's all being taped from down the block, in hopes of recording a scuffle for a civil suit. (Tonner 2005: A18)

It is not surprising that the claims by police officers that they are frequent targets of activist harassment are countered by activists who, in turn, declare themselves as victims of police harassment. For example, one Cop Watch member alleged that, while on patrol with other group members, "we were followed about 3 blocks on East Hastings with the cop practically stepping on our heels!" (Cop Watch report, December 3, 2003).

It is important to point out that other Cop Watch groups have been subject to more direct police intervention. In March 2005, three members of the Malcolm X Grassroots Movement's Cop Watch project in New York City were arrested for filming police behavior after being informed by police to discontinue (Cop Watch blog, March 7, 2005). An instance of police counter-countersurveillance occurred in Eugene, Oregon, when Eugene police used video surveillance equipment to spy on a Eugene Cop Watch press conference in which they announced their new website.

Some police officers have the view that the presence of Cop Watch cameras has an inverse effect on police performance from that desired by program participants. Cop Watch critics note that a number of the local organizations and individuals that support Cop Watch are also proponents of the decriminalization of narcotics. And yet it was felt by some of the officers interviewed that the presence of video cameras and documenting observers would make it *less,* rather than more, likely that they or other officers would be willing to exercise discretion in relation to offenses, including narcotics violations. For example, one officer noted:

The Cop Watch is ironic in itself because, if you see someone breaking the law, you can go, "If you leave the area, I'll just ignore the
fact that I saw you doing something bad. But if I see you again, I'm
going to have to arrest you." But if you have someone here with a
video camera following you around, as a police officer, for every little
thing, you're going to get a ticket.

This view is similarly illustrated within the following quote from an interview with a police officer who described a conversation that he had with
Cop Watch proponents:

I spoke to a few of them one time and said, "If I get a drug dealer out
at Carnegie Centre and I turn around and I've got a video camera on
me, I'll tell you what's going to happen. I'm going to arrest that drug
dealer and he's going to go jail. In the past I might have taken the
drug dealer's drugs off him and let him go." So I says, "You can bet
that I'm going to tell him that because that camera's on me, I have to
do everything to the letter of the law. So he's going to jail." I said, "I
think the drug dealer's going to be awfully pissed off when he finds
out that he could've gotten away." I told them, "You have to be very
careful with that camera thing."

Cop Watch members queried about these and other similar claims by
police disputed this characterization of their program's effects. One local
activist countered that for the police to "think that we would actually bring
the footage forward and say, 'Look, the Vancouver Police are not enforcing the Controlled Drug and Substances Act' is fairly [unlikely]." Furthermore, this individual contended, "We saw lots of cops take rocks off people
and let them go." Still other police officers apparently treat the Cop Watch
patrols and videotaping as something of a joke. Cop Watch members noted
that some police officers, upon spying the patrols, deliberately mug for the
camera: "Realistically, [the police] knew we were out there within thirty
seconds, and then they'd drive by, 'I'm on TV,' kind of thing."

Cop Watching as Sousveillance

Tonight was the first COPWATCH where we did not witness any
police misconduct (which is certainly not to say that none happened,
just that we didn't see any). If the VPD know when our patrols are
occurring (a distinct possibility), they may be instructing their members to be on their best behavior while we're on the street. If true, this
is not a bad thing: if a few watchful eyes and a video camera can deter
police brutality and harassment, even for a few hours, the outcome

for marginalized people can only be positive. (Cop Watch report, November 7, 2003)

We begin our analysis of this program by exploring the central premise underpinning Cop Watch's existence. Through the language that members employ, it is clear the organization justifies its work through the claim that it represents the residents of the DTES and the larger community of poor and marginalized peoples. We refer to the statement found in one of the group's reports: "By observing, recording and documenting police abuses *we* hold them accountable and send a message that *we* will not tolerate the systematic harassment and routine physical assaults on poor and marginalized people" (Cop Watch report, November 24, 2003). As this comment suggests, the means by which the police are to be held accountable is through the use of systematic surveillance, surveillance to be performed by those who see themselves as representing the people allegedly abused. In this fashion, supporters frame surveillance work as an exercise in supporting the democratic rights of the marginalized.

Steve Mann coined the term *sousveillance* to describe such activities. As Mann (n.d.) explains:

Sousveillance (roughly French for undersight) is the opposite of surveillance (roughly French for oversight). But by "sousveillance," I'm not suggesting that the cameras be mounted on the floor, looking up, rather than being on the ceiling looking down like they are now. Rather, I am suggesting that the cameras be mounted on people in low places, rather than upon buildings and establishments in high places. Thus the "under" (sight) means from down under in the hierarchy.

Mann further distinguishes between two forms of sousveillance: in-band, which arises from within an organization, and out-of-band, which is external to the organization and frequently arises from the perceived failure of surveillance mechanisms within institutions. It is not coincidental that "citizens videotaping police brutality and sending copies to news media" is used as an example of the latter form (Mann n.d.).

Sousveillance is a form of *reflectionism,* a term referring to the use of technology to mirror and confront bureaucracies and authoritative organizations such as police agencies. Reflectionism employs the tactic of appropriating tools of authoritative organizations and resituating those tools in a disorienting manner toward undercutting the privilege of the organization, in essence leveling (or attempting to level) the surveillance hierarchy (Mann, Nollman, and Wellman 2003: 333). Mann and colleagues (2003) write, "Reflectionism seeks to increase the equality between surveiller and the person being surveilled (surveillee), including enabling the surveillee to surveil the surveiller."

Mann's writings on sousveillance must be situated in the postpanoptic paradigm now coming into effect within the surveillance literature (cf. Boyne 2000). For decades the panopticon metaphor dominated scholarly and lay discussions of surveillance. In the *inspection house,* as Jeremy Bentham originally called it, jail cells on six stories would be positioned around a central observation deck, within which guards would be watching (or not) from behind blinded windows. The purpose was to render power "visible and unverifiable" so that inmates would not know if they were being monitored and would constantly modify their behavior in accord with institutional standards. Whereas violent forms of social control were bloody and had uncertain normalization effects on those being punished, the panopticon made discipline certain without blood (Lyon 1991: 600). The panoptic for Foucault (1977: 201) has the effect of inducing "in the inmate a state of conscious and permanent visibility that assures the automatic functioning of power" so to make the actual exercise of power unnecessary. The process of watching takes place within enclosed spaces, where subject populations are forced under the gaze. Foucault's appropriation of the panopticon metaphor, however, has not gone uncontested. David Lyon (1991: 608) critiques Foucault's usage of the panopticon in several ways. First, *Discipline and Punish* focuses on rational means and says little about resistance. Second, Foucault is guilty of "totalizing the partial," applying the panoptic metaphor to situations where it does not empirically correspond. Finally, the observer in the inspection house is always the watcher, never the watched (cf. Goodlad 2003). Many surveillance theorists have attempted to extend their analyses past the limitations of the panopticon (Mathiesen 1997; Bauman 1998; Deleuze 1992; Deleuze and Guattari 1987; Haggerty and Ericson 2000; Hier 2004; Walby 2005). Mann's work must be included in this cohort of writers raising questions about the plethora of other relationships between watchers and watched.

For Mann and other proponents, sousveillance is not simply a phenomenon to be described and analyzed but rather a process for rendering institutions democratically accountable and thus something to be promoted within the public sphere. This reading of Mann's purpose is clear: he sees sousveillance as a potential antidote not only to the problem of terrorism but moreover to the antidemocratic underpinnings that he suggests give rise to terrorism and totalitarianism: "Secrecy, not privacy, may be the true cause of terrorism" (n.d.). In his writings, surveillance (oversight) is depicted as employed exclusively by powerful institutions. The only effective remedy against the potential for institutions to abuse secrecy, and thus potentially citizens, is through sousveillance (undersight). Without effective undersight, surveillance-based states can become "unstable and tend toward totalitarianism" (Mann n.d.). Thus countersurveillance through the camera is viewed not only as a good thing but as necessary for democracy.

Mann and the members of Cop Watch are hardly alone in framing the use of surveillance of police as an appropriate form of community-based oversight of the institution. During the course of conducting interviews with several local organizations on their views of policing within the DTES, the subject of the Cop Watch patrols came up several times. One community group representative, although not claiming to represent the DTES constituency directly, expressed views that likely resonate with Cop Watch members and supporters. For this individual, who does represent an organization opposed to various forms of public surveillance, the Cop Watch program could be distinguished from objectionable forms of surveillance on the following grounds:

> I think there is some important distinctions here that … presumably, they're not doing this surreptitiously, and they shouldn't be ethically. Which means they can be in plain view. A police officer, they know they're being watched when they're in public. With that I don't have a problem. I think it enhances reciprocity. Again, as long as the videotape can be … it's plain what they're doing, and they're not interfering with any criminal investigations, then I don't have a problem with it.

When the activities of Cop Watch groups are conceptualized as sousveillance, countermonitoring from below using video recording equipment appears to be progressive and leveling of surveillance hierarchies.

Cop Watching as the Reproduction of Hegemonic Values

> People in the Downtown Eastside don't want to get taped by us, no more than anyone else. Who are we to tape? (Cop Watch organizer, interview)

In an essay titled "A Tack in the Shoe: Neutralizing and Resisting the New Surveillance," Gary Marx (2003b) identifies means employed by those who seek to escape the panoply of surveillance forms to which individuals are increasingly subjected. One of the measures identified is Mann's sousveillance, which Marx terms *countersurveillance*. In describing this form, Marx states that as an attempt at "democratizing the use of surveillance," countersurveillance strategies offer the potential to limit or inhibit the use of surveillance by others (Marx 2003b: 384). Furthermore, "if counter-measures uncover questionable practices, which are then publicized, it may lead, also, to their moderation or cessation" (Marx 2003b: 384). However, elsewhere Marx (1998) cautions that for surveillance use to be ethical, and surely this equally concerns the use of sousveillance, there must be openness regarding how data are collected and used. Indeed, he is quite clear on this point: "Openness regarding data collection can also help bring accountability to the data collectors; since it comes with an address, responsible behavior on their part may be more likely as a result" (Marx 1998: 177). Marx also raises another worrisome issue in relation to the ethical use of surveillance and surveillance-based technologies: "New technologies rarely enter passive environments of total inequality. Instead, they become enmeshed in complex pre-existing systems. They are as likely to be altered as to alter" (Marx 2003b: 371). Marx (1998: 179) speaks to these possible unintended consequences of surveillance proliferation when he writes:

> The democratization of surveillance as a result of low cost and ease of use can introduce a healthy pluralism and balance (as well as reciprocal inhibitions in use for fear of retaliation). On the other hand this may also help create a more defensive and suspicious society with an overall increase in anxiety-generating and resource-consuming surveillance and counter-surveillance.

In short, Marx suggests the uses of surveillance technologies are tied to the ideological agendas and private pursuits of those who employ them. Increasing surveillance, even as a resistance measure, is problematic.

Although Cop Watch members claim to represent their communities, many residents of Vancouver's DTES say that Cop Watch members do not represent them or their interests. Furthermore, some note that in keeping with the covert nature of their mission, Cop Watch leaders have not sought wider public input into their policies and practices or made those policies and practices publicly available. Critics also rightly note that no mechanisms for public oversight of Cop Watch's surveillance activities have been established. Thus the organization appears to be less than perfectly accountable to the community it claims to represent. Key questions thus become to what extent are the covertness and lack of public input necessarily bound up with the Cop Watch approach, and is Cop Watch simply a local phenomenon that could operate in a more publicly accountable and democratic fashion.

In interviews with DTES residents and community group members, we clearly see that the larger community is divided on the issue of Cop Watch and its tactics. This division is hardly surprising when one considers that there are literally hundreds of different social groups representing often divergent interests within this community. As one longtime community activist wryly noted, "If you put two people in a room in the Downtown Eastside you get a non-profit society. If you put three people in a room in the Downtown Eastside you get two non-profit societies." Many of these organizations are organized from within the community; others are primarily composed of interest groups from without who see themselves as filling need-gaps in local services. This latter fact leads some area residents to conclude that poverty activism has become "cool" for many youth from better neighborhoods, creating tensions with older residents and established community groups who prefer to work within the existing power structure to effect change. As one interviewee explained, "It's like the DTES, it's becoming a political symbol. It's like everyone's hobbyhorse for whatever political issue they're interested in." In relation to Cop Watch in particular, one area resident neatly summed the views of other critics within the community:

> The people doing the Cop Watch, did they come down and ask if the seniors or the single moms down here wanted a Cop Watch? I'm sure the drug dealers would love a Cop Watch. That would be great. Are you actually talking to people who actually live here, versus people who are using this community to prey on addicts or to sell drugs?

The unintended result of Cop Watch's philanthropic activism could be the undermining of democratic principles through the very means by which they intended to save them.

Concluding Remarks

Although earlier we discussed Cop Watch's use of the notions of sousveillance and reflectionism, Cop Watch activities also have a strong affinity with what the Situationist International (see Debord 1977) called *detournement*. Detournement is the rejection of hierarchy instead of the response to antagonism within the master discourse set by hierarchy. Such techniques often use the tools of hierarchal organization to create a counter-message with strong allusions to the organization in question as bases for subverting its primacy. Thus cop watching conceptualized as sousveillance is "reversing the panoptic gaze" and placing authorities under scrutiny through the use of camera surveillance equipment. Video activism is a very situationist practice that can cross-articulate with international movements against surveillance, like the Privacy International group in the United Kingdom. However, the Situationist International also provided us with another term for understanding social reproduction in capitalism: *recuperation*. Recuperation refers to the way capitalism can scoop up potentially subversive ideas and repackage them in a depoliticized form that is related to a broader question about hegemony and how a system of ideas and social practices becomes aligned with the dominant liberal–capitalist order. When conceptualized as an instance of recuperation, Cop Watch tactics might be considered as a more local manifestation of hierarchy at odds with the goal of making policing agencies more accountable to the public.

As David Lyon (2001: 3) points out, "The same process, surveillance—watching over—both enables and constrains, involves care and control." Surveillance must always be considered in the relation context in which it is put to work. Cop watching is certainly enabling for the Cop Watch members. Through their cop watching activities, Cop Watch members are reusing surveillance technologies against policing agencies with institutional power. No one would deny that Cop Watch participants are motivated by an ethics of care concerning the vulnerable populations within the DTES community. The potential for anyone to be the victim of police brutality extends this ethics of care indiscriminately. In this sense, the "watching over" done by Cop Watch members involves care.

There is nothing inherently democratic, however, about care or about caring through surveillance or is there anything that reeks of democracy inherent in the overprovision of cheap information and communication technologies. Although Cop Watch members and other proponents of sousveillance frame their work in democratic language, invoking concepts such as public accountability and formal and substantive equality to describe their activities, their critics offer an alternative means of conceptualizing their use of surveillance. Critics charge that, in effect, the Cop Watch program does little more than to reproduce the hegemonic values and strategies that its participants claim to resent. The flaw in the Cop Watch approach is that it speaks for the subject of police brutality (i.e., the homeless, the mentally ill, the underclass) instead of empowering the subject of police brutality to speak for herself, in effect forsaking an identity through the process of defending that identity. Fostering a less discriminating and less efficient relationship between organizations and their clientele is the key to resisting intensified surveillance (Rule et al. 1980),[2] not intensifying surveillance from below.

Cop Watch chapters share tactics and philosophy but have no formal overarching national or international organization. Cop watching can be understood as a loosely organized social movement (Tarrow 1998). In many social movement organizations, the tactics employed are compatible with, if not intrinsically bound up in, the political project they would like to realize through activism. In particular, the so-called new social movements such as environmentalism and feminism are often characterized by nonhierarchical organizational styles that mirror their emancipatory aims, "showing a preference for organizational forms that are decentralized, egalitarian, [and] participatory" (Buechler 2000: 48). In contrast, the Cop Watch chapter we studied adopted an organizational style that seems incommensurable with its political project.

The politics of countersurveillance cannot be divorced from the politics of collective action and activist organizing. The successes and failures of contentious political projects such as activism hinge in many ways on the enlisting of popular support. Enlisting such support requires the communicating of ideas and platforms to the public at large. The Cop Watch group in Vancouver has a paradoxical policy of not talking to the media about their ideas and activities. Cop Watch groups are not without a standpoint, but they very carefully choose the means by which they articulate that standpoint. On one level, this quiet approach could be a strategically sound tactic, for the media have a tendency through their editorial practices to frame the coverage of contentious political projects in a particular way, which is often damaging to the credibility of social movements (Gamson and Wolfsfeld 1993), partly because the police often have a hand in shaping media coverage (Ericson, Baranek, and Chan 1989; Doyle 2003). Such considerations are important for activist groups such as Cop Watch to account for in their organizing. The preference of the Cop Watch group in Vancouver to remain cloaked in secrecy is contradictory, however, because their mandate is public accountability and scrutiny of the police—on the grounds that the police ought not be permitted to operate in secrecy—and their antidemocratic organization disempowers the very people it purports to empower.

The particular usage of video surveillance equipment in cop watching activities also raises a number of interesting questions that might have implications for further activism in this field. Cop Watch members are not only watching over police but also more or less explicitly watching the people police come into contact with. If a surveillance camera of any sort is used to televisually capture the events that unfold, both the police officer and the people police encounter could potentially be videotaped. Although the Cop Watch group in Vancouver and most other Cop Watch groups offer instructions about what to do and what not to do with the camera (i.e., do not film criminal conduct if you see any, focus on the police, try not to record yourself getting into arguments with the police), unintended tapings of cops, themselves, and other members of the public will inevitably be recorded on videotape. What happens with this information? Do Cop Watch groups have a method for the destruction of personal information? How can Cop Watch groups ensure that members of the public desire that they be watched over in such a way? What happens if police or a government agency subpoenas such a tape? Civil libertarians often raise questions about police-operated surveillance cameras in public spaces. Do the same questions about surveillance and public space apply to activists filming police interactions with local citizens on those same streets?

We by no means wish to be seen as apologists for the inexcusable behaviors that police officers sometimes engage in, but rather we suggest that the unintended consequences of using video surveillance equipment as a technique in cop watching must be weighed against potential benefits. When any form of surveillance, be it surveillance pursued by authoritative organizations or grassroots activist groups, is thought of in terms of concrete social practices instead of a priori assumptions about the relative goodness or badness of social monitoring, it is possible to raise a number of ethical questions about those surveillance and countersurveillance practices. The answers to these questions are best proposed and enacted by activist groups in their own locales. We add a caveat, however: resistance groups that employ countersurveillance tactics and technologies need to consider not only the necessity of garnering local support through a careful articulation of their political aims but moreover, in reflexive fashion, how their politics of resisting organizational forms of power through surveillance activities create ripples throughout the communities they work within.

Notes

1. All interviews were taped with participants' knowledge and consent. Respondents were advised that their names and other personal information known about them would be kept strictly confidential. To help preserve anonymity, we stripped identifying information from interviews during the transcription process, and all interviewees were assigned to one of the generic categories identified earlier.
2. James Rule was one of Gary Marx's students, and their approaches to conceptualizing social monitoring, privacy, and the ethics of surveillance are compatible.

CHAPTER **10**

Defensive Surveillance
Lessons from the Republican National Convention

INSTITUTE FOR APPLIED AUTONOMY

Introduction

Meetings of high-profile transnational organizations like the World Trade Organization and G8 are, as a matter of routine, accompanied by equally high-profile demonstrations by labor, environmental, and antiglobalization activists. Anticipating protests, law enforcement agencies seal off areas surrounding meeting sites, transforming vast urban territories into militarized zones. Police rely on a dizzying array of surveillance and communications strategies to undermine activist strategies, including infiltrating activist groups, monitoring activist communications, making preemptive raids on activist meeting places, and videotaping protest actions for later analysis.

Activists counter police tactics with increasingly sophisticated tools and strategies. In recent years, protest strategy has evolved according to a distributed model of action, relying on coordinated actions aimed at multiple targets across a terrain. These tactics rely on intelligence gathering and information sharing to coordinate actions and react quickly to changing conditions. It is our contention that activists both appropriate military surveillance strategies and develop novel surveillance practices that proceed according to alternate logics.

We approach this topic as engaged practitioners. For several years, we have participated in local and global resistance movements as artists, engineers, and activists. In the summer of 2004, we worked with several activist groups to devise communications strategies for protesters of the Republican National Convention (RNC). This collaboration ultimately led us to develop TXTmob, a cell phone text messaging broadcast system that was widely used during the RNC protests.[1] Through deep engagement with activists, we have gained insight into the tactics and strategies employed by demonstrators to monitor and outmaneuver law enforcement agencies. Although it is imprudent to provide a detailed account of activist tactics (it is not our intention to betray the trust we have established with the activist community to present our findings to a research audience), we believe that an account of creative, active, operational resistance to dominant forms of power and control and a generalized description of activist practices will be of interest to the surveillance studies community. These practices identify means through which citizens have appropriated information and communication technologies to invert the power relations embodied by traditional surveillance regimes.

We present this chapter in several sections. First, we provide a brief discussion of protest tactics that have evolved over the past few years. We follow this with a more detailed look at the strategies used by demonstrators to monitor police activity during the RNC. Finally, we offer a set of reflections on how these practices reconfigure power relations ordinarily associated with surveillance practices.

Swarming

Street protest has evolved over the past several decades according to a model described by military theorists as "swarming"—the dispersion of command among many small, autonomous units that are able to collectively "attack an enemy from all directions" (Arquilla and Ronfeldt 2000). Unlike traditional protest marches, which tend to be organized by a small group of leaders working in cooperation with local police, swarm protests involve disparate, loosely coordinated, autonomous groups. The swarm model, in which groups of protesters converge on a central location from several directions to confound police and seize control of an area, emerged out of the "No Business as Usual" and "Stop the City" movements of the 1980s. It was used particularly effectively during the J18 (June 18) actions that paralyzed central London in 1999 and in the now-famous demonstrations that shut down a World Trade Organization meeting in Seattle later that same year.

After the J18 and Seattle protests, law enforcement adopted an aggressive approach to crowd control during large-scale demonstrations. Independent observers have come to call the current strategy the "Miami Model," named for its use during protests against the 2003 Free Trade Area of the Americas (FTAA) summit. The Miami Model has been described as "the criminalization of dissent" (K. Hughes 2004) and is characterized by the restriction of public access to large parts of the city; preemptive arrests of activist leaders; widespread use of nonlethal weapons including tear gas, pepper spray, and rubber bullets (Scahill 2003); and the use of mass arrests or "sweeps" that often involve detaining law-abiding citizens who are later released without charge (Reynardus 2004).

Aggressive crowd control measures are complemented by surveillance of activists and activist organizations. Police routinely videotape street protests to identify "troublemakers" and to create an evidentiary record for later prosecution. In addition, the well-publicized interrogation of activists in Colorado and Missouri by FBI agents in the spring of 2004 revealed that law enforcement agencies actively monitor activist groups on an ongoing basis (Lichtblau 2004).

Protest organizers' response to the consolidation of law enforcement resources around convention venues has been to distribute the sites of dissent throughout the city. Motivated by a need for inclusive approaches that "allow for a full spectrum of tactics and messages"[2] and a recognition that the Miami Model has effectively neutralized swarm tactics attempted in recent demonstrations, activists have adopted a strategy of radical decentralization. Rather than attempting a blockade of the 2004 RNC venue in New York City, organizers instead suggested various protest locations, including delegate hotels, government and corporate office buildings, and RNC event locations. The stated goal was not simply to disrupt the convention site but rather to "transform the streets … into stages of resistance and forums for debate."[3]

The capacity of activists to coordinate action in swarms is directly dependent on their ability to quickly share information about changing conditions with operatives dispersed throughout the city. This is accomplished by "comms affinity groups," which are collections of technically savvy activists who are responsible for intelligence gathering and information dissemination during protests. Comms groups use a variety of techniques, often relying on a network of activists distributed across the protest zone who maintain constant contact with each other and other activists by using two-way radios, cell phones, the Internet, radio, and word of mouth. During the RNC, comms groups relied on cell phone text messaging to an extent previously unrealized during highly anticipated mass mobilizations.[4]

Comms at the RNC

During the RNC, activist communications were coordinated by several local and national activist organizations.[5] Activists established communications centers at multiple locations around the city, where they monitored a variety of information sources, including overheard police communications, journalist accounts, activist websites and radio broadcasts, and reports from trusted comrades in the street. Information was then broadcast by text message to activists in the street and was also disseminated on the Internet and radio. In addition, several activist groups set up "open relays" that allowed protesters not formally affiliated with comms groups to send text messages to each other. Although many considered these relays to be less trustworthy than communications channels maintained by recognized groups, they were widely used and played an important role throughout the RNC.

Activists used communications networks to share information and coordinate actions. Significant traffic was dedicated to identifying undercover officers, reporting on police activity, and monitoring delegate movements. This enabled activists to coordinate a variety of actions across the city. Warned of police blockades and impending mass arrests, spontaneous demonstrations dispersed at a moment's notice, only to regroup minutes later several blocks away. Responding to reports of police violence, independent journalists were dispatched to videotape arrests all over the city, providing documentary evidence of police misconduct. Text message reports of delegates sitting down to brunch in quiet East Side restaurants resulted in groups of more than fifty demonstrators waiting to greet them by the time the check arrived.

The activist communications network, facilitated by cell phones, the Internet, text messages, and word of mouth, confounded law enforcement and co-opted police tactics. The weeklong series of coordinated actions across the city effectively shut down much of midtown Manhattan during the RNC. Despite more than 1,800 arrests, the police were unable to maintain control over the city. Rather than stifling activist activity, police strategies of spontaneous street closings and mass arrests at times only added to the chaos, contributing to the activists' stated goal of transforming midtown Manhattan into a theater of disruption and creative resistance.

Monitoring Strategies

During the RNC, activists documented police tactics and arrests, tracked delegate movements, and monitored police activity. Each of these practices represents a distinct model of surveillance and monitoring at play in the broader context of coordinated protest action.

It has become standard practice for protesters to produce photo and video documentation of police activity during demonstrations. It has been suggested that activist use of video cameras during street protests constitutes a sort of "inverse surveillance" that has the dual effect of mitigating police behavior and providing documentary evidence of police misconduct. These suggestions of the tables being turned and of inversions of hierarchical power structures to provide civilian oversight of official activity have become popular theoretical constructs among surveillance scholars and activists.[6] Particularly since the Rodney King case, inverse surveillance is considered a potent form that establishes independent review of police action.

During the RNC, independent journalists associated with the Indymedia network actively documented police crowd control and arrest procedures with videotapes and digital photographs. It is difficult to say with any certainty that this had a tempering effect on police conduct. Although many activists and independent observers complained about the mass arrests and unhealthy prison conditions, there were relatively few complaints of outright police brutality—a sharp contrast to the 2003 FTAA protests in Miami. Although personal imaging equipment was nearly ubiquitous among demonstrators, it is overly simplistic to claim that this in and of itself accounts for the relatively muted police response—for example, cameras were also omnipresent in Miami. Activists offer various explanations for the lack of police violence during the RNC beyond the very public scrutiny under which law enforcement was operating, including perceived affinities by New York police officers for the activists' opposition to the Republican Party.[7]

Although inverse surveillance may have had a limited impact on police behavior, it provided documentary evidence that played a crucial role in subsequent trials of activists arrested during the RNC. Images gathered by independent observers and independent analysis of police video records contradicted police officer courtroom testimony and has contributed to 400 charges against arrestees being dropped or dismissed. Video documentation of police conduct has also clearly shown police use of mass arrest sweeps, undermining official accounts of police arresting only those individuals who defied "clear warnings about blocking streets and sidewalks" (Dwyer 2005).

Video documentation of police conduct was mostly useful after the fact—in court cases and in the establishment of a historical record. Cell phone text messaging, on the other hand, had immediate operational value. By using text messaging to monitor police and delegate movements, activists were able to collectively share and act on an accurate representation of dynamic events unfolding across the city.

In tracking and engaging delegates in various locations around the city, activists employed command and control techniques reminiscent of the Defense Advanced Research Projects Agency's vision for small unit operations, in which small, highly mobile groups of soldiers rely on communication technologies to track and engage an enemy (Auger and Kievit 2004). Delegates observed wandering the midtown streets were quickly identified by vigilant activists. Their locations were conveyed to other activists by text messages, enabling protesters to swarm delegates at a moment's notice. During the "Mouse Bloc" actions of August 29, 2004, for example, groups of activists deployed throughout the theater district spent several hours intercepting delegates exiting *The Lion King* and other Broadway plays. In this case, visual monitoring of delegates coupled with rapid communications technology enabled activists to project operational influence, despite the ubiquitous presence of police in the area. This model of surveillance effectively mirrors the approach taken by both military strategists and public safety officials.

The use of text messaging to track delegate movements represents a militarized appropriation of consumer technology by civilian actors—that is, the goal is to identify and engage moving targets at moments of heightened vulnerability. This is an essentially offensive strategy, aimed at exercising power over delegates, limiting their movements, and subjecting them to chanting, shouting, and sign waving (and here we've reached the limits of our military metaphor). In contrast, activist monitoring of police movements is a fundamentally defensive strategy, representing a novel use of surveillance techniques to avoid rather than engage. During the RNC, activists relied on text messaging to warn each other of blockades and impending police action, enabling protesters to avoid arrest and find unobstructed routes through the city (Scahill 2004). This model, which we call "defensive surveillance," represents a departure from traditional surveillance regimes in that it involves active monitoring with the goal of avoidance rather than engagement.

Defensive Surveillance

Traditional surveillance is fundamentally about control—it is a means through which one group attempts to dominate another. This, of course, is why surveillance cannot be reduced to mere voyeurism—it is not about *looking* but rather about *doing*. It is the precursor to often violent action aimed at controlling or otherwise modifying the behavior of those who come under its gaze—or, at least, it makes a credible threat that such action will be forthcoming.

Surveillance is thus tied directly to operational models of power and action. Traditional surveillance regimes operate according to logics of force—of the watcher's ability to exercise his or her will on the body of the observed. Defensive surveillance undermines these regimes in that it reflects neither the exercise of official power nor the inversion of power hierarchies. Instead, defensive surveillance prepares an actor to leave the field of engagement entirely. It is a tactic of speed. If we employ a predator–prey metaphor to describe power relations in surveillance regimes, we might consider the difference between stereoscopic and peripheral vision. If surveillance is the predator's gaze (both eyes straight forward), defensive surveillance is the vision of the prey (an eye on each side of the head), like a gazelle that maintains a watchful eye on the lions lying in the tall grass, ready to flee to distant velds at the slightest rustle of the reeds.

Although surveillance and defensive surveillance are often copresent in visual monitoring practices (RNC activists were simultaneously targeting delegates and avoiding police), defensive surveillance practices aren't limited to probing an enemy's armor in preparation for an eventual attack. One is reminded of Harry Potter's "Marauder's Map," a fanciful technology that enables schoolchildren to track their teachers' movements so they can have clandestine meetings for plotting and root beer drinking. In a less literary vein, one can think of other cases—critical mass rides, floating crap games, graffiti writing—that are structured as perpetual cat-and-mouse games, in which the goal is not to confront an enemy but rather to maintain one's own autonomy in the face of overwhelming power.

For activists, swarming is fundamentally a speed strategy enabled by defensive surveillance tactics. Information gathered by individual actors is distributed—often openly—and acted upon instantaneously by many others. This rapid-reaction model is enabled by the flat organizational structure of protest swarms, in which decision making is distributed across a network of autonomous actors. Defensive surveillance thus meets the operational objectives of protest swarms while simultaneously embodying ideological commitments to liberty and self-determination.

Notes

1. See http://www.txtmob.com.
2. Bl(A)ck Tea Society, "International Call for Action and Support (Resist the DNC)," 2004, http://blackteasociety.org (accessed December 10, 2004).
3. August 31st Republican National Convention—Direct Action Information, 2004, http://www.a31.org (accessed December 10, 2004).
4. Text messaging had, of course, played a key role in previous demonstrations, particularly in popular uprisings in Spain and the Philippines—for example, see Rafael (2003). Unlike the protests in Madrid and Manila, however, the mass mobilization against the RNC was neither spontaneous nor unexpected. Activists and law enforcement officials had planned and trained for months in anticipation of open conflict in the streets of

New York. The RNC therefore represents the first widespread *strategic* use of text messaging in street protest.

5. Given the sensitive nature of this activity, we are withholding the names of the organizations and their members.

6. For example, see Brin (1998) or Mann (2004b).

7. Starhawk, "RNC Update Number 12: Guantanamo on the Hudson," http://www.starhawk.org/activism/activism-writings/RNC_update12.html (accessed May 7, 2005).

Mobilities and Insecurities

CHAPTER 11

Borderline Identities

The Enrollment of Bodies in the Technological
Reconstruction of Borders

IRMA VAN DER PLOEG

Social security scamming appears to come low on the list of priorities for the survivor of an "anti-terrorist" operation in Turkish Kurd-
istan who leaves his village on horseback, calls on his cousins, raises
the cost of a passage to sanctuary, travels by bus and truck to Izmir
or Istanbul, buys a place on a boat to Albania and, three months later,
still in the hands of a trafficking network, is invited to step out of a
lorry on the A3 and make his way to a police station in Guildford.

J. Harding (2000)

For a poor person from a poor country the border is not just a hard
to conquer barrier, but also a place where one finds oneself over
and over again, and where one finally stays continually, [it is] what
one becomes.

Lange (1998)[1]

Introduction

In our era of globalization, national borders, paradoxically, take on renewed significance. The globalization of Western economies is reflected in the opening of national borders by the institutionalization of free trade zones and common markets: the international agreements of the North American Free Trade Agreement in North America and Schengen in Europe legalize and symbolize the opening of borders to allow freer economic exchange. Because, however, the globalization of capitalism and free trade was not really intended to redistribute wealth in a more equitable way over the various parts of the globe, the result is, one might say, a system that is more open than ever but, at the same time, in a state that is further from equilibrium than ever. The intensification of cross-border traffic of capital, goods, jobs, and certain groups of people is accompanied in the Western world with increasing anxieties regarding state integrity. Jobs and capital may flow out of the country, out of reach of national governments and their policies; uncontrollable viruses threatening crops and cattle may come in. One particular anxiety, often distastefully exploited in national politics, concerns the increased cross-border flow of people. The facilitation of the free movement of people in the European Union (EU), as agreed in Schengen, goes hand in hand with the redefinition of immigration and asylum policies regarding persons from "third countries" and an extreme fortification of Europe's external borders, particularly the ones in the east. In the United States, the facilitation of cross-border trade with Mexico and Canada is accompanied by similar coordinated efforts to strengthen the external borders, particularly the border with Mexico, through which 95 percent of illegal border crossings is said to take place (Bean et al. 1994).

On both sides of the Northern Atlantic, external borders are reconstructed in ways that can be summed up as fortification, militarization, and informatization. Technology in many different varieties is central to these processes. A literal form of fortification includes road construction and the building of walls, as was done on the United States–Mexico border in the San Diego area; militarization involves increased patrolling by rapidly rising numbers of agents and the installation of every imaginable sort of detection device, from infrared and seismic scanners to high-power lamps and CO_2 scanners to detect exhaled air in containers and trucks.

But the most powerful novelty of recent years in both U.S. and European border control policy and enforcement consists of a range of new deployments of information technology. The practice of building databases, and indefinitely keeping growing numbers of records and files on traveling citizens, migrants, cross-border commuting workers, asylum seekers, and visiting business people, is extending hand over hand. These information systems can be divided into two categories: on one hand, there are systems whose purpose is to facilitate and accelerate border crossing (passage of immigration and customs inspections, etc.) of enrolled persons whose identities and records have been checked as posing no threat to immigration laws and policies; on the other hand, there are systems aiming at recognizing and stopping (expelled) migrants and refugees from (re)entering the country. And in the post-9/11 world, the identifying and stopping of potential terrorists is added to these purposes. Both types of systems are increasingly fitted with biometric systems that unequivocally tie the individual border crosser to the records on file.

In this chapter I argue that information technologies are profoundly political instruments implicated in the fortification of external borders of the Western world. Moreover, coupled with biometric technologies, the various systems in use for regulating border traffic, border patrol, immigration, and asylum policy establish forms of identity politics that transform geographical borders into lived and embodied identities. The next section describes some of the changing practices and policies regarding the United States–Mexico border and one of the EU's external borders, the Germany–Poland border, until the accession of ten new member states on May 1, 2004. The third section describes how, specifically in Europe, one traditional way to enter the first world legally, the application for political asylum, is gradually blocked, leaving many refugees little option but to join the ranks of the criminalized "illegal aliens," or *les sans-papiers*. The central role of two biometric databases in this process, IDENT and Eurodac, is also described. The fourth section is concerned with the contrasting type of system, the one that allows specific groups of people to pass the border more easily. Here, it is argued, the use of information technologies and biometrics, such as the Immigration and Naturalization Service Passenger Accelerated Service System (INSPASS), dedicated commuter lane (DCL), and secure electronic network for travelers rapid inspection (SENTRI) in the United States, are inscribing identities on bodies as well, but with somewhat different results. The final section discusses the way information technologies, and biometrics in particular, constitute increased levels of surveillance for both Western citizens and non-Western immigrants, refugees, and visitors in ways that more often than not are practically immune to democratic controls. In that sense, the informatization of the border is generally problematic. However, the different identities produced in this generalized surveillance require a careful differential assessment of the politics of technological identification rather than a treatment of it in general terms as one phenomenon.

Changes at the Border

Obviously, technology is not effecting these changes by itself, and it is not even the main actor, though it is an important one. However, to think that technology is merely an instrument in the execution of policy and law enforcement is to ignore some important aspects relating to the particular nature of these technologies as well. The extensive use of information technologies in maintaining national borders forms part of the intensifications and changes in external border-securing policies taking place in both the United States and Europe. Although there are, of course, significant differences in historical, cultural, and political backgrounds, the similarities in the transformations taking place in the late 1990s at the border between the United States and Mexico, on one hand, and the border between Germany and Poland, on the other hand, are striking enough to speak of a common process. The subsequent events of September 11, 2001, and the enlargement of the EU in 2004 led to an acceleration of this process that leave parliaments and civil liberties groups panting behind the facts.

The United States–Mexico border[2] has seen some quite visible changes, especially at the stretches of border that were part of the operations "Gatekeeper" in San Diego, California, "Hold the Line" in El Paso, Texas, and "Safeguard" south of Tucson, Arizona. Through the border areas, which used to be just snake-ridden arid terrain and mountainous desert with steep canyons and few bushes, are now miles-long stretches of twelve-foot-high metal walls that mark the border in a way that makes words such as *iron curtain* and *Chinese wall* spring to mind.

Broad new roads were constructed along these walls purely for patrolling purposes. In densely populated areas, with very busy ports of entry such as San Ysidro at San Diego, this wall, said to be built from old portable landing strips used in Vietnam, will be supplemented with a second one, a road in between. White four-wheel-drive border patrol vehicles are positioned on overlooking hilltops everywhere as "visual deterrents" (significantly diminishing job satisfaction among the agents who do nothing but sit static for hours on end, watching the area with binoculars). High-intensity stadium lamps, night-vision scopes, and a saturation policy regarding the numbers of agents now patrolling the twelve-mile stretch of border between San Diego and Tijuana has driven those trying to cross the border further and further east into the desert—a "tactical advantage" for the border patrol, because the distance to the nearest roads may involve days of walking, with many people ending up wounded and, occasionally, dead from accidents, heat exhaustion, and hypothermia as a consequence.

A new dirt road stretching along the border from the urban area eastward provides readable signs (footprints) and is patrolled by foot, on horseback, and by car. The areas between parallel roads are equipped with infrared beams, seismic sensors (that pick up vibrations from the occasional coyote), remote-control cameras, and, on top of the added hundreds of border patrol agents, thousands of National Guard troops, uniformed and armed with M16s. All this taken together represents the transformation of the border to a highly militarized war zone where the hunting down of men, women, and children seems to take place at all costs.

During the 1990s, the German Bundesgrenzschutz (BGS) saw similar, sharp increases in budget and personnel. After the downfall of the wall, BGS activities shifted from the border with East Germany to the Oder-Neisse line. Since then the budget of the BGS rose from 1.3 billion DM in 1989 to more than 3 billion DM in 1997, and the number of personnel in the BGS climbed from 24,000 in 1992 to about 30,000 in 1998. It also recruited some 1,200 "assistants" from the local residents, who, after a 10-week course, were set to work on the border as well. Thus it became the most heavily policed border in Europe, with an "agent density" in 1996 of 2.4 per kilometer (Forschungsgesellschaft Flucht und Migration 1998).

With the expansion of the EU by 10 additional countries in May 2004, which brought the total membership up to 25 countries, a new European border of some 4,000 kilometers came into existence. It stretches from the northern Baltic states of Estonia, Latvia, and Lithuania through Poland—which has more than 1,000 kilometers of border, the longest of any of the new EU countries—down to Slovakia and Hungary. It also includes the islands of Malta and Cyprus. As a condition of entry, the EU has insisted that Poland and the other, mainly former communist, states joining the EU must improve security on their eastern borders. This involves, for example, checking 6,000 pedestrians per day at the Medyka border crossing between Poland and the Ukraine, where the smuggling of cigarettes and vodka is a popular way to make a living. The rusty old watchtowers on the Ukrainian side of the border that were once used to guard the border between the Soviet Union and the East Bloc countries are, after a fifteen-year period of an open border policy, once again in use. Electric fences and trip wires have been installed, and the EU has provided other high-tech items: Land Rovers, Honda motorbikes, night-vision goggles, and thermal cameras. The border guards have even got their own plane—a Wilga light aircraft—and a helicopter. In the unlikely event of an ambush, they have 9mm pistols and submachine guns (L. Harding 2004).

Uncomfortable as they may feel about it—the only recently won freedom of movement was much enjoyed, and the reclosing of the border has a strong negative impact on the informal economy of the region—the Polish are doing their best to meet the EU's requirements. Visas, for example, were introduced immediately. They even had a visit from a couple of

Native Americans, employed by the American border guard on the United States–Mexico border, to instruct them on how to track humans by reading signs and traces such as broken branches and footprints (Papot 2004).

Asylum Policies and Illegal Migration: IDENT and Eurodac

The changing significance of national borders is reflected in the changing boundaries between legal and illegal migration. Although the boundary between legal and illegal migration becomes harsher, the once morally and politically highly relevant boundary between economic and political refugees is being erased. Fortress Europe is building its walls so high that even victims of political persecution find it increasingly impossible to acquire what in Cold War days was routinely granted by "the free world" to anyone escaping from communist countries: political asylum.

The Belgian government, trying as hard as the other EU countries to achieve the "harmonization" of immigration and asylum policies as laid down in many EU treaties, directives, resolutions, and "high level working group" action plans, has adopted a law that fines air carriers approximately 4,000 euros for every undocumented person they fly into the country. The Dutch government adopted a bill in 1999 (Wet Ongedocumenteerden—"Law on the Undocumented") that makes it possible to refuse entry, take in detention, or instantly deport asylum seekers who are not in possession of a valid passport—it is up to refugees to prove that they are not to blame for this lack. Asylum seekers whose applications are turned down are supposed to take care of their own eviction within four weeks—arranging their own travel documents and so on. Actual eviction is the bottleneck of the so-called return policy: unidentified persons, *les sans-papiers,* cannot be evicted to their presumed country of origin, because this country will not let them back in without proven identity either. They may also be taken in detention and deprived of all sorts of support. During this period, large numbers of these people of course go underground and slip into an illegal existence, resulting in the vicious circle of being caught again, getting new eviction orders, and going underground again, while being deprived of decent work opportunities, medical care, education for their children, and often even a roof above their heads.

Enactment of Europe's newly fortified borders is extended to the migrant-generating countries as well, where immigration workers are placed at foreign embassies to restrict the issue of visas and to fingerprint those who apply. Regional containment policies are set in motion to receive refugees from war and armed conflict in relief centers and camps in neighboring countries—often hardly out of danger as the examples of Kosovo and Rwanda made horribly clear, but all the same providing arguments to refuse entry and asylum in Europe.

In the United States, to determine "credible fear," an official from the Immigration and Naturalization Service (INS) interviews asylum seekers who have been stopped at the border and held in a detention center. Tens of thousands of Cubans, Haitians, and people with many other nationalities are held in detention camps here as well. If the judgment is "not credible," then there is no appeal; the applicant appears immediately before an immigration judge, whose negative verdict results in eviction within one day. According to the director of the asylum office in Los Angeles, the number of these interviews is quite high and rising, about 150 per month in Los Angeles and 4,000 per month nationwide. It is normal, however, for people to enter the country legally and then apply for asylum. The procedure to be followed then is more elaborate and involves two moments of fingerprinting: first at the location where the application is filed and then at the asylum office during the interview there. The first set of fingerprints is used for the background check with the FBI database for criminal records and so on, and the second set is stored in the INS's database IDENT and checked for matches to potential former applications, false identities, prior evictions, and so forth. At this point in the procedure, however, only twenty "double dippers" were found in a whole year. In Europe and the United States, the vast majority of "illegal aliens" enter the country legally and simply outstay their visas. They may then take the risk of applying for asylum—and the vast majority get negative decisions and end up as illegal aliens anyway—or they do not even try for asylum and steer clear of the authorities.

Thus, one can argue, the difference between refugees and illegal migrants is more the product of Western immigration and asylum policies and laws than a difference between actual flight reasons. The traditional distinction between political and economic refugees, deemed so significant in the ideologies of the Cold War days, has lost altogether its moral appeal at the expense of the notions of legitimate refuge and asylum. The very fact of being obliged to buy the services of illegal traffickers to arrive in a safe country, or of not possessing valid identity papers, may be enough to be refused asylum, or even prevented from applying for it, and to become a de facto "illegal person." Retrying is enough to become a criminal recidivist, affirming the attitude now rapidly becoming institutionalized and legalized that every application is probably bogus.

The fading line between illegal and economic migrants, on one hand, and genuine refugees and asylum seekers, on the other, is built into the databases on asylum seekers and illegal migrants that both the United States and Europe have been building over the past years. America's IDENT and Europe's Eurodac are information systems for the storage and automated retrieval and comparison of fingerprints of asylum seekers and caught illegal migrants.

The IDENT system, which is used at more than 400 INS sites along U.S. borders with Mexico and Canada, has a database containing records on aliens who have been deported for drug smuggling or more serious crimes. Within two years of its installation in 1997, this system had grown into a database containing fingerprints and facial photographs of hundreds of thousands of people, and it was growing at a fast pace. Located in Washington, D.C., IDENT consists of two databases: the "Lookout" and the "Recidivist." The Lookout has biographic data on "criminal aliens," and the Recidivist has biographic data on anyone apprehended for illegal entry; the latter contains, after being in use for only two years, records on 1.8 million people. IDENT can be accessed from any of the INS's law-enforcing branches, such as the border patrol stations, ports of entry (including airports), and asylum offices. Although the subject had come up before September 11, it was specifically after the terrorist attacks that the integration of IDENT with other government agencies' fingerprint databases, in particular the FBI's Integrated Automated Fingerprint Identification System (IAFIS) Criminal Master File database, which currently contains some 47 million records, has become a top priority. Furthermore, under the U.S. Visitor and Immigrant Status Indication Technology (US-VISIT) program that was started in 2004, visitors to the United States are routinely fingerprinted and face scanned, thus currently feeding into IDENT some 8,000 records on a daily basis. The capacity to run checks against the FBI's IAFIS database is planned to be enhanced to enable the handling of more than 20,000 such checks by the end of 2005 (U.S. Department of Justice 2004).

Every person registered in the Lookout database is also in the IAFIS database, which can be queried on request of any law enforcement agency. The registration process begins when the INS field agents capture a photographic image of the person and live scan the index fingers, which are then enrolled in the recidivist portion of IDENT. When the field agent gets a hit, it is provided to the fingerprint examiners at the IAFIS Data Center in San Diego for confirmation with the candidate's control number. The IAFIS Data Center is not actually involved in the enrollment of IDENT data, but it queries the database and provides the data relating to the IDENT hit number and a list of dates, times, locations, and photographs relating to each prior processing at an IDENT terminal (Wright 1996). In the asylum office in Anaheim–Los Angeles, however, the examination at the IAFIS center is bypassed and matches are decided by someone in the office with no particular claim to dactyloscopic expertise.

In Europe, the European Council has installed a system called Eurodac for the purpose of storing and comparing fingerprints of all asylum seekers ages fourteen years and older (Van der Ploeg 2005). This system, consisting of a central database to which member states can send fingerprints of asylum seekers met on their territory and an automated fingerprint comparison application, is intended to find out whether the person in question has already demanded asylum on an earlier occasion or in another of the member states. Following the decisions of the Dublin Convention of 1990, a "one-chance-only" policy for asylum applications is now in place for the whole of the EU, and Eurodac is intended as the main instrument for the realization of this policy. A separate protocol to the original convention on Eurodac determines that the database was going to include the fingerprints of illegal persons found anywhere in the EU, despite the fact that some countries considered this an uncomfortable amalgam of the issues of asylum and immigration, rendering Eurodac a disproportionate instrument of immigration control. Despite this discomfort and the opinion of the European Parliament, however, the plan was not changed. What did change was its status: it changed from being a "convention," for which ratification by the national parliaments is required, to a "regulation," for which no such compliance has to be sought. The system went live on January 15, 2003. After September 11, 2001, it also became regarded as a valuable tool in combating terrorism, because it can be used to track "third-country nationals" as well.

In June 2003, as part of its conclusions on the development of a common policy on illegal immigration and external borders, the Thessaloniki European Council stated, "A coherent approach is needed in the EU on biometric identifiers or biometric data, which would result in harmonized solutions for documents for third country nationals, EU citizens' passports and information systems." Invited to prepare appropriate proposals, the commission presented in September 2003 proposals for the adoption of biometric identifiers for visa and residence permits for third-country nationals, recommending face recognition as the primary biometric key and fingerprints as a secondary one. The increased worry about illegal foreigners living within the EU's borders spurred proposals to build a Visa Information System (VIS), a central database containing data on all applications for visas to enter the EU, including biometric data. Finally, there is the Schengen Information System (SIS), which was crucial to the Schengen Convention for it to become effective. It is a database intended to help to fortify the EU's external borders and to increase confidence of nation-states to open their internal borders to each other. It contains data on illegal migrants, lost and false travel documents, wanted or missing persons, and stolen goods. As of June 2002, some 10 million people were registered in the SIS. Most entries concerned forged or stolen identity papers, but 1.3 million concerned wanted or suspected criminals (Koslowski 2003).

Open Borders for Others?

In apparent contrast to biometric systems such as IDENT and Eurodac stands a rapidly growing field of application of biometric technology that facilitates border traffic through automation of identity checking.

The INSPASS, installed now in kiosks at the airports of Los Angeles, Miami, Newark, New York (JFK), San Francisco, Vancouver, and Toronto, allows automated inspection of frequent fliers upon entering the United States. The number of airports is steadily expanding; when the system is more failure proof, locations outside the United States where the INS conducts "prescreenings" might be included. Citizens of the United States, Canada, Bermuda, and the so-called Visa Waiver Pilot Program countries (a group of countries the citizens of which do not require a visa to enter the United States, including Australia, New Zealand, Japan, and most West European countries) who travel to the United States three or more times a year or who are diplomats, representatives to international organizations, or airline crews from the Visa Waiver Pilot Program nations can enroll in the system. The INS is planning to open the program to other "nonimmigrant classes and nationalities" in years to come but feels that the system must be performing more reliably and consistently first.

At an enrollment center, located, for example, at an airport, an INS inspector conducts an interview; valid passports have to be presented and then a digital facial photograph, fingerprints, and hand geometry are collected and stored. Here it turns out that sometimes the system carries out a selection of its own. As with the IDENT fingerprinting required for the asylum procedure, here it often turns out to be impossible to acquire a usable fingerprint from an individual. According to the inspectors working with the fingerprinting technology, this is often the case with Asian women and manual laborers. Similarly, the hand geometry required for INSPASS is biased against Asian women, whose hands, more often than those of others, are "too small" for the system. The fingerprints are used for a quick background check with the FBI's IAFIS database, and the photograph and hand geometry are stored on a personalized smartcard, the "portpass." Although storage on the smartcard in principle allows for deletion of the biometric data from the central system—a fact that biometrics advocates often cite to argue the "privacy-enhancing" potential of biometrics—the biometric data are stored somewhere in the system: a lost or damaged card can be replaced without the enrollee having to stop by at the enrollment center again to provide new data.[3]

INSPASS is the addition of automated inspection to the variety of already existing portpasses and border-crossing cards that, for example, are in use at several ports of entry along the southern border with Mexico.

It is available to Mexican citizens who, living near the border, regularly cross the border for shopping or work. However, according to a study for the U.S. Commission on Immigration Reform on the effects of "Operation Hold the Line" in El Paso (Bean et al. 1994), many Mexicans, who meet the criteria for acquiring such a pass, fail to get one, because of the difficulties in presenting the required documented proof of income, address, and employment demanded by the INS. This, according to the study, is in large part attributable to cultural differences in bookkeeping and administrative practices and to the fact that in Mexico many people are employed in the informal sector beyond the reach of government regulations. According to one Mexican businessman, "In my opinion the requirements the Americans demand [for the border-crossing card] are too tough. ... The problem is all the paperwork they ask for. A lot of people meet the requirements [of financial solvency], but getting the paperwork is impossible because we don't keep our books the way they want us to" (Bean et al. 1994: 112). A Mexican local government official explained, "Unlike in the United States, in Mexico not everybody is registered with the government. ... We don't have that mechanism, that kind of registry. ... In order to get a permit to enter the United States, they ask these people for many documents. The truth is that these people do have jobs. But they can't prove it because they aren't registered in any way like the United States has with Social Security" (Bean et al. 1994: 112).

Similarly, at the port of entry at Otay Mesa, near San Diego, an experimental automated inspection lane, recognizing vehicles and passengers in it, is used mostly by businesspeople and managers going back and forth between the "maquiladoras" (assembly plants) on the Mexican side of the border and the offices of these mostly American and Japanese electronics companies located in San Diego and Los Angeles. At this particular site, an experiment was conducted in 1997–98 with biometric facial-recognition and voice-verification systems to fully automate the inspection process at the special lane (DCL) already fitted with SENTRI. During the test, participants carried a handheld device in their car. Up to four people per car then spoke a set phrase into the device while in the SENTRI lane. The driver then had to point the device to a roadside receiver in the lane, transmitting the voice clips to a computer for analysis and comparison to the stored samples for each person. A facial-recognition system, composed of a set of cameras placed at the inspection booth and focused on the driver of the vehicle, was tested. The cameras fed live video clips, recorded while the car was in motion, to a computer for analysis. The system was designed to compare the results of the video clips against the SENTRI enrollment database of photographs for all participating drivers (Wing 1998). Both systems were designed to operate without the car having to stop, the aim being to reduce the time needed per inspection, to reduce waiting times, and to facilitate cross-border traffic. However, the major problem for both systems proved to be the failure to acquire usable biometric data from moving "targets." The rate of success improved significantly if people were required to actually look at a particular camera and speak into a fixed unit along the road, but then the gain in processing time per vehicle was lost again. In other inspection situations this may not pose a problem, and the INS changed its photographing policy from taking three-quarter profiles to taking full-frontal images to improve implementation of facial-recognition systems in a variety of applications in the future (Wing 1998).

After the experiment, the DCL at Otay Mesa reverted to the half-automated inspection process, in which each participant's car is fitted with a transponder, transmitting information upon approach to the computer at the inspection booth, thus triggering the relevant files with facial photograph, name, nationality, profession, and potential copassengers to appear on the screen at the booth for an inspector to compare with what he or she sees in the lane. As with INSPASS, enrollment here requires fingerprinting for an FBI background check and the taking of a facial photograph. As with the border-crossing card, proof of employment and income must be presented.

Today, several years after these first experiments and initial programs, their functioning is called into question. The status of INSPASS at present is unclear; its rollout has stalled, many of the kiosks are not even switched on anymore, and the time required by the enrollment process appeared to severely reduce the overall gains in efficiency of the border inspection process, which was its primary purpose. With the post-9/11 prioritization of improving border security, the INS is put under pressure from the Department of Homeland Security to update its technology and accelerate implementation (McMillan 2002). At the same time, a new program called Registered Traveler, quite similar to INSPASS but meant for the security checkpoints rather than INS inspection, and the use of biometric fingerprints and iris scans instead of hand geometry are now being tested at several airports by the Transportation Security Administration. Unlike INSPASS at the time, Registered Traveler spawns quite some debate about privacy issues and the proper roles of government and business (Frank 2005).

At Europe's ports of entry, automation of inspections is not as developed as in the United States, but at Schiphol Airport, Amsterdam, an iris-scanning system called Privium, open only to those in possession of a passport of the EU, has been in operation for about two years. The name is an allusion to the notion of privilege: the system is advertised as "an exclusive membership for frequent travelers who can appreciate priority, speed and comfort." But unlike the United States, of course, the EU consists of sovereign nation-states, which renders the opening of internal borders and abolishment of border inspections a quite significant change. For people who, like me, live on a national border—living in one country and working in another, thus unavoidably crossing the border several times a day—this system has made life much easier.

Although the internal EU borders have all but disappeared—the inspection booths have literally been taken down—random checks are carried out at regular intervals some kilometers behind the former border. If an individual is stopped on such an occasion, he or she faces an inspection that is more thorough than the one that was routine before: the individual now has to answer questions about where he or she lives and what the destination is, prove that the car is properly insured and has had its yearly technical test, and so forth. In the past, a passport or even a mere look in the car was sufficient. Identity checks can now be done everywhere on European territory, a practice that was not common before the opening of borders. Thus, although the opening of borders for (generally) first world citizens undoubtedly constitutes a privilege, this privilege is to an increasing extent dependent on intensified, gradually less voluntary, identification practices.

At present this trend is intensified by the post-9/11 international endeavor, led by the United States, to increase security of national borders and air travel, recently culminating in a standard for machine readable travel documents (MRTDs), developed by the International Civic Aviation Organization (ICAO 2004). This proposal, endorsed by the U.S. government, is now in the process of being adopted by the EU, Russia, and many other countries wishing to comply with the demands of the United States. It involves the inclusion of at least one, but preferably more, biometric feature in passports and travel documents.

It is significant that in discussing whether to store biometric images or templates on the travel documents, the ICAO concludes, "Each of the above state of play situations with respect to face, fingerprint, and iris biometrics all point to storage of the image as being the only reliable globally interoperable method for guaranteeing that the receiving State can process the data provided by the issuing State against the image of the MRTD holder they capture at the border" (2004: 31). Because the international interoperability of systems for automated identity checks is an unquestioned requirement, the ICAO gives the following recommendation: "For each biometric type stored on the MRTD, storage of the image is mandatory, and storage of an associated template is optional at the discretion of the issuing State" (p. 31). This directly undermines the claims of the International Biometric Industry Association about the privacy-enhancing nature of biometric technology, which is based on the use and irreversibility of templates rather than biometric images:

> Biometrics help protect privacy by erecting a barrier between personal data and unauthorized access. Technically, biometric capture devices create electronic digital templates that are encrypted and stored and then compared to encrypted templates derived from "live" images in order to confirm the identity of a person. The templates are generated from complex and proprietary algorithms and are then encrypted using strong cryptographic algorithms to secure and protect them from disclosure. Thus, standing alone, biometric templates cannot be reconstructed, decrypted, reverse-engineered, or otherwise manipulated to reveal a person's identity. In short, biometrics can be thought of as a very secure key: unless a biometric gate is unlocked by using the right key, no one can gain access to a person's identity. (International Biometric Industry Association 2005)

Thus, in recommending the storage of biometric data instead of the use of templates for interoperability reasons, which also avoids global dependence on one particular vendor's patented algorithm to create templates, the ICAO standard undermines the biometrics industry's claim that biometrics pose no threat to privacy. In the EU, the increased threat to privacy caused by this policy is planned to be compensated for by having the biometric data stored in encrypted form, with a public key infrastructure, enabling states to choose which countries are allowed to read the data.

Without such an encryption policy, the stored biometric information will be up for grabs, because, in addition, passports and travel documents will be endowed with contactless chips or radio frequency identification (RFID) technology, as the ICAO standard proposes (ICAO 2004). RFID tags are tiny computer chips connected to miniature antennas that can be placed on or in physical objects. The chips contain enough memory to hold unique identification codes for all manufactured items produced worldwide. When an RFID reader emits a radio signal, nearby tags respond by transmitting their stored data to the reader. With passive RFID tags, which do not contain batteries, the read range can vary from less than an inch to up to twenty or thirty feet, whereas active (self-powered) tags can have a much larger read range (Steinhardt 2004). The ICAO proposal involves fitting travel documents with RFID tags that allow the reading of the digital information, including biometric information stored on the chip, at a distance. That is, anyone carrying such a document may possibly be identified without the document even needing to be presented for inspection.

It is not surprising that the ICAO standard generated an outcry of protest. In an open letter to the ICAO, cosigned by some forty international human rights and civil liberties organizations, Privacy International expressed its alarm and called on the ICAO to significantly change its position (Privacy International 2004b). Nevertheless, under pressure from the demand by the United States to countries that participate in the Visa Waiver Pilot Program to have biometric MRTDs by October 26, 2006, in accordance with the ICAO requirements, many countries are currently developing MRTDs that will include biometric information. And although the EU so far did not follow up on the advice of RFID tagging, it has proposals in place to include fingerprints in passports and to install a central database for all biometrics; it also wants to have chips with more memory space than what is required by the ICAO (Commission of the European Communities 2004). Adding this to the new policies in the United States, such as the requirement of international carriers to share personal data on all incoming travelers and the US-VISIT program mentioned previously, which involves taking and storing facial photographs and fingerprints of visitors entering and exiting the United States (Yonkers and O'Conner Kelly 2003), reveals the proportions of the current informatization processes of border traffic. All in all, if all these plans and policies are established, incredibly huge databases with biometrics of billions of people will become instruments of surveillance and control to governments around the world in the next decade.

Conclusion

Information technology is at the heart of the current reconstruction of borders. In particular the combination of biometric and database technologies is leading to an increase in surveillance, the proportions of which are hard to overestimate: faces, license plates, fingerprints, and hand geometries are registered when individuals are passing through borders, applying for visas, or requesting asylum. Linked to a host of other personal data kept on files that can be accessed from many places besides the border, this *informatization of borders* is hoped to increase control over migration and combat terrorism, while facilitating low-risk border traffic at the same time. The freedom of increased international mobility for parts of the population thus goes hand in hand with citizens becoming better known and more transparent to authorities than ever before.

Although for Western citizens borders become less and less significant, it can be argued that facilitating systems designed to reduce waiting times at border crossings and so on are part of a set of systems that, geared toward convergence and integration, ultimately turn every citizen into an object of ubiquitous forms of mostly unobtrusive but nonetheless all-pervasive tracking and surveillance practices that are often immune to democratic controls. Echelon, the Schengen Information System, VIS, SIRENE, EIS, Europol, TECS, RINIS, Eurodac, and the EU–FBI system are information systems and databases that develop largely out of public sight, and when they claim to be about state security and the fight against terrorism, they develop hardly within the reach of any privacy and data protection regimes.[4] Meanwhile they contain, produce, and enable the international exchange of personal records on more and more intimate aspects of millions of peoples' lives. In this context, border-crossing systems may only add to what have been called "globalized networks of surveillance."

Surveillance, we know since Foucault, disciplines people (Foucault 1975, 1977), and in that sense surveillance levels in Western countries increase for everyone, in many cases in ways that are in blatant contradiction with traditional democratic procedures and parliamentary controls. Although one journalist's phrase "permanent electronic detention for every citizen," uttered in the context of a public debate on biometrics, may be quite overstating the point, it is naive to suppose that far more critical attention is not needed here. A political climate in which respect for relevant basic civil and human rights is the norm may change, as many claim it did since September 11, 2001. And it should be remembered that most data protection and privacy laws can be overruled as soon as state interests, in particular economic and security interests, are deemed to be at stake.

However, according to Foucault, surveillance disciplines through the production of subjectivities and identities. Although information technologies fitted with biometric systems increase the level of border surveillance in general, they do so with divergent effects for different groups of people. Some of the systems described render the border less visible and more easily permeable, making possible highly attractive and privileged identities—the mobile, postmodern, nomadic academic, for instance, or the cosmopolitan backpacking tourist forever in search of the most amazing landscapes on the globe. Other systems, on the other hand, increase the "stopping power" of borders for particular groups of people. Geographical borders have always had different political significance for different people. As selecting gates, borders have always constituted locations where different identities, tied to highly divergent life chances, find enactment.

The use of information technologies and biometrics, however, allows policies and forms of law enforcement that not only reinforce the border in its quality as a geographical line with this particular function but also achieve something that goes beyond that. It enables the extension of the function of the border as a selective and discriminating barrier beyond the actual geographical line to the inside of the country, effectively inscribing suspect identities on peoples' now machine-readable bodies (Van der Ploeg 2005).

Added to automated border inspections at geographical lines are the possibilities for online checks with information networks that extend to anywhere in the country. By virtue of the closer link established by information technology systems and biometrics between persons and their registered identities, the border becomes, more than ever before, part of the embodied identity of certain groups of people, verifiable at any of the many points of access to increasingly interconnected databases, and so increasingly difficult to get rid of wherever they find themselves. Moreover, with this growing interconnection of databases and (international) information sharing between governmental agencies, the classification of persons as suspected rather than trusted, as high risk rather than low risk may be attached to increasingly interchangeable group profiles: being registered in Eurodac or VIS or being a Muslim, Arabic, a suspected terrorist, a political publicist, an illegal recidivist, a look-alike of a face on a watch list, or a citizen from a refugee-generating state may result in significant decreases in freedom of movement and dignified treatment. It is therefore important to remember that the surveillance practices described produce infinitely better inhabitable identities for some people than for others. The enrollment of bodies in the technological reconstruction of borders and concomitant identities, therefore, requires an ethical and political research agenda that is sensitive to these differences.

Notes

1. "Für eine/n Arme/n aus einem armen Land ist die Grenze ... nicht nur ein schwer zu überwindendes Hindernis, sondern auch ein Ort, auf den man wieder und wieder trifft, und an dem man sich schließlich ständig aufhält, zu dem man 'wird' " (Lange 1998: 11).
2. In the fall of 1999, I spent three weeks in California interviewing INS officers, inspectors, border patrol agents, and various officers at the asylum office at Anaheim–Los Angeles, the Los Angeles airport, and the Otay Mesa border crossing between San Diego and Tijuana. I also joined an officer on his border patrol in that area.
3. Enrollees are not told about this storage. The inspector I asked about this at the Los Angeles airport did not know either, until the question about replacement of lost cards settled the matter. It also is not made clear whether records are kept about dates and locations of each border crossing.
4. The European Data Protection Working Party, set up under the Directive 95/46/EC of the European Parliament and of the European Council, already published two highly critical documents on biometrics, one specifically in relation to the proposals on the use of biometrics in residence permits and visas and the establishment of a central database for this purpose (VIS) (Data Protection Working Party 2003, 2004). Judging by the repeated demand to be heard, and to be given the opportunity to analyze the plans in detail prior to any decision making, the Working Party appears to seriously doubt whether its opinions will be taken into account by European Council legislators. According to the Working Party, the very establishment of the VIS as a central database containing all biometric data gathered on individuals in the course of applying for visas is judged to be disproportionate and highly threatening to fundamental rights, so the Working Party advises against it; whether this will suffice to halt the establishment of the VIS remains to be seen. The Working Party apparently fears that it might not; it continues to specify conditions for its establishment.

CHAPTER **12**
"Divided We Move"
The Dromologics of Airport Security and Surveillance

PETER ADEY

> We are segmented from all around and in every direction. The human being is a segmentary animal. Segmentarity is inherent to all the strata composing us. Dwelling, getting around, working, playing: life is spatially and socially segmented.

> **Deleuze and Guattari (1987: 208)**

> We only need refer to the necessary controls and constraints of the railway, airway or highway infrastructures to see the fatal impulse: the more speed increases the faster freedom decreases.

> **Virilio (1986: 142)**

Introduction

The title of this chapter "Divided We Move," a phrase taken from Zygmunt Bauman's (1998) *Globalization,* perfectly summarizes how access to and the experience of movement is becoming ever diverse. Using examples from the airport terminal, I argue that inequalities are emerging in the speed by which people and things move. I present the argument that

195

these inequalities represent a logic of speed, what I call a *dromo*logic. This is produced by neoliberal politics and economics that are combined with security fears and newly developing techniques to identify and distinguish one person from the next. The result is the increasing differentiation of movement into channels of faster and slower moving speeds, particularly at airports.

In the first section I explore the ideology of neoliberalism and its tendency, through competitive Darwinian market-led forces (Bourdieu 1998), to socially sort—to discriminate between the economically desirable and the economically undesirable. Combined with heightened senses of risk and fear, flows that are identified to be economically advantageous are becoming increasingly blurred with those that are recognized to be the most safe and secure. With a mounting faith in high technology and surveillance practices as the solution to fight terrorism, surveillant sorting is becoming increasingly prevalent (Lyon 2003d). The problem is not necessarily the intrusion on privacy and the erosion of civil liberties, although these are obvious issues, but the segmentation of mobilities into slower- and faster-moving channels, creating qualitatively different and sometimes severe experiences of mobility.

I follow this argument into the travel industry, using specific examples from developments within the U.S. security regime as the everyday ramifications of these neoliberal policies and surveillance systems. Building from my own work and others on airport surveillance (Adey 2004a), technological developments within fast-border bypass schemes, postnational citizenship programs (Sparke 2004), and biometric technologies (Van der Ploeg 1999a, 1999b, 2003), I examine the cultural life of neoliberal policies through the agreements and procedures that are facilitating the speeding up of the everyday mobility of a privileged few while slowing down the movement of other perhaps less desirable and untrustworthy people, or those who simply cannot afford to pay.

Situating Dromologics

Everyday experiences of airport security and surveillance are invariably framed and driven by policies and politics. Such policies can be perhaps pinned down to a form of politics or ideology that is notoriously difficult to locate: neoliberalism. Many commentators are beginning to notice how *neoliberalism* has become an all-encompassing successor term for *globalization*—leaving out the specificity and variations over which policies and practices take place. As the geographer Wendy Larner notes,

> We have moved from analyses of globalisation to analyses of neolib-
> eralism, but our labels continue to obscure the details and complex-
> ity of the processes involved. (Larner 2003: 509)

Neoliberalism has come to be seen as a coherent ideology owing its origins
to a Reagan and Thatcherite genesis (Peck and Tickell 2002; Peck 2004).
It is seen as the framing ideology that runs through the dominant transnational institutions such as the International Monetary Fund, the World
Bank, and the nation-states that it attempts to integrate and surpass.

Dominant approaches to neoliberalism have highlighted several particular characteristics. In terms of government, neoliberalism is seen as
a destructive project to "roll back" state regulation and indeed state service provision (Peck and Tickell 2002). Private companies are seen as more
efficient providers of services, taking advantages of "market opportunities." Controls over big business and corporations are shrunk considerably. Furthermore, state deregulation and privatization are expected to
work in tandem with the economic liberalization of trade. Treaties such
as the North American Free Trade Agreement are intended to tear down
the barriers to commerce so that people, capital, and goods may circulate
with comfort and without hurdles. Indeed, mobility, and the freedom of
movement, is woven into the neoliberal agenda, as much as it has been a
dominant ideological characteristic of nation-states and indeed extrana-
tional agreements and treaties. As Cresswell (2001: 22) writes, "The idea of
liberty and the idea of mobility have long been intertwined."

Yet as Doreen Massey (1991) argues, there is a danger in romanticizing
movement and reducing the differences and variations between mobilities to a process such as time–space compression. The equitable rhetoric
of movement is also rarely delivered. Mobilities can be *made* uneven; they
can be divided, segmented, or differentiated.

Such processes have been commonplace, particularly within Western
societies, as states, the traditional providers of infrastructural amenities,
have gradually "unbundled" their provision of services to the consumer's
door (S. Graham and Marvin 2001). The privatization of these services
and networks to corporate hands has seen the increasing collapse of the
modernist ideal of universal provision for all. The Darwinian competitive
characteristic of neoliberalism (Bourdieu 1998) sees private-sector service
providers "cherry pick" selected premium customers over less desirable
ones through an "infrastructural consumerism" (S. Graham 2000, 2002).
Improved and speedy infrastructural services are selectively provided to
premium customers, whereas reduced quality services are being offered
to others. The flows of water, electricity, and information are progressively
more segmented as differential access is offered to particular consumers.

In the context of cities, car drivers may buy the speed of their mobility through price-driven toll roads managed by Intelligent Transportation Systems. For instance, Stephen Graham and Simon Marvin (2001) and Holmes (2004) illustrate how access to decongested road space is priced and bought in examples such as the I-15 highway to San Diego in the United States and the CityLink project in Melbourne in Australia. Cyberspace is not immune to these differentiations, becoming itself another border (Marx 1997). Winseck (2003) illustrates how Internet users' data packets and bandwidth privileges may be identified through "technologies of discrimination." Internet service provider systems are being designed so that once the data packets are identified, they may be expedited and sped up. Other technologies are able to apply different bandwidth levels to different customers. Thus, premium customers experience faster and improved access.

But these disparities are occurring not only in the movement of cars and material and immaterial services, but also in transnational migrations and large global-scale mobilities where the differentiation of movement is increasingly tied to the differentiation of people (see also Hyndman 1997; Mitchell 2001: 181; Beaverstock 2002). Borders become the key sites from which to differentiate and sort some mobilities from others. Borders such as ports and airports become "permeable boundaries" (D. Wood and Graham forthcoming), conical-shaped sieves that force travelers to move through their space, while filtering wanted from unwanted flows (J. Anderson 2002). Thus, although neoliberal policies and economics open up borders and boundaries to mobilities through security and surveillance regimes, they do so in an incredibly uneven and differential way.

To differentiate between things, whether they be people, passengers, goods, animals, or weapons, requires identification. To differentiate services, businesses must be able to categorize their clients and separate them from one to the next. They must identify. Here, surveillance techniques are used to find differences between people, to sort them from others. Passports and codifications of the body are probably the most ancient of techniques (Torpey 2000; Salter 2003, 2004). Yet "dataveillance" is probably now the most ubiquitous. Service providers collect reams and reams of information on their customers and potential consumers, developing what is now well known as the "surveillant assemblage" (Haggerty and Ericson 2000). And yet, surveillance has become not just a passive tool for watching and identifying people but instead an active agent in the control and differentiation of mobile bodies, affecting their future decision-making abilities and choices (Lyon 2003d).

According to Oscar Gandy, a "panoptic sort" is occurring. He writes that in collecting swathes of information, surveillance systems are "used to coordinate and control their access to the goods and services that define life in modern capitalist economy" (Gandy 1993: 15; see also Elmer 2004). Thus as surveillance systems identify and differentiate people into informational categories, it is becoming increasingly clear that the surveillance systems are self-fulfilling prophecies, as their striations and categorizations are becoming overlain and reproduced upon society (Adey 2004b). According to Lyon these determine "who should be targeted for special treatment, suspicion, eligibility, access and so on." The system therefore "sieves and sorts for the purposes of assessment, of judgement. It thus affects people's lifestyles choices" (Lyon 2003c: 20).

Systems that were previously thought of as immune to society and politics are now being viewed as the ramifications of neoliberal political agendas. Stephen Graham (forthcoming) discusses how the Western world is increasingly "software-sorted." Politics, values, opinions, and more become embedded within the codes and categories that make these systems (Bowker and Star 1999). We are living in a "software-sorted society" (S. Graham 2004b), where people are separated through coded mediations such as intelligent transportation systems and algorithmic surveillance.

However, those who are sped up and slowed down are incredibly interrelated. Graham and Wood make this clear in their analysis of surveillance and information and communication technology (ICT) systems in an urban context:

> Within the context of the widespread privatisation of urban and mobility spaces across the world, software-sorting techniques are being socially shaped in two very different ways. On the one hand, the surveillance and monitoring capacities of ICTs are being shaped to prioritise and enhance the power and mobilities of privileged human bodies within the many scales of global, neoliberal capitalism. On the other, ICTs are being configured to *add* friction, barriers or logistical costs to the mobility and everyday lives of those deemed by dominant states or service providers to be risky, unprofitable, or undeserving of mobility. (D. Wood and Graham forthcoming)

Indeed, although these movements are sorted and processed through the latest security and surveillance techniques, the very need for and rationale behind the differentiation of movement progressively conflates issues of security and control with capital and consumerism. Matthew Sparke (2004) convincingly demonstrates how this is becoming the case for citizenship by using examples from the United States–Canada border regimes. Here, travelers may receive expedited mobility if they join specific citizenship programs. Yet their entry is decided on the basis of judgments over their "economic" security and furthermore "national" security. For Sparke, this reflects a new type of transnational citizenship that is offered to those who can afford it, what Calhoun describes as a "consumerist citizenship" (Calhoun 2003), or Hindess describes as a "neo-liberal citizenship" (Hindess 2002). This is what Sparke usefully labels a "neoliberal nexus" (forthcoming), as the dual and somewhat paradoxical necessities of free market economic trade and a nationalistic homeland security are focused on the border, supporting "a new political economy of consumer citizenship and individualized mobility and consumption" (S. Graham and Wood 2003: 234).

In short, my argument so far has been that implicit to security and surveillance regimes is a logic of speed and difference encouraged by neoliberal economics and politics. This is a logic of speed in that these regimes are often created to speed up things, such as trade, the movement of people, or security processing. But speed is also related to difference in that the regimes are based on the separation of mobilities into faster and slower moving groups. As I explore further, this happens often at the expense of other travelers, reproducing already existent inequalities or working to create new ones. Let us look in more detail at examples from airports in Canada and the United States to explore the ramifications of this dromo-logic on everyday airport life.

Speeding Up Airport Security

It is poignant that the social theorist Ulrich Beck (2001) points to neoliberalism as a primary contributor to 9/11—what he calls "Globalization's Chernobyl." Beck not only attributes blame to U.S. geopolitical foreign policy or globalization, but also finds that the answer lies in the liberalization of the travel industry. One example is the privatization of U.S. airport security, where he notes that some members of the highly flexible and part-time workforce earn even less than if they were to work in a fast-food restaurant.

Although international treaties have liberalized the movement of people and trade, the industries that support these agreements have become further privatized and deregulated. Take, for example, the U.S. aviation industry, which underwent enormous changes in the late 1970s through deregulation. The ruthless streamlining of airlines and the bloodbath of competition that followed saw the rationalization of airport security, which was controlled by the airlines (Martin 1993). Border crossing became a corporate affair. Yet the "rollback" of the state provision of border controls and security has, since 9/11, been restructured and redirected toward a creative "rollout," reflecting a "deeply interventionist agenda" (Peck and Tickell 2002).

The culture of speed begins here. At a policy level, speed was one of the main priorities of the U.S. Congress to federalize airport security under the Transportation Security Administration (TSA). The TSA was set up in November 2001 under the Aviation and Transport Security Act as a sharp response to 9/11. That said, private contractors continued to operate at five U.S. airports.

Although federal security services have been rolled out, the TSA is working closely with other partner groups in an attempt to roll back and secure limited contracts of private security services through the Screening Partnership Program, also known as "opt out." Moreover, they are working with and attempting to integrate with other elite and frequent traveler schemes that go on within airport and other border-crossing zones.

Federal security agencies are beginning to behave like business entities, privileging valued and premium customers as they come under pressure from business travelers and corporate America to treat passengers in a way that is other than universal. According to Stephan Graham, "Highly mobile and affluent business travellers can, increasingly, directly bypass normal arrangements for immigration and ticketing at major international airports" (2004a: 171). Using Paul Andreu's notion of tunneling, Graham explains how elite passengers can burrow through slow and laborious airport processes, whereas other not-so-affluent passengers must endure them.

Let us take one of the most written about bypass schemes: the Immigration and Naturalization Service Passenger Accelerated Service System (INSPASS) run by the U.S. Customs and Border Protection (CBP).

Passing the Border

INSPASS has been in place since 1996, and it is intended to accelerate border processing for authorized members of the scheme. People who are eligible are expected to be those traveling to the United States on business three or more times a year; they could be diplomats, representatives of international organizations, or airline crews, for example. Moreover, they must be citizens of the United States, Canada, or Bermuda or be legal permanent residents of the United States, although certain landed immigrants in Canada and citizens of countries involved in the Visa Waiver Program are also eligible.

The system works on the principle of preclearance. Preapproved passengers have had background checks and have provided further information. A preapproved traveler uses this system by arriving at the port of entry and proceeding to the INSPASS queue. Once at the front of the queue, the traveler inserts the INSPASS PortPASS card into the INSPASS automated kiosk. The traveler may then be invited to place his or her hand in a hand-geometry reader. This image is then compared with that recorded when the passenger enrolled. If the image is a match, the traveler will be printed a receipt and may make his or her way to baggage claim. It is expected that INSPASS will accelerate most users' passage to around fifteen to twenty seconds; the quickest passage could take eleven seconds. The system is currently available at four international airports in the United States and in two preclearance sites in Canada. However, the program is also linked to the Department of Homeland Security's perceived threat levels, so if the level reaches the "Threat Condition Orange," INSPASS is suspended.

NEXUS Air

Systems such as NEXUS, part of the U.S.–Canadian Smart Border scheme, are also moving into air travel mobilities with a pilot program that will operate until April 30, 2006. The scheme is an expansion of the land-border program explored previously by Sparke (2004). In Sparke's deconstruction of the postnational citizenship that underlies the NEXUS system, the successor to the Peace Arch Crossing Entry (PACE) system, the border has become bifurcated by emphasizing the dual purposes of increasing mobility for trade while reducing the threat of terrorism. Following the PACE system, NEXUS is designed to quicken the "pace" (Sparke 2004) of its precleared members while slowing down and making it harder for others.

NEXUS Air works on the same premise of prescreening and preapproving passengers so that they may proceed through airport processing with "little or no delay." These passengers are also obligated to pay a $50 fee for a year's membership. In this scheme, similar to the Privium program used at Schiphol Airport in Amsterdam, passengers must preenroll by having their iris recorded and their personal information taken. Upon entry to the United States or Canada, passengers may then physically bypass the security lanes that ordinary travelers must queue in, as NEXUS Air passengers are fed to the automated kiosks in the Federal Inspection Services area (U.S. preclearance) or the Canadian Inspection Services area. Not only are NEXUS passengers spatially sorted from others through these systems but they also experience automated questioning. Furthermore, if departing from the Vancouver airport, members of the scheme are also able to accelerate through security screening by gaining access to the priority lane.

The issues not only of speed differentiation within the airport terminal but also of how these elite bypass programs are integrated into other schemes such as priority lounges, car hire, car parking, and even connecting train links need to be considered (S. Graham and Marvin 2001; S. Graham 2004a).

Although these systems use spatial segregation and automated methods to increase the mobility speed of the low-risk or trusted passengers, they also work on the principle that the mobility of higher-risk passengers is slowed down. Thus they state:

> NEXUS Air also allows CBP officers and CBSA officials to concentrate their efforts on potentially higher-risk travelers and goods, which will help to ensure security and integrity at our borders. (CBP 2004)

The relationship between different airport mobilities must be seen here, for the possibility increases that passengers who are determined to be higher risk may be consequently slowed down by the increased time officers have to question them.

Registered Traveler

This trend is set to continue with other schemes that are focused less on immigration queues and more on relieving security wait times for select passengers. The "registered traveler program," piloted by the TSA in the summer of 2004 in several U.S. airports, is one case in point. The program, active at Boston, Los Angeles, Washington National, Houston, and Minneapolis–Saint Paul airports, is designed to help passengers bypass not immigration lines but security procedures. The program marks a minor shift from the criticized "trusted traveler" scheme. As Edward Hasbrouck notes:

> The name was changed (although not the essentials of the concept) to avoid the implication that registered travellers would be "trusted" and thus would automatically bypass security screening. That wouldn't do: the TSA thinks no one can be trusted. Registered travellers will still be treated with suspicion—they just won't be treated quite as suspiciously as unregistered travellers. (Hasbrouck 2004)

The program is intended for and was offered only to frequent fliers and priority members such as Northwest Airlines' "Platinum Elite Frequent Fliers." The Electronic Privacy Information Center (EPIC), an organization devoted to questioning the privacy implications of electronic media and information, has raised worries over this program in particular. In its comments to the TSA, EPIC questioned not only the privacy implications of the system but also how the "criteria for granting special 'status' to some travelers raises significant questions about the equity of the program and whether it would contribute to creating inequality in society" (EPIC 2003).

The assumption that frequent and high-fare-paying loyal customers are more trustworthy than others seems woven into the fabric of these schemes as they determine that some passengers are more trusted than others. Again there is a trade-off here. Passengers are required to *volunteer* background checks. They give their name, address, phone number, and date of birth, along with biometric identifiers. The TSA then conducts a security assessment of each volunteer. The TSA also confers with law enforcement and intelligence agency databases and makes checks of outstanding criminal warrants.

The subsequent movements of these registered elite members through the airport is meant to be substantially sped up (McGee 2004). It has been reported that members of the scheme may be able to avoid the procedures of removing shoes and coats and may be exempt from pat-down searches. Moreover, in some airports it may even be possible for the passengers to take entirely different routes through the terminal space. According to one report, members can even use the security channels and bypasses reserved for airline and airport staff (Burkeman 2004). The improved speed of the registered traveler, although free at the moment to only those selected, is expected to cost between $50 and $100 when the scheme is implemented properly.

However, these sped-up mobilities are not independent of the slower-moving economy ticket passengers. The registered elite passengers' movement is ever dependent on the slowing down of the less privileged. Although the TSA claims that allowing the registered passengers to bypass security systems will work to relieve congestion given the increased staff levels available for unknown or "high-risk" passengers, Edward Hasbrouck notes:

> Once travellers have the "choice" of registering and having all their movements logged, in exchange for avoiding the longer, slower, and more immediately intrusive "unregistered traveller" screening lanes, the treatment of the unregistered will likely be made sufficiently unpleasant, or at least sufficiently slow, that few who qualify for registration won't "choose" it. And if you don't want to register, you'll still be able to travel (for now, at least), as long as you show up at the airport three or four hours before your flight. (Hasbrouck 2004)

People effectively buy their speedy mobility at the expense of other slower-moving people. It is problematic, however, that some are unable to afford this speed. They may be ineligible to join frequent flier clubs. They may come from the wrong country or fail the inspectors' prescreening checks that could afford them a "low-risk" status. We may be left with two scenarios. First, in expediting frequent travelers who join the programs, standard travelers whose movement is slowed even more may feel forced to join registered traveler programs out of mere frustration. Second, for the elite bypass schemes to work effectively, there may be a cap applied to membership volume. Thus, the cost of membership of these programs may rise with demand, pricing people out of the programs to ensure a consistent speed of travel for those who can afford it. However, although slowing down some economy passengers may ignite class resentments and petty differences, there is the more serious issue of those who are then scrutinized more intently and slowed down more severely and intrusively by the very same surveillance technologies and procedures. Such concerns are most persistently evoked with regard to the TSA's use of passenger profiling systems discussed elsewhere.

Preemption

It is also worth mentioning how the differentiation of physical mobility in airports is reinforced by the speeding up of the systems that support it. The "technological fix" of surveillance systems to form solutions to our problems has dominated aviation security procurement and research. As many writers have described, technology has often been granted an almost religious or messianic place, particularly in the context of air travel (Corn 1983). Although security screening has become federalized, the TSA has created many other opportunities for security firms and technology developers. As David Lyon writes:

> There is tremendous commercial pressure to purchase new surveillance equipment. The current situation is seen as an unprecedented business opportunity by some who have seen their share prices rise several-fold since 9/11. American security companies in particular are hawking their wares around the world in the hope of taking advantage of the political climate of anti-terrorist activity. (Lyon 2003b: 84)

Contracts to provide the technology have so far been lucrative. The biometric technology provided for the U.S. Visitor and Immigrant Status Indicator Technology (US-VISIT) has led to the creation of a contract worth around $10 billion to the Accenture-led consortium (Wired 2004). The group, including corporations such as Raytheon, Dell, Sprint, and AT&T, has provided items such as inkless fingerprint-capturing systems and digital photography.

Indeed it is hardly surprising that corporations are lining up to secure contracts with the government, considering the potential rewards that have culminated in the "homeland security conference" and the increasing importance and focus on security technologies at aviation conferences and exhibitions (Dotinga 2004). Moreover, companies previously involved in unrelated technological developments such as CT scanners used at hospitals are suddenly finding their products have more profitable uses (T. Anderson 2005).

Following the military discourses that religiously emphasize the speed of information to increase strategic advantage (Haggerty forthcoming), accelerating speed through technology has been seen as a way to improve the efficiency of security while further expediting the mobility of the "kinetic elites." The speed of passengers' physical mobility is then paired with the speeding up of the information about them. Data captured by flight reservation systems and other sources are transferred prior to the passengers' arrival at their port of entry through records known as personal name records (Lyon 2003a; Bennett 2006).

Previously these records have been used in several of the notorious schemes known as Computer Assisted Passenger Pre-Screening (CAPPS) and CAPPS II, which were used to profile and categorize passengers according to their risk status, based on aspects of their racial group, country of origin, and destination (see Curry 2004 for a review of such systems). Increasingly, however, current systems are working on the premise not of presumption but of preemption. Since 9/11, airlines flying to the United States have been required to provide passenger and crew manifest data to the CBP for advanced processing in the Advanced Passenger Information System, which includes information stored in the personal name records or captured using machine-readable passports and tickets handed over at airport check-in counters and the departure gates. This information is then transferred electronically within fifteen minutes of a flight's departure. Upon receiving this data, the CBP uses the surveillant assemblage of the Interagency Border Inspection System to compare names and information to twenty-one other federal agencies and the FBI National Crime Information Center wanted-persons database (CBP 2003). On the basis of this information, the CBP may then make preemptive strikes on suspect passengers, either delaying their flight while more details are collected or even, in the well-publicized case of the artist formerly known as Cat Stevens (Kehaulani Goo 2004), diverting the flight to remove passengers before they even reach the airport of their destination.

It can be argued that the immediacy of this information may increase the amount of time given by security and immigration officers to "deliberate democratically" over the risk of one's entry. This departs from Virilio's (1986) provocative critique of the speed of the war machine to transmit instantaneous information that is acted upon with split-second decisions (Haggerty forthcoming). Yet the possible positive role of these speed systems, so often construed in negative dimensions (Connolly 2000), is problematic given that this information has previously been obtained without passengers' knowledge or permission, that it can be shared between multiple databases and users, and that deliberations over passengers' worthiness to enter the United States can be based solely on this information. Indeed, the effect of this acceleration can be the extreme deceleration for those declared to be risky.

Mark Salter (2004) has written about the delocalization of the border through a wider extension of the security and inspection regime. Perhaps these systems change not the spatiality but the *temporality* of the border, so that inspection deliberations take place before passengers even reach their destinations.

A Politics of Speed

What I have tried to show in this chapter is that the inequalities evident in airport security are reflective of wider societal changes to sort or differentiate movement into fast- and slow-moving groups. These societal stratifications are driven by a neoliberal political and economic agenda that increasingly conflates economic security with homeland security. It is problematic that although these programs tend to price people out of faster speeds of movement, there are also direct relations between these differential mobilities and more serious implications than queuing up for a long time or having to park far away from the terminal. For some people to be mobilized faster, it is sometimes necessary to make the mobility of others slower. As Saulo Cwerner writes on the topic of the "time politics" of asylum, "There is an unavoidable conflict between speed and democracy" (Cwerner 2004: 83). Although this has resulted in the freedom of mobility for some, for others this may mean more intensified forms of direct scrutiny, such as strip searches, interrogation, incarceration, and deportation, and more sustained forms of immobility. As Massey writes, "Differential mobility can weaken the leverage of the already weak" (Massey 1991: 240).

In recent studies, the scale of mobility has been seen as the deciding factor (Bauman 1998). The elite corridors of the business world resemble the exclusionary spaces of the gated community or business enclave. As Castells supports, there seems to be a growing number of transnational elites who enjoy these forms of mobility within highly segregated corridors of travel and work. He writes:

> Elites are cosmopolitan, people are local. The space of power and wealth is projected throughout the world, while people's life and experience is rooted in places. ... There is the construction of a (relatively) secluded space across the world along the connecting lines of the space of flows: international hotels whose decoration, from the design of the room to the color of the towels, is similar all over the world to create a sense of familiarity with the inner world, while inducing abstraction from the surround world; airports' VIP lounges, designed to maintain the distance *vis-à-vis* society in the highways of the space of flows. (Castells 1996: 415–17)

The motion of these kinetic elites is far reaching and long distant in comparison to that of the kinetic underclasses whose movements are perhaps local and shorter (Beaverstock, Hubbard, and Rennie Short 2004).

However, I wonder if it really is that simple. As Cresswell (2001) demonstrates, in the airport terminal an array of mobilities of airport workers, taxi drivers, homeless people, security personnel, flight attendants, migrants, and more coincide, more often than not to serve the elites—what could be labeled under Arjun Appadurri's terminology an "ethnoscape" (1990). Being "locally tied" or merely being able to move is too straightforward a description (Bauman 1998). Indeed, the kinetic underclasses may move in the same networks as the elites, although perhaps not in the same luxury. Of course, stories are abundant of economic migrants who are smuggled in suitcases and by other means. Sparke (2005) has shown the terrible irony of how a Gulfstream 5 jet, normally for the use of corporate executives and business elites, has been used to deport terror suspects to other countries with questionable human rights records by extraordinary rendition for "torture by proxy." As Ulf Hannerz suggests, "Being on the move ... is not enough to turn one into a cosmopolitan" (1990: 241). Rather it is the speed and, possibly more important, the control over and quality of movement that indicates these differences.

This does not mean that a politics of speed is necessarily a new phenomenon, for it has been shown historically how a dromological spatial politics was woven into British postwar planning. For Hubbard and Lilley, "Dromocrats (not technocrats) attempt[ed] to speed some things up by slowing others down" (2004: 277). We might argue, however, that neoliberal politics and economics are intensifying these inequalities through new agreements, changing structures of governance and a reliance on the instantaneity of technology and informational mobility.

Graham and Wood state, "Critical social policy research must work to expose the ways in which these systems are being used to prioritize certain people's mobilities ... while simultaneously reducing those of less favoured groups" (S. Graham and Wood 2003: 232). Although we try to think of the world, security, and surveillance in more mobile terms (Bennett and Regan 2004), we must also work to distinguish differential mobilities to see how they are *made* different. In this chapter, I have sought to do this through the language of speed, exposing different and interacting movements of varying velocities.

CHAPTER **13**

Why Where You Are Matters
Mundane Mobilities, Transparent Technologies,
and Digital Discrimination

DAVID LYON

Keeping Track, in Transit

Howard Boyle, the president of a fire sprinkler installation company in Woodside, New York, sends his workers out to sites where systems are established or serviced. In 2003 he gave five such workers company phones with a GPS (global positioning system) feature, though he did not tell them about the latter. He can now check if they have arrived at a site and whether they are moving around or sitting still. He hopes that he will be able to sort out billing queries where installation times are disputed, and he boasts that he can call his workers to ask "where are you now?" while looking at a screen that tells him just that (Harmon 2003).

Keeping track of where people are has always been important for families, employers, and authorities. They want to know that children are safe, workers are busy, and citizens are living lawfully. In the modern era, with its bureaucratic organizations and high mobility rates, schools, government departments, marketers, and law enforcement and emergency services also want to know where people are—as students, claimants, consumers, offenders, and accident victims. Anxiety, care, distrust, and opportunism can be strong incentives to find ways of finding people, of locating them at specific times.

In the past decade, the ability to trace people's whereabouts while in transit has grown enormously and very fast. Howard Boyle simply would not have been able to keep track of his employees by mobile (or cell) phone in the early 1990s,[1] and parents would not have been able to fit monitoring devices in their children's cars or in the pockets of their own parents afflicted with Alzheimer's. Tracing parolees by satellite would have sounded like science fiction, and posting invitations by text message to potential customers passing near Starbucks would have sounded like a marketer's fantasy. All these things now happen.

However, these tracking technologies develop, not because of some supposed "logic of technology" but because of an ongoing negotiation between social entities—cultural, economic, political—and social-technical systems. Although many analysts focus on the fast-moving, fragmented, and disembodied aspects of contemporary cultures, it is worth noting that those most affected by mobile technologies (above all I have in mind the mobile or cell phone) use them in relation to very mundane aspects of life. Indeed, e-mail addresses and phone numbers constitute fixed coordinates for relationships within the apparently blurred world of motion.[2]

It is a truism that some earlier technical innovations have contributed in extraordinary ways to fresh patterns of social relationship. The clock and the computer, mundane though they seem today, are paramount examples of such "exotic" technologies. Publicly coordinated synchronic time permits all manner of convenient meetings and management procedures, from school schedules to train timetables. Clocks became a vital part of the capitalist enterprise, particularly for measuring labor time down to the minute and thus for controlling workers. Computers, too, have contributed enormously to the surveillance capacities of all major social institutions, as an aspect of increasing efficiency and productivity.[3] These taken-for-granted technologies have far-reaching implications for power relations within the modern, bureaucratic, capitalistic contexts where they were developed.

In some similar ways, mobile technologies already show signs of being singularly significant within emerging patterns of "liquid" social life (Bauman 2001, 2005). Mobile technologies enter the empty gaps in social life, areas once thought of as "dead" time used for travel, and bring them back to life. As Nicola Green (2002: 290) says, such "Lazarus time" may be resurrected for family or business purposes. But it can equally be resurrected for surveillance purposes. Indeed, the surveillance aspects are the hidden side of what appear on the surface to be new freedoms—to be in touch anywhere and to make positive uses of those "dead" moments. It is a paradox that mobility was seen by modern sociologists, such as Georg Simmel, as liberating. People could stroll the streets of the big city anonymously, freed from the constraints of the villagers' watchful eyes (Simmel 1971). Today, movement in urban spaces is no longer a means of evading the gaze.

Mobile technologies both facilitate and inhibit mobility by easing open or closing off the channels of flow of persons, objects, and data. Although they may be linked with global systems, these mobile technologies are triggered or activated by their users. John Urry suggests, creatively, that in the twenty-first century it is appropriate to think of cars and mobile phones, for example, as "inhabited machines" that "come to life" as people use them (Urry 2001). To inhabit such machines is to be connected with sites across the world, which is an important aspect of globalization, helping to make the world feel like "one place." What Urry observes but does not elaborate is that "simultaneously such sites can monitor, observe and trace each inhabited machine."

It is such monitoring, observing, and tracing that I explore in this chapter. "Where you are" matters increasingly from the point of view of contemporary regimes of governance. Mobile phones, in conjunction with other technologies such as GPS, may be used to monitor, observe, and trace their users continuously and in real time. In this way, surveillance capacities are enhanced in various systems (intended to map the travels of consumers, employees, or citizens, for example). In particular, the number of points of contact between systems and subjects grows, with consequences for power relations between the two (Rule 1973; Lyon 1994: 51–52). Although mobiles may have unforeseen positive consequences for democratic processes, they may equally offer opportunities for the enhancement of other kinds of power. Surveillance—as monitoring, observing, and tracing—is not necessarily negative, but power relations are always present, for better or for worse.

As mobility is monitored more and more, it is easy to be distracted by the "privacy" debate. Let me put the question of privacy on one side at the outset. Some of the issues surrounding mobile telephony have to do with overheard conversations, and in this sense "privacy" seems to be a relatively trivial matter for many. Public places and mass transit systems are often alive with uninhibited, so-called private conversations. Other issues, more seriously, may relate to the extent to which the content of calls may be intercepted by unauthorized (or even authorized) others. This raises privacy questions of an informational rather than a place-based type. In this case, expectations and legal requirements—lawful access—are also significant. But the focus in this chapter is different again and does not start with privacy questions.

212 • David Lyon

Beyond the issue of the privacy of mobile communications lie questions of governance. Governance refers most broadly to modes of governing populations whether or not the nation-state is involved. Social order is achieved and maintained in myriad ways in contemporary societies, and what I refer to as "surveillance" has to be considered as one such way. Conventionally, surveillance was thought of as the practices of watching specific persons for specific purposes in specific, usually bounded, places (such as the "panopticon" prison). Today, in part because of its reliance on electronic technologies, surveillance is generalized across populations, for numerous, overlapping purposes, and in virtual and fluid "spaces" (see, e.g., Haggerty and Ericson 2000). As Majid Yar suggests, these now include "mobile, nomadic forms of control that utilize coded information to monitor, predict and direct the behaviour of individuals" (Yar 2003: 257) that are outside the old fixed panoptic spaces in what Giorgio Agamben calls "zones of indistinction" (Agamben 1997).

Although this chapter began with an example from production, it is more likely to be in the realm of consumption that mobile surveillance will be most manifest. As Mark Andrejevic argues, it is "m-commerce" that is becoming a dominant site of mobile surveillance, where the most mobile are also likely to be the most surveilled (Andrejevic 2004). At the same time, two other features should also be noted. First, although the analytic distinction between production and consumption may still hold, the processes discussed here help to blur those boundaries. Surveillance moves increasingly freely across and between those once more distinct realms. Second, the fact that commercial data may be most prominent in mobile surveillance does not exclude their use for law enforcement and other "state-related" purposes. Indeed, as a current example, the "war on terror" frequently uses commercial data in sorting for suspects (see O'Harrow 2005; Lyon 2003b).

Mundane Mobilities

Many people, young and old, women and men, in many countries now use mobile phones more than they use the Internet. The mobile phone offers person-to-person contact based on assumed constant availability (Wellman 2001). There is a sense of ordinariness of life with mobile phone use, especially if these devices are commonly visible—and audible—on the streets and in public transport in urban areas. Overheard conversations—or split conversations—are often about very mundane matters. People report their progress in traffic or at stations, or arrange meetings, or simply discuss exactly the same kinds of things that are discussed on landline phones.

Indeed, they often offer information about where they are, as reassurance or as a reason why they will miss the meeting.

The content of mobile calls may at times be of interest to parties other than the caller and called, but this does not seem to produce much care about what is said, even when intimacies are shared in very public places. Being audible and overheard by others is clearly an issue that relates to the context, so one might ask why locational data matters in one setting but not another. The answer suggested here is that locational data as consciously revealed by the phone user is unlikely to be thought of in surveillance terms, unless a fear—such as stalking—is brought into the picture. But locational data revealed by the device (rather than consciously by the person) is more likely to be regarded negatively when it is known about.

Much social analysis of mobile phones has examined behaviors and etiquette surrounding mobile culture. Sadie Plant (2001), for instance, compares several cities around the world, looking at uses of the mobile. The constant question (over)heard is "where are you?" but this is a personal, not usually a surveillance, question. She comments on the truism that landlines connected urban areas and nations of modernities, whereas mobiles appeared for a new—perhaps late- or postmodern—world of movement, of tourists and travelers, businesspersons and refugees, students and workers. Although this can be dismissed as soft technological determinism—it is mobile phones, inter alia, that help constitute the postmodern world as such—there is also an important sociological point here. In a general sense, in situations where mobility is lower than it is in the affluent and technologically advanced countries today, it is assumed that we know (more or less) where people are. Key means of communication today, such as e-mail and the mobile phone, do not yield any clues to the called party about the location of the person communicating. But such data are of interest to third parties; indeed, as we shall see there is potential economic (and other) benefit associated with those data.

Mobiles are used for mundane purposes. One can argue that the technologies are socially shaped by an era of growing mobility, even as that mobility is further enabled by them. In a world in which travel has become easier and quicker and covers larger terrains, and in which many things are done at a distance, corporations are in a constant quest for the means of connectivity. Customers are grateful when developing devices offer the chance to stay in touch despite dislocations of distance and schedules. If for some analysts the world is one of increasing disintegration and fragmentation, mobile technologies offer opportunities for holding things together, even if they require new skills to operate them (Agar 2003). This may mean that places change their meaning and significance or, possibly, that the means of communication become more significant.

What this assumes, however, is that the means of "holding things together" is created for the benefit of the consumer, the mobile user. However, the market for consumer data has grown hugely in recent decades, such that today the industries seeking to process personal data for a variety of purposes are valued in the multibillion-dollar range. With respect to locational data, a number of market analysts expect a large-scale growth (to hundreds of billions of dollars in some accounts) in traffic over the next few years, although as with any such market forecasts, considerable variation appears (Lyon, Marmura, and Peroff 2005). The aim, these analysts say, is to use locational data for mainly economic purposes, to exploit them for more precisely targeted marketing. In other words, it is above all marketers who will be better enabled to hold things together as they use locational data to coordinate their contacts with potential consumers.

It can be objected that in the case of GPS-enabled mobile telephony in the United States, user benefit was intended when ordinary devices became traceable for location by emergency services (the essential move that enabled commercial services to build on such traceability).[4] It seems hard to deny that users may be more quickly reached in an emergency using such techniques. Yet in the United States, despite considerable opposition by civil liberties groups, such devices are legally required to be switched on at all times (rather than having an emergency call trigger the switch). This means not only that emergency services have continual access and tracking affordances but that commercial enterprises do as well. This immediately places users in a situation in which information about their locations are available by default. The power relations embedded in such surveillance capacities are clearly unequal to say the least.

Many studies of new mobile telephony have remarked on the ways in which concepts of time and space are undoubtedly altering in relation to the new mobile technologies, although it does seem that small-scale, local, and immediate time–space paths are still vitally important to most people. As Boden and Molotch (1994) say, a "compulsion of proximity" still exists that encourages the ongoing persistence of face-to-face meeting, despite the potential for remote and now mobile communication. As Anthony Townsend neatly puts it, "The use of mobile phones offers an even finer level of identifying and exploiting minute variations in conditions between locations, the micromanagement of space as a result of the micromanagement of time and the always-accessible individual" (Townsend 2000: 101; cf. Fortunati 2002). Townsend puts an optimistic spin on this, suggesting that even as individuals struggle to sustain order and coherence in the face of accelerating time and compressing space, they also have the means of managing these forces and manipulating them as large-scale institutions tend to do.

However, there are other ways of thinking about the micromanagement of time–space. The mundane mobile may actually have some more exotic aspects to it (Michael 2003) that relate to a more radical kind of social change. But this idea cannot be discussed further until we have considered some ways in which the exotic aspects of mobile phones emerge. The device that is bought and sold with the promise of a reordering of opportunities and life pathways for the individual user (the mundane aspects) may also have a role in reordering such opportunities and everyday activities *of* that user (the exotic aspects, including surveillance). Neither of these is stable, however. The exotic and the mundane are likely to emerge together and in relation to one another.

Transparent Technologies

When a mobile phone is switched on, and every few minutes while it is working, it sends out a signal. All network base stations respond, and the provider allocates a phone to a station. On the highway, this may be up to 35 kilometers away, but in cities it is more likely to be within 500 meters. Picocells, with 50-meter radius, exist around shopping malls or office blocks. Which station the mobile uses is recorded, even if the call is simply to retrieve voice mail. The UK company Orange, for example, keeps this location information from the beginning and end of each call, whether outbound or inbound, for six months. BT Cellnet, another UK company, offers traffic news based on which station is nearest to the caller, and other such services are planned. But the data may be revealed to others, on application, under the Regulation of Investigatory Powers Act (2000) for a wide range of reasons: national security, crime, prevention of disorder, public health and safety, emergency protection of mental or physical health, and assessment or collection of taxes or other charges relating to government departments (Mathieson 2001).

One striking feature of almost every sociological and cultural examination of mobile phones is that the transparency of these technologies is unremarked. As I noted earlier, John Urry points out but does not discuss the ways that the sites to which people are connected by mobile devices also have the capacity to check up on them. Leslie Haddon and others (2001) mention that there is a potential for surveillance, using audit trails that reveal location, combined with databases to which service providers have access. And more than one author has noted that children and parents use mobile phones in contradictory ways. Teenagers may think that they can find more privacy out of their parents' earshot by using a mobile. At the same time, parents may use mobiles as "electronic leashes"—means of keeping tabs on where children are, either for their safety or because they do not trust them to act in an appropriate way when they are beyond range of their vision or hearing (Dong Kim 2002: 73).[5] However, existing research has yet to place mobile phones firmly within the context of contemporary surveillance practices and processes.

The focus of social science, by and large, is on the activities of the end user and how his or her direct social relationships are affected by mobile phone use (important exceptions include Gow and Ihnat 2004; Green and Smith 2004). A key assumption is that the mobile puts in the hands of individuals new means of communication, connection, and "micromanagement" of time and space. The emphasis is frequently on the liberating aspects of the new technologies that permit the "quicker, cheaper, convenient" connections, which free the individual from time-and-place constraints, or give those with no established landlines the chance to communicate by phone. All these features of the emerging social landscape no doubt exist, and it is perfectly proper to draw attention to them.

But as we have seen, mobile phones have other kinds of capacities in addition to those from which users benefit. They send signals and transmit the messages of their users. Third parties may discover where mobile users are at a given time and may under certain circumstances listen in to some messages.[6] It may well be the case that social movements are able to mobilize faster by using mobile phones—as happened classically in the protests against the World Trade Organization in Seattle in 1999—but it is also the case that mobile technologies are used to keep track of such protesters, in some countries in quite a detailed manner. The same technologies that provide the medium for coordination and micromanagement of individual activities can also provide the medium for institutional coordination and micromanagement, in ways that far transcend what may have been possible with landline phone systems.

Today, the transparency of mobile communications is becoming increasingly evident, and as this happens it will become clear why "where you are" matters to others as well as to friends, family, and colleagues. Three examples of this follow, relating to emergency services, marketing techniques, and antiterrorist activities. In each case, it is not so much the content of calls as their location that matters, although in policing and law enforcement contexts, phone tapping may also occur. In each case, too, an important feature of mobile surveillance is evident, namely, that location is continuously traceable, in real time. This is not the case with technologies such as radio frequency identification that require some kind of scanning device to obtain the locational data. It is useful to distinguish, then, between these "location technologies" and others that do not have quite the same capacities, for this distinction also has sociological and surveillance consequences (see Lyon, Marmura, and Peroff 2005).

In the United States and Canada, as well as in Europe, emergency calls from mobiles have become the focus of some attention from privacy advocates, because of their surveillance capacities and implications. Under so-called E911 ("E" for "enhanced" and 911 for emergency calls, as 999 in the United Kingdom) systems in the United States, and their equivalents elsewhere, emergency calls can be traced quickly. Conventional landline phones reveal their number and location to public services when an emergency number is called. But this used not to apply to mobile users, who had to give verbal information and instructions about how they could be reached. So the systems are being extended to mobile users, such that calls are traceable to within 20 to 50 meters of the phone (Bennett and Regan 2002). It remains to be seen how this will affect the "anonymous Samaritan" who calls on behalf of others but does not want to be identified.

In September 2003 a European Union directive (E112) came into force, requiring mobile phone networks to provide emergency services with any and all location information they can, again to try to speed up response times. By February 2004 the London Ambulance Service became the first to benefit from an initiative that is in line with the European directive, giving ambulance drivers accurate location information about the origin of emergency calls.[7] This is part of a process, the first stage of which was established at the start of 2004, to offer full coverage of the enhanced 999 service in the United Kingdom. The five mobile networks, plus BT Cellnet and cable and wireless, which connect emergency calls from mobiles, worked together with Ofcom, the regulator of U.K. communications, to provide the new services.[8]

For various reasons, network operators plan to take further such developments. If phone locations are traceable in an emergency, what is to prevent their being traceable in other circumstances as well? Commercial interests are evident in cases such as geography-sensitive traffic news services and the (celebrated but not very fully exploited) Starbucks coffee example. It seems that Starbucks has yet to take up on a large scale this opportunity for mobile marketing—as with a number of other companies, there is some hesitation about which is the best means of exploiting the mobile phone for consumer purposes. Some operators wish to recoup costs of making their systems comply with the emergency services directives, whereas others simply see other possibilities for using locational data. In the United Kingdom, Vodaphone customers can use their phone to find the nearest ATM, restaurant, or cinema, and another company, Zingo, offers to connect customers to the nearest taxi.[9] Other companies are offering specialized services, particularly for tracking employees and children. Although these systems are in their infancy, and thus have yet to be studied empirically, it is clear that they are of great interest to some companies in particular (Doward 2003).

Last but not least, the antiterror initiatives introduced since 9/11 have also included mobile phone location and message tracing as a means of both investigating and even preempting violent acts. To many observers, the dynamics of al Qaeda pointed up the changed rules of global guerrilla activities and perhaps of warfare too. So far from the "state-sponsored terrorism" feared by many governments, al Qaeda represents a network that operates independently of any state (and may in fact have states in its power rather than vice versa). Ease of travel, of funds transfers, and of communications, particularly using the Internet and mobile phones, enable this new modus vivendi (Neuman 2004). It is hardly surprising, then, that post-9/11 antiterrorist tactics include these three areas: travel, focusing on security at airports and borders; financial systems, focusing on curtailing the flow of funds to "terrorists"; and communications, focusing on the interception of suspicious messages.

Such concerns became even more pronounced after the Madrid bombings in March 2004. The European Union has appointed an "antiterror czar" who will, among other things, deal more diligently with the matter of sharing communications data. The idea is to track the activities of suspected conspirators, using their Internet and mobile phone logs (Brand 2004). It may be that the relative neglect of the surveillance aspects of mobile technologies is also related to the nature of these third-party uses. Questions of safety in relation to emergency calls have some prima facie priority over civil liberties or privacy questions (Black 2001). Questions about the uses of personal technologies for marketing and commercial surveillance are often deemed to be individual concerns, at worst of nuisance value, as in unwanted or repeat advertising calls. And in a climate of rising media-amplified fears and suspicions about the threat of terrorism, matters of national security appear to outweigh any queries about the necessity or efficacy of general surveillance sweeps for combating violence against civilians (Lyon 2003b).

Mobile phones are increasingly likely to be used for tracking purposes, in relation to both public and private services. Revealing timed locations is important, especially in an era of growing mobility. The systems described previously are all transparent technologies in the sense that they permit a greater visibility—as traceability—of their users to others. Some of those others have the public interest and personal safety in mind; others have profitability or personnel coordination in mind. Either way, the process of tracing and tracking people through devices they carry with them is likely to grow. What we do not yet know with any certainty is what the consequences will be, simply because of the newness of the systems described. However, several other factors should be noted.

First, mobile phones have multiplying functions. The ongoing integration of functions in one machine—voice, text, image, sound—is occurring at a very rapid rate. Some increased traceability relates to these proliferating combined functions. A Cambridge (United Kingdom) company, for instance, now offers to find customers when they are lost, if they can send a photo and 1 U.K. pound to their database. The image should depict a building or street where the customer is lost, which the company will identify by using image-recognition software. The company then sends back instructions to the customer on how to get back on track or further information about the buildings or street (Edward 2004: 5).

Second, cell phones are only one mobile technology among others; their combined use may be more significant than just telephone use. Other mobile technologies are rapidly coming on stream, which may also have significant social aspects. Much surveillance speculation attends such developments, but very little is known as yet about their use, let alone their unintended consequences. Onboard navigation systems for cars, transponders for electronic tolls at bridges or tunnels or on private highways, and black box sensors in cars offer multiple possibilities for generating mobile data. California resident Scott Knight, for example, was convicted in 2001 after a hit-and-run death when his OnStar system reported an airbag inflation. And Acme Rent-a-Car in New Haven, Connecticut, fined drivers $150 when their GPS system showed they had been consistently speeding (Schwartz 2003).

Third, the capacities of mobile technology surveillance are currently limited in significant ways. Legal requirements, though contradictory in some contexts, place limits on the extent to which mobile surveillance—relating to message content only—occurs. Tapping, for instance, still requires a warrant in most countries, and there are also curbs on the passing of data to third parties in privacy and data protection legislation. The technical capacity to engage in mobile surveillance is also limited. When it comes to message interception, this is particularly true. Only a fragment of the total messages of potential interest to surveillors is likely to be intercepted (Clarke 2003). Finally, mobile surveillance is costly. Even enhanced emergency services are expensive to establish, so it is not surprising that networks attempt to defray costs by considering other services as well as emergency ones.

Fourth, different kinds of transparency are produced by different kinds of mobile technology. Roger Clarke (2003) helpfully summarizes some of the differences, starting with the obvious self-disclosure of locational data in the course of a conversation. Landline phones have used versions of caller ID for some years now, and the prefix of the calling number discloses location to within a few kilometers in urban areas. Mobile phones disclose the cell from which the phone is operating, and this has now become a sought-after datum for law enforcement and antiterror purposes. There are also business incentives for obtaining access to this. E911 initiatives based on crisis stories lead to more precise location of calls, using GPS, triangulation, and directional antennas methods. Clarke also points to a further source of locational data: self-identification by devices as they pass detectors. These devices include smart cards, transponders (for example, for highway or bridge tolls), and radio frequency identification systems. As I observed earlier, however, such devices do not meet the criteria of locational technologies as defined here.

Having pointed out various limits on locational surveillance, I should also note that the trend is toward increasing traceability. The transparent technologies we have been discussing now help constitute everyday life in the affluent, technologically advanced societies. So all users can expect to become more traceable (if not more audible) to third parties the more they use such devices. This may mean that people find ways of reducing their visibility (by not using their devices or by encrypting them to prevent unauthorized or unwanted use) or possibly that they choose to go on using them in the belief that their benefits outweigh the possible negative aspects. Those who entertain doubts about mobile surveillance are likely to do so because they have strong views about their privacy or possibly because they believe that their civil liberties are jeopardized. However, there are more reasons for thinking carefully about mobile devices, which have to do with their place within a bigger picture of surveillance and governance in the twenty-first century.

Digital Discrimination

Accounts of mobile technologies that highlight how ordinary people reorder their daily time–space paths must be placed in a broader context. Although individual patterns of social life are constantly changing as people use new devices to coordinate their activities, the same devices are used by third parties, who also wish to have a say in coordinating those activities. The use of mobile technologies may also be considered as a new—locational—element within processes of governance. This may be rather obvious, as in the case of Howard Boyle, surreptitiously tracking his employees, or more likely be rather subtle, seen within a larger frame of digital discrimination. It also occurs, as we have seen, in relation to consumer surveillance. To explain this, I must shift the focus from how people actively use their mobile devices, even from how they might feel about the fact that their movements are traced, and from how behaviors and exchanges become visible, or knowable, to the purposes for which they are made visible.

Seen this way, surveillance is more than a mere threat to personal privacy, or even to civil liberties, important though these are. In most countries and cultures, having access to some inviolable spaces, or controlling the circulation of information about oneself, is important. In democratic societies, notions such as freedom of movement and the absence of the snooping, prying eye are held dear, and rightly so. But the kind of surveillance that has been burgeoning in the past couple of decades goes beyond any occasional and isolated cases of privacy infringement or limits on liberty. It is articulated with the general growth of mobilities and the emerging forms of governance—particularly those aimed at regulating the "means of movement" (Torpey 2000)—that are characteristic of social life in the early twenty-first century.

Garnering personal details without the individuals concerned knowing about—let alone consenting to—it has become routine. The organizations that engage in these practices proliferate rapidly and increasingly employ networking techniques such that the growth of personal data gathering is symbiotic. Deep changes are in process. James Rule goes so far as to say that the new technologies of "perpetual contact"—such as mobile phones—represent a "significant step in the movement toward what I have called 'total surveillance'—that is, a world in which every fact and every moment of every individual's life registers with a single, centralized agency of surveillance" (Rule 2002: 248). Although there may be other ways of reading this, the point about significant social change is crucial.

A final important feature of today's surveillance, whether in law enforcement, government administration, or consumer marketing techniques, is that it usually has to do with social sorting. Questions of social divisions and of social exclusion appear in this context. Simply put, surveillance seen as social sorting is a means of management, influence, and governance. The question is, how does it operate as such? The answer is that surveillance works in many ways, through multiple rationalities and techniques, to try to manage and manipulate behaviors. But it has some features in common across different fields of vision, different institutional areas. Increasingly, searchable databases are used to provide the means of digital discrimination. The aim is to segment populations according to certain criteria, sorting them into groups that will be treated differently. The idea is that levels of risk or of opportunity can be calculated from available data so that relevant groups can be targeted more accurately (Henman 2004).

The story of surveillance in the modern world has been told elsewhere, but some brief details do help. The twentieth century saw the quickening development of "information societies" around the world; the corollary is that surveillance societies also became more evident (Lyon 2001). Bureaucratic management, developed in the early part of the century, was augmented tremendously by computerization from the 1970s onward, with the result that systematic, routine monitoring of persons and populations for a range of purposes became commonplace in all but the poorest countries of the world by the turn of the twenty-first century. What once were fixed files became flows of personal data, first within and then between different kinds of organizations, from government departments to hospitals, schools, police, insurance brokers, credit card companies, and marketing corporations. Today's surveillance is not *caused* by information technology but certainly *enabled* by it.

Each transaction, exchange, purchase, and interaction we make now leaves a trail of electronic footprints. These fragments of personal data tell few tales on their own, but when they are combined with others they are a powerful means of predicting further actions, whether as consumers, offenders, claimants, travelers, or citizens. In the consumer sphere, for instance, geodemographic marketing works with probabilities based on neighborhood types that certain householders are good targets for specific products and so "place" and "past" become important elements of data images. As systems such as customer relationship management were promoted in the 1990s, deeper and richer records were created, using techniques such as data mining to draw together even more information (Gandy and Deanna 2002). The data image relating to an individual is created by combining such information. Certain well-heeled groups are targeted for special deals and privileges; others, with poorer postcodes, are passed by. As mobile lifestyles become more prevalent, the dead spaces of travel time also come to be of interest to personal data agencies.

So not only do exchanges and interactions attract surveillance attention but movement does as well. The most obvious case is that of video surveillance or closed-circuit television (CCTV). In countries such as the United Kingdom, where CCTV systems are densely distributed in urban spaces, ordinary citizens may expect to have their images monitored, if not recorded, several hundred times a day. In cases where they are recorded, details of geographical location become available to the security and police services that install or operate them. The evidence indicates, however, that the locations of certain groups—young black males especially, but, unofficially, young women—are disproportionately in focus (Norris 2003). The important difference between CCTV and the surveillance capacities of mobile phones is that although CCTV is clearly about some authorities "keeping watch," mobile phones are understood to be about ordinary people "keeping in touch." Surveillance is a side effect of mobile phone use. On the other hand, for some purposes mobile surveillance may have something in common with CCTV surveillance, including the fact that many (especially in the United Kingdom) assume that CCTV works and is a good thing. In so far as mobile surveillance is connected with emergency services, it would not be surprising to discover that similar assumptions reign.

The surveillance data garnered from locations may be added to the data image to inform new modes of governance. Because surveillance is ambivalent, the technologies linked with "care," such as emergency services, may also have some "control" motifs, such as targeting by police or commercial agencies. Law enforcement agencies clearly have an interest in where certain suspects are and will treat different groups differently depending on their interpretation of available data. Racial profiling has become especially marked since the serious antiterror campaigns were mounted following 9/11. Driving while black has been a cause for police interest for some time. Now flying while Arab or surfing while Muslim may also attract undue attention. But marketers also wish to target population segments so that they too can provide different levels of service or opportunity. Ideally, they want to induce users to follow particular commercial paths so they can target part of their individual lifetime value.

Each of these rationalities and techniques deserves exploration in its own right. They may have common elements, but there are many variations on the digital discrimination theme. The key point is that "where you are" matters because such information about location is fed into data images. These data images circulate, mutating as they travel, within the circuits of twenty-first-century surveillance. They enjoy levels of mobility far in excess of what their human referents could experience, moving faster, further, and through a greater range of fields than them. Where the consumer may have been could inform the data image retrieved by police investigating unrelated activities. How fast the driver was traveling could affect insurance premiums or invoices from car rental companies. All of this is a reminder that the data image is influential in real-life situations. It is flesh and blood embodied, social persons who are affected for better or worse by digital discrimination.

This interpretation of mobilities does not necessarily compete with those that put the accent on how people coordinate and control *their own* activities using mobile technologies. Rather, it dovetails with those focusing on action and the ways that people are better able to cope with conflicting schedules and what Helga Nowotny (1998) calls "overlapping times" by using mobile phones. This perspective emphasizes structural constraints on action, deriving from the demands of service providers for better information, which in turn may be used by commercial, safety, and security agencies within systems of (mobile and locational) governance. The one account does not cancel the other; rather, the two accounts together provide a more nuanced picture of mobile life with inhabited machines. It must be said, however, that the trend is toward greater use of locational data for governance of all kinds. And given the inequalities of access and power mentioned earlier, mobile surveillance could well become a more influential means of exacerbating existing social divisions.

What we do not yet know much about are the empirical details and the actual consequences of such mobile monitoring of locations over time. But the already existing systems, within which mobiles are now imbricated, are ones that contribute to digital discrimination, to the reinforcing of social division, and to social inclusion or exclusion. Some of this is unexceptional and socially benign, but other aspects are a cause for some concern, especially among civil libertarians and others who deplore the growth of digital discrimination. Many surveillance schemes that operate today tend to amplify stereotypes and to apply the most stringent and severe scrutiny to the most vulnerable—in socioeconomic, ethnic, and gendered terms. It is hard to imagine how locational data from mobile phones will be used differently. But it is worth finding out how they are used and worth remembering that other ways are possible.

Acknowledgments

An earlier version of this chapter was written while I was a visiting fellow at the Institute for Advanced Study in the Humanities, University of Edinburgh, during 2004 and was first presented at a "Life of Mobile Data" conference at the University of Surrey, United Kingdom, April 15–16, 2004.

Notes

1. I am using the term *mobile phone* (rather than the North American *cell phone*) because this chapter was first presented in the United Kingdom.
2. I am indebted to Heidi Campbell for this observation.
3. I discuss aspects of this in Lyon (1988) and Lyon (1994).
4. The Wireless Communications and Public Safety Act 1999.
5. In Ontario, where I live, Bell Canada recently (2005) launched its "Seek and Find" system that permits parents to track children by cell phone.
6. See http://www.poptel.org.uk/cgi-bin/dbs2/statewatch?query=mobile+phonesandmode =recordsandrow_id=20049.
7. See http://news.bbc.co.uk/1/hi/health/3485141.stm.
8. See http://www.ofcom.org.uk/media_office/news_archive/nr1_20040115.
9. See http://www.newscientist.com/hottopics/phones/phones.jsp?id=ns99994270.

CHAPTER 14

Using Intelligent Transport Systems to Track Buses and Passengers

Buses have been some of the least technologically advanced and glamorous of public transport options. However, in the wake of major event planning in already congested cities and the renewed focus on security in light of the attacks on public transport infrastructure in London in July 2005, buses are experiencing a high-tech renaissance. Airports, harbors, railway stations, and urban highways have been under technological surveillance since the most basic closed-circuit television (CCTV) cameras were introduced. The concentration of many travelers and goods in a small space makes these places some of the most intensively observed areas in our cities. Although subway and rail stations were prioritized for security audits and actions, buses have not always received the same treatment. In the years since 9/11, money has been made available in an effort to make surface public transport more secure and better tracked. Transit companies are looking to so-called intelligent transport systems (ITS) to increase their operating efficiency and passenger information.[1] ITS for buses work with bus priority measures to help keep buses moving in congested areas, for example, through queue jumper lanes, bus gates, and traffic signal priority. These improvements require reliable real-time vehicle location information. ITS can improve the speed and reliability of buses by deploying them in response to actual traffic conditions. ITS is also credited with increasing passengers' feelings of safety by providing more accurate and timely arrival information.[2] These technologies allow operators to know bus positions in real-time and know who is on (or was on) what bus (e.g., in the future, through cell phone ticketing). Today, law enforcement can request flight passenger manifests, taxi logs, and toll road information. Soon it will be possible to locate a passenger (or better put, a passenger's smart card) on a specific bus at a specific time. The storage of this information also allows for commercially exploitable data mining concerning a passenger's movement throughout the transport system. Newer digital and wireless technologies are creating options to secure and optimize bus travel but at the cost of more intense and automated surveillance.

In this chapter I discuss emerging themes in bus security and ITS by referring to research I have conducted with transport authorities in Vancouver and London as they adapt their systems for the 2010 and 2012 Olympic and Paralympic Games, respectively, in the face of new terrorist threats and demands for socially responsible, sustainable transit.[3] Although ITS and video surveillance can make contributions to safer and efficient transport and social integration, the technologies they introduce into the public sphere can also be used to track and trace passengers' movements and collect huge amounts of information on their behavior. This collected information can be used to define groups for specific treatment, leading ultimately to greater social fracturing. ITS and related systems improve public transport and create new questions for how we deal with the by-products of intense information collection.

The Case for Buses

Providing good bus service is seen by many transport authorities as a social equity issue. Translink in Vancouver writes, "Approximately half of bus riders do not have access to an automobile and use transit as their primary form of travel. Serving many of these riders is a matter of social and economic equity."[4] Transport for London makes similarly direct claims in the Social Inclusion Action Plan 2002–2004 Draft for Panels: Transport for London has a vision for a "transport system that serves the needs of all those who live, work or visit London, irrespective of economic status or social identity." Subsidies for public transport are redistributive.[5] Bus passengers are repeatedly found to be in the lowest socioeconomic groups of public transport users. When asked, many subway users indicate that they have other transport options and choose to take the subway for its convenience; however, bus travelers often do not have access to a car or a driver's license and use the bus as their sole transport source. Transport-dependent people are more often female. Buses in some jurisdictions, such as London but not Vancouver, are priced less expensive to use than subways or light rail. The relative accessibility of buses as surface transport, compared to the less-accessible rail and subways that usually involve climbing escalators or stairs, also means that buses attract more very young and older people to use them. Transport companies are confronted with two apparently contradictory priorities. As a public service, transport companies are entrusted to ensure that people can access their right to mobility to be part of their communities and travel to work, health care, and education. Second, public transport is part of a larger mobility policy to maintain quality of life through clean air and lack of congestion by enticing car users out of their cars and into transit. These are two different groups with different needs and power positions. One group tends to be more affluent commuters traveling longer distances on arterial routes from outside to the city core. The other group lives and works in the areas others want to speed through.

In addition to the social arguments for improving bus performance, investments to improve the capacity of surface transport are less costly than adding to underground or rail network infrastructure. Both Vancouver and London face similar challenges. Both are hosting the Olympics and Paralympics in the next years, and both must grow their capacity to move people and goods through their growing cities to stay competitive as economic centers. Vancouver is growing as the most important port on the west coast of North America and regional gateway to the Pacific Rim. London is increasing its populations and jobs at a remarkable rate. Public transport infrastructure has to be part of the solution if this growth and development is to be sustainable. Major events such as the Olympics create possibilities for extra resources from central governments to invest in public transit. They also awaken new security concerns. Vancouver's Translink writes, "[The 2010 Olympics] offers a unique opportunity to provide a wide range of travel choices that people might not ordinarily choose and, in doing so, will help shape future travel behaviour" (Greater Vancouver Transit Authority 2004a: 1).

Types of Bus Surveillance and ITS

Bus surveillance takes many forms. In some cities, human bus monitors still wait at bus stops with stopwatches and clipboards, noting times of arrival and departure. Supervisors drive through traffic pinch points ready to spring out during rush hour to see the problems on the ground as they occur and to request resources (e.g., call for tow trucks or police) to keep the traffic flowing. What originated in periscope mirrors to view the upper platforms and in conductors to greet passengers and watch the doors has evolved into both on- and off-bus camera systems, global positioning systems (GPSs) and beacon-based locator systems, bus mounting of sophisticated mobile data terminals to control traffic signals, and smart card trip tracking. I discuss each of these various technologies in turn before I conclude with some reflections on the surveillance implications of creating such an information-rich environment.

Cameras

Inward-looking cameras on buses are used to deter crime against the driver and passengers and criminal damage to the bus. The inward-looking cameras on the newest generation of buses in London are placed throughout the bus to capture everyone who boards the bus (see Figures 14.1 and 14.2).[6] Once the passengers are on the bus, the cameras can also view them from different angles. Signs indicate that video images are being captured and provide a telephone number for more information. Each of the cameras has a fixed viewing area and tapes the entire time the bus is turned on. The newer systems tape to hard disk, and the earlier analog systems record to tape. Some cameras did not work and were detected as defective only when law enforcement required a tape. Until recently the cameras on the buses did not provide a very high-resolution image. This lack of detail combined with the missing frames of the time-capture cameras sometimes made it difficult to satisfactorily identify suspects in assault, robbery, or criminal damage cases. Now, better guidelines concerning the placement of the

Figure 14.1 London buses.

Figure 14.2 Bus camera.

cameras, their testing, and their technical specification are leading to better image capture. Transport for London has now equipped the entire bus fleet with CCTV.

Having a tape depicting someone apparently committing a crime is only a small first step in pressing charges against him or her. In a city such as London, finding the people on the bus images would be near impossible if petty criminals did not restrict their crimes to areas they know well, according to the Metropolitan Police Service (MPS). Unlike the Underground and rail services policed by the British Transport Police, buses are the responsibility of the MPS. In addition to their normal bus-policing tasks, the MPS cooperates with Transport for London in a project called "Bus TAG" that is designed to stop criminal damage to Transport for London's bus company contractors. It is one of many steps to improve the cleanliness and safety of London buses for their passengers. Under this program, the Bus TAG team is alerted when substantial criminal damage occurs (usually graffiti but can also include destroyed upholstery or even arson). First the damage needs to be detected. Cleaning staff or the driver inspects the bus at the end of the day and notes if there is new graffiti or damage. If damage is found, a copy of the recording hard drive is made, and the original hard drive is put aside as possible evidence. The contents of the hard drive are viewed with proprietary software to see if the criminal act was captured on camera to a degree that makes identification possible. Video stills are then made of the assumed perpetrator and the damage. This goes into an evidence kit, which is given to the MPS along with a specific form developed by Bus TAG. This kit is checked for completeness, and then the MPS tries to find someone (e.g., local police officers, school staff, or parents) who recognizes the people depicted in the video stills. School-age youth who are responsible for most graffiti and tagging are easier to identify because most schools in England require their students to wear distinctive uniforms. The police justify this time-consuming work by claiming that it nips youth crime before it moves on to worse activities and puts pressure on the bus companies to keep their buses clean and welcoming. It has been argued that people feel safer on a clean, unscratched bus and that people are less likely to mark up a clean bus compared to a bus that is already in a bad state. The police also argue that some people arrested for antisocial behavior on the buses have had open warrants for more serious crimes. This approach to policing is often called the "broken windows" theory, which was developed by Wilson and Kelling and made famous by Los Angeles Police Department commissioner William J. Bratton, who applied it in his work, first as the head of the New York Transit Police (1991) and then in the New York Police Department (1994–96) under Mayor Giuliani.

Bus driver safety is another reason named for the use of cameras inside buses. Despite their enclosures, many bus drivers are accessible to passengers and interact with them to collect fares or check tickets and transfers. Dealing with passengers' money can lead to disagreements and violence. It is unfortunate that bus drivers in London are often harassed, assaulted, and spat on. Many drivers felt their requests for help were not sufficiently prioritized by the police services, and police were unsatisfied with the lack of evidence they needed to act on the information after the fact. Cameras were suggested as a way of both deterring assault and collecting evidence. Some drivers did not accept cameras that constantly recorded the driver. This led to cameras that record the space where passengers board beside the driver but not necessarily the driver while he or she is seated. It is not clear if the driver is safer, but there is a chance of better evidence gathering after an assault has taken place. Discussions on the role the cameras could play took place alongside the decision to phase out conductors on buses. People argued that keeping the conductor and getting better response times from the police were better deterrents than video cameras. However, cameras were seen to be a cost-effective solution with a deterrent effect because of their evidentiary value. Bus drivers also have been issued "spit kits" with swabs and latex gloves to do a DNA test on the saliva after a spitting assault. DNA kits were first issued in Scotland to transit personnel, and then they were issued in a pilot in August 2003 to selected London Underground staff and in August 2004 to parking attendants and bus drivers. The DNA sample would then be checked against a national DNA database.[7]

A final use of cameras inside the bus is for insurance claims in the case of accidents. This use is more of an issue in Canada and the United States than in Britain. After an accident, transport authorities are confronted with passengers claiming to have been injured while on their buses. Sometimes these people were not on the bus or are overstating their injuries. Other honest accident victims could not prove that they were on the bus. Video evidence protects the honest passengers and the transport companies while deterring those looking for an easy fraud target. When considering the evidentiary use of video surveillance, it is important to note that there are different possibilities of access for those who hold the tapes and those who may be depicted on them. In the United Kingdom, the Data Protection Act allows for viewing but only when certain conditions are met, which can in some cases present a large obstacle. Although in the case of a dispute going to court, evidence must be made available to both sides, other disputes do not necessarily require that all possibly relevant tapes be made freely available.

The deterrence function of these surveillance measures works only if the legal system supports the efforts of the transport authorities and bus companies. Once a better working relationship was achieved with the police, additional work needed to be done by bus companies to allow lawyers and judges to understand bus crime. Despite the efforts of the bus companies and police, many young people were not held responsible before the courts for their tagging and scratching activities. After damaging more than 50,000 pounds worth of windows, one young man was fined 50 pounds because it was only his first time before the court. This decision made many bus companies wonder if it was worth the time and expense to pursue youth crime or replace windows that were going to be scratched again. A leading London bus company invited magistrates to visit a garage and sit on a bus and experience bus travel in the hope that they would be more aware of the issues facing bus companies and take a harder line on young vandals. Many magistrates (like most higher earning Britons) had not been on a bus since their school days and had no appreciation of the discomfort and unease a messy, tagged-up bus with scratched windows gives to passengers. This type of action is aimed to show the effects of vandalism on the transport-dependent community and their transport options. Some transport-dependent people (especially older people) claim that they feel so unsafe because of the graffiti and young vandals that they do not use the buses and subsequently cut themselves off from participation in community life. The true cost of vandalism and antisocial behavior is social exclusion, not the price of replacing the windows. Both the introduction of Bus TAG and the work with judges highlight the importance of communication between various groups—communication that is not improved by technology investment. Many of the problems confronted by the drivers, the police, the bus companies, and the magistrates were communication and prioritization conflicts that had to be solved through other methods.

Much of the work of transport police is reactive in regard to the CCTV images and traces left by ticketing on buses. Only in the case of an event are the tapes or hard drives collected to see if there is useful information. Buses are a difficult environment for CCTV to function well because of the dirt and vibration. Often the cameras appear to be working, and only when the police request a tape is it made clear that the cameras are not working or that blind spots exist. After the bus bombing in London in July 2005, London's private bus companies did an audit to make certain that they had procedures in place to test for failing cameras, recorders, and hard drives. London's private bus companies are also required to meet standards set by the Data Protection Act for the images they collect, including destroying images after a certain amount of time if there has been no interest expressed by the police.

In London, outward-facing cameras are being used for a range of tasks from parking and bus lane enforcement to performance monitoring. Bus lanes are reserved for certain bus and emergency vehicle traffic during peak hours. Many double-decker buses in London have two cameras beside the route shield that record what is immediately in front of the bus while the bus is traveling in a bus lane. The driver does not have to start and stop the recording. Roadside beacons tell the driver when the bus goes in and out of a bus lane and controls the camera recording accordingly. While the bus is in the bus lane, the two cameras (one wide angle and one zoom) videotape the road and cars directly in front of the bus. These tapes are then collected by bus enforcement and carefully reviewed by staff to see if the vehicle driver was lawfully in the bus lane or in breach of the bus lane laws. (Automatic license plate recognition is not currently used for vehicle identification.) A ticket is then issued to the owner of the vehicle based on the information from a license plate database. The majority of bus lane enforcement takes place with CCTV and static cameras mounted on the street, but bus-mounted cameras play an important role. This system has been very successful in emptying the bus lanes in London. As with any bus priority measure, there is a debate about whether the goal should be completely empty bus lanes or if some mixed-use function would be a better use of road space.

Outward-facing cameras also monitor road quality and road use. How many cyclists use the bus lane? How many delivery vans? Where do people park illegally? What effect is construction having? Are all of the signs up to date and visible? Reviewing tapes of bus runs can answer these sorts of questions. Monitoring of bus lanes also reveals some details of passenger and driver behavior. How long does it take people to get on or off a bus? Which bus stops are too full? Which stops are hardly used? A human operator can use the information from the cameras to understand the details of various bus routes. Before using video monitoring, auditors would sit in buses with stopwatches or PDAs (personal digital assistants) and time the bus route and stops. Casual workers would be employed to sit in foldout chairs and count bicycles. Video-captured monitoring information, because it is available to be repeatedly viewed and checked, provides a verifiable information source that can then be input into modeling and simulation programs. Video monitoring can also provide more information than some roadside sensors; for example, sensors that count axels. The video monitor would be able to detect a fire truck, but the roadside sensor would detect just four axels.

GPSs and Beacons

People at rainy bus stops are not the only ones wondering where their bus is. Bus companies must pay for more buses to travel a route when the buses they have are not optimally deployed. Bus companies have used spotters and bus captains at turn-around points to try to keep buses on schedule. Before satellite GPSs were available, buses were tracked by passing radio beacons. In London, bus-fleet tracking is moving from beacons to GPSs. In younger cities such as Vancouver, where GPSs are already in place, they create a completely different operating environment by enabling real-time tracking.

The reliance of GPSs on satellites creates problems in an urban environment with garages, tunnels, and canyons created by skyscrapers. Current vehicle-tracking systems use GPSs with another technology, either dead reckoning or mapping software, or some combination of both. Dead-reckoning technology makes up for those areas where the satellite does not have line of sight to the vehicle. In these areas where too few satellites are available, dead-reckoning technology calculates the vehicle's position through distance and direction sensing. Distance is measured through odometer pulses, and direction is measured usually through vibrating microelectrical mechanical gyroscopes. These gyroscopes are like miniature tuning forks that vibrate when moved through a field. The vibration of the forks is picked up by sensors and turned into a voltage that then indicates the changes in direction. Unlike GPSs, dead-reckoning technology does not measure altitude. It could do so with the addition of a barometer, but because this application is for land travel, it is assumed that the altitude remains constant. When there is no satellite coverage, dead-reckoning systems make the calculations for vehicle location. When there is excellent GPS coverage, the GPS calibrates the dead-reckoning system by checking the odometer pulse and gyroscope voltages against the satellite readings.

In the case of partial coverage, new systems use Kalman filters, special algorithms that use the information available from both systems to correct errors and to calculate the most accurate location. With these enhanced GPSs, failures and dropouts due to tall buildings or deep garages are no longer an obstacle. Every bus can be tracked above and below ground. In addition to tracking the bus under normal conditions, GPS tracking is also advertised as a useful function in the case of an emergency situation where resources need to be redeployed or missing buses found.

Bus ITS and Mobile Data Terminals

Once location systems are installed for the bus network, a range of ITS technologies can be put into place to make the buses, in theory at least, run on time and as efficiently as possible.

The goal of bus ITS is to allow buses to avoid or react to congestion as they encounter it. Vancouver has special "B line" bus routes where the buses carry mobile data terminals that constantly compare the current position of the bus to where it should be and its place in respect to other buses (headways). If the bus is behind schedule, the mobile data terminals can change the traffic signals to allow the bus to get back on schedule and send messages to the upcoming bus stops to show a new time of arrival. Every bus and every bus stop is captured on dynamic real-time maps. All of this can be done without the bus driver's intervention.

Dynamic Maps and Crime Data

Many transport companies contribute route and other information to geographic information systems to create dynamic maps. London uses a Compstat (Comparative Statistics) management system and database, developed in New York, which is organized around the collection of geographical information about crimes and traffic. This information is plotted onto maps to be analyzed by police and transport representatives. The theory behind Compstat is that by mapping the locations of crimes, law enforcement has the chance to discover patterns and deploy resources more effectively.[8] This sort of data visualization is possible through GPS location information. London's Compstat system was lauded by the U.K. Department of Transport as "the most comprehensive system … in England and Wales."[9] This "intelligence-driven policing" approach again shows how the introduction of a specific technology—GPS location tracking—spawns many unforeseen applications.

Cashless Boarding

Alongside traffic congestion and road quality, passenger behavior has a great influence on bus reliability and speed. Transit authorities want to cut down on the time that a bus waits at a bus stop to load. This is accomplished through design changes like low-floor vehicles that do not require a passenger to climb steps (also good for wheelchairs and strollers) and more and wider doors. It is also accomplished through cashless multi-door boarding. Loading times on some busy Vancouver streets have been reduced from three minutes to thirty seconds by allowing all-door boarding. However, if the driver is not responsible for confirming that the passenger is boarding with a ticket, others have to do this job. In London the introduction of all-door boarding on some articulated bus routes led to some passengers' believing that they could ride for free and the articulated buses being nicknamed "happy buses."[10] It was necessary to start a press campaign to make certain that people boarded with valid tickets. The Revenue Protection Inspectors took over the responsibility to make certain that people boarded with tickets. The introduction of the new boarding methods increased the need for control and surveillance of the people who chose to benefit from faster boarding.

Cashless systems like those in place in downtown London save passengers time and companies money. Faster cashless buses save companies money in two ways. First, fewer buses have to be on the road, and second, the so-called transaction cost is lowered. Transaction cost refers to the individual costs per passenger. A large part of the transaction costs has been the money handling in the form of collecting huge amounts of coin from passengers and issuing paper tickets. There has been a three-pronged approach to this problem. The first is to move the coin collection off the bus. The second step is to replace paper tickets and transfers with plastic cards that the passenger uses repeatedly. The third is to do away with tickets altogether and introduce virtual tickets.

The West End of London is now a cashless zone. Each bus stop has a ticket machine, and no tickets can be bought on the bus. This removes the need for the driver to handle cash and issue tickets and cuts down dramatically on boarding time. In addition, small shops along the route sell tickets as licensed vendors.

Multiuse plastic cards are either magnetic swipe cards like those used in Vancouver or RFID cards (radio frequency identification) like those used for the Oyster system in London. The cards can be both read (does this card have enough money stored on it to pay for this trip?) and written to (record the station where this person boarded the bus). Although this read–write function is also possible with magnetic cards, I focus my remarks on the new RFID cards.

RFID cards have a small broadcaster and receiver in them. The cards do not have their own power supply but are recharged when they touch the reader devices. Passengers are encouraged to "touch in and touch out."

Some information is recorded on the card and downloaded every time it comes in contact with a reader. This information is then kept in large back office databanks. Unlike magnetic cards, which have to be swiped by a reading device, RFID cards, because they work through radio signals, do not actually need to contact the reading device to be read. This means that the cards can theoretically be read from a distance of ten to twenty centimeters, for example, while still in the passenger's wallet. Although not having to directly access a card can be convenient, it raises some important questions about the collection of information without explicit consent and the use of this travel information for purposes other than fare control. This data-capture element of RFID travel cards becomes increasingly important when paired with the use of the cards to buy products or make telephone calls. At individual points, all of this information is not very telling. However, brought together on a time line, transport information can give a detailed picture of the passenger's movement through the urban environment. Every trip and purchase could be tracked and timed to discover trends and target products to the user. If a passenger wants to remain anonymous, he or she can choose not to use Oyster cards or other smart cards or to use versions of them that do not require a full subscription with detailed personal information. However, often these other options are more expensive, and low-income bus riders are confronted with the dilemma of sacrificing their privacy or having to pay more. It is also not clear if these more anonymous options will be phased out in the name of efficiency and security in the future. The trend toward super cards for many applications is growing. The Danish government awarded a 200 million euro contract in September 2005 to roll out a travel card system that will be used across the country for public transport, trains, and purchases.[11]

Cashless boarding and GPSs have changed the way that transport companies collect passenger trip data. Transport companies regularly conduct surveys to find out their passengers' travel patterns so they can provide better-integrated service. These surveys have until recently taken the form of researchers questioning passengers in public transport about where they came from and where they are going to and with what mode of transport. This method is very time-consuming and error prone, because people may not accurately remember or even know how long they have been underway. Time-consuming surveys also do not always reach the busiest travelers, who then are underrepresented in the data. Other researcher methods included asking people to fill out detailed travel diaries, where the traveler notes the time, place, mode, and reason for travel for a period of time. This method also had problems with capturing levels of detail. Smart cards that passengers use to touch in and touch out can track chained trips and report on passenger travel behavior, which can provide more exact information about a certain group's (smart card users) traveling habits. However, this method leaves out the legs of travel not driven by smart cards, for example, those traveled by bicycle, foot, or car. To track these modes of travel, researchers in Florida[12] are prototyping a GPS PDA device that is carried by the transport user that records the location and the times of travel and prompts the user to explain what type of travel it is and for what purpose. This prototype is being watched with much interest by many research departments of transport authorities.

Another way for the transport companies to save money on the transaction costs is by removing tickets altogether. Rather than needing to print, distribute, and collect tickets, transport companies are looking at the use of cellular phones to transport virtual tickets. The same system used for parking or movie tickets will be available for transport services. Because mobile phones in North America are required to have built-in GPS capability, there are many interesting directions this technology could go. Phones could allow users to pay for the distance they travel on toll roads and could track what demographic groups use what services and when.

Privacy Protections

Some companies are marketing technologies as supporting privacy. Privacy-enhancing technologies are also being developed to cloak GPS signals and allow only a range of exactness measured in kilometers and not meters. Companies manufacturing RFID tags also argue that blocker tags could be made to invalidate active tags. Privacy advocates point out that blocker tags like any sort of promised privacy-enhancing technology could later be banned by government once the original RFID scanners were all in place. It would then be impossible to roll back the original installation of the offending devices. Accepting the argument of a technical fix assumes the acceptance of the original installation of the challenged technology. Once the challenged technology has been installed, the fix can be (for whatever reason) not installed.

A more promising approach taken by companies is their building steps of disclosure into their products, allowing people to gauge what amount of information is appropriate to be shared in a specific situation. For example, telecommunication companies are competing for clients and market share by offering more nuanced products that show that they respect people's need to control what is revealed by their behaviors. Understanding how to win customer acceptance and defining a privacy-protecting framework are new challenges that will need to be met by companies hoping to grow new market share.

The promise of real-time reporting is only now on the verge of being delivered because of the huge amounts of computing power required to process it and the need for high-speed mobile networks to collect and distribute it. The technical possibilities are there. How do we build in the safeguards to make these technologies politically realizable and socially acceptable?

As intelligent transport systems become more expensive to operate and maintain and more public–private partnerships are struck, the demand for access to transaction data, which may be of marketing value, can only increase. Public transport is run on a subsidy and is under pressure to make use of alternative income sources. Passengers need to be aware of the way data can be collected about their riding habits, movements, and behaviors so that they can be aware of when and how they are tracked and challenge inappropriate use.

Transport and advertising companies collect information on the demographics of bus passengers. This information can be used to market to bus passengers and also to provide an argument for the benefits of bus transport for other groups. Transport for London commissioned a "Town Centre Survey 2003–4" report from Accent Marketing and Research, which gathered purchasing and demographic information on bus passengers and asked leaders of local business associations about their impressions of bus riders and car drivers. Accent reported, "Respondents thought that retailers were keener to see shoppers visiting by using cars rather than by public transport—it was believed recognised that car-borne shoppers were likely to have higher disposable income and that bus users were limited by how much they could spend [or] by how much they could carry" (Accent Marketing and Research 2004: 24). Opinions of local business leaders are important because they can influence the implementation of new on-street parking regimes and other bus priority measures that affect the attractiveness of bus travel. Transport for London's managing director of surface transport Peter Hendy responded to the Town Centre report as follows: "These are fantastic results, the research dispels the myth that bus passengers have lower incomes and are less able to contribute to towns' economic growth. This together with the fact that many new passengers to buses are from social demographic AB [professionals and managers] means the rejuvenation of the bus network is a success and town centres all over the capital are benefiting from this investment."[13] Nonetheless, bus riders continue to be on the whole less affluent than users of other modes of transportation.

One of the advantages of bus-based advertising, according to those who sell it, is that it can be targeted to specific geographical areas and then offer point-of-purchase advertising. A bus deployed from a certain garage on a certain route can offer advertisements for local businesses where the passenger could go shop immediately. As the bus drives through the retail districts of the cities, people outside the bus also get an immediate rolling billboard message that may affect their immediate purchasing behavior.

The people on the bus are a captive audience for advertising, as they are for CCTV. Just as they cannot avoid the cameras, the advertising screens are also always flickering away. One can only choose not to look. Passengers cannot program out transit TV ads as they can with digital TV recorders or leave the viewing area like one can at home. GPS technology can allow advertisers to have their ads shown immediately before the bus stop where their product can be purchased. In London and across the United Kingdom, many bus companies are using the Crystaleyes system, where the CCTV cameras are linked into a dynamic news and advertising content provider. A small LCD flat screen is mounted in the top floor of a double-decker bus, obscuring part of the front window. The monitor displays news and advertising and CCTV images from the bus. The monitors' news and advertising content can be wirelessly updated, allowing for near real-time changes. This system is not yet linked into GPS technology in London, but it could be. With Crystaleyes, the viewing loop is closed. The passengers can watch themselves being watched.

Although the Data Protection Act does not allow the release of the in-bus videos to advertising researchers, there are other ways that the data are collected, either through surveys or through the information provided through the purchase of season tickets or smart cards. Sam Jaffe in his article "Easy Riders"[14] quotes a U.S. transit advertising research analyst arguing that transit advertising is an underused resource that is just beginning to get serious treatment from marketers: "If the transit system has electronic card readers and a good computer network, it's relatively easy to get a lot of information. ... The information is out there just waiting to be used." This information can be basic, such as whether the passenger holds a senior or a student pass, or can be personal, such as information given when purchasing the card or data on passenger e-mail and Internet use. The data the transport companies collect to provide better service are often the same information they need to sell advertising and profile their riders as potential consumers. Transport companies, like newspapers or television networks, are competing for advertising dollars by generating more detailed demographic data sets of their users.

What could possibly be wrong with a highly subsidized public service generating much needed additional revenue? Three answers come immediately to mind. First, public transport is a necessary public service and a monopoly. A large amount of bus riders are transport dependent and have no choice other than to be watched and tracked if they are to have any mobility and access to health care, employment, and education. Second, with a focus on creating increasingly detailed pitches to transport users based on their demographics and current locations, transport companies are constantly exposing the riders to a certain designed view of the world with certain prejudices. This is the case for communities struggling with liquor, drug, and unemployment issues who see only ads for pawnshops and beer in their neighborhoods. The social construction and exclusion of these groups is reinforced and amplified (Gandy 2003). The challenge for democratic societies is to protect against invasive profiling that rewards some behaviors and pushes others to invisibility. The risk is not solely a loss of privacy but growing social stratification (Lyon 2003d). Third, certain forms of public transport, such as short-trip bus travel, are predominantly used by the urban poor and especially working poor women. Security and tracking actions from the transit companies necessarily have a disproportional effect on these populations.

At the same time, the new focus on improving bus travel should be welcomed, as it is clear that priorities for spending have been more often on improving services to attract car owners rather than addressing the captured market of the transit dependent. Some of the technological improvements to buses to increase speed and reliability can be welcomed by all. Vancouver's Translink makes the argument that better information services and reliable transport information make it easier for transport-dependent passengers to make the best use of the system (Greater Vancouver Transit Authority 2004a: 36). The danger seems to lie in the expansion of demographic and transaction data collection to shape transport policy without an accompanying increase in the accessibility and transparency of the policy-development process. Bus users are some of the most marginalized in our societies to begin with, and care must be taken to ensure that new data collection methods do not detract from efforts to integrate more transport-dependent users in the development and implementation of transit priorities. It is not acceptable to simply watch and track passengers, because that assumes that the watchers and trackers already know what to watch and count and allows for answers and information solely along a predetermined schema. It removes people's ability to be part of setting what the choices are, rather than simply choosing between them. Just as democracy should not be just voting and polls but instead be an effort to include as many perspectives as possible in the agenda-setting and implementation process, public services such as transport will benefit from not just tracking their passengers but finding more time to carefully and openly listen to them.

Acknowledgments

I want to thank Dr. Barb Serfozo, Anne Enderwitz, and Ola Svenonius for their comments and assistance with this chapter.

Notes

1. In the United States, these systems are known as "intelligent transportation systems."
2. See http://www.tc.gc.ca/programs/environment/UTSP/intelligenttransportationsystems.htm (accessed October 15, 2005).
3. I conducted this research with my colleague at the Centre for Technology and Society, Dr. Leon Hempel.
4. "Three Year Plan and 10 Year Outlook," February 19, 2004, p. 14.
5. However, much research shows that rail, light rail, and underground services that are used by wealthier travelers are actually more subsidized than local bus services disproportionately used by the poor. See Hiroyuki Iseki and Brian D. Taylor, "The Demographics of Public Transit Subsidies: A Case Study of Los Angeles" (paper submitted for presentation at the 81st Annual Meeting of the Transportation Research Board, Washington, DC, 2001).
6. As of November 2005, Vancouver did not use cameras on buses but has been discussing their installation in other modes of transport.
7. See http://news.bbc.co.uk/2/hi/uk_news/england/london/3616156.stm (accessed October 15, 2005).
8. See http://www.nyc.gov/html/nypd/html/chfdept/compstat-process.html.
9. Department of Transport (2004: 9).
10. S. Lyon (2004).
11. See http://www.security.thalesgroup.com/press/pr_view.php?id=280 (accessed October 15, 2005).
12. Center for Urban Transport Research at the University of South Florida.
13. Transport for London press release, September 10, 2004.
14. American Demographics, March 1, 2004.

CHAPTER **15**

The Bundling of Geospatial Information with Everyday Experience

LANE DENICOLA

So long as everyday life remains in thrall to abstract space, with its very concrete constraints; so long as the only improvements to occur are technical improvements of detail (for example, the frequency and speed of transportation, or relatively better amenities); so long, in short, as the only connection between work spaces, leisure spaces and living spaces is supplied by the agencies of political power and by their mechanisms of control—so long must the project of "changing life" remain no more than a political rallying-cry to be taken up or abandoned according to the mood of the moment.

Lefebvre (1991: 60)

Introduction

No less a political luminary than Hannah Arendt described the 1957 launch of Sputnik, the first artificial satellite, as a technological event "second in importance to no other, not even to the splitting of the atom" (Arendt 1998: 1). Although her claim could reasonably be attributed in part to the still-reverberating sublimity of the event (*The Human Condition* first saw publication in 1958), she insightfully noted the theme of earthly escape in the ensuing popular discourse: "Nobody in the history of mankind has ever conceived of the earth as a prison for men's bodies or shown such eagerness to go literally from here to the moon" (Arendt 1998: 2). Arendt's juxtaposition of these human products—extraterrestrial artifice and the incarcerated body—is worth reflection, for it points to the ineluctable interdependence of the spatial aspects of a society's framing mythologies and the envelope of potential actions conceived of by the individuals within that society. As a general topic of social inquiry, this interdependence has a venerable literature. Durkheim suggested that "spatial [cosmological] organization was modeled on social organization and replicates it," that it was "the product of religious, and hence collective, representations" (Durkheim and Fields 1995: 11). Eliade likewise proposed space as socially constructed, a primordial dichotomy between the *profane space* of the everyday (and the modern) and the *sacred space* of religious experience (and the premodern), the latter being manifested as an "irruption" within the homogeneous, geometrically undifferentiated former (Eliade and Trask 1959: 20–23). One scholar of the past century in particular adopted not just space but the social and political significance of our everyday experience of it, as the focal abstraction for a potent social critique. Henri Lefebvre's *The Production of Space* (Lefebvre 1991), first published in 1974, offers an insight peculiarly appropriate to the analysis of an emerging sociotechnical phenomenon with significant implications for surveillance and security. I refer to this phenomenon—predicated on a specific type of technology, the *artificial satellite constellation*—as the "bundling" of geospatial information with everyday experience.

Critical analysis of the surveillance implications of geospatial information systems must contend with the obvious first-order connection they now enjoy through artificial satellites as a *symbol*. Thanks in no small part to the late twentieth-century rise of the "spy novel" and the "technothriller" as literary genres, few technological systems bear as potent a popular association with surveillance and security as the earth-orbiting satellite, particularly those systems used in position finding, eavesdropping, missile tracking, the monitoring of nuclear detonations, and the imaging of the terrestrial surface. The scale and expense of such systems, their emergence within a cold war landscape, and their highly centralized control, global scope, and inherent invisibility make the relevance of their development to issues of surveillance and security seem obvious. Now commonplace technology demonstrates that devices small enough to fit into a cell phone, in concert with an orbiting constellation of satellites and a supporting infrastructure on the ground, can instantly provide an individual's location nearly anywhere on the earth, to within an accuracy on the order of meters. Their value in the (overt or clandestine) surveilling of the movements of individuals and objects is presumably clear. Likewise, earth remote sensing (ERS) satellites are continuously collecting and archiving strategically chosen patches or contiguous ribbons of imagery of the earth's surface, with resolutions on the order of half a meter available to anyone willing to pay the price (give or take a few state-imposed restrictions), and even greater capabilities are afforded the most powerful national governments. Such systems have become almost synonymous with surveillance, their use the subject of popular speculation long before public acknowledgment of the American Keyhole program, the first satellite system used for espionage (Lindgren 2000).

Another first-order connection between surveillance and geospatial information systems (distinct from the analytic subject presented here) is their underpinning of geographic information systems. The data from position-finding and ERS systems are often merged with data gathered on the ground (e.g., physical measurements, marketing surveys, or census data) to produce a geographic information system, a heterogeneous database whose principal index is a set of terrestrial coordinates. Such spatialized databases are employed by a vast cross section of industries and organizations both public and private, pursuant to a variety of endeavors from petroleum prospecting to urban planning, environmental management to retail targeting, disaster preparedness to homeland security. Critical geographers and other scholars have led investigations into the social implications of geographic information systems, including discussion of matters of privacy and state control, the displacement of local knowledge systems, and possibilities for participation by communities in the design of any geographic information system in which they are a subject.[1] Examinations of the implications of such systems for social justice and democratic governance have contributed to the topics of surveillance and security, from the legality of the thermal imaging of private residences to the "locational privacy" infractions of cell phones to the "dataveillance" aspects of geocoded records.

A less-addressed dimension of surveillance as enabled through geospatial technologies—the dimension addressed in this chapter—can be approached through the topic of everyday experience by asking how a *reconfiguration of spatial perception* might contribute to a cultural matrix that is catalytic to surveillance. Distinct from the literal application of geospatial systems to surveillance, their shaping of the envelope of everyday practice is akin to "the capillary dispersion of suspicion throughout the carceral society" by means of, for example, the increased deployment of drug-use screening technologies in the workplace and elsewhere (Campbell 2004: 78; Chapter 4, this volume). Adopting the broad conceptual frame of the burgeoning geoinformatics industry, this chapter considers two forms of geospatial information—data in which the principal index is a set of coordinates within a globally scoped and globally standardized coordinate system. The first form is the index itself: *global location* or, more specific, the continuously updated stream of global coordinates for some set of bodies or objects. The second, crucially dependent on the first for its technical utility, is the *terrestrial image,* a photographic (or, more and more common today, digital) representation of the terrestrial surface and objects thereon, collected by devices on aircraft or satellites. Each of these two forms of information has been attached to everyday experience through different mechanisms, but consideration of a few of the central concepts from Lefebvre's *The Production of Space* yields valuable insights for the critical analysis of both and provides a framework by which their commonalities can be discerned. One objective of this chapter is to contribute to the pool of examples in which technological systems can operate as "bundling mechanisms," enmeshing a new spatial awareness in everyday experience—in Lefebvre's terms, "producing a new space"—and so following the empirical presentation of the chapter, I summarize relevant concepts from Lefebvre's work.

Satellite-based navigation (global location) and ERS (the terrestrial image) are only two of the most recent in the past two centuries of electronic and optical technologies to catalyze spatial reconfiguration. To set in relief those aspects in which they do set a new precedent, I briefly consider historiographic work on the effects on "everyday spatial awareness" of nineteenth-century technologies. First, the contemporaneous invention of the telegraph and the railroad shattered (over the course of several decades) European and American experiences of space, less from a raw acceleration in human activity than from the cleft that resulted (following the introduction of these technologies) between the previously unified activities of *communication* and *transportation.* The salience of these developments to the empirical analysis of the bundling of geospatial information rests in their illustration of how politics is enacted not simply through institutions and state actions or processes but within the space "produced" through everyday practice (a production mediated by technology). This is similarly illustrated in the second case I consider, specifically the nineteenth-century development of visual techniques and optical technologies (e.g., the stereoscope) and the concurrent shift toward *observation* and *attention* as pivotal capacities of a rational, mentally "healthy" subject. The argument is made that this development—the "production of an observer adequate to" a specific societal structure—was crucial to the wider demands of capitalist expansion. As a reading of a historical moment in technological development, it compels an equal scrutiny of the qualities of "locatability" and the "observer presumed by" the various systems unflinchingly collecting the *terrestrial image*. It likewise suggests the possibility of a profound synergy between capitalism and surveillance.

Global Location

Satellite-based navigation technically relies on three components: a constellation of radio-navigation satellites, a ground-control segment that manages the operation of these satellites, and the comparatively small receivers carried by individual users. The satellites maintain accurate time through ultraprecise onboard atomic clocks, transmitting this time and other signals to receivers on the ground. By comparison of the time signals received from three separate satellites (and in some applications, a separate receiver at a known location on the ground), position in three dimensions relative to some spatial reference system[2]—what I refer to generically here as *global location*—can be ascertained (typically in the form of latitude, longitude, and height above or below sea level). Satellite-based navigation began as the vision of the U.S. military in the mid-1960s, an organization with a strong interest in a global, all-weather, continuously available, highly accurate positioning and navigation system that could address the needs of a broad spectrum of users. A number of systems were devised and deployed and became operational during the late 1960s, but a joint initiative of the Air Force, Navy, and Army that began in 1968 was tasked in 1973 with the unification of several concept systems then on the drawing board into a single system, the Defense Navigation Satellite System, which eventually became the NAVSTAR Global Positioning System or GPS. The first developmental satellites were launched in the mid- and late 1970s, while the twenty-fourth "Block II" GPS satellite, launched in 1994, completed the deployment of the full constellation (though the system saw extensive use for many years prior to that). The cost to American taxpayers for the design, development, and deployment of GPS has run upward of $10 billion.[3]

The most important aspect of GPS for the discussion here is its availability to and proliferation among civilian users. Despite their intention from the program's earliest days to make GPS signals available for civil applications, the U.S. Department of Defense had argued strenuously against provision of the same level of capability to both civilian and military users. This resulted in a two-tiered system (dubbed "selective availability") where significantly greater positioning accuracy was made available to military equipment, but the scheme proved to be untenable for a number of reasons, and in the summer of 2000 this reduction in civil accuracy was simply turned off (though it was kept available for regional activation should national security be threatened). This sudden leap in accuracy enabled a wide variety of civil applications that previously were simply impossible, many with obvious implications for surveillance and security at the micro-level. "Equally adept at tracking vehicles, employees, adolescents, and convicted criminals, GPS is very much a surveillance technology, with credible threats to personal privacy. Just ask the former clients of Acme Rent-a-Car, a Connecticut firm that tracked its vehicles by satellite and fined customers exceeding 79 MPH" (Monmonier 2002: 13).

Again, what is of specific interest to the discussion here is not these clear and credible threats to "location privacy" but those threats that materialize through the shaping of our common everyday experience and so may be more difficult to discern. The position-finding capability provided by GPS underpins a vast (and growing) array of systems, from survey and cartography to resource management and transportation system control. Any civilian application involving measurements or observations made on the ground (from soil alkalinity to toxic releases, social demographics to the accounts of refugees) can easily include position as an additional datum, thereby permitting ready incorporation into a geographic information system. More generally, although situations where the lay user is interested in his or her actual coordinates are usually limited to recreational activities such as camping or sailing, onboard navigation systems providing contextual maps are becoming commonplace on aircraft, watercraft, and automobiles, particularly in the West. Thanks to the spread of cellular phones in the late 1980s and early 1990s—and the resulting explosion of emergency calls from cellular users who were unable to accurately describe their location—in 1996 the FCC ordered cellular providers to build position-finding capability into their networks (the so-called E911 initiative). Although several schemes for providing such capability were conceived, the microminiaturization of GPS receivers down to a single chip is today a reality. The routine availability and precision of position that is possible with GPS has been recognized as a widely marketable commodity, and a new sector of "location-based services" has emerged in recent years.[4] These include both user-centered services (such as the ability to quickly locate by cell phone the ATM or restaurant nearest to one's current location) and business services (for example, automated advertising for a restaurant on the cell phones of potential customers in its immediate vicinity).

Two recent developments serve to underline the growing pervasiveness and importance of global location. Executive Order 12906, signed by President Clinton in 1994 and amended in 2003 by President Bush, established the Federal Geographic Data Committee, responsible for coordinating the development of a National Spatial Data Infrastructure, the sum total of "technology, policies, criteria, standards and people necessary to promote geospatial data sharing throughout all levels of government, the

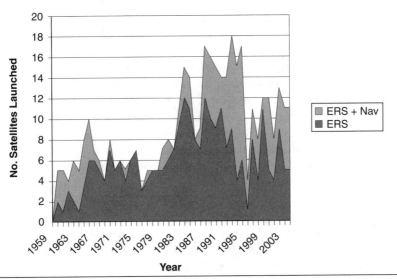

Figure 15.1 Annual number of satellite launches for civil earth remote sensing and navigation applications. Data from Wade (2005).

private and non-profit sectors, and academia." The stated objective is "to support public and private sector applications of geospatial data in such areas as transportation, community development, agriculture, emergency response, environmental management, and information technology" (Executive Order 12906 1994). The United States, however, is hardly the only nation to be enamored of geospatial information technologies. Beginning in the late 1990s, the European Commission undertook its first major technical venture: its own satellite-based navigation system, called *Galileo*, to be deployed and operational by 2008. Its many touted improvements over GPS include civil control (GPS remains under the ultimate control of the U.S. Air Force) and a multileveled system of legal guarantees against signal interruption, including a "life-critical" level of service (European Commission Directorate-General of Energy and Transportation 2004). It is telling that the current U.S. administration, predicated in part on the Department of Defense's doctrine of "space domination," has publicly been quite vocal in expressing disapproval of the European Union's move toward an independent positioning system under civil control (Ball 2004).

The Terrestrial Image

The second case of geospatial information bundling I now consider critically depends in nearly all contemporary cases on the satellite-based location systems discussed earlier but is wholly distinct in the manner of its proliferation through everyday experience.[5] ERS—the science and craft of collecting, processing, and interpreting images of the earth's surface from high altitude—yields the geospatial information form I refer to here as the *terrestrial image*.[6] The canonical origin of ERS—another geospatial technology unquestionably of military derivation (Cloud 2001)—is traced to the first known aerial photograph, taken by Parisian photographer Gaspard Félix Tournachon[7] in 1858 from a tethered balloon, eighty meters above the French town of Bievre. The airplane did not see use as a photographic platform until 1908, five years after its invention, but with the opening of World War I, the military use of aerial reconnaissance photographs was made clear. In 1934 the American Society of Photogrammetry (now the American Society of Photogrammetry and Remote Sensing) was established by former military specialists who had commercialized aerial photography for surveying applications (Lillesand and Kiefer 2000: 57). With the advent of radar by the British in 1935, "sight at a distance" was extended both in range and in sensitivity (as well as into new regions of the electromagnetic spectrum), and the role of both these early remote sensing technologies only increased over the course of World War II. Within the first decade of the Cold War, President Eisenhower would empower the defense establishment to develop the three photoreconnaissance systems pivotal to postwar American strategic foreign policy: the U-2 aircraft (used primarily from 1956 until the aircraft of pilot Francis Gary Powers was shot down in 1960), the SR-71 aircraft (operational beginning in 1966, though never actually used for its originally intended mission of Soviet surveillance), and the Corona system of earth-orbiting satellites, which took up where the U-2 left off, becoming operational in 1960 (Lindgren 2000). It was in this same year that the first *civil* satellite system for imaging came online: the Television and Infra-Red Observation Satellite, or Tiros, a system for weather observation.

ERS is only one of the principal space industries—also composed of telecommunications, space transportation, and (as discussed earlier) satellite-based navigation—and by some measures it generates a relatively small portion of those industries' direct revenue: US$300 million in 2002 or less than 5 percent (Office of Space Commercialization 2001). In terms of growth, however, although only a handful of imaging satellites were in orbit in the 1970s, more than 60 were continuously monitoring the state of the earth by 2002, with more than 100 additional imaging satellites scheduled for deployment over the next decade (Aschbacher 2002). ERS likewise has scientific significance disproportionate to the direct revenue it generates,[8] and industry privatization and technical innovations in sensor resolution and computing have precipitated significant challenges to orthodox concepts of national sovereignty[9] and intellectual property, destabilized privacy protections and the regulation of geospatial information, swamped analysts with vast streams of data, and opened up new questions about the role of expertise and local knowledge in environmental policy making.

The central question here concerns the process by which ERS is substantively shaping our common, everyday experience and in particular what "space" it is contributing to the production of. In part this question can be treated empirically. Three mechanisms through which such shaping might occur are considered here:

- the reconfiguration by ERS of everyday understandings of social or quasi-social concepts (e.g., sovereignty),
- the embedding of ERS products within civil practices (such as environmental management and urban planning) and the resultant influences on everyday life, and
- the proliferation and circulation of ERS imagery and technology as a cultural symbol.

It is noteworthy that a defining millennial moment was experienced with an unparalleled immediacy—and by the vast majority of the world's population—in no small part through ERS technology. When the attack on the World Trade Center and the Pentagon occurred on September 11, 2001, all nonmilitary aircraft were immediately grounded or forbidden from entering U.S. airspace. As a result, the event was visually captured, transmitted around the globe, and inscribed into history not only through photographs and video taken by local observers but by the Kodak-built camera on the IKONOS high-resolution imaging satellite, lofted into orbit twenty-four months earlier by the Space Imaging company. The then-and-now comparison of the lower Manhattan mise-en-scène, the prominent twin towers from months before on one side, the smoking hole left in the prickling urban terrain on the other, was so compelling an image that Space Imaging made medium-resolution versions available for free on the Internet, a testament to the power of their primary product. The 9/11 aftermath—the rescue and recovery efforts, the forensic data collections, the colossal cleanup task, and the early stages of the reconfiguration into a commemorative space—reverberated in the new register of the terrestrial image. The event marked the emergence of a new popular visual genre.[10] Many people in and outside the West have experienced American operations in Afghanistan, the ongoing war in Iraq, and most recently the catastrophic December 2004 tsunami in Asia as a stream of annotated, up-to-the-minute, high-resolution satellite images, reproduced on television, in newspapers and magazines, and particularly online as "interactive features," where viewers can zoom in to inspect individual buildings in the

American military base in Mosul or the trees and buildings scoured from what was once the Sumatran town of Lhoknga.

Particularly for Americans engaged in distant state-sponsored conflicts, many with family or friends directly involved in the activity, our daily conversations and concerns have been visually extended to the public (and, in some cases, what were effectively private) spaces of physically remote communities. This disruption of the boundary between public and private has also developed more locally and arises from the prosthetic sensory nature of ERS. The use of thermal-imaging capabilities to confirm illicit activities within enclosed buildings or to verify compliance with environmental law within the confines of multibuilding industrial complexes has in some cases been upheld within American courts, in other cases not (Brilis, Gerlach, and Van Waasbergen 2000; Markowitz 2002). More generally, ERS imagery has been employed within the judicial process to corroborate environmental conditions or events described in testimony and to disambiguate regional boundaries and the disputed location of photographed events. In introductory comments at a UN General Assembly in October 2004, the UN Office of Outer Space Affairs suggested that "now is the right time for the space and development agendas [of the UN] to be fully integrated" and that space technology "can be key in relation to a whole number of core items on the [UN] agenda" (Environmental News Service 2004). Nongovernmental organizations such as VERTIC and GlobalSecurity.org have advocated and even successfully employed ERS imagery in exposés of state or corporate violations of international agreements (Pike 2005; Verification Research, Training, and Information Center 2005). Global Monitoring for Environment and Security (2005), a joint initiative of the European Commission and the European Space Agency that depends heavily on ERS data sources and infrastructure, has the stated aim "to support Europe's goals regarding sustainable development and global governance, in support of environmental and security policies, by facilitating and fostering the timely provision of quality data, information, and knowledge."

Today, ERS also operates on the level of symbol, an unsurprising development given that psychologists working in the field of human factors refer to ERS data as "nonliteral imagery," visual representations that (in contrast to mere photographs, whose content is presumably transparent) demand a specialized technical literacy to interpret (R.R. Hoffman and Markman 2001). It is not only through the popular news media that the nonspecialist is exposed to ERS. It is a visual form that has bled into the realm of *representational space* (a Lefebvrian concept to be discussed shortly), and here its signification varies according to the conventions of genre. Susan Roberts and Richard Schein (1995: 192) suggested a decade ago that "advertisements may be the most 'public' face of geographic technologies"

Figure 15.2 The website of Space Imaging, a leading commercial provider of high-resolution satellite imagery. (Courtesy of Space Imaging.)

and analyzed the dialectical relationship of such advertisements with the inhabited world and with the technologies being advertised (also drawing on the work of Lefebvre in their analysis). Popular films have likewise capitalized on the omnipresent, high-technology connotations of ERS capability, "conjuring"[11] the superlative technical authority it symbolizes in a spectacle of state power.[12] In July 2002, the U.S. Geological Survey celebrated the thirtieth anniversary of the Landsat satellite's first image-collection activity by opening its popular "Earth as Art" traveling exhibit, in which images taken by the Landsat 7 satellite and "selected on the basis of aesthetic appeal" were displayed (U.S. Geological Survey 2002a). The exhibit is now being expanded in an online version hosted by NASA's Goddard Space Flight Center (U.S. Geological Survey 2002b). The most prominent high-resolution imagery providers (e.g., Space Imaging and DigitalGlobe) maintain significant galleries of free downloadable images of sites relevant to current events, and in the case of Space Imaging, a separate online store has been established to allow people to purchase poster-size prints of its terrestrial images, whose subjects range from states and cities to specific urban features such as stadiums, monuments, university campuses, golf courses, racetracks, or even one's own residence. NASA is well positioned to capitalize on this new demand; the agency maintains a number of unique online ERS resources, intended more for the general public than for professional interpreters.[13] Even the technology is cast as something to be recreationally observed. Some websites provide "satellite profiles" and locale-specific flyover times so that satellites can be observed in the same manner as astronomical phenomena (Peat 2005), and software is available for the home PC that generates visualizations of satellites in flight, including ground tracks, sensor footprints, and other graphical embellishments (XtremeMac 2005).

Everyday Experience and the Production of Space

The "conquering of time and space" through technological means is a well-worn trope of modernity, and it has enjoyed intensification in contemporary narratives of the Information Revolution.

> Perhaps the most significant challenge posed by the linking of computers and telecommunications is the prospect that the basic structures of political order will be recast. Worldwide computer, satellite, and communication networks fulfill, in large part, the modern dream of conquering space and time. These systems make possible instantaneous action at any point on the globe without limits imposed by the specific location of the initiating actor. Human beings and human societies, however, have traditionally found their identities within spatial and temporal limits. They have lived, acted, and found meaning in a particular place at a particular time. (Winner 1988: 116)

Narratives of technological manifest destiny and the unyielding march of progress tout the "end of geography" and the annihilation of the meaning of distance (Cairncross 1997), but this understanding of the effects on space suffers from two major flaws: its equation of *distance* and *geography*, and its dependence on a purely *physical* understanding of geography. The significance of geographic characteristics that are independent of distance and the "symbolic, social, and cultural construction" of place belie the annihilation thesis, and this broad set of changes is instead more accurately understood as a *transformation* of space.[14] In *The Production of Space*, Lefebvre pressed for an even stronger shift in our conceptualization of the past two centuries of spatial reconfiguration, a shift built less on a model of space as a passive medium or empty container ready to be filled with things but rather on a model of space as *actively producing and produced by social relations*.[15] Central to this reconceptualization is the recognition of such social relations in the realm of everyday experience:

> A revolution that does not produce a new space has not realized its full potential; indeed it has failed in that has not changed life

itself, but has merely changed ideological superstructures, institutions or political apparatuses. A social transformation, to be truly revolutionary in character, must manifest a creative capacity in its effects on daily life, on language and on space—though its impact need not occur at the same rate, or with equal force, in each of these areas. (Lefebvre 1991: 54)

In analyzing the significance of geospatial information to critical issues in surveillance and security, it is worthwhile to ask what such a reconceptualization of space might yield for that analysis. Where is the relationship between state and civic practices and everyday experience? What aspects of "observation" as a common experience are encoded in the circulated terrestrial image? At what point does sovereignty explicitly become a spatial matter, or, alternatively, at what point does global location become a matter of the body?

Two concepts developed by Lefebvre in sketching the broad outlines for a "history and science of space" are especially useful here. First, Lefebvre describes a broad historical division between *absolute space,* the heterogeneous, historical, civil, and religious space of premodern society, and *abstract space,* the homogeneous, ahistorical, quantitative, and fluid space of modernity. Absolute space is epitomized in such forms as the premodern village, the nave of a cathedral, and (near the historical transition to abstract space) the medieval town with its surrounding network of roads spanning the local countryside. "Capitalism and neocapitalism," meanwhile, "have produced abstract space, which includes the 'world of commodities,' its 'logic' and its worldwide strategies, as well as the power of money and that of the political state. This space is founded on the vast network of banks, business centres and major productive entities, as also on motorways, airports and information lattices" (Lefebvre 1991: 53). Furthermore, "abstract space, the space of the bourgeoisie and of capitalism, bound up as it is with exchange (of goods and commodities, as of written and spoken words, etc.) depends on consensus more than any space before it … One of its contradictions is that between the appearance of security and the constant threat, and indeed occasional eruption, of violence" (p. 57). This dichotomy presents at once an apparently straightforward reading of the bundling of geospatial information—what else does it entail but the provision of an abstract space, one both globally homogeneous and quantitatively reductive? There are ruptures in that reading, however. Given their technical similarities, on what basis does the civil management of the proposed Galileo system and its adherence to free market principles challenge the hegemony of America's GPS? More concretely, the terrestrial image seems in many instances to cathect abstract space and the "global implosion" effected by information networks with a revitalized sense of local particularity.

Another of the concepts developed in *The Production of Space* with obvious relevance to this analysis is Lefebvre's distinction between "three moments" of social space:

> The *spatial practice* of a society secretes that society's space; it propounds and presupposes it, in a dialectical interaction; it produces it slowly and surely as it masters and appropriates it. From the analytic standpoint, the spatial practice of a society is revealed through the deciphering of its space ... *Representations of space* [are] conceptualized space, the space of engineers, planners, urbanists, technocratic subdividers and social engineers, as of a certain type of artist with a scientific bent—all of whom identify what is lived and what is perceived with what is conceived ... *Representational spaces* ... [are those] directly *lived* through [their] associated images and symbols, and hence the space of "inhabitants" and "users," but also of some artists and perhaps of those, such as a few writers and philosophers, who *describe* and aspire to do no more than describe. This is the dominated—and hence passively experienced—space which the imagination seeks to change and appropriate. (Lefebvre 1991: 38–39)

Spatial practice, representations of space, and representational spaces are each a crucial intersection within the program Lefebvre proposes for a "science of space," but it is their distinctions and mutual interaction and shaping that Lefebvre foregrounds in that program. As the principal commodity of urban planners and technical geographers, geospatial information—as inscribed, for example, within geographic information systems—is clearly a representation of space. The empirical evidence considered here, however, unsettles this triad, illustrating how global location and the terrestrial image appear to straddle these moments in their traces on everyday lives and material conditions, complicating and enriching any reading of geospatial information technologies. The slippage and catalytic interaction between the three is an aspect of the terrestrial image that is central to its spatially productive power.

As a segue from the theoretical framework I take from Lefebvre, I next consider two important historiographic cases, each similar in its own way to the present analysis insofar as both approach the social study of science and technological development by examining the phenomenology and shaping of everyday spatial experience. The examples serve first by providing a comparative perspective on the framework developed by Lefebvre ("absolute space/abstract space" and "spatial practice/representations of space/representational spaces"), a perspective that effectively illustrates my interpretation of that framework. Just as important, each of these two cases serves to corroborate the analytic approach taken here in understanding how spatial awareness can be bundled (or unbundled, as the case may be) with everyday experience.

Communication and Transportation

In his analysis of and argument for cultural approaches to the study of "mass communications," James Carey outlines what he takes as the two primary conceptions of communication in the American context, both of which are essentially of religious derivation:

> The *transmission view* of communication is the commonest in our culture—perhaps in all industrial cultures—and dominates contemporary dictionary entries under the term. ... It is formed from a metaphor of geography or transportation. ... Our basic orientation to communication remains grounded, at the deepest roots of our thinking, in the idea of transmission: communication is a process whereby messages are transmitted and distributed in space for the control of distance and people ... The *ritual view* of communication, though a minor thread in our national thought, is by far the older of those views—old enough in fact for dictionaries to list it under "Archaic." ... A ritual view of communication is directed not toward the extension of messages in space but toward the maintenance of society in time; not the act of imparting information but the representation of shared beliefs. (J. Carey 1989: 15–16)

This dyad bears clear similarities to Lefebvre's conceptualization of abstract space and absolute space. A society that adheres more strongly to the transmission view of communication (as inscribed in technologies such as the printing press and electronic media) "reduces space and time to the service of a calculus of commercialism and expansionism," which is to say that it produces *abstract* space. Social interaction built on the ritual view, meanwhile, valorizes local and historical particularity and the interpretive process, producing *absolute* space. In addition to underpinning his espousal of anthropological approaches to communications, these seemingly dichotomous views of the communicative process are the armature on which Carey subsequently builds an argument concerning the social significance of two deeply intertwined technologies: the railroad and the telegraph.

Beginning with the telegraph, electronic communication technologies created a schism in what had previously been a unitary experience, a division yielding the distinct phenomena of *communication* and *transportation*. Historically, information had most commonly traveled only as quickly as humans could transport physical objects through space, but with the development of the telegraph, a split was effected that "not only allowed messages to be separated from the physical movement of objects; it also allowed communication to control physical processes actively" (J. Carey 1989: 203), as in the case of telegraphic control of rolling stock by railroad switching. In the emerging cultural metaphor of control theory, the telegraph and the railroad became the "nerves and muscles," respectively, of the modern state. This technologically induced abstract space, Carey argues, "evens out markets in space. The telegraph puts everyone in the same place for the purposes of trade; it makes geography irrelevant" (pp. 217–221). This had the effect of decontextualizing local market peculiarities, making prices uniform across large geographic regions, and allowing commodities to flow independently from the receipts that represent them—the spatial and informational prerequisites for economic innovations such as futures markets. Particularly relevant here, however, is that Carey is considering not simply the effects of these technologies as tools of commerce but also how they "altered the spatial and temporal boundaries of human interaction, brought into existence new forms of language as well as new conceptual systems, and brought about new structures of social relations" (p. 204). This is precisely the manifestation of a "new space" Lefebvre explains is at the heart of all genuinely revolutionary social transformation.

This split between communication and transportation (and Carey's approach to it) is relevant to the present discussion of the geospatial. It is suggestive of the means through which our technologically mediated everyday experience—our *space*—can have profound political implications. It illustrates the sort of change I am referring to as "bundling," though in the inverse form of "unbundling"; an activity and an understanding common to a wide population were quite suddenly cleft into two very distinct concepts. Also, in looking ahead to the geospatial information systems to be discussed, I could say that our everyday experience of surveillance is refining the bodily metaphor of nerves and muscles by further splitting communication into the "afferent" versus the "efferent" neurological functions (the nerves that effect muscle control versus the sensory systems that convey bodily status and environmental conditions), confining communication to the former and establishing surveillance (through a capillary dispersion of specific social relations) as the latter within the secure body politic.

Observation and Attention

Another set of nineteenth-century technological developments had important implications for our everyday experience. In his potent analysis of the changes—realized through the optical technologies of both art and science—in Western understandings of human physiology and sensation, Jonathan Crary advocates an analytic distinction between optical devices and the "observer identity" presumed by such devices. Marking a pivotal transition in the early 1800s, Crary examines the stereoscope, a "quintessentially nineteenth-century optical technology" that enjoyed great popularity:

> Although "set to work" may sound inappropriate in a discussion of optical devices, the apparently passive observer of the stereoscope and phenakistiscope, by virtue of specific physiological capacities, was in fact made into a producer of forms of verisimilitude. And what the observer produced, again and again, was the effortless transformation of the dreary parallel images of flat stereo cards into a tantalizing apparition of depth. The content of the images is far less important than the inexhaustible routine of moving from one card to the next and producing the same effect, repeatedly, mechanically. And each time, the mass-produced and monotonous cards are transubstantiated into a compulsory and seductive vision of the "real." (Crary 1990: 132)

Crary's approach to the analysis of optical technologies and "observational technique" is of manifold relevance to the theorization of geospatial information being attempted here. First, it foregrounds a common entertainment modality as a part of everyday experience in the nineteenth century, with the requisite sensitivity to bodily presentation espoused by Lefebvre. It is the "observational architecture" that arises through the stereoscope as a popularly distributed device and (in contrast with passive models of observation) the *active participation* of the observer within a web of visual signification that are at the heart of matter. This shaping of the "presumed observer" in discourse and practice was part of a tectonic shift in the economic and cultural terrain, one that demanded "a more adaptable, autonomous, and productive observer ... to conform to new functions of the body and to a vast proliferation of indifferent and convertible signs and images" (Crary 1990: 149). The move toward homogeneity and fluidity of exchange Crary reads into this shaping of everyday observational technique is in close congruence with the move Lefebvre describes from absolute to abstract space. Crary notes, in fact, that "according to critical theorists [Lefebvre among them], our insistence on an actual, objectively understandable, representable kind of space promotes certain political agendas" (p. 79).

Another of Crary's analytic subjects is the coincident development, within the human sciences but in particular through the field of psychology, of "attention" as a—even *the*—fundamental issue in the demarcation of rationality and cognitive health. Juxtaposing his analysis with much of the contemporary critical literature on spectacle, he writes:

> Spectacle is not primarily concerned with a *looking at* images but rather with the construction of conditions that individuate, immobilize, and separate subjects, even within a world in which mobility and circulation are ubiquitous. In this way attention becomes key to the operation of noncoercive forms of power. This is why it is not inappropriate to conflate seemingly different optical or technological objects: they are similarly about arrangements of bodies in space, techniques of isolation, cellularization, and above all separation. Spectacle is not an optics of power but an architecture. Television and the personal computer, even as they are now converging toward a single machinic functioning, are antinomadic procedures that fix and striate. They are methods for the management of attention that use partitioning and sedentarization, rendering bodies controllable and useful simultaneously, even as they simulate the illusion of choices and "interactivity." (Crary 1999: 74–75)

It is important to maintain the distinction between these conceptions of spectacle (visual fascination versus noncoercive control) in understanding the political implications of geospatial information. The politics of observational modalities dwell not simply in the literal content we observe, and likewise the politics of locational modalities can be found outside the more orthodox concerns of "surveillance" (privacy, consent, disclosure, accessibility, etc.). The deepest changes effected by optical (and geospatial) technologies occur more subtly but just as concretely on the level of bodily control and arrangement in space, on the level of "life as lived," which is to say that politics resides just as powerfully in the everyday experience of specific bodily dispositions. In decoding their meaning for surveillance and security, a commensurate level of nuance in that register must be sustained. Crary also makes clear that taking an analytic focus on loosely related or seemingly unrelated technologies may in some situations be warranted in their parallel effects on everyday experience. In considering both satellite-based navigation (global location) and ERS (the terrestrial image), two technically similar systems with quite distinct products and applications, I take the commonalities in their ability to arrange bodies in space, to fix, striate, and separate, as more deeply informative than either case considered on its own.

Conclusions

Surveillance inherently entails a bundling, the attachment (or the potential attachment) of new recording mechanisms, inconspicuous or overt, to commonplace, otherwise anonymous activities. It is true that the *culmination* of surveillance hinges on "linking," the establishment of connections. Closed-circuit video of a person committing a crime, their fingerprints or DNA at the scene, and recordings of their phone conversations before and after the alleged crime are of use to the state when they *corroborate* each other, when that person becomes "ready at hand" or that data are linked with a "documented identity" (residential location, tax or financial records, employment records, medical records, familial relationships, social and political affiliations, etc.). Data collected on our everyday actions (patterns of entertainment, consumption of goods and services, civic participation) become of use to marketers through correlation and connection in demographic analyses. The mode of surveillance, however, is a bundling: video recording with department store perusal, drug testing with employment, "lifestyle segmentation profiling" with the use of consumer credit. Surveillance can be employed to verify compliance (and deter noncompliance), to enable after-the-fact analysis or classification, and to inform predictive models of future action, but in all cases there is a process of bundling. Although the inverse may hold true—anonymity demands an *un*bundling—the converse need not; that is, not all bundling enables surveillance.

The bundling of geospatial information arguably represents in reified form the abstract space described by Lefebvre. Aside from the literally practical, syncretic drive toward a standardized coordinate system, global location is coded (in the cultural sense) virtuous through its underlying qualities: homogeneity, universal applicability, quantitative certainty, and fluidity in exchange and manipulation. A trade journal advertisement for a GPS receiver for surveyors asks, "Got centimeters?" (Ashtech Precision Products 2001). In a play on the popular and widely mimicked "Got milk?" advertising campaign of an American dairy industry association, positional accuracy stands in for a homogenized, organic, and fluid sustenance. The rhetoric of the geospatial information industry echoes that of the wider information technology sector, touting the security of digital data and formats over time, the facile utility of geo-coded data, and the as-yet untapped commercial potential latent in geospatial archives, an information matrix awaiting the entrepreneurial data-mining prospector. The shift toward abstract space is effected not so much through some coercive imposition by the state of a uniform spatial standard—Lefebvre makes clear that any such endeavor is likely doomed to failure—but instead through an integration of the geospatial with civil discourse and practice; abstract space is "secreted by" and reciprocally constitutes a particular set of social relations, part of the constellation of everyday experience that (if only in the modern moment) is always technologically mediated.

Consider further Lefebvre's stance that "the genesis of a far-away order can be accounted for only on the basis of the order that is nearest to us—namely, the order of the body" (Lefebvre 1991: 405). From that perspective it becomes significant that global location (arguably an order less tangible, more remote, and inaccessible than almost any other), and in particular *locatability*, the quality of being continuously situated on a global (or globally referenced) spatial grid, is increasingly woven into the fabric of lived experience: how we communicate and interact with our families and others, how advertisements and other cultural forms are presented to us, how our immediate environments are designed and negotiated, where and what we consume. Beginning in the nineteenth-century, attention became (according to Crary) a normative category, the keystone capacity of a cognitively healthy subject, and he notes that "it is becoming clearer that a concurrence of panoptic techniques and attentive imperatives now functions reciprocally in many social locations" (Crary 1999: 76). Through spatial data infrastructures, the panoply of geospatial technologies involved, and the ubiquity of global location as a principal information substratum, the normative quality of locatability has been established—it is in fact becoming a crucial measure of the *secure subject*.

Returning again to the central question of this chapter—how might the bundling of geospatial information (in particular global location and the terrestrial image) with everyday experience be catalytic to a culture of surveillance—I suggest that "security" as a social need is a quality that both produces and is produced by a particular *space*, a space that must be read as constituted through social relations. Far more at issue than the "Big Brother" scenario of routine tracking and observation of individual citizens by orbiting satellites are the very real changes effected through such technologies in our everyday experience. Satellite-based navigation and observation contribute through the variety of mechanisms described to a broad shift in our sense of the secure, sovereign subject, thereby entrenching their continuous signals as unavoidably vital to contemporary society. Literally emplaced within the heavens, these megalithic systems are beyond the reach of all but the most powerful nations, offering little in the way of rapid adaptability to changing social concerns. Although their global transmissions cannot in and of themselves generate an abstract space, the attendant consumer technologies, spatial representations, and changes to civic practice can. Lefebvre wrote that abstract space

> functions *positively* vis-à-vis its own implications: technology, applied sciences, and knowledge bound to power. Abstract space may even be described as at once, and inseparably, the locus, medium and tool of this "positivity." How is this possible? Does it mean that this space

could be defined in terms of a reifying alienation, on the assumption that the milieu of the commodity has itself become a commodity to be sold wholesale and retail? (Lefebvre 1991: 50)

The evidence presented here demonstrates that global location and the terrestrial image are now commodities of increasing importance to environmental stewardship and the conduct of civic affairs. Although issues of the environment and state security may traditionally be quite distinct or even diametrically opposed, it is through the commodified terrestrial image that both are understood as aspects of the same fundamentally reconfigured space, a space with a global horizon but nonetheless secreted through micro/local practice. It is conceivable that the rhetoric of "earthly escape" noted by Arendt in the 1950s was in fact an expression (however unconscious) of a popular revulsion to the predominance of abstract space heralded by the artificial satellite. Recent clashes over the militarization of (outer) space and its protection as an international domain for peaceful endeavors compels us to inquire into the relations of surveillance and the newest mechanisms of capitalism, not to mention the significance in those relations of that space referred to as "low earth orbit."

Notes

1. Particularly relevant examples include Aitken and Michel (1995), Pickles (1995), Robbins (2003), Sheppard (1995), Sieber (2004), and Yapa (1995).
2. In the case of GPS, that reference system is referred to as the World Geodetic System 1984 (WGS84), an earth-coordinate system standard developed and refined by the U.S. National Imagery and Mapping Agency (2000).
3. See "Appendix B: GPS History, Chronology, and Budgets" in Pace et al. (1995). Also see Erickson (1995).
4. Satellite-based navigation systems such as GPS are only one of a number of possible frameworks on which location-based services could be built. See Preissl, Bouwman, and Steinfield (2004).
5. For the phenomena framed in ERS images to be accurately correlated with observations on the ground ("ground truth"), fiducial marks on the images must often be matched or registered with precisely known locations on the earth's surface, or in some cases the position of the sensor must be known. This information can be provided by satellite-based positioning systems such as GPS.
6. It is worth noting that the form of these images and the material practices used in their collection vary widely. They may exist as photographic negatives or in electronically stored digital files. They may rely on the transmissions and reflections of the earth and other natural sources, or they may require the illumination of the earth by an artificial source (e.g., a radar or laser beam). In either case the electromagnetic signals collected may mimic the human response pattern (i.e., visible light), some portion of the spectrum invisible to humans (e.g., the infrared), or a number of variations and combinations thereof.
7. Also known by the pseudonym "Nadar."
8. By early estimates "the international global change research program, which relies primarily on satellite observations for its data, is likely to become the largest research project in human history" (Litfin 1998: 194).
9. ERS is contributing to an unbundling of territoriality, deterritorializing state practices by making them "globally transparent" on one hand but enhancing the territorial sov-

ereignty of developing countries with remote regions (and reterritorializing the political practices of local environmental and indigenous groups) on the other hand. See Litfin (1998).

10. Even since before the 1999 launch of Space Imaging's IKONOS satellite, news media and journalism professional associations have lobbied to have ERS imagery enjoy the legal protections afforded "photojournalism." See Livingston (2001).

11. "In the gap between [lay and expert understandings of science in America after the mid-1800s], there arose a certain kind of mischief, namely, the conjuring of science. One could use the common symbols and imagery of science, as understood by nonscientists, to make it seem that scientists were bestowing the plenary authority of science on various ideologies that had nothing to do with science" (Toumey 1996: 8).

12. *Patriot Games* (1992), *Enemy of the State* (1998), and *The Bourne Identity* (2002), for example, each include scenes where characters are viewing satellite imagery or involve stylized special effects that imply that imaging satellites are being used to surveil them.

13. For example, Earth Observatory is a site focused on climate and environmental change, the stated purpose of which is "to provide a freely-accessible publication on the Internet where the public can obtain new satellite imagery and scientific information about our home planet" (NASA 2005). Even more recently NASA has established World Wind, a site that "lets you zoom from satellite altitude into any place on Earth. Leveraging Landsat satellite imagery and Shuttle Radar Topography Mission data, World Wind lets you experience Earth terrain in visually rich 3D, just as if you were really there" (NASA Ames Research Center 2005).

14. "Rather than think about this as the death-of-distance, it is more useful to refer to the *transformation of space* made increasingly salient by the introduction of information and computer technology (ICT). In the sense of physical geography, the use of ICT reconstitutes the spatial map by revalorizing locations and the relations between them. It also reconstitutes what we now call cyberspace. Cyberspace is typically conceived of as something new, a product of ICT applications. Yet this formulation perpetuates myths of revolution that suggest that everything now changes with the arrival of this technology, creating a radical rupture in history that diminishes the value of the past because cyberspace provides an entirely new start to time. Notwithstanding the value of such mythic formulations that have received extensive attention, cyberspace is not new, but rather a deepening and extension of those shared communication spaces created over the history of communication technology and accelerating with the telegraph, telephone, and broadcast technologies. ICT applications contribute to reshaping or remapping the contours of cyberspace just as they remap physical geography. Perhaps more important is that these dual transformations interact so that physical geography and cyberspace are mutually constitutive" (Mosco 2000: 41).

15. "Social relations, which are concrete abstractions, have no real existence save in and through space. *Their underpinning is spatial.* In each particular case, the connection between this underpinning and the relations it supports calls for analysis. Such an analysis must imply and explain a genesis and constitute a critique of those institutions, substitutions, transpositions, metaphorizations, anaphorizations, and so forth, that have transformed the space under consideration" (Lefebvre 1991: 404).

CHAPTER **16**

Techniques of Preparedness

ANDREW LAKOFF

In this chapter I describe some of the techniques involved in bringing together diverse forms of threat—ranging from a biological attack, to a flu epidemic, to an environmental catastrophe or a hurricane—into a coherent space of knowledge and intervention. Contemporary security expertise approaches an uncertain future through a distinctive temporal orientation embedded in these techniques, an orientation I call "preparedness." Preparedness is arguably the primary strategic logic through which threats to collective life are now being taken up in the United States. To understand the implications of the centrality of preparedness for questions of social vulnerability and inequality, I find it helpful to contrast it with another possible way of approaching threats to collective life: "population security." Although population security works through ongoing attention to the health and well-being of members of the population, preparedness focuses on temporally limited interventions to preserve governmental and economic order. In what follows, I use discussions of the failures of response to Hurricane Katrina as a case to illustrate how preparedness operates as a form of security rationality. The contrast between preparedness and population security helps us understand why, despite the initial outcry that Katrina provoked, its political implications have been limited.

* * *

One evening the week after Hurricane Katrina struck, the intrepid news correspondent Anderson Cooper was featured on the Charlie Rose show. Cooper was still on the scene in New Orleans, the inundated city in the background and a look of harried concern on his face. He told Rose that he had no intention of returning to his comfortable life in New York City anytime soon. Cooper had been among the reporters to challenge official accounts that the situation was under control, based on the contradiction between disturbing images on the ground and government officials' claims of a competent response effort. He seemed shocked and dismayed by what he had seen in New Orleans, but he was also moved, even transformed by his role as witness to domestic catastrophe. He had covered disasters in Somalia and Sri Lanka, he said, but he never expected to see images like these in the United States: widespread looting, hungry refugees, corpses left on the street to decompose. Toward the end of the interview, Rose asked him what he had learned from the event. Cooper paused, reflected for a moment, and then answered, "We are not as ready as we can be."

Insofar as the hurricane and its aftermath could be said to have a shared moral, it is this: *we are not prepared*—whether for another major natural disaster, a chemical or biological attack, avian flu, or some other type of disastrous event. This lesson has structured response to the hurricane in terms of certain kinds of interventions and not others. And the basic elements of possible response were already in place. This implies that the potential for Katrina to be a politically transformative event may be limited; it is more likely to intensify and redirect processes that are already underway. To see this, we must analyze the emergence and extension of preparedness as a guiding framework for domestic security in the United States—one that constitutes a field of salient threats and systematizes measures for addressing them.

Preparedness names both an ethos and a set of techniques for reflecting about and intervening in an uncertain, potentially catastrophic future (Collier, Lakoff, and Rabinow 2004). Unlike other issues potentially raised by Hurricane Katrina, such as racial inequality, concentrated urban poverty, the social isolation of older people, the shortsightedness of environmental planning on the Gulf Coast, or endemic governmental corruption, the demand for preparedness is a matter that enjoys widespread political agreement on the necessity of state-based intervention. In other words, in the imperative of preparedness, we find a shared sense of what "security" problems involve today. To be prepared is an injunction that must be followed. What can be a source of dispute is not *whether* we need to be prepared but *how* to prepare and what we need to prepare *for*. The problem then becomes one of technical improvement rather than of political transformation.

Preparedness organizes a set of techniques for maintaining economic and social order in a time of emergency. It assumes the disruptive, potentially catastrophic nature of certain events. Because the probability and severity of such events cannot be predicted, the only way to avert catastrophe is to have plans to address them already in place and to have exercised for their eventuality; in other words, to maintain an ongoing capability to respond appropriately. First responders are trained, relief supplies are stockpiled, and the logistics of distribution are mapped out. During the event itself, real-time situational awareness is critical to the coordination of response. The duration of direct intervention by a preparedness apparatus is limited to the immediate onset and aftermath of crisis. But the requirement of vigilant attention to the prospect of crisis is ongoing, permanent. Techniques such as early warning systems make possible such sustained attention. The following is a list of types of preparedness techniques:

- Scenario planning and simulation exercises
- Early warning and monitoring systems
- Stockpiled supplies
- Plans for the coordination of response among diverse entities
- Information sharing and information analysis
- Assessment techniques, such as readiness metrics

It should be noted that these techniques are not unique to U.S. domestic security: scenarios and simulations, early warning and detection systems, and plans for coordinating response can also be found in humanitarian relief, environmental monitoring, and international health organizations—in any field oriented toward managing potential catastrophe. Preparedness is an "abstract technology" that can be made concrete in diverse ways, according to different political aims.[1]

* * *

Preparedness is not wholly new, but it has assembled and redirected disparate elements of already existing security apparatuses. I focus here on its relation to two types of collective or public security that have coexisted in complementary relation over the course of the past century: population security and nation-state security. These two types of security differ in their aims and objects, and in the forms of knowledge on which they rely. I suggest that some of the tensions we have seen in the response to Katrina and in discussions of other security threats emerge from conflicting imperatives that are embedded in the techniques that preparedness has adopted from these two other types of security.

Population security aims to foster the health and well-being of human beings understood as members of a national population (Foucault 2003). Its mechanisms work to collectivize individual risk—of illness, accident, infirmity, poverty. Through calculation of the rates of such events across large populations over an extended period, population security apparatuses find regularities—birth and death rates, illness prevalence, patterns of consumption. They can then intervene to increase and sustain life. Examples of mechanisms connected to population security include: efforts to know and improve the public health, the promotion of social welfare through means such as guaranteed pensions, the construction of public works to improve urban hygiene, health and safety regulations on industrial development or on the circulation of commodities, and collective means of mitigating the risks presented by natural disasters. I will return below to this latter set of techniques, which are now a part of the field of "emergency management."

Nation-state security, in contrast, seeks to defend the territorial integrity of a nation-state against external enemies through military and other means. Examples of efforts toward national security include: the military-industrial system of weapons development and procurement, intelligence gathering and threat assessment operations, economic aid programs designed to contain enemy expansion, and civil defense systems oriented toward protecting the defense and industrial infrastructure in the event of an attack on the homeland. The intersection of the legacy of Cold War–era civil defense with the expanding field of emergency management has provided the basis for many of the practices now associated with preparedness.

* * *

U.S. civil defense programs were developed in response to the rise of novel forms of warfare in the mid-twentieth century: first, air attacks on major cities and industrial centers in World War II, and then the prospect of nuclear attack during the Cold War. One key problem civil defense approached was how to maintain the nation's war-fighting and postwar recuperation capacities even in the face of a devastating attack. For civilian strategists such as Herman Kahn, this question was imperative, given U.S. military doctrine: for the strategy of deterrence to work, the enemy had to be convinced that the United States was prepared to engage in a full-scale nuclear war and had thus made concrete plans both for conducting such a war and for rebuilding in its aftermath (Ghamari-Tabrizi 2005). Kahn invented a method for "thinking about the unthinkable" that would make such planning possible: scenario development. Drawing up nuclear war scenarios and playing them out as simulations helped generate knowledge of current vulnerabilities in order to develop programs to mitigate them. The technique of scenario development went on to have a prolific career in other areas concerned with managing an uncertain future, such as corporate strategy, environmental protection, and international public health. The lesson of a successful simulation based on a scenario is typically the same as the one that Cooper gleaned from Katrina: "We are not prepared." However, it is focused on experts and leaders rather than on the public.[2]

As an extension of local civil defense efforts, the field of emergency management expanded in the 1960s and early 1970s in response to a series of devastating natural disasters. Federally based emergency management had begun with efforts to systematize response to natural disasters, especially floods and fires, in the 1930s. These programs included both mitigation efforts, such as levee construction and forest management, and recovery mechanisms, such as the declaration of federal disasters to release assistance funds. In the 1970s, emergency management further extended its purview to human-caused disasters such as toxic spills, nuclear accidents, and refugee crises.[3]

In contrast to civil defense, which operated according to the norms of hierarchical command-and-control associated with national security, emergency management had a distributed, decentralized structure. Although its broader vision was federally coordinated, a good deal of planning efforts took place at state and local levels and involved loosely coupled relations among private sector, state, and philanthropic organizations (Waugh 2003). Despite these organizational differences, civil defense and emergency management shared a similar field of intervention: potential future catastrophes. Thus emergency planners borrowed techniques for gauging and improving current readiness, such as scenarios and simulations, from civil defense. However, there was often dispute over whether locally based emergency management programs should focus their planning efforts more on nuclear war or on likely natural disasters. These tensions foreshadow some of the issues raised in the wake of Hurricane Katrina, such as the role of the military and the distribution of responsibility between federal and local agencies in emergency situations.

* * *

In the aftermath of Katrina, it was common to see comparisons made between the failed governmental response to the hurricane and the more successful response to the attacks of 9/11. To an observer a decade before, it might have been surprising that a natural disaster and a terrorist attack would be considered part of the same problematic. And the image, three weeks after Katrina, of George W. Bush flying to the Northern Command in Colorado—a military installation designed for use in a national security crisis—to follow the progress of Hurricane Rita as it hurtled toward Texas might have been even more perplexing. Discussions of the potential role of the military in responding to an influenza pandemic can be added to this list. To explain the seemingly intuitive association of these disparate types of events under the aegis of security, it is important to understand the rationality through which civil defense and emergency management were institutionally merged.

When the Federal Emergency Management Agency (FEMA) was founded during the Carter administration, the new agency consolidated federal emergency management and civil defense functions under the rubric of "all-hazards planning." All-hazards planning assumed that for the purposes of emergency management, many kinds of catastrophes could be treated in the same way: earthquakes, floods, industrial accidents, and enemy attacks could be brought into the same operational space, given their common characteristics. Needs such as early warning, the coordination of response by multiple agencies, public communication to assuage panic, and the efficient implementation of recovery processes were shared across these various sorts of disasters. Thus all-hazards planning focused not on assessing specific threats but on building capabilities that could function across multiple threat domains.

What was forged through the consolidation of multiple forms of disaster planning under the all-hazards rubric was not only a set of techniques and protocols but also a shared ethos: the injunction to be prepared. The threats that preparedness experts approach cannot necessarily be avoided: for such events, it is "not a question of if, but when." The point is to reduce current vulnerabilities and put in place response measures that will keep a disastrous event from veering into unmitigated catastrophe. Scenarios and simulations are tools for such planning.

* * *

In the two and a half decades since the establishment of FEMA, the agency has faced ongoing tension between its natural disaster planning task and its civil defense function. Whereas Democratic presidents have tended to emphasize the former, Republican administrations have focused on the latter (Ward, Wamsley, Schroeder, and Robins 2000). FEMA's assimilation into the Department of Homeland Security (DHS) in the wake of 9/11 once again shifted its orientation more toward civil defense—in this case, toward preparation for a terrorist attack. Nonetheless, it is noteworthy that DHS characterized its overall mission in the terms of "all-hazards" planning familiar from emergency management. As Secretary Michael Chertoff said in 2005 in unveiling DHS's new "National Preparedness" plan,

> The Department of Homeland Security has sometimes been viewed as a terrorist-fighting entity, but of course, we're an all-hazards Department. Our responsibilities include not only fighting the forces of terrorism, but also fighting the forces of natural disasters.[4]

The National Preparedness plan proposed a linked set of mechanisms to bring disparate forms of threat into a common security field. These may be termed "techniques of preparedness": examples include detection and early warning systems, simulation exercises, coordinated response plans, and metrics for the assessment of the current state of readiness. In its plan, the DHS selected 15 disaster scenarios as "the foundation for a risk-based approach." These possible events—including an anthrax attack, a flu pandemic, a nuclear detonation, and a major earthquake—were chosen on the basis of plausibility and catastrophic scale. The detailed scenarios made it possible to generate knowledge of current vulnerabilities and the capabilities needed to mitigate them. Using the scenarios, DHS developed a menu of the critical tasks that would have to be performed in various kinds of major events; these tasks, in turn, were to be assigned to specific governmental and nongovernmental agencies. Scenario 10 was "Natural Disaster—Major Hurricane."[5]

From the vantage of preparedness, the failed response to Hurricane Katrina did not undercut the utility of all-hazards planning. Rather, it pointed to problems of implementation and coordination, of command and control. This indicates why, in response to the failure, we have seen the redirection and intensification of already-developed preparedness techniques rather than a broad rethinking of security questions—for example, thinking about the conditions of production of vulnerable populations. On the one hand, as official inquiries into the catastrophe have gotten under way, there are continued struggles over how to attribute blame for the failures in response. But along with this, there are demands, addressed to various agencies charged with security tasks, to enact reforms that will improve our national preparedness. Such reforms would be primarily technical: in the context of the Gulf Coast, rebuild the flood protection infrastructure; in large cities, improve evacuation plans. For preparedness planning in general, ensure that there are coherent systems of communication and coordination in crisis. Meanwhile, there will be broader scrutiny of the relationship between federal, local, and state responsibility for dealing with various aspects of disaster preparedness. One possible direction of reform is toward an increased federalization—and militarization—of emergency management.

* * *

In this process of attributing blame and developing technical reforms, it is important not to lose sight of the larger questions that the hurricane and its aftermath raise about the uses and meanings of "security" today. Here it is worth noting some of the differences between the objects and aims of population security and those of preparedness. In contrast to population-security-based tasks such as public health provision and poverty relief, preparedness is oriented to crisis situations and to localized sites of disorder or disruption. These are typically events of short duration that require urgent response (Calhoun 2004). Their likelihood in a given place demands a condition of readiness rather than a long-term work of sustained intervention into the welfare of the population. The object to be known and managed differs as well: for preparedness the key site of vulnerability is not the health of a population but rather the critical infrastructure that guarantees the continuity of political and economic order. If population security builds infrastructure, preparedness catalogs it and monitors its vulnerabilities. And although preparedness may emphasize saving the lives of "victims" in moments of duress, it does not consider the living conditions of human beings as members of a social collectivity.

* * *

Techniques of preparedness generate ongoing knowledge of vulnerabilities to potential catastrophe and direct security planners to means of mitigating these vulnerabilities. It should be emphasized that these techniques are not unique to U.S. domestic security: early warning and detection systems, plans for coordinating response, and scenarios and simulations can also be found in humanitarian relief, environmental monitoring, and international health organizations—in any field oriented toward managing potential catastrophe.

What kind of politics do techniques of preparedness have? To consider Katrina a problem of preparedness rather than one of population security is to focus political questions about the failure around a fairly circumscribed set of issues. For the purposes of disaster planning, whose key question is "Are we prepared?" the poverty rate or the percentage of people without health insurance are not salient indicators of readiness or of the efficacy of response. Rather, preparedness emphasizes issues such as hospital surge capacity, the coherence of evacuation plans, the condition of the electrical grid, or the ways of detecting the presence of E. coli in the water supply. From the vantage of preparedness, the conditions of existence of members of the population are not a political problem. One task for critical intervention, then, is to keep attention focused on the role such conditions played in turning Katrina from disaster into catastrophe.

Notes

1. For a discussion of insurance as an abstract technology, see Francois Ewald (1991).
2. For an example from international public health, see Laurie Garrett (1994).
3. See http://www.fema.gov/about/history.shtm.
4. "Secretary Michael Chertoff, U.S. Department of Homeland Security, Second Stage Review Remarks," July 13, 2005, House Security Committee, http://www.dhs.gov/dhspublic/interapp/speech/speech_0255.xml.
5. See the following documents, available online: *National Preparedness Guidance: Homeland Security Presidential Directive 8: National Preparedness,* Office of Homeland Security, April 27, 2005, http://www.ojp.usdoj.gov/odp/docs/NationalPreparednessGuidance.pdf; and *Planning Scenarios: Executive Summaries,* The Homeland Security Council, July 2004, http://www.globalsecurity.org/security/library/report/2004/hsc-planning-scenarios-jul04_exec-sum.pdf.

CHAPTER 17

Technology Studies for Terrorists
A Short Course

LANGDON WINNER

During the weeks that followed the terrorist attacks of September 11, 2001, I devoured dozens of newspapers, magazines, and online documents trying to gain a better understanding of the origins and significance of those awful events. From the stack of material, one item leaped out. An essay by political scientist Thomas Homer-Dixon in *Foreign Policy* noted, "Langdon Winner, a theorist of politics and technology, provides the first rule of modern terrorism: 'Find the critical but non-redundant parts of the system and sabotage ... them according to your purposes.'"[1]

Oh wonderful, I thought to myself, this is just what I need—to be known as the person who formulated the first rule of modern terrorism. I imagined the FBI knocking at my door: "Mr. Winner, we'd like you to come down the office to answer a few questions." The musings about sabotage that Homer-Dixon had unearthed came from a chapter I'd written thirty years earlier, a contribution to a book on an apparently drab theme—organized social complexity.[2] As I worked on the piece back then, it occurred to me that knowledge about inner workings of technological systems could, perversely, be used by system wreckers. The context was America in the early 1970s, when a rash of bombings spread across the United States, blasts targeted at banks and other public buildings in twisted protest of the war in Vietnam. My thoughts about sabotage occurred as I was moving from a background in classical political theory to ponder the social theories of

technology. Both bodies of thought emphasize the building and maintenance of frameworks of order in human affairs. But, I wondered, couldn't
the same understandings be applied to projects of destruction? Over the
years I'd forgotten that the question had ever crossed my mind.

Following Homer-Dixon's prompt, the topic reemerged while I strug-
gled with my misgivings about the nation's response to 9/11. As someone
who lives just two hours from the site of the World Trade Center and who
spends a good amount of time in New York City, I experienced the catastrophe with feelings of shock, outrage, and sadness shared by millions
around the globe. During the hours and days that followed, politicians
and pundits gravely intoned, "This is the day everything changed." But
what exactly was it that had changed? For the nation's political leaders and
much of the American populace as well, there seemed to be but one answer.
September 11, 2001, was as a day of infamy equivalent to Pearl Harbor, a
provocation that propelled the nation into a life-and-death struggle called
"the war on terror." Required now was a massive military campaign to
punish the perpetrators wherever they could be found, thus defending the
nation from any further terrorist threat.

The metaphor of "war" has gained currency in American public discourse in a wide range of contexts during the past forty years. In the
1960s President Lyndon Johnson declared "war on poverty." In the 1970s
President Nixon boldly declared "war on crime." Nixon and subsequent
presidents moved on to declare an aggressive "war on drugs." Not to be
outdone, President Jimmy Carter argued that the energy crisis of the 1970s
required the nation to eliminate its dependence on foreign sources of oil,
an initiative that Carter called "the moral equivalent of war."

Among these so-called wars is a crucial similarity. They have all been
lost or at least not decided in a way that even remotely resembles victory.
Poverty and crime still loom as chronic problems in American life, with
scant signs of victory over their sources or the damage they cause. Although
it is extremely violent and costly, the war on drugs has not significantly
reduced drug use in the country or the social decay that accompanies it.
Despite much political hand-wringing and well-meaning research programs on renewable energy, the nation's dependency on foreign oil is now
greater than in the late 1970s. By now these incessant calls to war reflect the
torpor of our political speech. But even to address that fact would probably
require yet another declaration of war: "My fellow Americans, the crisis
before us demands a bold and decisive response—the war on metaphorical
exhaustion!"

It is true that the 9/11 attacks by al Qaeda were acts of war in the most
direct, compelling sense. Yet I wondered then, as I do now, if conceiving
our situation post-9/11 as a state of war with all that implies is the most

appropriate and productive response. Could it be that our leaders have launched yet another ambiguously defined "war" clouded with uncertainty and motivated by the quest for domestic political advantage?

America's lockstep march into the "war on terror" has been extremely costly, especially as it involves the conquest and occupation of Iraq. Hundreds of billions of tax dollars squandered, thousands of American soldiers killed and wounded, mounting evidence of torture in U.S. detention centers in Iraq and elsewhere, rampant corruption among contractors and quislings in Iraq, and a sharp decline in the reputation of the country as a force for peace, international law, and human rights around the globe all stem from the hasty, ill-conceived consensus that formed after 9/11. It seems altogether likely that the nation's bellicose response has spawned many more terrorists than had existed previously, a fact that could vex the United States, Europe, and other countries for decades to come. Even more disturbing (but seldom emphasized) are the tens of thousands of deaths and injuries of innocent Iraqi civilians in this conflict, casualties that are not simply "collateral damage" but more accurately war crimes committed in pursuit of a hasty, vengeful, ill-considered policy.

Among the costs at home are ones directly related to the theme of this book, increasing surveillance in social life. Justified by the supposed need to discover and eliminate covert terrorist plots such as those hatched by Mohammed Atta and his associates, new varieties of police power have been devised and implemented. Antiterrorist legislation and the use of technologies to monitor the activities of citizens have vastly expanded possibilities for the government to shadow people's daily comings and goings while diminishing legal and practical resistance to such spying. Among the casualties of the ongoing "war" in this setting are some of our cherished rights and liberties.

At this writing, four years after the attacks, it is increasingly clear that opportunism has been a crucial feature of post-9/11 politics. The neoconservative clique around President George W. Bush quickly adapted the fears and passions of the moment to justify their long-standing plans for renewed militarization at home and bellicose policies abroad, all in the name of asserting the United States as the world's "lone superpower." This has resulted in an extraordinary reallocation of public funds toward the Pentagon and projects in "homeland security" while starving public spending on social needs. Yet so powerful has been the metaphor, that even months after 9/11 there was essentially no debate about whether the crisis confronting the nation was best, or even adequately, defined as another war. There has been little or no discussion about possible alternate conceptions and strategies. Our elected officials, journalists, and media pundits, as well as our scientists and scholars in universities and think tanks, have

been notably silent on the matter. Is the cause a mistaken sense of patriotism, a desperate hope for national unity, an abject failure of imagination,
or something else? Whatever the case, few Americans were prepared to ask
the following questions: What is our predicament really? Which strategies
now make sense? And shouldn't there be widespread public deliberation
about what should be done?

Given the heavy costs, foreign and domestic, incurred in the "war on
terror," it seems imperative to reconsider our situation and renew the
search for alternatives. The article that fingered me as the author of the
"first rule of modern terrorism" gave rise to a question: Is there anything in
my field of research and teaching—the field of technology studies (broadly
construed)—that might contribute a fresh understanding of the terrible
problems that loom before us? Upon reflection, there are several themes in
social and political studies of technology that could be usefully brought to
bear on problems of terrorism. I briefly comment on four of them here: the
interweaving of technology and society, the phenomenon of technological
style, the dynamics of risky technology and "normal accidents," and the
social construction of technological systems.

Interweaving

A common insight has emerged from the historians, sociologists, anthro-
pologists, political scientists, and philosophers who have studied the social
dimensions of technology in recent years. There is growing awareness that
technological devices, systems, and routines are thoroughly interwoven
with the structures and processes of social and political life. Conceptions
of this kind have largely replaced the view in earlier scholarship that one
could identify a clear, obvious boundary between technology on one hand
and society on the other.[3]

From my own standpoint, this insight is crucial for understanding
modern political society. As people design technologies, negotiate their
features, and introduce them into the broader realm of human affairs,
they are engaged in something far more profound than improving material well-being, for technological devices and systems reflect and, indeed,
materially and institutionally embody forms of social and political life.
Technical things bear responsibilities, express commitments, and assume
roles as agents in the realm of human relationships. In an era in which
computerized devices have become important intermediaries in many
parts of everyday life, an awareness of the social and political qualities of
technical objects has become increasingly common.

Studies of interweaving of this kind are often directed at the effects of
new technological developments within political culture. For example, in

the United States in recent years we have seen the rise of interconnected patterns in architecture, transportation, information, and communications packaged as "gated communities." People live in clusters of buildings, behind walls, using electronic passkeys to enter and leave, driving to work and back, watching endless hours of video on elaborate home entertainment systems. These costly structures respond to concerns for personal security that are rife in America today. But this rapidly spreading sociotechnical pattern has been criticized as an unfortunate development in America, for it realizes a return of segregation and the dismantling of community as a living, face-to-face experience (see Blakely and Snyder 1997).

By the same token, we can employ lessons about interweaving to identify materially embodied social reforms that merit praise for their political effects. For example, during the past thirty years, an array of changes in technology and architecture have made it possible for millions of people with disabilities—including paraplegics and quadriplegics—to enter domains of social life where they had previously been excluded, an overwhelmingly positive, democratic development (Shapiro 1993).

From this vantage point the horrifying events of 9/11 present phenomena of interweaving and new challenges for political society. The acts of terrorism caused a rupture within the complex interconnection of technical systems and political culture, for the consequences of the attacks were not merely in the lives lost, people injured, and material structures destroyed; they soon extended crucially and directly to ramifications in the country's social and political order. Indeed, the institutional responses to 9/11 have caused far more damage than the initial attack did. Many of these responses involved the kinds of surveillance mentioned earlier, passage of several draconian laws, and the creation of a wide range of antiterrorist policies and practices. Most notorious of these is a law passed shortly after the 9/11 attack: "Uniting and Strengthening America by Providing Appropriate Tools Required to Intercept and Obstruct Terrorism," or USA PATRIOT Act in its acronym. Federal initiatives of this kind are echoed in a host of antiterrorist laws passed at the state level, all of which extend government mechanisms for the routine monitoring of everyday life in airports, schools, offices, libraries, banks, online communications, and the like. Not to be outdone, the Pentagon has expanded its secretive Counterintelligence Field Activity, using "leading edge information technologies and data harvesting" to determine who within the U.S. population is a security threat (Pincus 2005).

Groups concerned about the erosion of rights and liberties—the American Civil Liberties Union, the Electronic Privacy Information Center, and the American Library Association, among others—fear that government snooping far exceeds any legitimate concern to prevent criminal, terrorist conspiracies. One concern centers on the 30,000 "national security letters" issued by the FBI in recent years to obtain a wide range of information about citizens whose innocuous communications make them suspect, triggering a comprehensive, clandestine search. As reported in the *Washington Post*:

> Senior FBI officials acknowledged in interviews that the proliferation of national security letters results primarily from the bureau's new authority to collect intimate facts about people who are not suspected of any wrongdoing. Criticized for failure to detect the Sept. 11 plot, the bureau now casts a much wider net, using national security letters to generate leads as well as to pursue them. Casual or unwitting contact with a suspect—a single telephone call, for example—may attract the attention of investigators and subject a person to scrutiny about which he never learns. (Gellman 2005)

Amid the smoking wreckage of the World Trade Center one finds other debris, including significant parts of the U.S. Constitution, including the fourth and sixth amendments of the Bill of Rights. Traditional protections of civil liberties have been badly weakened by Congressional legislation, overshadowed by the expanding powers of the executive branch and undermined by the virtually unlimited scope of information technologies used for surveillance. Within the new security apparatus of "homeland security," individuals are defined not as citizens but as suspects.

Developments of this kind suggest an updated version of Winner's first rule of modern terrorism: find the nonredundant parts of the system that also have great symbolic significance and strike there. This will not only bring the greatest damage to material infrastructures but produce generalized damage to the country's political order as well. In this light, what the response to 9/11 revealed, unfortunately, is an astonishing *lack of resilience* in the fundamental techno-political institutions of American society. Scholars in the field of technology studies could well have predicted this. Among other results, the thorough, complex interweaving of large-scale technical systems and political society leaves us vulnerable, not only in a physical sense but in cultural and political ways as well.

Technological Style

Another idea in contemporary technology studies relevant to our predicament is the theme of technological style. Historians of technology have tried to explain how it is that societies in different historical periods prefer different technical forms (see Staudenmaier 1985; T.P. Hughes 1983). It appears that making and using technology sometimes reflect an overall pattern or style in contrast to other technical possibilities available in principle. In his cultural history of technology *Leonardo to the Internet,* Tom Misa argues that political conditions often determine which technological style is chosen in a particular historical setting. As illustration he shows how some of the most prominent technical accomplishments of fifteenth- and sixteenth-century Europe expressed a distinctive conception of power and authority, one that favored the grandeur of the patron over the prosperity of the general populace. "Characteristically," he observes, "Leonardo and his fellow Renaissance-era technologists had surprisingly little to do with improving industry or making money in the way we typically think of technology today. Instead, Renaissance-era courts commissioned them for numerous technical projects of city-building, courtly entertainment, and dynastic display, and for the means of war" (Misa 2004: 3).

From this vantage point we can ask the following question: What aspects of contemporary technological style are called into question by prospects of terrorism? One element that seems especially significant is the style of openness and trust expressed in many of the technological systems on which modern life depends. In democratic societies where freedom and equality are key ideals, a long-standing, largely unstated assumption has been that the linkages that hold together systems in energy, communications, transportation, water supply, food supply, and the like could be left essentially open and unprotected. People trust crucial technical systems of this kind to operate efficiently; in turn, ordinary people are trusted not to interfere with or damage the apparatus. Thus, even the structures of relatively hazardous technological systems, plants that process toxic chemicals, for example, have long presupposed qualities of openness that could make them susceptible to attack. We generally assume that no one would be so malicious or foolish to destroy technologies on which their well-being depends.[4]

For the September 11 terrorists, the American technological style based on openness and trust provided a golden opportunity. For example, in retrospect the airport gate checks were far too trusting; no one tried to confiscate the box cutters that Atta and his men carried as weapons. For a time even after the planes had been hijacked, the trust among the passengers continued. The terrorists reassured the passengers that, as in hijackings of the past, they would eventually land and be set free.

Recognition that sociotechnical arrangements based on trust are also sources of insecurity bought a widespread, highly costly refurbishing of many technological devices and systems. This is clearly visible at airports, where the gate check has become a time-consuming, intrusive exercise orchestrated by guards who guide passengers through a variety of electronic and electromechanical stages. In countless sociotechnical settings, as fear has replaced trust, institutions have retooled in ways that replace openness with closure. What used to be readily available information about the structure and workings of large-scale systems—water systems, transit systems, energy systems, and the like—is now restricted or secret. More and more of infrastructure and public architecture are placed behind fences and concrete barriers. The new technological style seems to be, "You can't be too careful."

The creation of an increasingly closed technological style in post-9/11 sociotechnical arrangements also has ramifications for habits of mind in society at large. An obsession with security fuels the rising popularity of what are called "conservative" ways of thinking—fear and loathing expressed in a variety of socially divisive ways, including suspicion of immigrants, protests against teaching the theory of evolution in the schools, and open contempt of unconventional political ideas, for example, gay rights. Where democratic, live-and-let-live tolerance once prevailed, there is often a bellicose insistence in traditional cultural norms as the identifying signs of public virtue. Whether the al Qaeda terrorists intended to achieve these effects, a clear consequence of 9/11 has been an abrupt closure of intellectual horizons and policy perspectives common in American public life. In a thoroughly interwoven sociotechnical world, a shift in technological style involves profound changes in the ways people think about social life in general.

Risky Technologies

Of all the topics explored in the literature of technology studies, the one with most obvious relevance for understanding terrorist attacks is the large body of research on risk and risky technologies. Scholars in psychology, philosophy, sociology, management, political science, and engineering have all contributed to our knowledge here, focusing on recurring risks associated with technology in everyday life but also on accidents in large-scale systems.[5] What has been learned from research on risk that might be useful in this context?

One might begin by rejecting the war metaphor and equivalent terms altogether. Rather than define the possibility of terrorist attack as something that would immediately require a military response, one might think about it as a particular category of risk that challenges us to study which human–machine systems harbor dangerous malfunctions and what might be done to prevent them from being realized as catastrophes. One could study these possibilities, analyze their dynamics, and propose serviceable remedies.

A common finding in studies of risk that might be helpful is that people find it very difficult to judge the likelihood of the real dangers they face and how such dangers arise. The hazards we imagine to be most likely and consequential are often not ones that square with statistical probabilities of the dangers that await us. For example, in the United States about 40,000 people die in car accidents each year, but cars are still manufactured and driven in ways that are remarkably unsafe. By comparison, 3,011 people died in the 9/11 attack. We now agonize endlessly about the 3,011 but take the 40,000 for granted.

Yes, it is unseemly to compare levels of death. One death is always too many. But it may be that looking at terrorist attacks from the standpoint of technological risk would be more reasonable and more fruitful than defining terror as an ill-defined, perpetual war waged in numerous locations around the globe. Social analysis of risk, a well-developed field of research, could make it possible to distinguish between possibilities for terrorism that are greatly worrisome and those that are less so. It might help us compare and judge remedies for terrorism that focus on truly urgent yet manageable problems as compared to measures that are of little use and may even make matters worse.

Thus, how can we judge the level of risk presented by Muslim and Middle Eastern immigrants studying and working in the United States—the kinds of people we are now deporting by the hundreds? Many immigrants of this description are peaceful, productive persons, not dangerous in the least. Why are they identified as especially dangerous? Is religion or country of national origin a good predictor of harmful intentions? By comparison, the dangers contained within technological systems crucial to our way of life—the international containerized cargo system, for example—seem to pose a much greater threat. Why we are we more vigilant about supposedly dangerous immigrant groups than we are with familiar, possibly vulnerable, complex systems? The literature on risk assessment (Mary Douglas's *Purity and Danger* is a classic in this genre) notes that cultural meanings inform our sense of who or what is dangerous, judgments that are sometimes far from reasonable (Douglas 1966). At a time in which the presence of immigrants is a gnawing issue in the United States, it is perhaps not surprising to find ideas about dangers from terrorism centered on them rather than on the refinery down the road that processes tons of toxic substances each week using outdated equipment.

The same kinds of questions can be asked about other conceptions and measures now applied in antiterrorist surveillance. In the United States, one option government officials can employ is to obtain records of what persons are reading from libraries and bookshops. Librarians must release the list of books a patron has checked out if the FBI requests it; they break the law if they refuse or if they tell anyone about the search. As in the McCarthy period of the 1950s, special danger is now attributed to the strange ideas and information Americans get from the books they read. But compared to other possible dangers in the age of terrorism, how significant are library books? If someone checks out a copy of the Qur'an, will he or she be flagged as suspicious?

The body of research on risky technology that may be most relevant to understanding possibilities of terrorism concerns the operation of large-scale technical systems. Of special relevance is the research of sociologist Charles Perrow on what he terms "normal accidents." Looking at a variety of cases—marine collisions, airline traffic control, accidents in chemical and nuclear plants, and others—Perrow identifies patterns of events that often lead to system failures, the worst of which become catastrophes with significant loss of life and property. Typically what happens is that two or more failures occur with results that interact in surprising ways. For example, a failure in a key technical component is compounded by operator error, amplified by a breakdown in communications. He explains:

> Occasionally ... two or more failures, none of them devastating in themselves in isolation, come together in unexpected ways and defeat the safety devices—the definition of a "normal accident" or system accident. If the system is also tightly coupled, these failures can cascade faster than any safety device or operator can cope with them, or they can even be incomprehensible to those responsible for doing the coping. If the accident brings down a significant part of the system, and the system has catastrophic potential, we will have a catastrophe. (Perrow 1999: 356–57)

Although Perrow's studies do not pay much attention to catastrophes caused by acts of terrorism, his analysis and recommendations can easily be applied in this context. The initial cause of calamity is no longer a component failure or operator error but a deliberate, malicious act. Nevertheless, the chain of events may proceed in ways his theory anticipates. Much of the 9/11 Commission Report released in the summer of 2004 reads like an extended description of a normal accident in terrorist mode. The ability of the hijackers to get through security screening, the communications mix-ups among federal agencies, and the failure of U.S. air defense to intercept the aircraft all follow the typical pattern of a Perrowian calamity. In one passage of this kind, the report observes, "Existing protocols on 9/11 were unsuited in every respect for an attack in which hijacked planes were used as weapons. ... A shootdown authorization was not communicated to the NORAD air defense sector until 28 minutes after United 93 had crashed in Pennsylvania. Planes were scrambled, but ineffectively, as they did not know where to go or what targets they were to intercept."[6]

The commission's account of what happened after the planes hit the World Trade Center also corresponds closely to what happens in catastrophic "normal accidents." Firemen and police could not communicate adequately for a variety of reasons, including channel overload. A repeater system in the World Trade Center that could have greatly improved communications had two buttons; someone switched on one of them but not the other. First responders on the scene had a less accurate overview of their predicament than people watching the disaster on CNN.

Terrorists could learn a great deal reading the literature on large-scale technical systems and the 9/11 report, namely, how it is possible to outmaneuver, disrupt, and destroy highly costly, highly sophisticated systems of contemporary technology by using clever planning and simple tools. It is likely that the more studious of them know much of this already. By the same token, it is possible to read such studies with the purpose of finding ways to anticipate and prevent similar calamities in the future. Decades of research and analysis on risky technologies have much to offer our understanding of the circumstances in which acts of terrorism could occur. Who among serious students of these situations will pass the final exam—wrongdoers seeking to achieve maximum damage or those people hoping to frustrate any such malign intentions?

Social Construction

The final range of topics in contemporary technology studies I want to emphasize is the social construction of technology. Constructivist research is especially good at mapping the complex negotiations that go into the creation of technical artifacts and systems. Donald MacKenzie's *Inventing Accuracy* offers an excellent case study of this kind, following an extensive collection of individuals, groups, and institutions involved in deciding which guidance system would control the flight of U.S. ballistic missiles (MacKenzie 1990). Rather than identify one inventor or handful of innovators, we should chart the contributions of numerous actors involved in shaping technical outcomes.

In this vein, the sports utility vehicle, the wildly popular but highly problematic vehicle, emerged not as a simple response to market pressure but within a complex set of initiatives and negotiations lasting several decades, ones that involved dozens of groups with seemingly different interests— manufacturers, government officials, labor unions, trade associations, environmentalists, and consumers among the most prominent. The design of the sports utility vehicle was not a single, isolated accomplishment. It was the product of complex deliberations, deals, and compromises (Bradsher 2002).

As applied to social processes of technological design, there are often a variety of constituent groups that influence the eventual outcome. Although it may seem odd, from today's perspective terrorists can be seen as one among many constituencies with needs and problems that are somehow communicated and fed into the mix of social construction. Of course, it may be difficult to determine in advance of their "use" of technological systems exactly what their input entails. They don't (as far as we know) come to focus group meetings or attend design charrettes to make their preferences known. Nevertheless, terrorist influence on the processes of social construction can be formidable. Especially after 9/11, their silent presence must be taken into account by those who hope to derail their murderous interventions.

A chapter in terrorist social construction of technology surfaced in preparations to build the Freedom Tower in New York, a 1,776-foot-tall symbolic skyscraper designed by architect Daniel Liebeskind as a replacement for the World Trade Center and tribute to the 9/11 victims. In May 2005, very late in the process, someone in the New York City police department called attention to the fact that in its existing design, the edifice was open to a blast from a truck bomb parked on the city's West Side highway.[7] Heeding the warning, planners delayed construction of the building while the blueprints were modified to prevent an attack from that angle. Thus, as silent, shadow participants, imaginary terrorists had a substantial influence on the design of a monumental work of architecture, in fact the very tower meant to defy terrorist schemes in perpetuity.

How could one make such unseen terrorist presence a continuing contribution to technology shaping in the post-9/11 world? What kinds of research, development, and testing are suited to the challenge? One ingenious approach surfaced in October 2003, when Nathaniel Heatwole, a student at Guilford College in Greensboro, North Carolina, revealed that over a period of months, he had carried box cutters and other dangerous devices onto commercial airliners. His aim, he explained later, was to show the inadequacies of newly installed airline security systems. In the end, Heatwole left some of his implements on two airplanes and sent the authorities an e-mail indicating where the items could be found. He was promptly arrested and charged with several felonies.[8] It is fortunate for Heatwole that the judge in the case recognized that he was not a dangerous criminal and sentenced him to a $500 fine and 100 hours of community service.[9]

Following Heatwole's example, one might propose funding groups of covert surrogate terrorists whose work it would be to find ways to breach security arrangements and disrupt large-scale technological systems, going just far enough to demonstrate conclusively what is possible in principle and then stopping any further penetration. Rather than throw them in jail, one could award them graduate fellowships and support them in novel dissertation projects. If nothing else, this could give a new surge of energy to research on the social construction of technology, a field that, for all its virtues, has become a little dull and repetitive in its range of application.

Conclusion

This brief exploration suggests some ways in which social studies of technology might be applied to the realm of terrorism and counterterrorism. My comments about the interweaving of society and technology, technological style, the analysis of risk technologies, and the social construction and deconstruction of technology may even point to more fruitful strategies than those commonly employed in today's "war" on terror. It is possible to achieve a broader and deeper understanding of the specific circumstances of our vulnerability and to map more sensible and productive paths of actions. This idea is not new with me or even especially radical. An emphasis of this kind has emerged within a series of studies by think tanks and blue ribbon panels, most notably the 9/11 Commission, that have noted how ill prepared the United States remains in confronting the real prospects of terrorist attacks on its own soil.[10] Evidently, President George W. Bush and his administration have been so fixed on the strategy of "taking the battle to the enemy" overseas that more urgent locations of vulnerability, including ones that are obviously the most crucial—badly controlled stockpiles of nuclear materials in the former Soviet Union and elsewhere—have been woefully neglected. As the Harvard Project on Managing the Atom concluded in May 2005, "Unfortunately, the on-the-ground progress in securing, consolidating and eliminating nuclear stockpiles in the last year remained slow, when compared to the urgency of the threat" (Brunn and Wier 2005: v).

Closer to home, the nation has been notoriously slow and ineffective in its response to the vulnerability of containerized cargo systems. Each month millions of crates are brought in, which are poorly scanned for hazardous materials, including nuclear bombs and dirty bombs—crates that are loosely monitored in their movement from origin to destination. The same can be said of the vulnerability of the nation's 15,000 chemical plants, built under now dubious assumptions of openness and trust.

As we own up to the nation's lax, ill-focused, wildly bellicose response to the real problems unearthed by 9/11, the literature of technology studies offers a wealth of concepts, theories, and case studies that could be applied to research on possibilities for terrorist attacks and reasonable strategies for preventing them. An interesting conclusion in Charles Perrow's work, for example, is that it is actually rather difficult to bring about catastrophe in large-scale systems either by accident or by malicious intention. Exactly the right arrangement of causes and effects, of failures and blunders have to be in place. Research findings of that kind should be reassuring to us. Perrow suggests a variety of reforms to diminish the odds of disaster, ones that involve strategies for loose coupling of components in technical systems so that one diminishes the chance of cascading failures. He argues for greater flexibility in the communications and behaviors of the people who work in and around large-scale systems. Yes, there is a cost to such measures, a loss in efficiency, speed, and volume of throughput in the hazardous systems of modern life. To achieve much greater security, we would have to give up a measure of the productivity and convenience Americans and Europeans have gotten used to. However, if one is willing to live with these costs, the likelihood of catastrophic normal accidents and, by implication, catastrophic consequences from terrorist strikes can be substantially reduced.

Specific detailed proposals about ways to reduce vulnerability through reform in the design and management of key technological systems are the focus of Stephen Flynn's book *America the Vulnerable*. Although Flynn buys much of the bombastic, misleading rhetoric of the war on terror, he draws on his experience as a commissioned officer in the Coast Guard and subsequent academic research on risky technologies to identify areas of blindness in America's response to 9/11 and to outline paths of improvement. Containerized cargo crates could be redesigned to include sensors, global positioning systems, and communications devices. The global system of containerized cargo could be rearranged to include a limited number of institutional gateways where safe practices could be installed. Flynn upholds the total reorganization of material and social frameworks at Boston Logan Airport after 9/11 as a model of reform. What he finds there are well-rehearsed practices that emphasize open not closed communication and flexibility in the choices made available to employees (Flynn 2004).

In writings like these—technology studies broadly interpreted—one finds useful ideas in the quest to create more resilient and reliable institutions in our sociotechnical landscape. The path to a safer, more secure society involves projects in the reengineering of systems that loom as targets for catastrophic attack. In this mode one identifies vulnerabilities and fixes them, using the best social wisdom and technological ingenuity available. One continually monitors the workings of such systems to make sure that the worst possibilities for damage are anticipated and prevented. Rigorous, intellectually responsible studies of the broader horizons of terrorism suggest that remedies of this kind are the best focus for our efforts and money.

An important implication of this insight is that the destructive focus of the "war on terror" in its domestic setting—the making of systems for thoroughgoing surveillance of civilians—actually has little relevance to the nation's safety and security. Yes, it makes sense of be vigilant against criminal conspiracies, watchful of purchases of explosives and other devices that could be used in terrorist plots. But it is likely that, following the Oklahoma City bombing of 1996 and the attacks of 9/11, local and federal police are already well prepared to uncover and intercept insidious plots that involve mass destruction on American soil. Beyond that, the greatest threats to domestic security are ones that involve the structure and operation of technological complexes—the airlines, nuclear plants, chemical plants, dams, containerized cargo, and so forth—whose protection involves comprehensive monitoring and the installation of technical fixes that have nothing to do with routine surveillance of everyday life. This is actually the best, tough-minded advice from those who have studied the real prospects for terrorism: watch technological systems, not people's everyday activities.

In sum, the best strategy for an age in which terrorism has entered the picture is to attend to specific, very real circumstances of our vulnerability and correct them, taking steps that could, in fact, enhance rather than degrade our way of life. Is this not a better approach than fanning endless fears about terrorists and lobbing 500-pound bombs at strange neighborhoods in distant lands? Alas, this is probably not a great rallying cry: let us join together in a campaign to understand and systematically reduce our vulnerability, achieving new levels of resilience within the sociotechnical frameworks of modern life. I realize that my plea would probably have little appeal on television talk shows.

The day after the 9/11 attack, I went to the university to teach a class of undergraduates in a course on law, values, and public policy. By then it was known pretty much who the hijackers were and who had instigated the attack. In my class that term, about a quarter of the students were Muslim, and a good number of those were of Middle Eastern origin. I began by asking everyone to express their thoughts and feelings about what had happened. There ensued a series of angry outbursts.

"Your people did this!" shouted a young man from the New York suburbs, pointing to a young woman wearing a head scarf.

"I'm as American as anybody in this room," she responded, fighting back tears, "and I hate the terrorists as much as you."

Echoing calls commonly heard on talk radio, some of the students exclaimed that America should just nuke all the capital cities in the Middle East and get it over with.

After about a half hour of this, I suggested that we turn to the readings for the day. It happened that we were wrapping up discussion of the *Oresteia* by Aeschylus. I'd assigned the book to raise the following question: How did people handle disputes before there was any system of law?

In the drama we behold Agamemnon's return from the Trojan War and a sequence of bloody murders that breaks out within the royal family. One killing leads to another within a moral order in which family members must enact retribution. Just as things are spinning out of control, the goddess Athena appears. She proclaims that the revenge killings have gone on long enough. From now on the city will be governed by the rule of law. There will be courts, trials, and juries within an enduring framework of civil order. For the spirits of revenge, the Furies, Athena creates a new role as the Eumenides, the kindly ones, asked to protect their new home, the city of Athens.

I asked my students, How would Aeschylus view the discussion we've been having today? Most of them got the point. Even when the crimes suffered are horrendous, acting out raw feelings of hatred may not be the best way to proceed. Perhaps there are more rational, more peaceful, more fruitful ways to confront these horrible problems and our deepest feelings about them.

I recognize that the body scholarship in technology studies is less profound than the dramas of Aeschylus. But it may contain ideas and proposals that point in some promising directions. Better the wisdom of Athena than the counsels of crazed vengeance our leaders still prefer.

Acknowledgment

An earlier version of this essay was given as the Tenth Annual Hans Rausing Lecture for the Department of History and Philosophy of Science, University of Cambridge, May 19, 2005.

Notes

1. Quoted in Thomas Homer-Dixon (2002).
2. The original text appeared in Langdon Winner (1975). The full quote is as follows: "The study of redundancy is one direction in which any future discussion of social complexity ought to investigate. In particular, it illuminates a whole category of action which has stood in the shadows of political thought for thousands of years but which now seems entirely relevant to the technological society—*sabotage*. A first rule, for example, might be: 'Find the critical but nonredundant parts of the system and sabotage (or protect) them according to your purposes'" (p. 69).

3. There is now a vast literature in this genre. See, for example, Langdon Winner (1986); Wiebe Bijker, Thomas Hughes, and Trevor Pinch (1987); Wiebe Bijker and John Law (1992); Donna Haraway (1997).

4. I expand on this point in Langdon Winner (2004).

5. See, for example, Joseph G. Morone and Edward J. Woodhouse (1986).

6. *The 9/11 Commission Report: Final Report of the National Commission on Terrorist Attacks upon the United States: Executive Summary,* http://www.9-11commission.gov/report/911Report_Exec.htm.

7. "Bomb Risk Forces NY Tower Rethink," BBC News, May 5, 2005, http://news.bbc.co.uk/1/hi/world/americas/4515759.stm.

8. "College Student Admits Planting Box Cutters on Planes," CNN, October 17, 2003, http://www.cnn.com/2003/US/10/17/suspicious.baggage/.

9. "Student in Box-Cutter Case Gets Probation," Newmax, June 24, 2004, http://www.newsmax.com/archives/articles/2004/6/24/122102.shtml.

10. More than a year after the release of the final report of the 9/11 Commission, members of the commission, reassembled in a private group called the 9/11 Public Discourse Project, complained that few of the remedies they had proposed had been implemented. See Lara Jakes Jordan, "Sept. 11 Panel: U.S. Remains Unprepared," *Washington Post,* December 5, 2005. Other reports warning that U.S. approaches to terrorism are badly conceived include one written before the 9/11 attack, *Roadmap for National Security: Imperative for Change,* The National Commission on National Security/21 Century, February 15, 2001, http://www.google.com/url?sa=U&start=4&q=http://govinfo.library.unt.edu/nssg/PhaseIIIFR.pdf&e=912.

Contributors

Peter Adey is currently an ESRC Postdoctoral Fellow at the Institute of Geography and Earth Sciences, University of Wales, Aberystwyth. His research tries to take the space of the airport seriously, examining the mobilities airports produce and are produced by, while exploring their grounding within social, cultural, and political contexts. He has published work concerning airport surveillance, materiality, and identity and is currently working on developing two research projects concerning British airport architecture and the historical construction of airspace.

Heather Cameron is a research fellow at the Centre for Technology and Society at the Technical University of Berlin and a research associate at the Canadian Centre for Policy Analysis in Science and Technology at Simon Fraser University in Vancouver. Her research concerns tracking and tracing technologies in transport and the social and political consequences.

Nancy D. Campbell is the author of *Using Women: Gender, Drug Policy, and Social Justice* (Routledge 2000) and of articles on drug testing in *Science, Technology, and Human Values* and *Surveillance and Society*. Her forthcoming book *Science Says: The Laboratory Logics of Substance Abuse Research* is based on extensive interviews with addiction researchers and is a history of the social organization of knowledge production in the drug sciences. She is an assistant professor in the Department of Science and Technology Studies at Rensselaer Polytechnic Institute. Her Ph.D. is from the History of Consciousness program at the University of California, Santa Cruz. Her dissertation was titled "Cold War Compulsions: U.S. Drug Science, Policy, and Culture" (1995).

Simon A. Cole is an assistant professor of criminology, law, and society at the University of California, Irvine. He studies the interactions between science, technology, law, and criminal justice. He is the author of *Suspect Identities: A History of Fingerprinting and Criminal Identification* (Harvard University Press 2001). His current interests are the sociology of forensic science and the development of criminal identification databases and biometric technologies. He teaches courses on forensic science and society, surveillance and society, and science, technology, and law.

Lane DeNicola is a doctoral candidate in science and technology studies at Rensselaer Polytechnic Institute. His research interests include the cultural and political dimensions of information technology, modeling and simulation, and space industrialization. His dissertation research examines the development of remote sensing capability, expertise, and policy in India, particularly in the context of the global "environmental informatics" market. Prior to graduate study, he spent six years as a programmer and analyst at the Johns Hopkins University Applied Physics Laboratory and later the Lincoln Laboratory and the Center for Space Research at MIT.

Aaron Doyle is an associate professor in the Department of Sociology and Anthropology at Carleton University. His books include *Arresting Images: Crime and Policing in Front of the Television Camera* (2003), *Insurance as Governance* (with Richard Ericson and Dean Barry, 2003), *Uncertain Business: Risk, Insurance and the Limits of Knowledge* (with Richard Ericson, 2004), and *Risk and Morality* (coedited with Richard Ericson, 2003). His current research includes work on surveillance and the mass media, on jails and remand centers, and on the relations between risk, fear, blaming, and punitiveness.

Virginia Eubanks is an assistant professor in the Department of Women's Studies at the University at Albany, SUNY. Eubanks came to her research—"high-tech" development and women's urban poverty in the United States—through a history of activism in community media and technology center movements. She is currently working on a book project titled *Popular Technology: Citizenship and Inequality in the Information Economy.* Eubanks also cofounded the Popular Technology Summer Workshops, a popular education and technology series held annually at the YWCA of Troy-Cohoes. The workshop is a place for ordinary people to come together to define a high-tech equity agenda and is grounded in the idea that ordinary people have the ability and the right to create their own tools to promote economic, political, social, and cultural democracy. More information is available at www.populartechnology.org.

Jill A. Fisher is an assistant professor in the Women and Gender Studies Program and the Consortium for Science, Policy, and Outcomes at Arizona State University. As a scholar of science and technology studies, her work focuses on the politics of medicine in the United States, particularly the ways in which health care is being shaped by neoliberal ideologies. She is currently completing a book that examines the privatization of clinical trials—the process of pharmaceutical companies' outsourcing their drug research to private practice physicians around the country.

Laura Huey teaches in the Criminology Department at Kwantlen University College and is the author of several theory and research articles on policing and social exclusion. Her most recent work examines surveillance and the policing of skid-row districts.

The **Institute for Applied Autonomy** is an anonymous collective of artists, activists, and engineers united by the cause of individual and collective self-determination. The group's stated mission is to develop technologies that extend the autonomy of human activists in the performance of real-world, public acts of dissent. Since its founding in 1998, the IAA's projects have included robots that write graffiti and distribute subversive literature, geographic information system tools for monitoring and avoiding surveillance cameras, and mobile computing applications that support massively distributed street protest. The IAA has exhibited its works throughout the United States, Europe, and Asia, and it lectures widely on a variety of topics. See www.appliedautonomy.com for more information.

Cindi Katz is a professor of geography in environmental psychology and women's studies at the Graduate Center of the City University of New York. Her work concerns social reproduction and the production of space, place, and nature; children and the environment; and the consequences of global economic restructuring for everyday life. She is the editor (with Nancy K. Miller) of *Women's Studies Quarterly.* She is the editor (with Janice Monk) of *Full Circles: Geographies of Gender over the Life Course* (Routledge 1993) and of *Life's Work: Geographies of Social Reproduction* (with Sallie Marston and Katharyne Mitchell) (Blackwell 2004). Her book *Growing up Global: Economic Restructuring and Children's Everyday Lives* (University of Minnesota Press 2004) received the Meridian Award for outstanding scholarly work in geography from the Association of American Geographers.

Andrew Lakoff is an assistant professor of sociology and science studies at the University of California, San Diego. He is the author of *Pharmaceutical Reason: Knowledge and Value in Global Psychiatry* (Cambridge 2005) and coeditor of *Global Pharmaceuticals: Ethics, Markets, Practices* (Duke

2006). He is currently working on a study of forms of future-orientation among security planners in the United States.

David Lyon is Queen's Research Chair in sociology and director of the Surveillance Project at Queen's University, Kingston, Ontario. His most recent books are *Surveillance after September 11* (Polity 2003) and *Surveillance as Social Sorting: Privacy, Risk, and Digital Discrimination* (ed., Routledge 2003). He is a founding editor of the online journal *Surveillance and Society*.

Gary T. Marx, professor emeritus M.I.T., is a lapsed sociologist and electronic (garymarx.net) and occasionally itinerant scholar. His most recent book is *Windows into the Soul: Surveillance and Society in an Age of High Technology* (University of Chicago Press forthcoming).

Torin Monahan is an assistant professor of justice and social inquiry at Arizona State University. He has training in the field of science and technology studies, and his scholarly research focuses on the design of information technology infrastructures and their associated political and social ramifications. He is author of *Globalization, Technological Change, and Public Education* (Routledge 2005). He is currently conducting research on surveillance systems in public places. For further information, visit PublicSurveillance.com.

Henry N. Pontell is a professor of criminology, law, and society in the School of Social Ecology and a professor of sociology in the School of Social Sciences at the University of California, Irvine. He has written on numerous topics in crime, criminal justice, and law and society. His books include *A Capacity to Punish: The Ecology of Crime and Punishment, Social Deviance, Prescription for Profit: How Doctors Defraud Medicaid, Profit without Honor: White Collar Crime and the Looting of America, Big Money Crime: Fraud and Politics in the Savings and Loan Crisis*, and *Contemporary Issues in Crime and Criminal Justice: Essays in Honor of Gilbert Geis.* In 2001 he received the Albert J. Reiss Jr. Distinguished Scholarship Award from the American Sociological Association and the Donald R. Cressey Award from the Association of Certified Fraud Examiners.

Irma van der Ploeg (Ph.D.) holds a degree in philosophy and science and technology studies and is currently employed as a senior researcher at the Institute for Healthcare Management and Policy, Erasmus University Medical Centre, Rotterdam, the Netherlands. She has published extensively on philosophical, normative, and gender aspects of medical reproductive technologies and information and communication technologies. She is author of *Prosthetic Bodies: The Construction of Couples and Fetuses* *as Patients in Reproductive Technologies* (Kluwer 2001) and *The Machine-Readable Body: Essays on Biometrics and the Informatization of the Body* (Shaker 2005).

Kevin Walby is a Ph.D. candidate at Carleton University. His interests include critical criminology, surveillance and governance studies, institutional ethnography, and the sex trade in Canada.

Langdon Winner is a political theorist who focuses on social and political issues that surround modern technological change. He is the author of *Autonomous Technology* and *The Whale and the Reactor* and the editor of *Democracy in a Technology Society*. As Thomas Phelan Chair of Humanities, he teaches courses in technology studies and the politics of design in Rensselaer Polytechnic Institute's Department of Science and Technology Studies. He lectures frequently in the United States, Europe, and the Far East. A committed activist, he is involved in a number of environmental and social causes, especially ones that involve direct, democratic participation. At present he is writing a book on sustainable technologies and local politics. His blog Technopolis offers running commentaries on events and ideas he finds interesting.

References

Accent Marketing and Research. 2004. *Town Centres Survey 2003–4: Summary Report.* July 2004. London.

Acsys Biometrics. 2004. Acsys Biometrics and Hummingbird Defense Systems to Develop the "Safe Schools Program" in Maricopa County, Arizona. Burlington, ON Canada, http://www.nxsgrp.com/html/press_releases/PR%2002%2024%2004%20Acsys%20Hummingbird%20Maricopa.pdf.

Adey, P. 2004a. Secured and Sorted Mobilities: Examples from the Airport. *Surveillance and Society* 1 (4): 500–519.

———. 2004b. Surveillance at the Airport: Surveilling Mobility/Mobilising Surveillance. *Environment and Planning A* 36 (8): 1365–1380.

Agamben, Giorgio. 2005. *State of Exception.* Chicago: University of Chicago Press.

———. 2000. *Means without End: Notes on Politics.* Minneapolis: University of Minnesota Press.

———. 1997. *Homo Sacer: Sovereign Power and Bare Life.* Stanford, CA: Stanford University Press.

Agar, Jon. 2003. *Constant Touch: A Global History of the Mobile Phone.* Cambridge: Ikon Books.

Agre, Philip. 2001. Changing Places: Contexts of Awareness in Computing. *Human-Computer Interaction* 16 (2–4): 177–192.

Aitken, Stuart C., and Suzanne M. Michel. 1995. Who Contrives the "Real" in GIS? Geographic Information, Planning and Critical Theory. *Cartography and Geographic Information Systems* 22 (1): 17–29.

Allan, Darin, and Joel Volinski. 2001. *Cops, Cameras, and Enclosures: A Synthesis of the Effectiveness of Methods to Provide Enhanced Security for Bus Operators.* Center for Urban Transportation Research University of South Florida: Tampa, Florida.

Allard, Patricia. 2002. *Life Sentences: Denying Welfare Benefits to Women Convicted of Drug Offenses.* Washington, DC: The Sentencing Project.

Alpert, S. 2003. Protecting Medical Privacy: Challenges in the Age of Genetic Information. *Journal of Social Issues* 59 (2).

Altheide, David L. 2006. *Terrorism and the Politics of Fear.* Lanham, MD: AltaMira.

———. 2002. *Creating Fear: News and the Construction of Crisis.* New York: Aldine de Gruyter.

American Civil Liberties Union. 2003a. Complaint in *Alexander, et al v. Goose Creek Police Dept., et al.* Charleston, NC, http://www.aclu.org/Files/getFile.cfm?id=14577.

———. 2003b. Interview with George McCrackin [video], http://www.aclu.org//drugpolicy/gen/10672prs20031215.html (cited July 3, 2004).

———. 2001. Safety in Schools: Are We on the Right Track? Boulder, CO, http://www.aclu-co.org/news/letters/paper_boulderschools.htm.

_____. 1999. *Drug Testing: A Bad Investment*. New York: American Civil Liberties Union.

Anderson, J. 2002. Borders after 11 September 2001. *Space and Polity* 6 (2): 227-232.

Anderson, T. 2005. Guardian Uses Xray Technology for Airport Security. *Washington Business Journal,* March 21, 2005.

Andrejevic, Mark. 2004. Monitored Mobility in the Era of Mass Customization. *Space and Culture* 6 (2): 132–150.

Appadurai, A. 1990. Disjuncture and Difference in the Global Cultural Economy. In *Global Culture: Nationalism, Globalization and World Culture,* ed. M. Featherstone. London: Sage.

Aquia Harbour. 2004. Security, http://www.aquiaharbour.org/pages/security.asp (cited May 16, 2004).

Arendt, Hannah. 1998. *The Human Condition*. 2nd ed. Chicago: University of Chicago Press.

Armitage, Rachel. 2002. To CCTV or Not to CCTV? London: Nacro, http://www.nacro.org.uk/data/briefings/nacro-2002062800-csps.pdf.

Arquilla, J., and D. Ronfeldt. 2000. *Swarming and the Future of Conflict*. RAND National Defense Research Institute.

Aschbacher, Josef. 2002. Monitoring Environmental Treaties Using Earth Observation. In *The Verification Yearbook 2002,* ed. T. Findlay and O. Meier. London: VERTIC.

Ashtech Precision Products. 2001. *Geospatial Solutions* 11 (1). (back cover advertisement)

Associated Press. 2005. "ID Theft Insurance Not Always Good Option," October 2, 2005.

_____. 2003. Raid Might Have Broken Drug-Dog Rules, *TheState.com,* December 8, 2003, http://www.thestate.com/mld/thestate/news/local/7440066.htm.

Auger, J.D., and J. Kievit. 2004. SUO—Special Operations Forces for the 21st Century. *Special Operations Technology* 2 (5), August 18, 2004.

Ball, Philip. 2004. Hostile Space, *news@nature.com,* November 12, 2004, http://www.nature.com/news/2004/041108/pf/041108-19_pf.html (cited February 24, 2005).

Barney, Darin. 2000. *Prometheus Wired: The Hope for Democracy in the Age of Network Technology*. Chicago: University of Chicago Press.

Barr, Stephen. 2004. GAO Gets New Name, Permission to Launch New Compensation System, *WashingtonPost.com,* July 12, 2004, B02, http://www.washingtonpost.com/wp-dyn/articles/A43080-2004Jul11.html.

Barstow, David. 1999. A.T.M. Cards Fail to Live Up to Promises to Poor. *New York Times,* August 16, 1999, http://www.nytimes.com/library/politics/081699ny-welfare-atm.html.

Bartholow, Jessica, and Debra Garcia. 2002. An Advocate's Guide to Electronic Benefit Transfer (EBT) in California: Consumers Union, http://www.consumersunion.org/finance/ebt/ebt-rpt1.htm.

Bauman, Zygmunt. 2005. *Liquid Life*. Cambridge: Polity Press.

_____. 2001. *Liquid Modernity*. Cambridge: Polity Press.

_____. 1998. *Globalization: The Human Consequences*. New York: Columbia University Press.

BBC. 1999. Americas Columbine Shooting Footage Aired on TV, London, http://news.bbc.co.uk/1/hi/world/americas/473379.stm.

Bean, Frank D., Roland Chanove, Robert G. Cushing, Rodolfo de la Garza, and Gary P. Freeman. 1994. *Illegal Mexican Migration and the United States/Mexican Border: The Effects of Operation Hold the Line on El Paso/Juarez*. U.S. Commission on Immigration Reform. Austin, TX: Population Research Center, www.utexas.edu/lbj/uscir/respapers/imm-jul94.pdf.

Beaverstock, J.V. 2002. Transnational Elites in Global Cities: British Expatriates in Singapore's Financial District. *Geoforum* 33 (4): 525–538.

Beaverstock, J.V., P. Hubbard, and J. Rennie Short. 2004. Getting Away with It? Exposing the Geographies of the Super-Rich. *Geoforum* 35 (4): 401–407.

Beck, U. 2001. Globalization's Chernobyl. *Financial Times*.

Becker, C. 2004. The Next Generation: RFID Could Save Millions of Dollars; HDMA Study. *Modern Healthcare* 34 (46): 18.

Becker, Howard S. 1963. *Outsiders: Studies in the Sociology of Deviance*. New York: Free Press.

Bennett, C. 2006. What Happens When You Book an Airline Ticket (Revisited): The Computer Assisted Passenger Profiling System and the Globalization of Personal Data. In *Global Surveillance and Policing: Borders, Security, Identity,* ed. E. Zureik and M.B. Salter. Cullompten: Willan.

Bennett, C., and P. Regan. 2004. Surveillance and Mobilities. *Surveillance and Society* 1 (4): 449–455.

———. 2002. What Happens When You Make a 911 Call? Privacy and Regulation of Cellular Technology in the USA and Canada. Paper presented at the Canadian Political Science Association, May 31, 2002.

Bergman, Lowell, and David Rummel. 2004. *The Secret History of the Credit Card.* PBS.

Best, Joel. 2002. Monster Hype: How a Few Isolated Tragedies—and Their Supposed Causes—Were Turned into an "Epidemic." *Education Next,* Summer, http://www.findarticles.com/p/articles/mi_m0MJG/is_2_2/ai_87209076.

———. 1999. *Random Violence: How We Talk about Crimes and New Victims.* Berkeley: University of California Press.

Bijker, Wiebe E., Thomas Hughes, and Trevor Pinch, eds. 1987. *The Social Construction of Technological Systems: New Directions in the Sociology and History of Technology.* Cambridge, MA: MIT Press.

Bijker, Wiebe E., and John Law, eds. 1992. *Shaping Technology/Building Society: Studies in Sociotechnical Change.* Cambridge, MA: MIT Press.

Bimber, Bruce A. 1996. *The Politics of Expertise in Congress: The Rise and Fall of the Office of Technology Assessment.* Albany: State University of New York Press.

Black, Jane. 2001. No Hiding from a Cell Phone. *Business Week Online,* June 21, 2001, http://www.businessweek.com/bwdaily/dnflash/jun2001/nf20010621_803.htm.

Blakely, Edward, and Mary Gail Snyder. 1997. *Fortress America: Gated Communities in the United States.* Washington, DC: Brookings Institution Press.

Blanchette, Jean-François, and Deborah G. Johnson. 2002. Data Retention and the Panoptic Society: The Social Benefits of Forgetfulness. *The Information Society* 18:33–45.

Boden, Diedre, and Harvey Molotch. 1994. The Compulsion to Proximity. In *NoWhere: Space, Time, and Modernity,* ed. R. Friedland and D. Boden. Berkeley: University of California Press.

Bonsen, G.Z., D. Ammann, M. Ammann, E. Favey, and P. Flammant. 2005. "Continuous Navigation: Combining GPS with Sensor Based Dead Reckoning," *www.gpsworld.com* (accessed October 3, 2005).

Bourdieu, Pierre. 1998. The Essence of Neoliberalism. *Le Monde Diplomatique,* December, http://mondediplo.com/1998/12/08bourdieu.

———. 1977. *Outline of a Theory of Practice.* Trans. R. Nice. Cambridge, MA: Cambridge University Press.

Bowker, G.C., and S.L. Star. 1999. *Sorting Things Out: Classification and Its Consequences.* Cambridge, MA: MIT Press.

Boyd, Graham. 2002. Collateral Damage in the War on Drugs. *Villanova Law Review* 47:839–845.

Boyne, Roy. 2000. Post-Panopticism. *Economy and Society* 29 (2): 285–307.

Bradsher, Keith. 2002. *High and Mighty: SUVs—The World's Most Dangerous Vehicles and How They Got That Way.* New York: Public Affairs.

Brand, Constant. 2004. EU Nations Set to Name Anti-terror Czar. *The Guardian,* March 19, 2004, http://www.guardian.co.uk/worldlatest/story/0,1280,-3880554,00.html.

Branigin, William. 2003. Stafford Teens Charged in Burglary Ring. *Washington Post,* July 14, 2003.

Brat, Ilan. 2004. Always under Surveillance. *The State Press (Arizona State University),* April 28, 2004, 1, 8–9.

Brewer, Alexander, Nancy Sloan, and Thomas L. Landers. 1999. Intelligent Tracking in Manufacturing. *Journal of Intelligent Manufacturing* 10 (3–4): 245–250.

Brilis, George M., Clare L. Gerlach, and Robert J. van Waasbergen. 2000. Remote Sensing Tools Assist in Environmental Forensics—Part I: Traditional Methods. *Journal of Environmental Forensics* 1: 63–67.

Brin, David. 1998. *The Transparent Society.* Reading, MA: Perseus Books.

Bromley, Hank. 1998. Introduction: Data-Driven Democracy? Social Assessment of Educational Computing. In *Education/Technology/Power: Educational Computing as a Social Practice,* ed. H. Bromley and M.W. Apple. Albany: State University of New York Press.

Brotherton, David C. 1996. The Contradictions of Suppression: Notes from a Study of Approaches to Gangs in Three Public High Schools. *The Urban Review* 28 (2): 95–117.

Brown, Justine K. 2004. A Face in the Crowd. *Government Technology,* April, http://www.govtech.net/magazine/story.php?id=89806&issue=4:2004.

Browning, Dan, and Chris Graves. 2002. The Identity Crisis. *Minneapolis Star Tribune,* February 10, 2002, 1A.

Brunn, Matthew, and Anthony Wier. 2005. *Securing the Bomb 2005: The New Global Imperatives*. Cambridge, MA: Belfer Center for Science and International Affairs.

Buechler, Steven. 2000. *Social Movements in Advanced Capitalism: The Political Economy and Cultural Construction of Social Activism*. Oxford: Oxford University Press.

Burkeman, O. 2004. Fee Buys Right to Skip Air Security. *The Guardian Online*, http://www.guardian.co.uk/airlines/story/0,1371,1239079,00.html (cited July 2005).

BurleCCTV. 2004. *Philips–Burle CCTV*, http://www.burlecctv.com/ (cited July 5, 2004).

Burns, Ronald, and Charles Crawford. 1999. School Shootings, the Media, and Public Fear: Ingredients for a Moral Panic. *Crime, Law and Social Change* 32: 147–168.

Bush, Corlann Gee. 1997. Women and the Assessment of Technology. In *Technology and the Future*, ed. A.H. Teich. New York: St. Martin's Press.

Bush, George W. 2004. Executive Order 13335. Washington, DC, http://www.whitehouse.gov/news/releases/2004/04/20040427-4.html.

————. 2001. President Unveils Back to Work Plan. Washington, DC: White House, http://www.whitehouse.gov/news/releases/2001/10/20011004-8.html.

Cahill, S. 1990. Childhood and Public Life: Reaffirming Biographical Divisions. *Social Problems* 37 (3): 390–402.

Cairncross, Frances. 1997. *The Death of Distance: How the Communications Revolution Will Change Our Lives*. Boston: Harvard Business School Press.

Calavita, Kitty, Henry N. Pontell, and Robert H. Tillman. 1997. *Big Money Crime: Fraud and Politics in the Savings and Loan Crisis*. Berkeley: University of California Press.

Caldeira, Teresa P.R. 2000. *City of Walls: Crime, Segregation, and Citizenship in São Paulo*. Berkeley: University of California Press.

Calhoun, Craig. 2004. A World of Emergencies: Fear, Intervention, and the Limits of Cosmopolitan Order. *The Canadian Review of Sociology and Anthropology* 41 (4): 373–395.

————. 2003. The Class Consciousness of Frequent Travelers: Toward a Critique of Actually Existing Cosmopolitanism. In *Conceiving Cosmopolitanism: Theory, Context and Practice*, ed. C. Vertovec and R. Cohen. Oxford: Oxford University Press.

California Department of Consumer Affairs. 2003. *How to Use the California Identity Theft Registry: A Guide for Victims of "Criminal" Identity Theft*, http://ag.ca.gov/idtheft/index.htm.

Calvaneso, George. 1999. Where's Your Equipment When You Need It? *Health Management Technology* 20 (10): 20–21.

Cameron, Heather. 2004. CCTV and (In)dividuation. *Surveillance and Society* 2 (2–3): 136–144, http://www.surveillance-and-society.org/articles2(2)/individuation.pdf.

Campbell, Nancy D. 2005. Suspect Technologies: Scrutinizing the Intersection of Science, Technology, and Policy. *Science, Technology, and Human Values* 30 (3): 374–402.

————. 2004. Technologies of Suspicion: Coercion and Compassion in Post-disciplinary Surveillance Regimes. *Surveillance and Society* 2 (1): 78–92.

————. 2000. *Using Women: Gender, Drug Policy, and Social Justice*. New York: Routledge.

Campbell, Nancy, and Virginia Eubanks. 2004. Making Sense of Imbrication: Popular Technology and "Inside-Out" Methodologies. Paper read at Participatory Design Conference, Toronto, Canada.

Caponetto, T.R. 2004. Identity Theft Is a Major Problem in America, *KansasCity infoZine*, http://www.infozine.com/news/stories/op/storiesView/sid/2215/.

Carey, Corinne A. 1998. Crafting a Challenge to the Practice of Drug Testing Welfare Recipients. *Buffalo Law Review* 46, Lexis-Nexis (accessed July 23, 2001).

Carey, James W. 1989. *Communication as Culture: Essays on Media and Society*. Boston: Unwin Hyman.

Castells, M. 1996. *The Rise of the Network Society*. Oxford: Blackwell.

Caulkins, Jonathan P., Peter Reuter, Martin Iguchi, and James Chiesa. 2003. *Drug Use and Drug Policy Futures*. Santa Monica, CA: Rand Corporation, IP 246-DPRC.

Center for Reproductive Rights. 2002. Court Upholds Rights of Pregnant Women: Medical University of South Carolina Drug Testing Scheme Found Unconstitutional, www.reproductiverights.org (accessed January 19, 2003).

Chandler, Kathryn A. 2004. *Crime and Safety in America's Public Schools: Selected Findings from the School Survey on Crime and Safety*. Washington, DC: National Center for Education Statistics, http://nces.ed.gov/pubs2004/2004370.pdf.

Chapin, A. 2005. Arresting DNA: Privacy Expectations of Free Citizens versus Post-Convicted Persons and the Unconstitutionality of DNA Dragnets. *Minn. L. Rev.* 89.

Chasnoff, Ira. 1990. The Prevalence of Illicit-Drug or Alcohol Use During Pregnancy and Discrepancies in Mandatory Reporting in Pinellas County, Florida. *New England Journal of Medicine* 322.17 (26 April): 1202–1206.

ChoicePoint: More ID Theft Warnings. 2005. *CNN/Money*, February 17, 2005, http://money.cnn.com/2005/02/17/technology/personaltech/choicepoint/index.htm (cited July 26, 2005).

City of Vancouver. 2001. Downtown Eastside Community Monitoring Report, http://www.city.vancouver.bc.ca/COMMSVCS/PLANNING/dtes/pdf/MonitorRpt2001.pdf.

Clarke, Roger. 2003. Wireless Transmission and Mobile Technologies, http://www.anu.edu.au/people/Roger.Clarke/EC/WMT.html.

———. 1989. The OECD Data Protection Guidelines: A Template for Evaluating Information Privacy Law and Proposals for Information Privacy Law, Canberra: Xamax Consultancy, http://www.anu.edu.au/people/Roger.Clarke/DV/PaperOECD.html(accessed December 2005).

Cloud, John. 2001. Imaging the World in a Barrel: CORONA and the Clandestine Convergence of the Earth Sciences. *Social Studies of Science* 31 (2): 231–251.

CNN. 2000. Columbine Report, http://www.cnn.com/SPECIALS/2000/columbine.cd/frameset.exclude.html (cited July 3, 2004).

Coaffee, Jon. 2004. Rings of Steel, Rings of Concrete and Rings of Confidence: Designing out Terrorism in Central London pre and post September 11th. *International Journal of Urban and Regional Research* 28 (1): 201–211.

Coates, Vary. 1995. On the Demise of OTA. *TA-Datenbank-Nachrichten* 4 (4), http://www.itas.fzk.de/deu/TADN/TADN1295/inst.htm.

Cohen, Stanley. 1972. *Folk Devils and Moral Panics*. Oxford: Blackwell.

Cole, Simon A. 2001. *Suspect Identities: A History of Fingerprinting and Criminal Identification*. Cambridge, MA: Harvard University Press.

Colker, David. 2005. ID Theft Coverage Draws Criticism. *Los Angeles Times*, May 27, 2005, C1, C10.

Colker, David, and Joseph Menn. 2005. ChoicePoint CEO Had Denied Any Previous Breach of Database. *Los Angeles Times*, March 3, 2005, C1, C6.

Collective Opposed to Police Brutality. 2002. http://users.resist.ca/~copb-van/ (accessed November 23, 2002).

Collier, Stephen J., Andrew Lakoff, and Paul Rabinow. 2004. Biosecurity: Towards an Anthropology of the Contemporary. *Anthropology Today* 20 (5): 3–7.

Collins, M.F., and D. Weatherburn. 1995. Unemployment and the Dynamics of Offender Populations. *Journal of Quantitative Criminology* 11 (3): 231–245.

Comaroff, Jean, and John L. Comaroff. 2000. Millennial Capitalism: First Thoughts on a Second Coming. *Public Culture* 12 (2): 291–343.

Commission of the European Communities. 2004. *Proposal for a Council Regulation on Standards for Security Features and Biometrics in EU Citizens' Passports*. Brussels: Commission of the European Communities.

Conde, Caspar. 2004. *The Long Eye of the Law: Closed Circuit Television, Crime Prevention and Civil Liberties*. St. Leonards, Australia: Centre for Independent Studies, http://www.cis.org.au/IssueAnalysis/ia48/IA48.pdf.

Connell, Sally Ann. 2004. Students Face Possibility of Identity Theft. *Los Angeles Times*, August 29, 2004, B5.

Connolly, W.E. 2000. Speed, Concentric Cultures, and Cosmopolitanism. *Political Theory* 28 (5): 596–618.

Cooper, Caroline S. 2003. *Drug Courts—Just the Beginning: Getting Other Areas of Public Policy in Sync*. Washington, DC: Justice Programs Office, American University.

Cop Watch blog. 2005. March 7, 2005, http://cop-watch.blogspot.com/2005/03/copwatch-activists-arrested.html (accessed September 26, 2005).

Corn, J.J. 1983. *The Winged Gospel: America's Romance with Aviation, 1900–1950*. New York: Oxford University Press.

Cornelius, Wayne A. 2001. Death at the Border: Efficacy and Unintended Consequences of US Immigration Control Policy. *Population and Development Review* 27 (4): 661–85.

Courtwright, David. 2001. *Forces of Habit: Drugs and the Making of the Modern World*. Cambridge, MA: Harvard University Press.

Crary, Jonathan. 1999. *Suspensions of Perception: Attention, Spectacle, and Modern Culture*. Cambridge, MA: MIT Press.

_____. 1990. *Techniques of the Observer: On Vision and Modernity in the Nineteenth Century*. Cambridge, MA: MIT Press.

Cressey, Donald R. 1953. *Other People's Money: A Study in the Social Psychology of Embezzlement*. Glencoe, IL: Free Press.

Cresswell, T. 2001. The Production of Mobilities. *New Formation*, 11–25.

Cronkite, Walter. 2003. The New Inquisition. *Denver Post*, September 21, 2003, http://www.thezephyr.com/cronkite/cronkite092503.htm.

Crowley, Thomas. 2005. Interview with the author, June 18, 2005, Orlando, Florida.

_____. 1984. Contingency Contracting Treatment of Drug-Abusing Physicians, Nurses, and Dentists. In *Behavioral Intervention Techniques in Drug Abuse Treatment*. NIDA Research Monograph 46: 68–83.

Cruikshank, Barbara. 1999. *The Will to Empower: Democratic Citizens and Other Subjects*. Ithaca, NY: Cornell University Press.

Curry, Michael R. 2004. The Profiler's Question and the Treacherous Traveller: Narratives of Belonging in Commercial Aviation. *Surveillance and Society* 1 (4): 475–499.

Cusack, Rebecca. 2003. Interview with Virginia Eubanks, September 4, 2003.

Cwerner, S.B. 2004. Faster, Faster and Faster: The Time Politics of Asylum in the UK. *Time and Society* 13 (1): 71–88.

Daniels, Alan. 1999. Drugs, Crime Threaten Tourism, Harcourt Says. *Vancouver Sun*, April 27, 1999, DI.

Daniels, Cynthia. 1993. *At Women's Expense: State Power and the Politics of Fetal Rights*. Cambridge, MA: Harvard University Press.

Dash, S. 2004. *The Intruders*. New Brunswick, NJ: Rutgers University Press.

Data Protection Working Party. 2004. *Opinion No7/2004 on the Inclusion of Biometric Elements in Residence Permits and Visas Taking Account of the Establishment of the European Information System on Visas (VIS)*, August 11, 2004, Brussels.

_____. 2003. *Working Document on Biometrics*, August 1, 2003, Brussels.

Davies, S. 1995. Welcome Home Big Brother. *Wired*, May 1995, 58–62.

Davis, Kristin. 2001. Anatomy of an ID Fraud. *Kiplinger's Personal Finance*, March 1–6, 2001.

Davis, S. 2004. Tagging Along: RFID Helps Hospitals Track Assets and People. *Health Facilities Management* 17 (12): 20–24.

Dawson, T. 1994. Framing the Villain. *New Statesman and Society*, January 28, 1994.

Debord, Guy. 1977. *Society of the Spectacle*. Detroit: Red and Black.

de Certeau, Michel. 1984. *The Practice of Everyday Life*. Trans. S. Rendall. Berkeley: University of California Press.

de Certeau, Michel, Luce Giard, and Pierre Mayol. 1998. *The Practice of Everyday Life*. Trans. T.J. Tomasik, ed. L. Giard. New revised and augmented ed., Vol. 2: Living and Cooking. Minneapolis: University of Minnesota Press.

DeCew, Judith Wagner. 1997. *In Pursuit of Privacy: Law, Ethics, and the Rise of Technology*. Ithaca, NY: Cornell University Press.

Deleuze, Gilles. 1992. Postscript on the Societies of Control. *October* 59: 3–7, http://www.nadir.org/nadir/archiv/netzkritik/societyofcontrol.html.

Deleuze, Gilles, and Félix Guattari. 1987. *A Thousand Plateaus: Capitalism and Schizophrenia*. Trans. B. Massumi. Minneapolis: University of Minnesota Press.

Demers, Amanda. 2004. Interview with Virginia Eubanks, February 2, 2004.

Department of Transport. 2004. *Links between Bus Related Crimes and Other Crimes: A Briefing Paper*. London, October 2004.

Derrida, Jacques. 1988. *Limited Inc*. Trans. S. Weber and Jeffrey Mehlman. Evanston, IL: Northwestern University Press.

DeVoe, Jill, Katharin Peter, Sally Ruddy, Amanda Miller, Mike Planty, Thomas Snyder, and Mike Rand. 2003. *Indicators of School Crime and Safety: 2003*. Washington, DC: National Center for Education Statistics, http://nces.ed.gov/pubs2004/2004004.pdf.

d'Hont, Susy. 2002. *The Cutting Edge of RFID Technology and Applications for Manufacturing and Distribution*. Texas Instrument, http://www.rfidusa.com/pdf/manuf_dist.pdf.

Dickman, Fred J., William G. Emener Jr., and William S. Hutchison Jr., eds. 1986. *Counseling the Troubled Person in Industry.* Springfield, IL: Charles C. Thomas.

Dillon, Sam. 2003. Cameras Watching Students, Especially in Biloxi. *New York Times,* September 24, 2003, B9.

Ditton, Jason, Emma Short, Samuel Phillips, Clive Norris, and Gary Armstrong. 1999. *The Effect of Closed Circuit Television Cameras on Recorded Crime Rates and Public Concern about Crime in Glasgow.* Edinburgh: Scottish Office Central Research Unit, http://www.scotcrim.u-net.com/researchc2.htm.

Dong Kim, S. 2002. Personal meanings. In *Perpetual Contact: Mobile Communication, Private Talk, Public Performance,* ed. James E. Katz and Mark Aakhus. Cambridge and New York: Cambridge University Press.

Dotinga, R. 2004. Make a Killing from Antiterrorism. *Wired,* http://www.wired.com/news/business/0,1367,64215,00.html.

Douglas, Mary. 1966. *Purity and Danger: An Analysis of Concepts of Pollution and Taboo.* London: Routledge and Kegan Paul.

Doward, Jamie. 2003. Big Brother Latest: Now Your Phone Can Be Used to Track You Down, *The Observer,* December 7, 2003, http://observer.guardian.co.uk/libertywatch/story/0,1373,1101729,00.html.

Doyle, Aaron. 2003. *Arresting Images: Crime and Policing in Front of the Camera.* Toronto: University of Toronto Press.

Dreifus, Claudia. 2005. A Conversation with—David Wong; A Bloodless Revolution: Spit Will Tell What Ails You. *New York Times,* April 19, 2005, F2.

Drug Court Clearinghouse and Technical Assistance Project. 2000. *Drug Court Survey Report.* Washington, DC: School of Public Affairs, American University.

Duggan, Lisa. 2003. *The Twilight of Equality? Neoliberalism, Cultural Politics, and the Attack on Democracy.* Boston: Beacon Press.

Durkheim, Emile, and Karen E. Fields. 1995. *The Elementary Forms of Religious Life.* New York: Free Press.

Dwyer, J. 2005. Videos Challenge Accounts of Convention Unrest. *New York Times,* April 12, 2005.

Edward, Rhianna. 2004. Lost? Help Is Just a Mobile Phone Photo Away. *The Scotsman,* April 13, 2004, 5.

Eglash, Ron, Jennifer L. Croissant, Giovanna Di Chiro, and Rayvon Fouché. 2004. *Appropriating Technology: Vernacular Science and Social Power.* Minneapolis: University of Minnesota Press.

Eldridge, Marge, and Rebecca Grinter. 2001. Studying Text Messaging in Teenagers. Workshop on Mobile Technologies at CHI 2001, Seattle, WA, www.cs.Colorado.edu/~palen/chi_workshop/papers/EldridgeGrinter.pdf/.

Electronic Privacy Information Center. 2005. Brief of *Amicus Curiae.* U.S. Court of Appeals for the Fifth Circuit. No. 05-30541. Case No. 3:03-cv-00857-JJB-CN.

———. 2003. In the Matter of Privacy Act Notice Concerning Aviation Security Screening Records, http://www.epic.org/privacy/airtravel/tsacomments2.24.2003.html (cited June 2005).

Eliade, Mircea, and Willard R. Trask. 1959. *The Sacred and the Profane: The Nature of Religion.* 1st American ed. New York: Harcourt Brace.

Elmer, Greg. 2004. *Profiling Machines: Mapping the Personal Information Economy.* Cambridge, MA: MIT Press.

Environmental News Service. 2004. Space Focus Shifts to Environment, Development, http://www.ens-newswire.com/login/index.asp?q=/ens/oct2004/2004-10-19-03.asp (cited November 2, 2004).

Erickson, Caroline. 1995. *GPS Positioning Guide.* 3rd ed. Ottawa, Ontario: Natural Resources Canada.

Ericson, Richard, Patricia Baranek, and Janet Chan. 1989. *Negotiating Control: A Study of News Sources.* Toronto: University of Toronto Press.

Etzioni, Amitai. 1999. *The Limits of Privacy.* New York: Basic Books.

Eubanks, Virginia. 2004. Popular Technology: Citizenship and Inequality in the Information Economy. Doctoral diss., Science and Technology Studies, Rensselaer Polytechnic Institute, Troy.

European Commission Directorate-General of Energy and Transportation. 2004. Galileo: European Satellite Navigation System 2005, September 30, 2004, http://europa.eu.int/comm/dgs/energy_transport/galileo/index_en.htm (cited March 1, 2005).

Ewald, Francois. 1991. Insurance and Risk. In *The Foucault Effect: Studies in Governmentality*, ed. Graham Burchell, Colin Gordon, and Peter Miller. Chicago: University of Chicago Press.

Executive Order 12906—Coordinating Geographic Data Acquisition and Access: The National Spatial Data Infrastructure. 1994. *Federal Register* 59 (71): 17671–17674.

Farmer, Paul. 2004. *Pathologies of Power: Health, Human Rights, and the New War on the Poor.* Berkeley: University of California Press.

_____. 1999. *Infections and Inequalities: The Modern Plagues.* Berkeley: University of California Press.

_____. 1992. *AIDS and Accusation: Haiti and the Geography of Blame.* Berkeley: University of California Press.

Feig, Bruce E. 2001. *Audit of Office of Temporary and Disability Assistance Electronic Benefit Transfer System.* New York: Office of the State Comptroller, http://www.osc.state.ny.us/audits/allaudits/093001/99s51.pdf.

Folbre, Nancy. 1987. *Who Pays for the Kids: Gender as a Structure of Constraint.* New York: Routledge.

Forschungsgesellschaft Flucht und Migration. 1998. Die Grenze. Flüchtlingsjagd in Schengenland. *Zeitschrift für Flüchtlingspolitik in Niedersachsen* 5 (55).

Fortun, Kim. 2004. Environmental Information Systems as Appropriate Technology. *Design Issues* 20 (3): 54–65.

Fortun, Michael, and Herbert J. Bernstein. 1998. *Muddling Through: Pursuing Science and Truths in the 21st Century.* Washington, DC: Counterpoint.

Fortunati, Leopoldina. 2002. The Mobile Phone: Towards New Categories and Social Relations. *Information, Communication, and Society* 5 (4): 513–528.

Foucault, Michel. 2003. *"Society Must Be Defended": Lectures at the College de France, 1975–76.* New York: Picador.

_____. 2000. Truth and Juridical Forms. *Essential Works of Michel Foucault, 1954–1984.* Vol. 3. Ed. James D. Faubion, trans. Robert Hurley and others. New York: New Press.

_____. 1994. The Ethics of Concern for the Self as a Practice of Freedom. *Essential Works of Michel Foucault, 1954–1984.* Vol. 1. Ed. Paul Rabinow, trans. Robert Hurley and others. New York: New Press.

_____. 1988. The Political Technology of Individuals. *Technologies of the Self.* Ed. L.H. Martin, H. Gutman, and P.H. Hutton. Amherst: University of Massachusetts Press.

_____. 1980. *Power/Knowledge: Selected Interviews and Other Writings, 1972–1977.* Brighton, Sussex: Harvester Press.

_____. 1977. *Discipline and Punish: The Birth of the Prison.* New York: Vintage Books, Random House.

_____. 1975. *The Birth of the Clinic: An Archaeology of Medical Perception.* New York: Vintage/Random House.

_____. 1972. *The Archaeology of Knowledge.* New York: Random House.

Flynn, Stephen. 2004. *America the Vulnerable: How Our Government Is Failing to Protect Us from Terrorism.* New York: HarperCollins.

Frank, Thomas. 2005. Biometric IDs Could See Massive Growth. *USA Today,* 1–5.

Freire, Paulo. 1998. *Pedagogy of Freedom: Ethics, Democracy, and Civic Courage.* New York: Rowman and Littlefield.

_____. 1997. *Pedagogy of the Oppressed.* New York: Continuum. (Orig. pub. 1970.)

_____. 1973. *Education for Critical Consciousness.* New York: Continuum.

French, Michael T., M. Christopher Roebuck, and Pierre Kebreau Alexandre. 2001. Illicit Drug Use, Employment, and Labor Force Participation. *Southern Economic Journal* 68 (2).

Friedman, Thomas L. 2005. *The World Is Flat: A Brief History of the Twenty-first Century.* New York: Farrar, Straus, and Giroux.

Furedi, Frank. 2005. *Culture of Fear: Risk-Taking and the Morality of Low Expectation.* New York: Continuum.

Gamson, William, and Gadi Wolfsfeld. 1993. Movements and Media as Interacting Systems. *Annals AAPSS* 528 (July 1993): 114–125.

Gandy, Oscar H. 2003. Data Mining and Surveillance in the Post 9/11 Environment. In *The Intensification of Surveillance: Crime Terrorism and Warfare in the Information Age,* ed. K. Ball and F. Webster. London: Pluto.

———. 1993. *The Panoptic Sort: A Political Economy of Personal Information.* Boulder, CO: Westview.

Gandy, Oscar, and A. Deanna. 2002. All That Glitters Is Not Gold: Digging beneath the Surface of Data Mining. *Journal of Business Ethics* 40: 373–386.

Garfinkel, Simson. 2002. Future Tech: One Face in 6 Billion, *International Biometric Group,* http://www.biometricgroup.com/in_the_news/discover.html (cited July 6, 2004).

———. 2000. *Database Nation: The Death of Privacy in the 21st Century.* Beijing: O'Reilly.

Garland, David. 2001. *The Culture of Control: Crime and Social Order in Contemporary Society.* Chicago: University of Chicago Press.

Garrett, Laurie. 1994. *The Coming Plague: Newly Emerging Diseases in a World out of Balance.* New York: Farrar, Straus, and Giroux.

Gellman, Barton. 2005. The FBI's Secret Scrutiny: In Hunt for Terrorists, Bureau Examines Records of Ordinary Americans. *Washington Post,* November 6, 2005, A01.

General Accounting Office. 1995. *Electronic Benefits Transfer: Use of Biometrics to Deter Fraud in the Nationwide EBT Program.* Washington, DC: General Accounting Office, http://www.gao.gov/archive/1995/os95020.pdf.

General Electric. 2004. Surveillance Technology from GE, http://www.ge.com/stories/en/20138.html?category=Products_Business (cited July 5, 2004).

Ghamari-Tabrizi, Sharon. 2005. *The Worlds of Herman Kahn: The Intuitive Science of Thermonuclear War.* Cambridge, MA: Harvard University Press.

Gibson, Cuemi. 2003. Interview with Virginia Eubanks, August 8, 2003.

Gill, Martin. 2004. Offenders' Views and CCTV. Paper read at CCTV and Social Control, January 8–9, Sheffield, United Kingdom.

Gilliom, John. 2001. *Overseers of the Poor: Surveillance, Resistance, and the Limits of Privacy.* Chicago: University of Chicago Press.

Girolami, Liz. 2003. Interview with Virginia Eubanks, July 15, 2003.

Giroux, Henry A. 2004. *The Terror of Neoliberalism: Authoritarianism and the Eclipse of Democracy.* Boulder, CO: Paradigm.

Glabman, M. 2004. Room for Tracking: RFID Technology Finds the Way. *Materials Management in Health Care* 13 (5): 26–28, 31–34, 36.

Glassner, Barry. 2000. *The Culture of Fear: Why Americans Are Afraid of the Wrong Things.* New York: Basic Books.

Global Monitoring for Environment and Security. 2005. European Commission/European Space Agency, February 17, 2005.

Global Security. 2002. Raytheon, http://www.globalsecurity.org/military/industry/raytheon.htm (cited July 5, 2004).

Goode, Erich, and Nachman Ben-Yehuda. 1994. *Moral Panics.* Oxford: Blackwell.

Goodlad, Lauren M.E. 2003. Beyond the Panopticon: Victorian Britain and the Critical Imagination. *PMLA: Modern Language Association of America* 118 (3): 539–56.

Goold, Benjamin J. 2004. *CCTV and Policing: Public Area Surveillance and Police Practices in Britain.* Oxford and New York: Oxford University Press.

Gow, Graham, and Mark Ihnat. 2004. Prepaid Mobile Phone Service and the Anonymous Caller: Considering Wireless E-911 in Canada. *Surveillance and Society* 1 (4): 555–572.

Grabosky, Peter N., Russell G. Smith, and Gillian Dempsey. 2001. *Electronic Theft: Unlawful Acquisition in Cyberspace.* Cambridge: Cambridge University Press.

Graham, Jamie. 2005. Media Release 2005-03-31, *Vancouver Police Department,* http://www.vancouver.ca/police/media/Releases/050331.htm (accessed April 14, 2005).

Graham, S. Forthcoming. Software-Sorted Geographies. *Progress in Human Geography.*

———. 2004a. FlowCity: Networked Mobilities and the Contemporary Metropolis. In *Urban Mutations: Periodization, Scale Mobility,* ed. T. Nielson, N. Albertsen, and P. Hemmersam. Denmark: Arkitektskolens Forlag.

———. 2004b. The Software Sorted City: Rethinking the Digital Divide. In *The Cybercities Reader,* ed. S. Graham. Oxford: Blackwell.

———. 2002. Bridging Urban Digital Divides? Urban Polarisation and Information and Communications Technologies (ICTs). *Urban Studies* 39 (1): 33–56.

_____. 2000. Constructing Premium Network Spaces: Reflections on Infrastructure Networks and Contemporary Urban Development. *International Journal of Urban and Regional Research* 24 (1): 183–200.

_____. 1998. Towards the Fifth Utility? On the Extension and Normalisation of Public CCTV. In *CCTV Surveillance and Social Control*, ed. C. Norris and G. Armstrong. Avebury: Gower.

Graham, S., and S. Marvin. 2001. *Splintering Urbanism: Networked Infrastructures, Technological Mobilities and the Urban Condition.* London and New York: Routledge.

Graham, S., and D. Wood. 2003. Digitizing Surveillance: Categorization, Space, Inequality. *Critical Social Policy* 23 (2; Issue 75): 227–248.

Grand, J. 2002. The Blooding of America: Privacy and the DNA Dragnet. *Cardozo L. Rev.*

Grant, B.F., and D.A. Dawson. 1996. Alcohol and Drug Use, Abuse, and Dependence among Welfare Recipients. *American Journal of Public Health* 86 (10): 1450–1454.

Greater Vancouver Transit Authority. 2004a. 2005–2007 Three Year Plan and Ten Year Outlook: Strategic Transportation Plan Amendment, February 2004.

_____. 2004b. B Line Bus Rapid Transit, September 2004.

Green, Nicola. 2002. On the Move: Technology, Mobility, and the Mediation of Social Time and Space. *The Information Society* 18: 281–292.

_____. 2001. Who's Watching Whom? Monitoring and Accountability in Mobile Relations. In *Wireless World: Social and Interactional Aspects of the Mobile Age*, ed. Barry Brown et al., 32–45. London: Springer.

Green, Nicola, and Sean Smith. 2004. "A spy in your pocket?" The Regulation of Mobile Phone Data in the UK. *Surveillance and Society* 1 (4): 573–587.

Greene, Thomas C. 2004. Feds Approve Human RFID Implants: Solution Desperately Seeking a Problem. *The Register*, October 14, 2004.

Greenhouse, L. 2001. High Court Bars Some Drug Tests. *New York Times*, March 22, 2001.

Guston, David H., and Daniel R. Sarewitz. 2002. Real-time Technology Assessment. *Technology in Society* 24: 93–109.

Haddon, Leslie, et al. 2001. *From Mobile to Mobility: The Consumption of ICTs and Mobility in Everyday Life.* COST269 Mobility Workgroup, http://www.cost269.org/working%20group/cost_workgpr_mobility.htm.

Haggerty, K.D. Forthcoming. Visible War: Information War, Surveillance and Speed. In *The New Politics of Surveillance and Visibility*, ed. K.D. Haggerty and R.V. Ericson. Toronto: University of Toronto Press.

Haggerty, Kevin D., and Richard V. Ericson. 2000. The Surveillant Assemblage. *British Journal of Sociology* 51 (4): 605–622.

Hannerz, U. 1990. Cosmopolitans and Locals in World Culture. In *Global Culture: Nationalism, Globalization and World Culture*, ed. M. Featherstone. London: Sage.

Haraway, Donna J. 1997. *Modest_Witness@Second_Millennium.FemaleMan_Meets_Onco- Mouse: Feminism and Technoscience.* New York: Routledge.

Harding, Jeremy. 2000. On Refugees and Illegal Migrants. *London Review of Books* 22 (3): 1–25.

Harding, Luke. 2004. On Patrol along the EU's New Eastern Frontier. *Guardian Unlimited*, April 28, 2004, http://www.guardian.co.uk/eu/story/0,7369,1204973,00.html (cited November 5, 2004).

Hardt, Michael, and Antonio Negri. 2000. *Empire.* Cambridge, MA: Harvard University Press.

Harmon, Amy. 2003. Lost? Hiding? Your Cellphone Is Keeping Tabs. *New York Times*, December 31, 2003.

Harrell, Adele, and Mark A. Kleiman. 2000. Drug Testing in Criminal Justice Settings. *The Urban Institute*, September 19, 2000.

Hasbrouck, E. 2004. TSA Requests Proposals for "Registered Traveller" Program, *The Practical Nomad*, http://hasbrouck.org/blog/archives/000191.html (cited June 2005).

Heaviside, Sheila, Cassandra Rowand, Catrina Williams, and Elizabeth Farris (Westat, Inc.). 1998. *Violence and Discipline Problems in U.S. Public Schools: 1996–97.* Washington, DC: National Center for Education Statistics, http://nces.ed.gov/pubs98/98030.pdf.

Henman, Paul. 2004. Targeted! Population Segmentation, Electronic Surveillance, and Governing the Unemployed in Australia. *International Sociology* 19 (2): 173–191.

Herbeck, Dan. 2004. Raids Target Drug Dealing in Housing Projects. *Buffalo News*, February 26, 2004.

Hess, David. 1997. *Science Studies: An Advanced Introduction*. New York: New York University Press.

Hess, Ed. 2003. The New Just-in-Time: Wal-Mart's Pushing RFID (Radio Frequency Identification), but What's the Ultimate Payoff? *Integrated Solutions,* http://www.integratedsolutionsmag.com/Articles/2003_11/031109.htm.

Hier, Sean P. 2004. Risky Spaces and Dangerous Faces: Urban Surveillance, Affective Governance and CCTV. *Social and Legal Studies* 13 (4): 541–554.

Hill, Jim. 1999. Arizona Criminals Find Jail Too In-'tents,' *CNN.com,* July 27, 1999, http://www.cnn.com/US/9907/27/tough.sheriff/.

Hindess, B. 2002. Neo-liberal Citizenship. *Citizenship Studies* 6 (2): 127–144.

Hiroyuki, Iseki, and Brian D. Taylor. 2001. The Demographics of Public Transit Subsidies: A Case Study of Los Angeles. Paper submitted for presentation at the 81st Annual Meeting of the Transportation Research Board.

Hochschild, A. 2000. The Nanny Chain. *American Prospect* 11 (4).

Hoffman, Morris B. 2000. The Drug Court Scandal. *North Carolina Law Review* 78: 1437–1534.

Hoffman, Robert R., and Arthur B. Markman, eds. 2001. *Interpreting Remote Sensing Imagery: Human Factors*. Boca Raton, FL: Lewis Publishers.

Hollinger, Richard C., and Lonn Lanza-Kaduce. 1988. The Process of Criminalization: The Case of Computer Crime Laws. *Criminology* 26 (1): 101–126.

Holmes, D. 2004. The Electronic Superhighway: Melbourne's CityLink Project. In *The Cyber Cities Reader,* ed. S. Graham. London: Routledge.

Holstein, James A., and Gale Miller, eds. 2003. *Challenges and Choice: Constructionist Perspectives on Social Problems*. New York: Aldine de Gruyter.

Homer-Dixon, Thomas. 2002. The Rise of Complex Terrorism. *Foreign Policy,* January–February 2002.

Hubbard, P., and K. Lilley. 2004. Pacemaking the Modern City: The Urban Politics of Speed and Slowness. *Environment and Planning D* 22 (2): 273–294.

Huey, Laura. 2005. Negotiating Demands: The Politics of Skid Row Policing in Edinburgh, San Francisco and Vancouver. Unpublished manuscript.

Hughes, K. 2004. Criminalizing Dissent? In *NOW with Bill Moyers.* PBS.

Hughes, Thomas P. 1983. *Networks of Power: Electrification in Western Society, 1880–1930*. Baltimore: Johns Hopkins University Press.

Hui, Stephen. 2003. Witnessing the Downtown Eastside. *The Simon Fraser University Peak,* May 5, 2003, 4–7.

Hummingbird Defense Systems, Inc. 2004. *Hummingbird Defense Systems, Inc.,* http://www.hbird.net/ (cited July 3, 2004).

Hussar, William J., and Debra E. Gerald. 2003. *Projections of Education Statistics to 2013.* Washington, DC: National Center for Education Statistics, http://www.nces.ed.gov/pubs2004/2004013.pdf.

Hyndman, J. 1997. Border Crossings. *Antipode* 29 (2): 149–176.

Identity Theft Resource Center. 2005. 2005 Disclosures of U.S. Data Fraud Incidents, http://www.idtheftcenter.org/datadisclosure_2005.pdf.

Inciardi, James A., and Karen McElrath, eds. 2004. *The American Drug Scene.* 4th ed. Los Angeles: Roxbury Publishing.

Institute for Applied Autonomy. 2004. http://www.appliedautonomy.com/.

Institute for a Drug-Free Workplace. 1988. *The Drug-Free Workplace Report.* Washington, DC: Institute for a Drug-Free Workplace.

International Biometric Industry Association. 2005. http://www.ibia.org.

International Civic Aviation Organization. 2004. Biometrics Deployment of Machine Readable Travel Documents, http://www.icao.int/mrtd/download/documents/Biometrics%20deployment%20of%20Machine%20Readable%20Travel%20Documents%202004.pdf.

Iseki, Hiroyuki, and Brian D. Taylor. 2001. The Demographics of Public Transit Subsidies: A Case Study of Los Angeles. Paper submitted for presentation at the 81st Annual Meeting of the Transportation Research Board.

Ivy, M. 1993. Have You Seen Me? Recovering the Inner Child in Late Twentieth-Century America. *Social Text* 37: 227–252.

Jackson, Janine, and Peter Hart. 2002. *Fear and Favor 2001: How Power Shapes the News.* New York: Fairness and Accuracy in Reporting, http://www.fair.org/reports/ff2001.html.

Jaffe, Sam. 2004. Easy Riders. In *American Demographics*, http://www.adage.com/section. cms?sectionId=195.

Jakes Jordan, Lara. 2005. Sept. 11 Panel: U.S. Remains Unprepared. *Washington Post*, December 5, 2005.

Jenkins, Philip. 1998. *Moral Panic: Changing Concepts of the Child Molester in Modern America*. New Haven, CT: Yale University Press.

Jenness, Valerie. 2004. Explaining Criminalization: From Demography and Status Politics to Globalization and Modernization. *Annual Review of Sociology* 30: 147–171.

Jenness, Valerie, and Ryken Grattet. 2001. *Making Hate a Crime: From Social Movement to Law Enforcement*. New York: Russell Sage.

Johnson, Kevin R. 2004. *The "Huddled Masses" Myth: Immigration and Civil Rights*. Philadelphia, PA: Temple University Press.

Jossi, F. 2004. Electronic Follow-up: Bar Coding and RFID both Lead to Significant Goals—Efficiency and Safety. *Healthcare Informatics* 21 (11): 31–33.

Katz, Cindi. 2001. The State Goes Home: Local Hypervigilance of Children and the Global Retreat from Social Reproduction. *Social Justice* 28 (3): 47–56.

_____. 1995 Power, Space, and Terror: Social Reproduction and the Public Environment. Paper presented at Landscape Architecture, Social Ideology, and the Politics of Place Conference, Harvard University, Graduate School of Design, Cambridge, MA, March 17–18.

Katz, D.M. 1998. Worried about the Babysitters? Tape Them. *New York Times*, April 5, 1998, Section 14LI: 4.

Kehaulani Goo, S. 2004. Cat Stevens Held after DC Flight Diverted. *Washington Post*, September 22, 2004, A10.

Kent, Jonathan. 2005. Malaysia Car Thieves Steal Finger, *BBC News*, March 31, 2005, http:// news.bbc.co.uk/go/pr/fr/-/2/hi/asia-pacific/4396831.stm (cited April 1, 2005).

Kingsbury, Nancy. 2003. *Border Security: Challenges in Implementing Border Technology*. Washington, DC: General Accounting Office, http://www.gao.gov/new.items/d03546t.pdf.

Klein, Hans K., and Daniel Lee Kleinman. 2002. The Social Construction of Technology: Structural Considerations. *Science, Technology, and Human Values* 27 (1): 28–52.

Konovsky, M.A., and R. Cropanzano. 1993. Justice Considerations in Employee Drug Testing. In *Justice in the Workplace: Approaching Fairness in Human Resource Management*, ed. R. Cropanzano. Hillsdale, NJ: Lawrence Erlbaum.

Koskela, Hille. 2000. "The Gaze without Eyes": Video-surveillance and the Changing Nature of Urban Space. *Progress in Human Geography* 24 (2): 243–265.

Koslowski, Rey. 2003. Information Technology and Integrated Border Management. Paper read at Managing International and Inter-Agency Cooperation at the Border, Geneva, March 13–15.

Kossan, Pat. 2003. Phoenix School First to Install Face Scanners. *Arizona Republic*, December 11, 2003, http://www.azcentral.com/arizonarepublic/local/articles/1211edsecurity11.html.

Kupchik, Aaron. 2006. *Judging Juveniles: Prosecuting Adolescents in Adult and Juvenile Courts*. New York: New York University Press.

Kupchik, Aaron, and Torin Monahan. Forthcoming. The New American School: Preparation for Post-Industrial Discipline. *British Journal of Sociology of Education*.

Kuzma, Lynn M. 2004. Security versus Liberty: 9/11 and the American Public. In *The Politics of Terror: The U.S. Response to 9/11*, ed. W. Crotty, 160–188. Boston: Northeastern University Press.

Kyllo v. United States 99.8508 (2001).

LaFree, Gary. 1998. *Losing Legitimacy: Street Crime and the Decline of Social Institutions in America*. Boulder, CO: Westview.

Landt, Jeremy, and Barbara Catlin. 2001. *Shrouds of Time: The History of RFID*. Aim Publication, http://www.itee.uq.edu.au/~madhan/7.%20files/shrouds_of_time.pdf.

Lange, Matthias. 1998. Grenzen, Gewalt und Identitätspolitik. In *Die Grenze. Flüchtlingsjagd in Schengenland. Zeitschrift für Flüchtlingspolitik in Niedersachsen*. Forschungsgesellschaft Flucht und Migration e.V.

Larner, W. 2003. Neoliberalism? *Environment and Planning D* 21 (5): 509–512.

Latour, Bruno. 1987. *Science in Action: How to Follow Scientists and Engineers through Society*. Cambridge, MA: Harvard University Press.

Lawrence, Richard, and David Mueller. 2003. School Shootings and the Man-Bites-Dog Criterion of Newsworthiness. *Youth Violence and Juvenile Justice* 1 (4): 330–345.

Lazer, David, ed. 2004. *DNA and the Criminal Justice System: The Technology of Justice.* Cambridge, MA: MIT Press.

Lees, Loretta. 1998. Urban Renaissance and the Street: Spaces of Control and Contestation. In *Images of the Street: Planning, Identity, and Control in Public Space,* ed. Nicholas R. Fyfe. London: Routledge.

Lefebvre, Henri. 1991. *The Production of Space.* Oxford and Cambridge: Blackwell.

Lemert, Edwin M. 1958. The Behavior of the Systematic Check Forger. *Social Problems* 6: 141–149.

Leo, R. 1992. From Coercion to Deception: The Changing Nature of Police Interrogation in America. *Crime, Law and Social Change,* September 1992.

Lessig, Lawrence. 1999. *Code and Other Laws of Cyberspace.* New York: Basic Books.

Lewin, Tamar. 2003. Raid at High School Leads to Racial Divide, Not Drugs. *New York Times,* December 9, 2003, A20, http://teachers.altschools.org/tnellen/nyt/raid.html.

Lewin Group. 2005. *Health Information Technology Leadership Panel: Final Report.* Washington, DC: Department of Health and Human Services, http://www.os.dhhs.gov/healthit/HITFinalReport.pdf.

Lewis, S. 1995. *It Can't Happen Here.* New York: Signet Classics.

Lewis, Tyson. 2003. The Surveillance Economy of Post-Columbine Schools. *Education, Pedagogy, and Cultural Studies* 25: 335–355.

Lichtblau, Eric. 2004. F.B.I. Goes Knocking for Political Troublemakers. *New York Times,* August 16, 2004.

Lichtblau, Eric, and John Markoff. 2004. Accenture Is Awarded U.S. Contract for Borders. *New York Times,* June 2, 2004.

Lighty, Todd, and Todd Gibson. 2001. Fraud, ID Theft Finance Terror. *Chicago Tribune,* November 4, 2001, 1.

Lillesand, Thomas M., and Ralph W. Kiefer. 2000. *Remote Sensing and Image Interpretation.* 4th ed. New York: Wiley and Sons.

Lindgren, David T. 2000. *Trust but Verify: Imagery Analysis in the Cold War.* Annapolis: Naval Institute Press.

Litfin, Karen. 1998. Satellites and Sovereign Knowledge: Remote Sensing of the Global Environment. In *The Greening of Sovereignty in World Politics,* ed. K. Litfin. Cambridge, MA: MIT Press.

Livingston, Steven. 2001. Remote Sensing Technology and the News Media. In *Commercial Observation Satellites: At the Leading Edge of Global Transparency,* ed. J.C. Baker, K.M. O'Connell, and R.A. Williamson. Santa Monica, CA: RAND and the American Society of Photogrammetry and Remote Sensing.

Lombardi, K.S. 1997. New Surveillance: Day-Care Cyber Visits. *New York Times,* March 16, 1997.

Low, Setha M. 2003. *Behind the Gates: Security and the New American Dream.* New York: Routledge.

Lynch, Mona. 2004. Punishing Images: Jail Cam and the Changing Penal Enterprise. *Punishment and Society* 6 (3): 255–270.

Lyon, David. 2003a. Airports as Data Filters: Converging Surveillance Systems after September 11th. *Journal of Information Communication and Ethics in Society* 1 (1): 13–20.

———. 2003b. *Surveillance after September 11.* Malden, MA: Polity Press.

———. 2003c. Surveillance as Social Sorting: Computer Codes and Mobile Bodies. In *Surveillance as Social Sorting: Privacy, Risk, and Digital Discrimination.* London and New York: Routledge.

———. 2003d. *Surveillance as Social Sorting: Privacy, Risk, and Digital Discrimination.* London and New York: Routledge.

———. 2003e. Technology vs "Terrorism": Circuits of City Surveillance since September 11th. *International Journal of Urban and Regional Research* 27 (3): 666–678.

———. 2001. *Surveillance Society: Monitoring Everyday Life.* Buckingham, UK: Open University.

———. 1994. *The Electronic Eye: The Rise of Surveillance Society.* Cambridge: Polity/Malden, MA: Blackwell.

_____. 1991. Bentham's Panopticon: From Moral Architecture to Electronic Surveillance. *Queen's Quarterly* 98 (3): 596–617.

_____. 1988. *The Information Society: Issues and Illusions.* Cambridge: Polity/Malden, MA: Blackwell.

Lyon, D., S. Marmura, and P. Peroff. 2005. *Location Technologies: Mobility, Surveillance and Privacy,* Report for the Office of the Privacy Commissioner (Ottawa), www.Queensu.ca/sociology/Surveillance/.

Lyon, Sawer. 2004. How Thousands Avoid Bus Fares. *Evening Standard,* November 25, 2004.

MacDonald, Scott, and Samantha Wells. 1994. The Impact and Effectiveness of Drug Testing Programs in the Workplace. In *Research Advances in Alcohol and Drug Problems, Volume II: Drug Testing in the Workplace,* ed. Scott Macdonald and Paul M. Roman, 121–142. New York: Plenum.

MacKenzie, Donald A. 1990. *Inventing Accuracy: An Historical Sociology of Nuclear Missile Guidance.* Cambridge, MA: MIT Press.

MacPherson, Donald. 2001. *A Framework for Action: A Four Pillar Approach to Drug Problems in Vancouver.* City of Vancouver.

Malone, Robert. 2005. To RFID or Not? *Forbes,* November 1, 2005, http://www.forbes.com/technology/2005/11/01/rfid-walmart-savings-cx_rm_1031rfid2.html.

Mann, Steve. 2004a. Sousveillance, Not Just Surveillance, in Response to Terrorism, http://www.chairetmetal.com/cm06/mann-complet.htm (accessed March 11, 2005).

_____. 2004b. Sousveillance: Inverse Surveillance in Multimedia Imaging. In *Proceedings of the 12th Annual ACM International Conference on Multimedia.* New York.

_____. n.d. Sousveillance: Secrecy, Not Privacy, May Be the True Cause of Terrorism, http://www.wearcam.org/sousveillance.htm (accessed March 11, 2005).

Mann, Steve, Jason Nollman, and Barry Wellman. 2003. Sousveillance: Inventing and Using Wearable Computing Devices for Data Collection in Surveillance Environments. *Surveillance and Society* 1 (3): 331–355.

Markowitz, Kenneth J. 2002. Legal Challenges and Market Rewards to the Use and Acceptance of Remote Sensing and Digital Information as Evidence. *Duke Environmental Law and Policy Forum* (Spring).

Martin, B. 1993. *In the Public Interest? Privatization and Public Sector Reform.* London Atlantic Highlands, NJ: Zed Books in association with Public Services International.

Marx, Gary T. Forthcoming. Varieties of Personal Information as Influences on Attitudes toward Surveillance. In *The Politics of Surveillance and Visibility,* ed. R. Ericson and K. Haggerty. Toronto: University of Toronto Press.

_____. 2005. Seeing Hazily (but Not Darkly) through the Lens: Some Recent Empirical Studies of Surveillance Technologies. *Law and Social Inquiry* 30: 339–399.

_____. 2003a. Some Information Age Technofallacies. *Journal of Contingencies and Crisis Management* 11 (1): 25–31.

_____. 2003b. A Tack in the Shoe: Neutralizing and Resisting the New Surveillance. *Journal of Social Issues* 59 (2): 369–390.

_____. 1998. Ethics for the New Surveillance. *The Information Society* 14: 171–185.

_____. 1997. The Declining Significance of Traditional Borders and the Appearance of New Borders in an Age of High Technology. In *Intelligent Environments,* ed. P. Droege. North-Holland: Elsevier Science.

_____. 1996. Electric Eye in the Sky: Some Reflections on the New Surveillance and Popular Culture. In *Computers, Surveillance, and Privacy,* ed. D. Lyon and E. Zureik. Minneapolis: University of Minnesota Press.

_____. 1988. *Undercover: Police Surveillance in America.* Berkeley: University of California Press.

_____. 1981. Ironies of Control: Authorities as Contributors to Deviance through Escalation, Nonenforcement, and Covert Facilitation. *Social Problems* 28 (3): 221–233.

Massey, D. 1991. A Global Sense of Place. In *Exploring Human Geography,* ed. S. Daniels and R. Lee. London: Arnold.

Massing, Michael. 1998. *The Fix.* New York: Simon and Schuster.

Mathieson, S.A. 2001. You Can Ring, but You Can't Hide. *The Guardian,* November 29, 2001, http://www.guardian.co.uk/print/0,3858,4309424-110837,00.html.

Mathiesen, Thomas. 1997. The Viewer Society: Michel Foucault's "Panopticon" Revisited. *Theoretical Criminology* 1 (2): 215–34.

McCahill, Michael. 2002. *The Surveillance Web: The Rise of Visual Surveillance in an English City.* Cullompton, Devon: Willan Publishing.

McCahill, Michael, and Clive Norris. 2003. *CCTV Systems in London: Their Structures and Practices.* Hull, UK: UrbanEye Project, http://www.urbaneye.net/results/ue_wp10.pdf.

———. 2002. *CCTV in London.* Hull, UK: UrbanEye Project, http://www.urbaneye.net/results/ue_wp6.pdf.

McCarthy, Michael. 2004. World Report: Healthy Design. *The Lancet* 364: 405–406.

McDaniel, Joanne. 2001. *School Resource Officers: What We Know, What We Think We Know, What We Need to Know.* Raleigh, NC: Center for the Prevention of School Violence, http://www.ncdjjdp.org/cpsv/Acrobatfiles/whatweknowsp01.pdf.

McGee, W. 2004. Speed Trap? "Registered Travelers" Might Race through Airport Security but at What Cost? *T & E,* August, 13–18.

McGeehan, Patrick. 2004. The Plastic Trap. *New York Times,* November 21, 2004.

McMillan, Robert. 2002. The Myth of Airport Biometrics. *Wired News,* 1–5.

Menn, Joseph. 2005a. Fraud Ring Taps into Credit Data. *Los Angeles Times,* February 16, 2005, A1, A20.

———. 2005b. Hackers Tap 40 Million Credit Cards. *Los Angeles Times,* June 18, 2005, A1, A32.

———. 2005c. Firms Hit by ID Theft Find Way to Cash In on Victims. *Los Angeles Times,* August 22, 2005, A1, A14.

Meyrowitz, Joshua. 1986. *No Sense of Place: The Impact of Electronic Media on Social Behavior.* New York: Oxford University Press.

Michael, Mike. 2003. Between the Mundane and the Exotic: Time for a Different Sociotechnical Stuff. *Time and Society* 12 (1): 127–143.

Mihm, Stephen. 2003. Dumpster-Diving for Your Identity. *New York Times Magazine,* December 21, 2003.

Misa, Thomas J. 2004. *Leonardo to the Internet: Technology and Culture from the Renaissance to the Present.* Baltimore: Johns Hopkins University Press.

Mitchell, K. 2001. Transnationalism, Neo-liberalism, and the Rise of the Shadow State. *Economy and Society* 30 (2): 165–189.

Mizzell, Angie. 2003. *School Drug Raid Causes Uproar.* Goose Creek, SC: MSNBC, http://www.msnbc.com/news/990598.asp?0cv=CB10&cp1=1.

Monahan, Torin. Forthcoming. Counter-surveillance as Political Intervention? *Social Semiotics.*

———. 2006. Radio Frequency Identification (RFID). In *Encyclopedia of Privacy,* ed. W.G. Staples. Westport, CT: Greenwood.

———. 2005a. *Globalization, Technological Change, and Public Education.* New York: Routledge.

———. 2005b. The School System as a Post-Fordist Organization: Fragmented Centralization and the Emergence of IT Specialists. *Critical Sociology* 3 (4): 583–615.

———. 2004. Just Another Tool? IT Pedagogy and the Commodification of Education. *Urban Review* 36 (4): 271–292.

Monmonier, Mark S. 2002. *Spying with Maps: Surveillance Technologies and the Future of Privacy.* Chicago: University of Chicago Press.

Morgan, John P. 1988. The "Scientific" Justification for Urine Drug Testing. *University of Kansas Law Review* 36: 683–697.

Morone, Joseph G., and Edward J. Woodhouse. 1986. *Averting Catastrophe: Strategies for Regulating Risky Technologies.* Berkeley: University of California Press.

Mosco, Vincent. 2000. Webs of Myth and Power: Connectivity and the New Computer Technopolis. In *The World Wide Web and Contemporary Cultural Theory,* ed. A. Herman and T. Swiss. New York: Routledge.

Mother Jones. 2005. Off Track. *Mother Jones,* September/October 2005, 17.

Murphy, Jean V. 2003. Get Ready! Wal-Mart Mandate Puts RFID, Smart Tags On Fast Track. *Global Logistics and Supply Chain,* September 2003.

Musheno, Michael C., James P. Levine, and Denis J. Palumbo. 1978. Television Surveillance and Crime Prevention: Evaluating an Attempt to Create Defensible Space in Public Housing. *Social Science Quarterly* 58 (4): 647–656.

Nahas, Brigitte M. 2001. Drug Tests, Arrests, and Fetuses: A Comment on the U.S. Supreme Court's Narrow Opinion in *Ferguson v. City of Charleston. Cardozo Women's Law Journal* 105 (8).

NASA. 2005. Earth Observatory, http://earthobservatory.nasa.gov/ (cited March 1, 2005).

NASA Ames Research Center. 2005. World Wind, January 26, 2005, http://worldwind.arc.nasa.gov/ (cited March 1, 2005).

National Consumer Coalition. 2003. Privacy Villain of the Week: Overton County Schools, TN, http://www.nccprivacy.org/handv/030710villain.htm (cited July 3, 2004).

National Imagery and Mapping Agency. 2000. *Department of Defense World Geodetic System 1984, Its Definition and Relationships with Local Geodetic Systems.* St. Louis, MO: National Imagery and Mapping Agency.

Neil, R. 2005. On a Roll: RFID Moves toward Patient Safety. *Materials Management in Health Care* 14 (3): 20–23.

Nelson, Barbara. 1984. Women's Poverty and Women's Citizenship: The Political Consequences of Economic Marginality. *Signs* 10 (21): 209–231.

Neuman, Peter R. 2004. Why Nobody Saw 9/11 Coming. *New York Times*, March 27, 2004.

New Jersey v. T.L.O. 1985. 469 U.S. 325, 351, 83 L. Ed. 2d 720, 105 S. Ct. 733.

Newman, Graeme R., and Megan M. McNally. 2005. *Identity Theft Literature Review.* National Institute of Justice, http://www.ncjrs.gov/pdffiles1/nij/grants/210459.pdf.

Newman, Oscar. 1972. *Defensible Space.* New York: Macmillan.

New York Surveillance Camera Players. 2002. How to Make Maps of Camera Locations, http://www.notbored.org/map-making.html.

Nieto, Marcus. 1997. *Public Video Surveillance: Is It an Effective Crime Prevention Tool?* Sacramento: California Research Bureau, http://www.library.ca.gov/CRB/97/05/.

Nieto, Marcus, Kimberly Johnston-Dodds, and Charlene Wear Simmons. 2002. *Public and Private Applications of Video Surveillance and Biometric Technologies.* Sacramento: California Research Bureau, http://www.library.ca.gov/crb/02/06/02-006.pdf.

Nisbet, R. 1975. *The Twilight of Authority.* New York: Oxford University Press.

Nock, Steven L. 1993. *The Costs of Privacy: Surveillance and Reputation in America.* New York: Aldine De Gruyter.

Normand, Jacques, Richard O. Lempert, and Charles P. O'Brien, eds. 1994. *Under the Influence? Drugs and the American Work Force.* Washington, DC: National Academy Press.

Norris, Clive. 2004. Introductory Remarks. Paper read at CCTV and Social Control, Sheffield, United Kingdom, January 8–9.

———. 2003. From Personal to Digital: CCTV, the Panopticon, and the Technological Mediation of Suspicion and Social Control. In *Surveillance as Social Sorting: Privacy, Risk and Digital Discrimination,* ed. D. Lyon. London: Routledge.

Norris, Clive, and Gary Armstrong. 1999. *Maximum Security Society: The Rise of CCTV.* London: Berg.

Nowotny, Helga. 1998. *Time: The Modern and Postmodern Experience.* Oxford: Blackwell.

Obe, Don. 1960. Skid Road Aid Picks Pockets of Taxpayers, Expert Says. *Vancouver Sun*, December 2, 1960, 1, 2.

O'Brien, Timothy L. 2004. Gone in 60 Seconds. *New York Times*, October 24, 2004, 1–5.

Office of Inspector General. 2003. *HIPAA Readiness: Administrative Simplification for Territories with Medicaid Programs.* Washington, DC: Department of Health and Human Services.

Office of Space Commercialization. 2001. *Trends in Space Commerce.* Washington, DC: U.S. Department of Commerce.

O'Harrow, Robert, Jr. 2005. *No Place to Hide.* New York: Free Press.

———. 2003. Identity Crisis. *Washington Post*, August 10, 2003, W14.

Ostbye, Truls, David F. Lobach, Dianne Cheesborough, Ann Marie M. Lee, Katrina M. Krause, Vic Hasselblad, and Darryl Bright. 2003. Evaluation of an Infrared/Radiofrequency Equipment-Tracking System in a Tertiary Care Hospital. *Journal of Medical Systems* 27 (4): 367–380.

Pace, Scott, Gerald Frost, Irving Lachow, David Frelinger, Donna Fossum, Donald K. Wassem, and Monica Pinto. 1995. *The Global Positioning System: Assessing National Policies.* Arlington, VA: RAND.

Paltrow, Lynn M. 2001. The War on Drugs and the War on Abortion. *Southern University Law Review* 28 (3): 201–253.

Papot, Thijs. 2004. *Poland's EU Border Challenge*. Radio Netherlands Wereldomroep, http://www.rnw.nl/hotspots/html/pol040429.html.

Patton, Jason. 2000. Protecting Privacy in Public? Surveillance Technologies and the Value of Public Places. *Ethics and Information Technology* 2: 181–187.

Peat, Chris. 2005. Heavens Above, *Heavens-Above GmbH*, January 26, 2005, http://www.heavens-above.com/ (cited March 1, 2005).

Peck, J. 2004. Geography and Public Policy: Constructions of Neoliberalism. *Progress in Human Geography* 28 (3): 392–406.

Peck, J., and A. Tickell. 2002. Neoliberalizing Space. *Antipode* 34 (3): 380–404.

Perrin, R.A., and N. Simpson. 2004. RFID and Bar Codes: Critical Importance in Enhancing Safe Patient Care. *Journal of Healthcare Information Management* 18 (4): 33–39.

Perrow, Charles. 1999. *Normal Accidents: Living with High-Risk Technologies*. Princeton, NJ: Princeton University Press.

Philips. 2004. Philips Semiconductors, http://www.semiconductors.philips.com/ (cited July 5, 2004).

Phillips, David J. Forthcoming. *Knowing Glances: Identity, Visibility, and Power in Information Environments*. Cambridge, MA: MIT Press.

Phillips, David J., and Michael Curry. 2003. Privacy and the Phenetic Urge: Geodemographics and the Changing Spatiality of Local Practice. In *Surveillance as Social Sorting: Privacy, Risk, and Digital Discrimination*, ed. D. Lyon. London: Routledge.

Phoenix, AZ, Cop Watch. 2005. http://www.phoenixcopwatch.org/ (accessed September 25, 2005).

Pickles, J., ed. 1995. *Ground Truth: The Social Implications of Geographic Information Systems*. New York: Guilford.

Pike, John. 2005. *GlobalSecurity.org*, http://www.globalsecurity.org/ (cited March 1, 2005).

Pincus, Walter. 2005. Pentagon Expanding Its Domestic Surveillance Activity Fears of Post-9/11 Terrorism Spur Proposals for New Powers. *Washington Post*, November 27, 2005, A06.

Piven, Frances Fox, and Richard Cloward. 1971. *Regulating the Poor: The Functions of Public Welfare*. New York: Vintage.

Pivot Legal Society. 2005. PIVOT Calls for Public Review. *PIVOT Post*, April 2005, 1.

———. 2002. To Serve and Protect, http://www.pivotlegal.org (accessed May 23, 2003).

Plant, Sadie. 2001. On the Mobile: The Effects of Mobile Telephones on Social and Individual Life, www.motorola.com/mot/documents/0,1028,333,00.pdf.

Pontell, Henry N. 2003. "Pleased to Meet You, Won't You Guess My Name?" Identity Fraud, Cyber Crime, and White-Collar Delinquency. *Adelaide Law Review* (January): 305–328.

Pontell, Henry N., and Anastasia Tosouni. 2005. *The 2003 and 2004 Victimization Surveys Conducted by the Identity Theft Resource Center: A Preliminary Analysis*. San Diego, CA: Identity Theft Resource Center.

Poon, Martha. 2005. From Operations Research to Revenue Scores: How Consumer Credit Scoring Has Become the Social Science of the Finance Industry. Paper presented at Making Society, Knowing Society, University of California, San Diego, June 4.

Poster, Mark. 2006. *Information Please: Culture and Politics in the Age of Digital Machines*. Durham, NC: Duke University Press.

Preissl, Brigitte, Harry Bouwman, and Charles Steinfield, eds. 2004. *E-Life after the Dot Com Bust*. Heidelberg: Physica-Verlag.

Privacy International. 2004a. *Mistaken Identity: Exploring the Relationship between National Identity Cards and the Prevention of Terrorism*. London, http://www.privacyinternational.org/issues/idcard/uk/id-terrorism.pdf.

———. 2004b. An Open Letter to the ICAO: A Second Report on "Towards an International Infrastructure for Surveillance of Movement," http://www.privacyinternational.org/article.shtml?cmd[347]=x-347-103018.

Pugh, Tony. 2005. Crooks Seem to Have Upper Hand in Identity Theft Crimes, Experts Say. *Knight Ridder*, June 29, 2005.

Pulsipher, L.M. 1993. "He Won't Let She Stretch She Foot": Gender Relations in Traditional West Indian Houseyards. In *Full Circles: Geographies of Women over the Life Course*, ed. C. Katz and J. Monk, 107–121. London: Routledge.

Quayle, Dan. 1983. American Productivity: The Devastating Effects of Drug and Alcohol Abuse. *American Psychologist* 38 (4): 454–458.

Radianse. 2005. Press Release, January 11, 2005, http://www.radianse.com/press-HUP-011105.htm.

Rafael, Vicente L. 2003. The Cell Phone and the Crowd: Messianic Politics in the Contemporary Philippines. *Public Culture* 15 (3): 399–425.

Rafter, Nicole. 1990. The Social Construction of Crime and Crime Control. *Journal of Research on Crime and Delinquency* 27 (4): 376–389.

Raitano, Zianaveva. 2003. Interview with Virginia Eubanks, October 4, 2003.

Ramsey, Matthew. 2003. Arrested Woman Wants Officers Fired, Watch on Rest. *Vancouver Sun*, December 5, 2003, B1.

Raytheon. 2004. Thermal-Eye, http://www.thermal-eye.com/ (cited July 5, 2004).

Regan, Keith. 2001. AOL, Phillips Eye New E-Commerce Platforms. *EcommerceTimes*, July 12, 2001, http://www.crmbuyer.com/story/11949.html.

Reid, J.L. 2004. Radarfind Finds Market in Real Time Inventory. *Triangle Tech Journal*, http://www.triangletechjournal.com/news/article.html?item_id=605.

Reiman, Jeffrey. 2000. *The Rich Get Richer and the Poor Get Prison: Ideology, Class, and Criminal Justice.* 7th ed. Boston: Pearson.

Reinarman, Craig, and Harry G. Levine. 1997. *Crack in America: Demon Drugs and Social Justice.* Berkeley: University of California Press.

Reynardus, J.E. 2004. *The Free Trade Area of the Americas (FTAA) Inquiry Report: Civilian Oversight of Miami–Dade Police and Corrections and Rehabilitation Departments.* Miami, FL: Independent Review Panel.

Rice-Oxley, Mark. 2004. Big Brother in Britain: Does More Surveillance Work? *Christian Science Monitor*, February 6, 2004, http://www.csmonitor.com/2004/0206/p07s02-woeu.htm.

Riesman, D., et al. 2001. *The Lonely Crowd.* New Haven, CT: Yale University Press.

Riley, Claudette. 2003. Parents Demand Limits for School Cameras, *Tennessean.com*, July 9, 2003, http://www.tennessean.com/local/archives/03/07/35666846.shtml.

Robbins, Paul. 2003. Beyond Ground Truth: GIS and the Environmental Knowledge of Herders, Professional Foresters, and Other Traditional Communities. *Human Ecology* 31 (2): 233–253.

Roberti, Mark. 2005. A Look Back at 2005. *RFID Journal*, December 19, 2005, http://www.rfidjournal.com/article/articleview/2048/1/128/.

Roberts, Dorothy. 1997. *Killing the Black Body: Race, Reproduction, and the Meaning of Liberty.* New York: Pantheon Books.

Roberts, Mike. 2005. Watchdog Puts Heat on Police Chief. *Vancouver Province*, April 10, 2005, A8.

Roberts, Susan M., and Richard H. Schein. 1995. Earth Shattering: Global Imagery and GIS. In *Ground Truth: The Social Implications of Geographic Information Systems.* New York: Guilford.

Robins, Lee N. 1973. *A Followup of Vietnam Drug Users.* White House Special Action Office Monograph, Series A, #1. Washington, DC: U.S. Government Printing Office.

Robins, Lee N., D.H. Davis, and D.W. Goodwin. 1974. Drug Use in U.S. Army Enlisted Men in Vietnam: A Follow-up on Their Return Home. *American Journal of Epidemiology* 99: 235–249.

Rose, D. 1993. Local Childcare Strategies in Montréal, Québec: The Mediations of State Policies, Class, and Ethnicity in the Life Courses of Families with Young Children. In *Full Circles: Geographies of Women over the Life Course*, ed. C. Katz and J. Monk, 188–207. London: Routledge.

Rose, Nikolas. 1999. *Powers of Freedom.* New York: Routledge.

Rosen, Jeffrey. 2004. *The Naked Crowd: Reclaiming Security and Freedom in an Anxious Age.* 1st ed. New York: Random House.

———. 2001. A Cautionary Tale for a New Age of Surveillance. *New York Times Magazine*, October 7, 2001, http://www.schizophonia.com/archives/cctv.htm.

Rosoff, Stephen M., Henry N. Pontell, and Robert H. Tillman. 2004. *Profit without Honor: White-Collar Crime and the Looting of America.* 3rd ed. Saddle River, NJ: Prentice Hall.

Rosser, N. 2004. DNA Kits to Stop Bus Spit Attacks. *Evening Standard*, September 1, 2004.

Roth, Rachel. 2002. The Perils of Pregnancy: Ferguson v. City of Charleston. *Feminist Legal Studies* 10: 149–158.

Rothstein, Mark A. 1991. Workplace Drug Testing: A Case Study in the Misapplication of Technology. *Harvard Journal of Law and Technology* 4 (Fall): 65–93.

Rule, J.B. 2002. From Mass Society to Perpetual Contact. In *Perpetual Contact: Mobile Communication, Private Talk, Public Performance,* ed. James E. Katz and Mark Aakhus. Cambridge and New York: Cambridge University Press.

———. 1973. *Private Lives, Public Surveillance.* London: Allen-Lane.

Rule, James, Douglas MacAdam, Linda Stearns, and David Uglow. 1980. *The Politics of Privacy: Planning for Personal Data Systems as Powerful Technologies.* New York: Elsevier.

Rushlo, Michelle. 2003. Phoenix Installs Face Scanners in School. *Boston Globe,* December 15, 2003, http://www.boston.com/news/nation/articles/2003/12/15/phoenix_installs_face_scanners_in_school/.

Ryan, Barbara Ann. 2003. Interview with Virginia Eubanks, August 4, 2003.

Ryan, William. 1976. *Blaming the Victim.* Rev. ed. New York: Vintage Books.

Salter, M.B. 2004. Passports, Mobility, and Security: How Smart Can the Border Be? *International Studies Perspectives* 5 (1): 71–91.

———. 2003. *Rights of Passage: The Passport in International Relations.* Boulder, CO: Lynne Rienner.

San Francisco Bay Guardian. 2001. Food stamps and ATMs. June 6, 2001, http://www.sfbg.com/News/35/36/36edwelf.html.

San Francisco Bay View. 2004. Lawsuit Filed after SWAT Raids High School. January 14, 2004, http://www.mapinc.org/tlcnews/v04/n092/a09.htm?155.

Sarewitz, Daniel R. 1996. *Frontiers of Illusion: Science, Technology, and the Politics of Progress.* Philadelphia, PA: Temple University Press.

Scahill, J. 2004. The New York Model: Indymedia and the Text Message Jihad. *Counterpunch,* September 9, 2004.

———. 2003. The Miami Model: Paramilitaries, Embedded Journalists and Illegal Protests: Think This Is Iraq? It's Miami. *Counterpunch.*

Schabner, Dean. 2004. Police See Growing Link between ID Theft, Crystal Meth Use, *ABC News Internet Ventures,* http://abcnews.go.com/Business/YourMoney/story?id=89748&page=1 (cited March 24, 2004).

Schneider, Anne, and Helen Ingram. 1997. *Policy Design for Democracy.* Lawrence: University Press of Kansas.

———. 1993. Social Construction of Target Populations: Implications for Politics and Policy. *American Political Science Review* 87 (2): 334–347.

Schram, Sanford F. 2003. *Praxis for the Poor.* New York: New York University Press.

———. 2000. *After Welfare: The Culture of Postindustrial Social Policy.* New York: New York University Press.

Schumer, Charles E. 2003. *Senate Judiciary Committee Holds Hearing on New Wiretap Powers Review.* Washington, DC: American Civil Liberties Union, http://www.aclu.org/Privacy/Privacy.cfm?ID=13469&c=130.

Schwartz, John. 2003. This Car Can Talk: What It Says May Cause Concern. *New York Times,* December 29, 2003.

Sclove, Richard E. 1995. *Democracy and Technology.* New York: Guilford.

Seghetti, Lisa M. 2002. *Immigration and Naturalization Service: Restructuring Proposals in the 107th Congress.* Washington, DC: Congressional Research Service, http://212.111.49.124/news-archive/crs/10094.pdf.

Shapiro, Joseph. 1993. *No Pity: People with Disabilities Forging a New Civil Rights Movement.* New York: New York Times Books.

Shepard, Edward M., and Thomas J. Clifton, et al. 1998. *Drug Testing and Labor Productivity.* Research Paper No. 18. Syracuse, NY: Institute of Industrial Relations, LeMoyne University, http://www.lindesmith.org/library/shepard2.cfm (accessed October 7, 2005).

Sheppard, Eric. 1995. GIS and Society: Towards a Research Agenda. *Cartography and Geographic Information Systems* 22 (1): 5–16.

Shesgreen, Deidre, and Denise Hollinshed. 2001. Computer Glitch Leaves Food Stamp Recipients in Lurch. *St. Louis Post-Dispatch,* August 18, 2001.

Short, Emma, and Jason Ditton. 1995. *Does Closed Circuit Television Prevent Crime? An Evaluation of the Use of CCTV Surveillance Cameras in Airdrie Town Centre.* Edinburgh: Scottish Office Central Research Unit, http://www.scotland.gov.uk/cru/resfinds/crf08-00.htm.

Sieber, Renee E. 2004. Rewiring for a GIS/2. *Cartographica* 39 (1): 25–39.

Simmel, Georg. 1971. The Metropolis and Mental Life. In *George Simmel on Individuality and Social Forms*, ed. D. Levine. Chicago: University of Chicago Press. (Orig. pub. in German 1903.)

Simon, Bart. 2005. The Return of Panopticism: Supervision, Subjection, and the New Surveillance. *Surveillance and Society* 3 (1): 1–20.

Singer, Linda. 1993. *Erotic Welfare: Sexual Theory and Politics in an Age of Epidemic*. New York: Routledge.

Smith, Dorothy. 1999. *Writing the Social: Critique, Theory, and Investigations*. Toronto, Canada: University of Toronto Press.

———. 1974. Women's Perspective as a Radical Critique of Sociology. *Sociological Inquiry* 44 (1): 7–13.

Smith, Graham. 2004. Rethinking Police Complaints. *British Journal of Criminology* 44: 15–33.

Soss, Joe. 1999. Lessons of Welfare: Policy Design, Political Learning, and Political Action. *American Political Science Review* 93: 363–380.

Sparke, M. Forthcoming. A Neoliberal Nexus: Economy, Security and the Biopolitics of Citizenship on the Border. *Political Geography*.

———. 2005. Plenary Session: Geographies of Fear and Hope I; Economies, Politics and Peace. Paper read at the Association of American Geographers Annual Meeting, Denver.

———. 2004. Passports into Credit Cards. In *Boundaries and Belonging*, ed. J. Migdal. Cambridge: Cambridge University Press.

Stanford, Vince. 2003. Pervasive Computing Goes the Last Hundred Feet with RFID Systems. *IEEE Pervasive Computing*, April–June 2003, http://dsonline.computer.org/0306/d/bp2app.htm.

Staples, William G. 2000. *Everyday Surveillance: Vigilance and Visibility in Postmodern Life*. Lanham, MD: Rowman and Littlefield.

Staudenmaier, John M. 1985. *Technology's Storytellers: Reweaving the Human Fabric*. Cambridge, MA: MIT Press.

Stegman, Michael A., Jennifer S. Lobenhofer, and John Quinterno. 2003. *The State of Electronic Benefit Transfer (EBT)*. Chapel Hill: Center for Community Capitalism, University of North Carolina at Chapel Hill, http://www.kenan-flagler.unc.edu/assets/documents/cc_ebt.pdf.

Steinhardt, Barry. 2004. ACLU Testifies to Congress on Dangers of Biometric Passports, http://www.privacyinternational.org/article.shtml?cmd[347]=x-347-60594.

Stern, Mark J. 1988. Economic Change and Social Welfare: Implications for Employees' Assistance. In *Evaluation of Employee Assistance Programs*, ed. Michael J. Holosko and Marvin D. Feit, 7–23. Binghamton, NY: Haworth Press.

Strathern, M., ed. 2000. *Audit Cultures: Anthropological Studies in Accountability, Ethics and the Academy*. London: Routledge.

Strohm, Chris. 2004. Lawmaker Questions Demise of Government Technology Task Force, *GovExec.com*, August 20, 2004, http://www.govexec.com/dailyfed/0804/082004c1.htm.

Surveillance Camera Players. 2003. Ten Predictions Concerning Cell Phones, http://www.notbored.org/cell-phones.html.

Sullivan, Bob. 2004. Criminals Taking Advantage of Online Banking, Gartner Says, *MSNBC.com*, June 14, 2004.

Tarrow, Sidney. 1998. *Power in Movement: Social Movements and Contentious Politics*. 2nd ed. Cambridge: Cambridge University Press.

Think & Ask. 2002. Media Giants: Who Owns What? http://www.thinkandask.com/news/mediagiants.html (cited July 5, 2004).

Tice, Karen. 1998. *Tales of Wayward Girls and Immoral Women: Case Records and the Professionalization of Social Work*. Chicago: University of Illinois Press.

Tonner, Mark. 2005. Officer Says Activists Cruise Streets, Looking for Conflict with the Law. *Vancouver Province*, April 10, 2005, A18.

Torpey, J.C. 2000. *The Invention of the Passport: Surveillance, Citizenship, and the State*. Cambridge and New York: Cambridge University Press.

Toumey, Christopher. 1996. *Conjuring Science: Scientific Symbols and Cultural Meanings in American Life*. New Brunswick, NJ: Rutgers University Press.

Townsend, Anthony. 2000. Life in the Real-Time City: Mobile Telephones and Urban Metabolism. *Journal of Urban Technology* 7 (2): 85–104.

UC, Irvine Police Department, Irvine Police Department, UC, Irvine Student Center, and UC, Irvine Scheduling and Conference Services. 2004. Identity Theft: The Fastest Growing Crime in America! Panel presentation, March 4.

United States Postal Service. 2005. Safeguard Your Personal Information, Pub. 280, http://www.usps.com/postalinspectors/pub280txt.htm.

Urry, John. 2001. Inhabiting the Car. In *Collective Imagination: Limits and Beyond,* ed. E.R. Larreta, 277–304. Rio de Janeiro: UNESCO.

U.S. Citizenship and Immigration Services. 2002. *Yearbook of Immigration Statistics.* Washington, DC: Office of Immigration Statistics, http://uscis.gov/graphics/shared/aboutus/statistics/Illegal2002.pdf.

U.S. Congress. 1994. House Committee on the Judiciary. *Criminal Aliens: Hearings before the Subcommittee on International Law, Immigration, and Refugees.* 103d Cong., 2d sess.: 165.

———. 1989. House Select Committee on Children, Youth, and Families. *Born Hooked: Confronting the Impact of Perinatal Substance Abuse.* 101st Cong., 1st sess., April 27: 121.

U.S. Customs and Border Protection. 2004. *INS Passenger Accelerated Service System.* U.S. Customs and Border Protection, http://www.customs.gov/xp/cgov/travel/frequent_traveler/nexus_air.xml (cited July 2005).

———. 2003. *Advance Passenger Information System (APIS) Fact Sheet.* U.S. Customs and Border Protection, http://www.customs.gov/xp/cgov/travel/inspections_carriers_facilities/apis/apis_factsheet.xml (cited August 2005).

U.S. Department of Commerce. 2005. *Radio Frequency Identification: Opportunities and Challenges in Implementation.* Washington, DC, http://www.google.com/url?sa=U&start=3&q=http://www.technology.gov/reports/2005/RFID_April.pdf&e=10313.

U.S. Department of Justice. 2004. *Follow-up Review of the Status of IDENT/IAFIS Integration.* Washington, DC: U.S. Department of Justice.

U.S. Geological Survey. 2002a. *Celebrating 30 Years of Imaging the Earth 2005,* July 22, 2002, http://www.usgs.gov/public/press/public_affairs/press_releases/pr1608m.html (cited March 1, 2005).

———. 2002b. Our Earth as Art 2005, http://earthasart.gsfc.nasa.gov/index.htm (cited March 1, 2005).

U.S. Medicine Institute for Health Studies. 2004. Beyond the Electronic Health Record: Anticipating the Direction of Future Technologies, Roundtable Discussion, Washington, DC, December 6, 2004, http://:www.usminstitute.org/EHRtranscript.pdf.

Vancouver Cop Watch Manual. 2005. http://crow.riseup.net/brady/propaganda/pdf/cop_watch_manual.pdf (accessed September 26, 2005).

Vancouver Police Department. 1977. Annual Report. City of Vancouver Archives, Police Department Fonds (PDS25).

Vancouver Police Department Discussion Document. 2001. Neighbourhood Safety Watch: A Safer Community Option for the Downtown Eastside, Strathcona, Chinatown and Gastown Area.

Van der Ploeg, I. 2005. *The Machine-Readable Body: Essays on Biometrics and the Informatization of the Body.* Maastricht: Shaker.

———. 2003. Biometrics and Privacy: A Note on the Politics of Theorizing Technology. *Information Communication and Society* 6 (1): 85–104.

———. 1999a. The Illegal Body: "Eurodac" and the Politics of Biometric Identification. *Ethics and Information Technology* 1 (4): 295–302.

———. 1999b. Written on the Body: Biometrics and Identity. *Computers and Society* 29 (1): 37–44.

Vary, Meredith. 2003. Interview with Virginia Eubanks, August 21, 2003.

Verification Research, Training, and Information Center. 2005. VERTIC 2005, http://www.vertic.org (cited March 1, 2005).

Vernonia School Dist. 47J v. Acton. 1995. 515 U.S. 646, 132 L. Ed. 2d 564, 115 S. Ct. 2386.

Virilio, Paul. 1986. *Speed and Politics: An Essay on Dromology.* New York: Columbia University.

Wacquant, Loïc. 2001. Deadly Symbiosis: When Ghetto and Prison Meet and Mesh. *Punishment & Society* 3 (1): 95–134.

Wade, Mark. 2005. Encyclopedia Astronautica, http://www.astronautix.com (accessed: August 5, 2005).

Wailoo, Keith. 1997. *Drawing Blood: Technology and Disease Identity in Twentieth-century America.* Baltimore, MD: Johns Hopkins University Press.

Walby, Kevin. 2005. Open-Street Camera Surveillance and Governance in Canada. *Canadian Journal of Criminology and Criminal Justice* 47 (4): 655–683.

Walker, R. 2004. The Corporate Manufacture of Word of Mouth. *New York Times Magazine,* December 5, 2004.

Walker, S. 2004. Police DNA "Sweeps" Extremely Unproductive: A National Survey of Police DNA Sweeps. Unpublished paper, Department of Criminal Justice, University of Nebraska.

Ward, Robert, Gary Wamsley, Aaron Schroeder, and David B. Robins. 2000. Network Organizational Development in the Public Sector: A Case Study of the Federal Emergency Management Administration (FEMA). *Journal of the American Society for Information Science* 51 (11): 1018–1032.

Waugh, William L., Jr. 2003. Terrorism, Homeland Security and the National Emergency Management Network. *Public Organization Review* 3: 373–385.

Weber, Max. 2000. *The Protestant Ethic and the Spirit of Capitalism.* New York: Routledge.

Weinberg, Alvin M. 2003. Can Technology Replace Social Engineering? In *Technology and the Future,* ed. A.H. Teich, 9th ed. Belmont, CA: Thomson/Wadsworth. (Orig. pub. 1966.)

Weissbourd, R. 1999 How Society Keeps Fathers away from Their Children. *American Prospect* 11 (2).

Wellman, Barry. 2001. Physical Space and Cyberspace: The Rise of Personalized Networking. *International Journal of Urban and Regional Research* 25.

Wikipedia. 2004. James Bulger Murder Case, http://en.wikipedia.org/wiki/James_Bulger_murder_case (cited May 20, 2004).

Williams, Granville. 2001. Media Ownership 2001: MediaChannel, http://www.mediachannel.org/ownership/chart.shtml.

Wilson, James Q., and George E. Kelling. 1982. Broken Windows: The Police and Neighborhood Safety. *Atlantic Monthly,* March 1982.

Wing, Bradford. 1998. *Facial and Voice Verification Test for SENTRI.* Washington, DC: Office of Strategic Information and Technology Development, U.S. Immigration and Naturalization Service.

Winner, Langdon. 2004. Trust and Terror: The Vulnerability of Complex Socio-technical Systems. *Science as Culture* 13 (2): 155–172.

———. 1988. Mythinformation. In *Questioning Technology,* ed. A. Carnes and J. Zerzan. St. Louis, MO: Left Bank Books.

———. 1986. *The Whale and the Reactor: A Search for Limits in an Age of High Technology.* Chicago: University of Chicago Press.

———. 1979. Technology as Legislation. In *Technology and Change: A Courses by Newspaper Reader,* ed. J.G. Burke and M.C. Eakin. San Francisco: Boyd and Fraser.

———. 1977. *Autonomous Technology: Technics-out-of-Control as a Theme in Political Thought.* Cambridge, MA: MIT Press.

———. 1975. Complexity and Human Understanding. In *Organized Social Complexity: Challenge to Politics and Policy,* ed. Todd R. La Porte (pp. 40–76). Princeton, NJ: Princeton University Press.

Winseck, D. 2003. Netscapes of Power: Convergence, Network Design, Walled Gardens and Other Strategies of Control in the Information Age. In *Surveillance as Social Sorting: Privacy, Risk and Digital Discrimination,* ed. D. Lyon. London: Routledge.

Wired. 2004. Big Bucks for Biometrics, http://wired-vig.wired.com/news/privacy/0,1848,63683,00. html (cited 2005).

Woliver, Laura R. 2002. *The Political Geographies of Pregnancy.* Urbana and Chicago: University of Illinois Press.

Wood, Chris. 2001. The Electronic Eye View: The War on Terror Is Making Surveillance Systems More Popular Than Ever. *Maclean's* 114 (47): 94.

Wood, D., and S. Graham. Forthcoming. Permeable Boundaries in the Software Sorted Society: Surveillance and Differentiations of Mobility. In *Mobile Technologies of the City,* ed. M. Sheller and J. Urry. London: Routledge.

Woodhouse, Edward J., and Dean Nieusma. 2001. Democratic Expertise: Integrating Knowledge, Power, and Participation. In *Knowledge, Power and Participation in Environmental Policy Analysis,* ed. M. Hisschemöller, R. Hoppe, W.N. Dunn, and J.R. Ravetz (pp. 73–96). New Brunswick, NJ: Transaction.

Woodward, John D., Nicholas M. Orlans, and Peter T. Higgins. 2003. *Biometrics.* New York: McGraw-Hill/Osborne.

Woolgar, Steve, ed. 2002. *Virtual Society? Technology, Cyberbole, Reality*. Oxford: Oxford University Press.

Wright, L. 1996. Who's Who at the Border. The Ident System—Operation Gatekeeper. *In the Print* 12 (2): 3.

Wrigley, J. 1999. Hiring a Nanny: The Limits of Private Solutions to Public Problems. *Annals AAPSS* 563: 162–174.

XtremeMac. 2005. Freefall—Satellite Simulator and Screen Saver, http://www.xtrememac.com/freefall/index.shtml (cited March 1, 2005).

Yamaguchi, Ryoko, Lloyd D. Johnston, and Patrick M. O'Malley. 2003. Relationship between Student Illicit Drug Use and School Drug-Testing Policies. *Journal of School Health* 73 (4): 159–164.

Yapa, L. 1995. Is GIS Appropriate Technology? *International Journal of Geographical Information Systems* 5: 41–58.

Yar, Majid. 2003. Panoptic Power and the Pathologisation of Vision: Critical Reflections on the Foucaldian Thesis. *Surveillance and Society* 1 (3): 254–271.

Yonkers, Steven, and Nuala O'Conner Kelly. 2003. *US-VISIT Program, Increment 1 Privacy Impact Assessment*. Washington, DC: Department of Homeland Security.

Young, D. 2004. FDA Embraces RFID to Protect Drug Supply. *American Journal of Health-System Pharmacy* 61 (24): 2612, 2615.

Youth Violence Project. 2003. *Violence in Schools*. Charlottesville: School of Education, University of Virginia, http://youthviolence.edschool.virginia.edu/violence-in-schools/national-statistics.html (cited July 4, 2004).

Zeller, Tom, Jr. 2005. Identity Crises. *New York Times*, October 1, 2005, B1, B3.

Zhekun, Li, Rajit Gadh, and B.S. Prabhu. 2004. Applications of RFID Technology and Smart Parts in Manufacturing. Proceedings of ASME 2004 Design Engineering Technical Conferences and Computers and Information in Engineering Conference, Salt Lake City, UT, September 28–October 2, 2004.

Zimmer, Lynn, and James B. Jacobs. 1992. The Business of Drug Testing: Technological Innovation and Social Control. *Contemporary Drug Problems* 19 (Spring): 1–26.

Zimring, Franklin E., and Gordon Hawkins. 1992. *The Search for Rational Drug Control*. New York: Cambridge University Press.

Zinberg, Norman. 1984. *Drug, Set, and Setting: The Basis for Controlled Intoxicant Use*. New Haven, CT: Yale University Press.

Index

O

Observation, 246, 258–260
Odor identification, 7, 41
Office of Technology Assessment, 5
Oil, national dependency on foreign, 276
Onboard navigation systems, 219, 248.
    See also Locational data
Online banking fraud, 135
Online bill paying, 135
Opacity, in IT surveillance technologies,
    95–96
Open borders, through automated
    identity checking, 185
Openness
    and 9/11 attacks, 281
    replacement by closure, 282
Operant conditioning, for drug-
    dependent physicians, 68
Operation Gatekeeper, 180
Operation Hold the Line, 180, 187
Operation Safeguard, 180
Opportunism, in post-9/11 politics, 277
Organized crime, and identity theft, 137
Otay Mesa crossing, 187
    biometric recognition at, 187
Outcomes, unintended, 12
Outliers, and biometrics, 8
Outsourcing, and identity fraud, 136

P

Panoptic sorting, 198–199
Panopticon metaphor, 159
Paper shredders, 52
Parent-to-child surveillance, 70. *See also*
    Child protection industry
    locational data, 210
    mobile phones as electronic leashes,
    215–216
Parenting, as form of community
    policing, 35
Participatory action research, 92
Passports, biometrics in, 189
Patient bracelets, RFIDs in, 80
Patient records, centralizing of, 77
Patients' rights, 5
Pell grants, ineligibility based on drug
    tests, 59

Pepper spray, 28
Personal information
    garnering without subject
        knowledge, 221
    misuse on Internet, 134
    obtaining by e-mail fraud, 134–135
    out of individual control, 146
    protecting through technology
        design, 51
    storage in mass databases, 131–132
    trading for rewards and convenience,
        38, 48
Personnel tracking, 84–88
Philips Electronics, ties to AOL
    TimeWarner CNN, 120
Phishing, 134–135
PIVOT Legal Society, 154
Plea bargaining, as disguised coercion,
    38
Police, as agents of discipline and
    control in schools, 117
Police harassment, Cop Watch claims
    of, 156
Police misconduct/brutality
    cop watching to prevent, 152–157
    deterrence by Cop Watch
        organizations, 150
    independent journalist evidence at
        RNC 2004, 170
Police power, 277
Political asylum, blocking of
    applications for, 179
Political learning
    for low-income women, 91
    through technology implementation,
        100–104
    in welfare system, 89–90
Poor people
    critical ambivalence toward, 92
    deserving versus nondeserving, 57
    increased dependency and
        disempowerment by
        surveillance, 16
    marginalization by surveillance, 16
    targeting by EBT systems, 14–15
    as test populations for technologies
        of surveillance, 90–92
    unequal surveillance of, 5
Popular Technology Workshops, 106

S

in reconstruction of national borders,
177, 191
role in bypassing consent, 40
side effects, 11, 13
as separate from society, 11, 17
social construction of, 285–287
social theories of, 275–276
for sorting by economic desirability,
196
valence of, 87
Telegraph, implications for spatial
awareness, 246
Telephone voice changers, 28
Temporary Aid to Needy Families
(TANF), 103
Terminator, The, 27
Terrestrial image, 246, 249–254
importance to civic affairs, 263
Terrorism
applying social construction of
technology to, 287
defining as category of risk, 282, 283
evaluating from risk standpoint, 283
failure of biometrics to deter, 8
links to identity theft, 132
surveillance as response to, 6–7
and technological vulnerabilities,
275, 285
versus identity theft, 125
Thatcher, Margaret, and origins of
neoliberalism, 197
Thermal cameras, at Germany–Poland
border, 181
Thermal face print scans, 7
Third World therapeutics, 72
Three strikes laws, 59
Time-space micromanagement, 215, 216
Toll roads
differential access to, 198
transponder devices for, 219, 220
Total surveillance, 221
Tracking. *See* Locational data
Tradeoffs
belief contingent on efficacy, 10
questioning veracity of, 2
rationale for beliefs in, 11–14
reductive nature of concerns about,
10
in security debate, 2

Traffic violations
CCTV efficacy in preventing/
generating revenue from, 5
deterrence by surveillance, 21
reduction with surveillance, 6
Transnational elites, mobility of, 207
Transparency
absence in IT surveillance, 95–96
of mobile technologies, 209, 215–220
Transparent lockers, in public schools,
110
Transportation, historical split from
communication, 257–258
Transportation Security Administration
(TSA), 201
Travelers
central databases on, 178
sorting by economic desirability, 196
Trojan horse programs, 135
Truro, Massachusetts, case, 37
Trust
changes after 9/11 attacks, 281
replacement by fear, 282
Two-way radios, use in protest
demonstrations, 169
TXTmob, 168

U

U-2 aircraft, 250
Undisclosed information sharing, 96
Unequal power relations, structuring by
surveillance, 12
United Kingdom. *See* Great Britain
United States, surveillance by private
companies, 5
Urine testing, 57, 98
for drug-dependent physicians, 68
history of, 63
and power relations, 62
socio-structural contexts of, 60
U.S.-Canada border regimes, 199–200,
202–203
U.S. Customs and Border Protection,
(CBP), 201, 203, 206
U.S.–Mexico border, 178, 179, 180–182
militarization of, 180, 181